Lecture Notes in Computer Science 3088

Commenced Publication in 1973
Founding and Former Series Editors:
Gerhard Goos, Juris Hartmanis, and Jan van Leeuwen

T0223606

Josep Lladós   Young-Bin Kwon (Eds.)

Graphics Recognition

Recent Advances and Perspectives

5th International Workshop, GREC 2003
Barcelona, Spain, July 30-31, 2003
Revised Selected Papers

 Springer

Volume Editors

Josep Lladós
Universitat Autònoma de Barcelona
Computer Vision Center, Department of Computer Science
Edifici O, Campus UAB, 08193 Bellaterra, Spain
E-mail: josep@cvc.uab.es

Young-Bin Kwon
Chung-Ang University, Department of Computer Engineering
221, Heuksukdong, Dongjakku, Seoul 156-756, Korea
E-mail: ybkwon@visionnet.cse.cau.ac.kr

Library of Congress Control Number: 2004111114

CR Subject Classification (1998): I.5, I.4, I.3.5, I.2.8, G.2.2, F.2.2, H.4

ISSN 0302-9743
ISBN 3-540-22478-5 Springer Berlin Heidelberg New York

Springer is a part of Springer Science+Business Media

springeronline.com

© Springer-Verlag Berlin Heidelberg 2004
Printed in Germany

Typesetting: Camera-ready by author, data conversion by Scientific Publishing Services, Chennai, India
Printed on acid-free paper   SPIN: 11301134   06/3142   5 4 3 2 1 0

Preface

This book contains refereed and improved papers presented at the 5th IAPR[1] International Workshop on Graphics Recognition (GREC 2003). GREC 2003 was held in the Computer Vision Center, in Barcelona (Spain) during July 30–31, 2003. The GREC workshop is the main activity of the IAPR-TC10, the Technical Committee on Graphics Recognition[2]. Edited volumes from the previous workshops in the series are available as Lecture Notes in Computer Science: LNCS Volume 1072 (GREC 1995 at Penn State University, USA), LNCS Volume 1389 (GREC 1997 in Nancy, France), LNCS Volume 1941 (GREC 1999 in Jaipur, India), and LNCS Volume 2390 (GREC 2001 in Kingston, Canada).

Graphics recognition is a particular field in the domain of document analysis that combines pattern recognition and image processing techniques for the analysis of any kind of graphical information in documents, either from paper or electronic formats. Topics of interest for the graphics recognition community are: vectorization; symbol recognition; analysis of graphic documents with diagrammatic notation like electrical diagrams, architectural plans, engineering drawings, musical scores, maps, etc.; graphics-based information retrieval; performance evaluation in graphics recognition; and systems for graphics recognition. In addition to the classic objectives, in recent years graphics recognition has faced up to new and promising perspectives, some of them in conjunction with other, affine scientific communities. Examples of that are sketchy interfaces and on-line graphics recognition in the framework of human computer interaction, or query by graphic content for retrieval and browsing in large-format graphic documents, digital libraries and Web applications. Thus, the combination of classic challenges with new research interests gives the graphics recognition field an active scientific community, with a promising future.

Following the tradition of the previous workshops in the series, the scientific program of GREC 2003 was organized in a single-track 2-day workshop. It comprised eight sessions dedicated to specific topics. For each session, there was an overview talk, followed by a number of short presentations. Each session was concluded by a panel discussion. The workshop had 47 registered participants from 15 different countries. After the workshop, all the authors were invited to submit enhanced versions of their papers for this edited volume. The authors were encouraged to include ideas and suggestions that arose in the panel discussions of the workshop. Every paper was evaluated by three reviewers. At least one reviewer was assigned from the attendees to the workshop. As a result of the reviewers' comments, many of the papers that appear in this volume were

---

[1] International Association for Pattern Recognition, http://www.iapr.org
[2] http://www.iapr-tc10.org

thoroughly revised and improved. Hence, we feel that the scientific contents of this book have excellent quality.

This volume is organized into seven sections, reflecting the session topics in the workshop: platforms, architectures and document knowledge models; technical documents, maps and charts; perceptual organization, indexing and graphical signatures; image analysis and low-level processing; symbol recognition, graphical matching and classification; on-line processing and user interfaces; and performance evaluation and contests.

Two contests were held during GREC 2003: The *Second Arc Segmentation Contest*, organized by Liu Wenyin, with two participants. And the *First Symbol Recognition Contest*, organized by Ernest Valveny and Philippe Dosch, with four participants. The contests were a big success, and the inclusion of them has become a key issue in GREC workshops. Contests are useful not only to evaluate the state-of-the-art on algorithms related to different problems of graphics recognition, but also to provide evaluation databases and ground-truth to the community. This time, all the material used in the contests was distributed in a CD among GREC 2003 delegates and can be downloaded from the TC10 Web page.

We owe special thanks to the contributing authors, the reviewers and also to the workshop chairs that stimulated active panel discussions at the end of the sessions. We also especially acknowledge the support provided by the sponsors of the workshop: the IAPR (International Association for Pattern Recognition), CVC (Computer Vision Center), UAB (Universitat Autònoma de Barcelona), AER-FAI (Asociación Española de Reconocimiento de Formas y Análisis de Imágenes), DURSI (Departament d'Universitats Recerca i Societat de la Informació, Generalitat de Catalunya), MCyT (Ministerio de Ciencia y Tecnología, TIC2002-11614-E), and HP (Hewlett-Packard). Many thanks also to Javier Jiménez, Enric Martí, Oriol Ramos, Gemma Sánchez, and Ernest Valveny, who were responsible for local arrangements, and worked hard both for the organization of the workshop and during the preparation of this book.

The 6th Graphics Recognition Workshop (GREC 2005[3]) will be held in Hong Kong, China, in August 2005, and it will be organized by Dr. Liu Wenyin.

April 2004   Josep Lladós
                                                                Young-Bin Kwon

---

General Chair

Josep Lladós, Spain

Program Co-chair

Young-Bin Kwon, Korea

Program Committee

Sergei Ablameyko, Belarus
Gady Agam, USA
Adnan Amin, Australia
Dorothea Blostein, Canada
Eugene Bodansky, USA
Atul Chhabra, USA
Luigi Cordella, Italy
David Doermann, USA
Dave Elliman, UK
Georgy Gimelfarb, New Zealand
Jianying Hu, USA

Chew Lim Tan, Singapore
Gerd Maderlechner, Germany
Enric Martí, Spain
Daisuke Nishiwaki, Japan
Lawrence O'Gorman, USA
Jean-Marc Ogier, France
Tony Pridmore, UK
Karl Tombre, France
Toyohide Watanabe, Japan
Liu Wenyin, China
Marcel Worring, Netherlands

Additional Referees

Sébastien Adam, France
Bertrand Coüasnon, France
Philippe Dosch, France
Pasquale Foggia, Italy
Alexander Gribov, USA
Joaquim Jorge, Portugal
Pierre Leclerq, Belgium
Sergei Levachkine, Mexico

Jean-Yves Ramel, France
Gemma Sánchez, Spain
Carlo Sansone, Italy
Eric Saund, USA
Eric Trupin, France
Ernest Valveny, Spain
Adam Winstanley, Ireland
Su Yang, China

Table of Contents

Perceptual Organization, Indexing and Graphical Signatures

Image Analysis and Low-Level Processing

Symbol Recognition, Graphical Matching and Classification

On-line Processing and Sketchy Interfaces

Performance Evaluation, Contests

Author Index

Strategy for Line Drawing Understanding

Jean-Yves Ramel[1] and Nicole Vincent[2]

[1] LI / Polytech'Tours - Université François Rabelais de Tours,
37250 Tours, France
ramel@univ-tours.fr
[2] Lab. SIP, Université Paris 5, 45, rue des Saints Pères,
75270 Paris Cedex 6, France
nicole.vincent@math-info.univ-paris5.fr

Abstract. In this paper, we present different strategies for localization and recognition of graphical entities in line drawings. Most systems include first a segmentation step of the document followed by a sequential extraction of the graphical entities. Some other systems try to recognize symbols directly on the bitmap image using more or less sophisticated techniques. In our system, an intermediate representation of the document provides a precise description of all the shapes present in the initial image. Thereafter, this representation constitutes the main part of a shared resource that will be used by different processes achieving the interpretation of the drawings. The actions (recognition) done by these different specialists are scheduled in order to read and understand the content of the document. The knowledge that is provided by the shared representation is used instead of the bitmap image material to drive the interpretation process. In the current system, the specialists are trying, during several cycles to interpret the drawings in an intelligent way by interpreting the simplest parts of a drawing first and making the shared representation evolve until the total understanding of the document.

1 Introduction

Most of the works achieved in the field of line drawing analysis and recognition, concern low level processing [1, 2] or symbol recognition [3, 4, 5] but very few studies deal with interpretation strategies or knowledge management in interpretation systems. Recently, Song [18] described and compared some algorithms that realize line or curve extraction in one or two step methods but do not deal with higher level processing. Nevertheless, it is obvious the way the different elementary tasks are performed and linked is of great importance, indeed, a better use of the techniques would improve quality of results. We are proposing a general approach for line drawing study, relying on an image representation that can evolve along the process and can be used by some actors to achieve any specific processing. In the first part of this paper, the classical strategies used for line drawing interpretation are presented from the extracted knowledge management point of view. Next, we propose another way to tackle the understanding problem. In our system, we have chosen to extract first the easy to recognize graphical entities such as text, curves and other high level symbols.

J. Lladós and Y.-B. Kwon (Eds.): GREC 2003, LNCS 3088, pp. 1–12, 2004.

Then, the more complex or more ambiguous cases benefit from the previously acquired knowledge. This extraction strategy we have called "from the simplest to the most complex" is detailed in section 4. In a last part, we illustrate the cyclic aspect of the strategy (notion of perceptive cycles) that allows the contextual extractions.

Thanks to the images presented all along the paper, we show the experimental results we have obtained on engineering drawings and how this system can be adapted to the analysis of different other types of drawings such as maps.

2 Traditional Interpretation Strategies

Here, we are to briefly recall the most traditional interpretation strategies. They can be divided in two classes. On one hand are the methods that rely on a multi-layer approach and on the other hand those that look for entities directly in the bitmap image.

2.1 Sequential Analysis

Traditional pattern recognition methods divide an interpretation process into two successive phases: the segmentation (low level processing) and the recognition (high level processing).

For line drawings, in most of the systems, the algorithms involved in the segmentation process are highlighting a layer organization of these documents [1, 6]. Their physical structure is generally composed of a thin line layer that contains the major part of the information and that can be divided in several other sub-layers, of a filled shape layer, of a text layer corresponding to annotations, and of some other possible layers that may be small symbols (arrowheads, disks, ...).

When all the layers have been extracted, the high level entities have to be rebuilt during the recognition stage. Then, we do not speak anymore of the physical structure of the drawing but rather of the underlying syntax. These syntactical rules are specifying the relations that may occur between shapes and that allow to recognize the different symbols. Numerous recognition methods (structural, syntactic, statistical, ...) could then be applied and a semantic analysis can bring some help to the analysis [7, 8].

Unfortunately, since the different parts of the high level entities can be dispatched among several layers, some difficulties may arise. Besides, the inconsistencies between information provided by different layers may be numerous and they are very difficult to handle because the segmentation result cannot be modified. So, the approach has to be limited quite simple drawings in order to act correctly. The figure 1a summarizes the classical architecture of such automatic reading systems.

It can be noticed (figure 1a) that low level processes P1, P2, ... use only the static bitmap image and some a priori knowledge to achieve the layer segmentation. The high level processes use the results of the segmentation (in the different layers) and some syntactic or semantic rules to interpret the drawing [9, 10, 11]. It is regrettable that no communication between processes of high and low levels or even of the same level exists when this processing scheme is adopted.

2.2 Direct Analysis

Some other systems use algorithms dedicated to symbol recognition which work directly on the image without any previous segmentation step. In this case, two classical ways to proceed can be mentioned :

- comparison of the connected components of the image with the different symbols or shapes we want to localize and that have been stored in a dictionary [12].
- looking for some particular configurations of lines in the image (closed loops, junctions, end points, ...) corresponding to potential symbols [8, 17].

If different processes are used to recognize these different shapes, their order of activation have to be defined. In this case, the processes can be managed by a controller (expert system). The activation of the recognition algorithms is then realized according to a set of rules specifying prerequisites for the extractions. We can also choose to create a hierarchical structuration of the recognition processes. Low level processing will be at the bottom of the tree and algorithms dedicated to high level object recognition will be at the top. Recognition algorithms should be adapted before being plugged in a such system and then we can speak of multi-agent systems.

These systems use a more opportunistic analysis method in order to understand the drawings, nevertheless the cooperation and activation of the different agents are very difficult to manage (implementation of the controller or cooperation). This is probably why we do not hear a lot about such processes. Figure 1b summarizes the architecture needed for direct analysis of drawings.

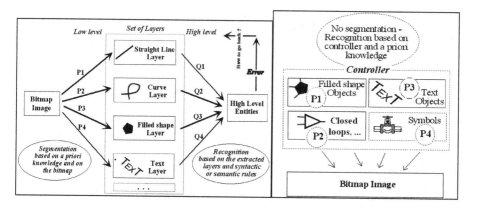

Fig. 1. (a) Sequential or (b) direct interpretation of a drawing

Finally, we can conclude that the extraction of graphical entities in a document is most often achieved either in a sequential or a hierarchical way [11, 13]. The global task is then decomposed into a succession of elementary stages and an entity of a given level can always be considered as a composition of some lower level elements.

We are now to present how we propose to deal with the problem. First we precise the different tools we have defined and the architecture of the process. Then the strategy is the object of the last section.

3 Cyclical Interpretation

We have decided to mix the two previous approaches. To do that, first a representation has been defined to describe and manage all the present shapes and all the available information known about in the studied document. Both the use of a powerful representation that enables an easy share of the information and of several agents each one achieving a precise task makes it possible, during the document analysis, to put segmentation and recognition processes at the same level. We have also tried to separate the a priori knowledge and the extracted information from the interpretation algorithms.

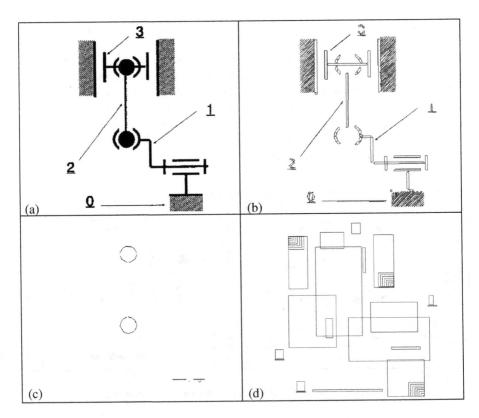

Fig. 2. (a) Initial image and its representation (b) Quadrilaterals and (c) contours Vectors, (d) Connected Components (CC)

3.1   The Image Representation

The representation to be shared by different processors will replace the initial bitmap image and evolve along the recognition process. It is achieved by a contour vectorisation step followed by a structural graph construction [14]. The elementary entities are such as quadrilaterals and vectors. Our vectorisation algorithm can be compared to Shimotsuji's [15] or Shih's [16] methods. Through a one step computation it provides several interesting pieces of information (figure 2):

- a set of quadrilaterals for the representation of the thin shapes (lines)
- a set of contour vectors for the filled shapes
- all the connected components of the image

Next, a structural graph was found the most adapted way to represent topological relations (parallel, corner, intersection, above, below, ...) between the elements present in the built representation. The patterns (vectors, quadrilaterals, ...) label the nodes of the graph while the arcs describe the nature of the existing topological relations between these patterns (figure 3).

Examples of patterns in the representation					
Topological relation	T junction T(1,2)	X (Intersection) X(1,2)	P (Parallel) P(1,2)	L junction L(1,2)	S (Successive) S(1,2)

Fig. 3. Topological relations between patterns

As we tend towards understanding of the document, we have modeled the way human observer can focus on any of the patterns by the definition of an influence zone. Figure 4 describes the graph construction process applied to the influence area (the dotted rectangle) of a Quadrilateral pattern (in gray). After the construction of the sub-graphs corresponding to all the patterns present in the representation, we obtain the global image structural graph.

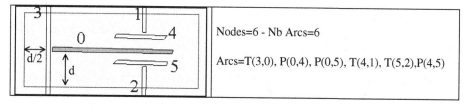

Nodes=6 - Nb Arcs=6

Arcs=T(3,0), P(0,4), P(0,5), T(4,1), T(5,2),P(4,5)

Fig. 4. Influence area of the Quadrilateral 0 and the corresponding sub-graph

3.2   Perceptive Cycles

The interpretation of the drawings is achieved using different processes we have called specialists. No controller is needed to activate these specialists, the chosen architecture includes a mechanism of "perceptive cycles" (figure 5). During the cycles, the specialists are activated sequentially. Progressively, they contribute to simplify and to improve the image representation . The shared representation can then be compared to a Blackboard structure where all the useful information is easily accessible and can be modified by any specialist. As can be seen in figure 5, knowledge and extracted data are in the shared resource and are clearly separated from recognition processes.

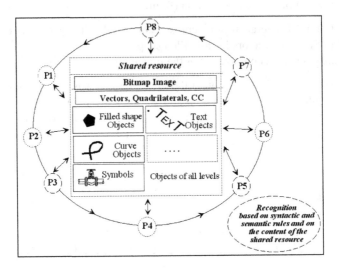

Fig. 5. Cyclical interpretation of a drawing

The specialists use the shared representation as a context to generate hypotheses. They analyze and recognize the symbols, they merge simple objects to build more complex entities (curves, mechanical elements,...) and thus, they make the representation evolve. For example, at the beginning the representation contains no text area, but cycle after cycle more and more text areas will be localized. The context management is therefore achieved automatically and allows the specialists to take into account previously extracted entities. Thus, we obtain a better use of the information acquired during the interpretation process.

The specialists have to extract only reliable data at the present instant: the evidences. Then, the number of mistakes is limited during the analysis and less incoherencies appear minimizing the snowball effects. Besides, we can mention the approach brings another interest as it enables to overstep explicitly and rationally the decision conflicts. No specific controller is needed.

The chosen method, combining perceptive cycles minimizing error risk, enables to change the specialists activation order without modifying the final results. Only the interpretation process speed will increase or decrease. Some objects are more easily located than others or they constitute a prerequisite to the location of higher level entities, nevertheless all of them will be detected in the same way in a more or less long period of time. Indeed, some data, ambiguous at a given instant, for a given specialist, could be an evidence for an other specialist. So, during all the cycles the number of ambiguities decreases with regard to the current state of interpretation.

Depending on the type of the drawing to be analyzed, the user (the expert) decides the investigation strategy to be followed in order to extract, as best as possible, the different types of graphical entities. That is to say, the user chooses, within one cycle, the type of the specialists and their activation order. For example, for the kinetic diagrams, we have chosen the following cycle: Text → Filled shapes → Dotted lines → Curves → Annotations → Symbols → 3D reconstruction.

4 From the Simplest to the More Complex

Every decision taken by a specialist is considered as a definitive result. After each cycle, an analysis of the shared representation content is achieved in order to decide whether the analysis is achieved or not. If necessary, a new cycle is restarted to solve some complex problems that remain. To emphasis the incremental aspect of the strategy, it is interesting to increase the adaptation capacities of the specialists along the cycles, modifying some parameters specifying these specialists.

In addition to the knowledge provided by the shared representation, a specialist uses (unfortunately !) different parameters in order to achieve its task. The values of these parameters, are fixed in a severe way to restrict error risk at the beginning (for extraction of reliable data), then we make them evolve, cycle after cycle, in order to become less and less coercive. The table 1 shows how can evolve the parameters used by some specialists during the interpretation of kinetic diagrams.

Table 1. Evolution of the parameters (Nc=number of the cycle in progress)

Text Specialist		Curve Specialist		Symbol Specialist	
Parameter	Value	Parameter	Value	Parameter	Value
Max length of quadrilaterals	Constant	Max length of quadrilaterals	Constant	Max length of quadrilaterals	Constant
Size of virtual text component : Tv	$Tv<Nc *100$	Number of Successive quadrilaterals : Nq	$Nq > 6 - Nc$ $(Nc < 6)$	Size of the influence area	$d = 100 +$ $20 * Nc$
Real connected component presence	Needed during the first cycle only	Error : E	$E < (e\_moy$ $* Nc)/2$ $e\_moy =$ line thickness		
Proximity of other text areas : dt	$dt = +\infty$ for $Nc < 2,$ $dt<Nc*100$ after				

In table 1, we have indicated the knowledge (rules) used by the Text specialist during the cycles: The length of the quadrilaterals (the elementary straight lines) should be lower than a constant threshold, the size of the virtual text component (corresponding to a set of these small connected quadrilaterals) should be lower during the first cycle, the virtual text component should overlap a real connected component, after the first cycle the only constraint on virtual text component is to be close to an already detected text area.

Some successive stages of an extraction process are shown in figure 6. The first perceptive cycle starts by the activation of the Text specialist. We can notice on image 2), that at the beginning of the first cycle, the number of zones focused (virtual text components) that will be studied by this specialist is quite important. Nevertheless most of the characters (drawn in black in image 3) are detected without any problem. We can also notice that the x and y axes arrowheads have been considered as characters.

Image 4) describes the results obtained by the process that isolates the curves in the image. In our system, curves are modeled by Bezier curves. Then, the mechanical entities associated with specific graphs are correctly isolated in image 5); only a stationary swivel was disconcerted with a slippery swivel (framed by a dotted line). The mistake is due to the bad representation of a line: a hand drawn line (not perfectly straight) has been figured by 2 quadrilaterals instead of one.

From image 6), the second cycle is concerned. Evidences have been extracted and the specialists can now try to solve more complex problems. As can be seen in image 6), during the second activation of the Text specialist the number of focusing zones has decreased a lot. Some problematic zones (during the first cycle) for this specialist have constituted evidences for some other specialists (curves, mechanical elements,...). As these ambiguities have been solved, new text zone localization is made easier, as shown by dotted rectangles on image 7) and parameters have been modified. The specialist can use previously recognized objects (text, curves, symbols, ...) to generate new hypotheses. Moreover, as explained before, it uses less restrictive parameters to recognize new text areas in the same drawing.

In all the images of the figure 6, the gray parts are corresponding to low level features that have still not been interpreted at the given instant in the current perceptive cycle. We can notice that, after each step, this representation is simplified with respect to the previous state. During the cycles, as the used parameters are less restricting, new entities are extracted and both simplification and improvement of the shared resource occur (creation of new objects). Interpretation ends when a whole perceptive cycle brings no more modification to the shared resource. The understanding is complete if the data stored in the representation present no more unlabelled objects. Other wise, the system will ask the user to help the system towards understanding. The user has to solve the problems remaining after the automatic process is stopped.

5 Conclusion

In the proposed architecture, knowledge management and interpretation strategy problems are solved thanks to both the use of a shared representation and by the cyclical activation of specialists.

Each specialist, during several cycles, uses the information at its disposal in order to send back some coherent data of higher complexity level. It analyses the consistency of a shared representation from its own point of view by a confrontation of the representation with its own knowledge (parameters, syntactic or semantic rules, ...). Until now, a specialist cannot use an entity already used by an other specialist. However it could be possible without a lot of modifications in the system. It would probably bring new results but it would also raise many problems; among them we can mention the difficulty:

- to evaluate the results coming from different processings
- to merge results provided by different processings
- to define the rules that lead to choose one process rather than an other one

In most other systems, management of recognized entities (hatched area, text, ...) raises problems by increasing the complexity of the recognition of the other elements. Our representation and its evolution mechanism solve this difficulty and enable detection of objects that are elements in several entities.

Generally, during the detection or the recognition of high semantic level entities, the difficulty occurs at the beginning of the interpretation when the context on which the analysis is based is too poor. It appeared to us that the extraction of reliable data first, during perceptive cycles, would be a good solution to limit this problem as well as the inconsistencies resolution stages and their avalanche of undesirable effects.

The chosen architecture is based on specialists that realize a specific task and so preserve a possible generalization. Indeed, the list of the specialists could be modified or completed according to the problem to be solved without any modification of the global architecture. The set of specialists could be plugged in a tool box. Then, each tool could be used and could be activated in a different way according to the type of the drawing we want to interpret.

The tests we have done until now give us encouraging results and let us think that our architecture can prove to be efficient to build a software allowing the analysis or the indexation of different types of line drawings (image 10 in figure 6).

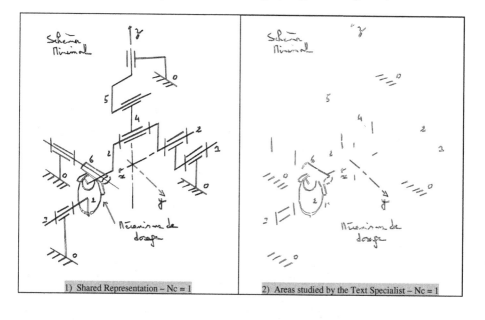

1) Shared Representation – Nc = 1 2) Areas studied by the Text Specialist – Nc = 1

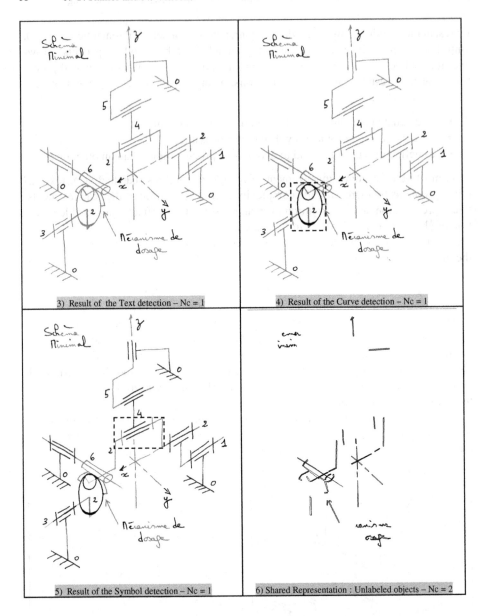

3) Result of the Text detection – Nc = 1

4) Result of the Curve detection – Nc = 1

5) Result of the Symbol detection – Nc = 1

6) Shared Representation : Unlabeled objects – Nc = 2

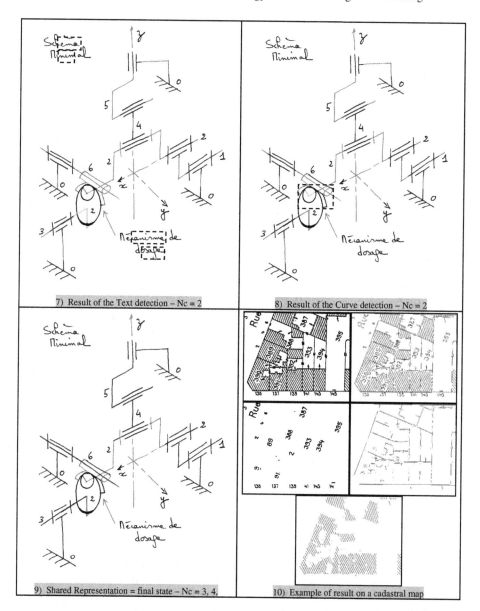

Fig. 6. Some views describing the state of the interpretation process (Nc = number of the in progress cycle)

References

1. Hilaire, X. Tombre, K. Improving the accuracy of skeleton based vectorization. Graphics recognition – algorithms and applications. In lecture notes in computer sciences. Springer verlag. Volume 2390. 2002, p. 273–288.
2. Dori, D. And Tombre, K. Form engineering drawings to 3D CAD models: are we ready now? Computer Aided Design, 1995, Vol. 29, no. 4. p. 243–254.
3. Ah-Soon, C. Tombre, K. Architectural Symbol recognition using a network of constrainst. Pattern Recognition Letters, 2001. Vol 22(2). p. 231–248
4. Adam, S. Ogier, JM. Cariou, C. Mullot, R. Labiche, J. Gardes J. Symbol and Character recognition: application to engineering drawings. International Journal of Document Analysis and Recognition. 2000. Vol 3(2). p. 89–101.
5. Cordella, LP. Vento, M. Symbol recognition in documents: a collection of techniques. International Journal of Document Analysis and Recognition. 2000. Vol 3(2). p. 73–88
6. Shimotsuji, S. Hori, O. Asano M. Robust drawing recognition based on model-guided segmentation. IAPR Workshop on document analysis systems. Kasserslautern (Allemagne) 1994. p. 337–348.
7. Bunke, H. Error correcting graph matching. On the influence of the underlying cost function. IEEE transaction on PAMI. 1999. Vol 21(9), p. 917–922.
8. Yu, D. Samal, A. Seth, S. A system for recognizing a large class of engineering drawings. IEEE Transaction of Pattern Analysis and Machine Intelligence. 1997, Vol. 19, no. 8, p. 868–890.
9. Joseph, S.H. and Pridmore, T.P. Knowledge directed interpretation of mechanical engineering drawings. IEEE Transactions on Pattern Analysis and Machine Intelligence, 1992, Vol. 14, no. 9, p. 928–940.
10. DenHartog, JE. TenKate TK. Gerbrands JJ. Knowledge based interpretation of utility maps. Computer Vision and Image Understanding. 1996, Vol. 63, no. 1, p. 105–117.
11. Ogier, JM. Mullot, R. Labiche J. Lecourtier Y. Semantic coherency: the basis of an image interpretation device – application to the cadastral map interpretation. IEEE Transaction on Systems, Man and Cybernetics. 2000, Vol. 30, no. 2. p. 237–244.
12. Llados, J. Valveny E, Sanchez G, Marti E. Symbol recognition: current advances and perspectives. In lecture notes in computer sciences. Springer verlag. Volume 2390. 2002, p. 104–127.
13. Pasternak, B., Neumann, B. ADIK: An adaptable drawing interpretation kernel. International Joint Conference on artificial Intelligence. Avignon, 1993. Vol. 1. p. 531–540.
14. Ramel, JY. Vincent, N. Emptoz H. A structural representation for understanding line drawing images. International Journal on Document Analysis and Recognition. Special issue on Graphics Recognition, Volume 3, no. 2 - Décembre 2000. p. 58–66.
15. Shimotsuji, S. Hori, O. Asano, M. Suzuki, K. Hoshino, F. Ishii, T. A robust recognition system for a drawing superimposed on a map. Computer in USA. 1992, Vol. 25, no. 7, p. 56–59.
16. Shih, C. and Kasturi, R. Extraction of graphic primitives from images of paper based line drawings. Machine Vision and Applications, 1989, Vol. 2, p. 103–113.
17. Kadonaga, T. and Abe, K. Comparison of methods for detecting corner points from digital curves. Lecture Notes in Computer Science no. 1072. Graphics Recognition, Methods and Applications. R. Kasturi and K. Tombre Eds. 1995. p. 23–34.
18. Song, J. Su, F. Tai, M. and Cai, S. An Object-Oriented Progressive-Simplification-Based vectorization system for engineering drawings: model, algorithm, and performance. IEEE Transaction on Pattern Analysis and Machine Intelligence. Vol 24. no. 8, 2002. p. 1048–1060.

DocMining: A Cooperative Platform for Heterogeneous Document Interpretation According to User-Defined Scenarios

Eric Clavier[1], Gérald Masini[2], Mathieu Delalandre[3], Maurizio Rigamonti[4],
Karl Tombre[2], and Joël Gardes[1]

[1] France Télécom R&D, 2 Avenue Pierre Marzin, 22307 Lannion Cedex, France
{rntl.ball001, Joel.Gardes}@rd.francetelecom.com
[2] LORIA, B. P. 239, 54506 Vandœuvre-lès-Nancy Cedex, France
{Gerald.Masini, Karl.Tombre}@loria.fr
[3] PSI Laboratory, Université de Rouen, 76821 Mont Saint Aignan, France
Mathieu.Delalandre@univ-rouen.fr
[4] DIUF, Université de Fribourg, Chemin du musée, 31700 Fribourg, Switzerland
Maurizio.Rigamonti@unifr.ch

Abstract. The DocMining platform is aimed at providing a general framework for document interpretation. It integrates document processing units coming from different sources and communicating through the document being interpreted. A task to be performed is represented by a scenario that describes the units to be run, and each unit is associated with a contract that describes the parameters, data and results of the unit as well as the way to run it. A controller interprets the scenario and triggers each required document processing unit at its turn. Documents, scenarios and contracts are all represented in XML, to make data manipulation and communications easier.

1 Introduction

The design of document analysis systems requires the integration of various components and algorithms (image processings, character and symbol recognition, interpretation tasks, etc.), especially when it has to deal not only with textual components but also with graphics and images. If the aim is the design of a versatile system, the components must be able to cooperate in a flexible way and the domain knowledge must be easy to integrate into the system.

The classical way to process a textual document consists in segmenting the document into homogeneous zones to apply character recognition methods followed by "linguistic" post-processing steps: Dictionary lookup, application of language models, etc. There is good know-how in building such systems [2], as well as systems, like smartFIX, dedicated to more general "business documents" [7].

Mature systems are available for specific domains, such as check processing [10], recognition of tables [17], or recognition of forms [13]. However, especially when graphics-rich documents are concerned, most of the working systems

J. Lladós and Y.-B. Kwon (Eds.): GREC 2003, LNCS 3088, pp. 13–24, 2004.
© Springer-Verlag Berlin Heidelberg 2004

designed up to now appear to be specific to a given application area. For example, the system by IBM Italy for the Italian land register maps encapsulates all the domain knowledge in its core [3]. Arias et al. also describe a system for the analysis of manhole drawings for a telephone company [1], whereas Dosch et al. propose an interactive system for architectural drawings analysis [9]. Some systems are designed to analyze drawings made of symbols and connecting lines [19], and the MAGELLAN system exploits the connections of legends to extract information from maps [16]. Only very little work has been done to build generic tools. In most cases, this implies that the system only offers low-level tools, or that it supplies complex and exhaustive knowledge representation schemes. The work by Pasternak [14], based on a hierarchical and structural description coupled with triggering mechanisms, and the DMOS method, based on syntactical techniques [4], belong to this category.

In this paper, we present an approach that may seem less ambitious, as we do not aim at representing all the domain knowledge, but that is probably more realistic when the purpose is to be able to process a large number of heterogeneous documents and to allow users to define their own knowledge. This approach is based on strategic knowledge acquisition and instrumentation. The knowledge describes the tools to be used to extract objects from documents and the chaining relations between these tools [15]. Scenarios, *i.e.* sequences of calls to *document processing units* (DPU's), may subsequently be constructed and executed, using available libraries of such units.

More precisely, the paper describes the DocMining platform that provides a general framework for document interpretation. The platform architecture is plug-in oriented, so that users can conveniently integrate new processing units. Document visualization and manipulation tools are designed according to the same principle, so that a user is able to fully customize the interactions with the platform. DPU's communicate through the document to be processed, that contains not only graphical objects and data, but also traces of the execution of the DPU's, in order to avoid the problems of data scattering usually met in classical document processing chains. Running a scenario results in collecting some user's experience, that becomes part of the scenario itself. The scenario may then be transformed into a new DPU corresponding to a higher-level granularity.

As a user can create his own objects, integrate his own DPU's into the platform, design his own interfaces and define his own scenarios, all the users share and exchange knowledge through the platform. In this way, the platform may be used for various purposes:

- Domain specific platform design: Document processing units available for a particular kind of document can be integrated into the platform as plug-in's. The domain knowledge is taken into account through domain specific scenarios and may be manipulated by interfaces especially defined by users.
- Evaluation of the results quality and of the influence of parameters and thresholds tuning, thanks to the trace recorded during the execution.
- Evaluation of the efficiency of a processing unit according to the nature of the input documents.

- Benchmarking: Such a task consists in a predefined scenario describing a full processing chain. Each process to be experimented is associated with a so-called contract and each corresponding algorithm is implemented according to the specifications of its contract. When the scenario is run, the efficiency of the processing units can be directly measured.
- Experimentation of various implementations of a same algorithm: As users share the same integration framework, they can exchange processing units. They do not have to re-implement units already implemented by partners.

This project is supported by the DocMining consortium, including four academic partners, PSI Lab (Rouen, France), Project Qgar (LORIA, Nancy, France), L3I Lab (La Rochelle, France), DIUF Lab (Fribourg, Switzerland), and one industrial partner, GRI Lab from France Télécom R&D (Lannion, France). It is partially funded by the French Ministry of Research, under the auspices of RNTL (*Réseau National des Technologies Logicielles*).

2   Overview of the DocMining Platform

The platform architecture includes five main components (Fig. 1). The document base contains images of documents associated with metadata, the so-called document structures. A document structure represents the structure of the corresponding document at a given time, as well as information expressing how this structure has been produced. Users can define their own document structures, according to their needs.

The document processing base provides the ability to (re)use document processing units from various (remote) libraries. The platform makes them interoperate by providing a common integration framework based on the notion of contract, defined between each DPU and the document structure. Any user interface connected to the platform may access and manipulate the whole document structure or part of it, as all the users' interactions with the document are defined according to the same plug-in approach.

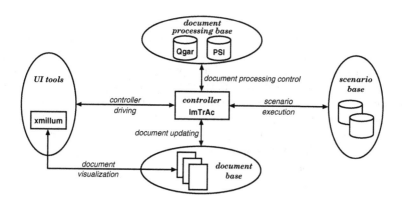

Fig. 1. The DocMining platform architecture

An interpretation task is represented by a scenario expressing the user's strategic knowledge, *i.e.* the parameters of the processing units, and the objects and data manipulated by the different units. The controller is responsible for running scenarios, updating the document structure, simulating processings, and so on. Its main task consists in controlling how processing units and scenarios access the document structure. It selects the required document elements to be processed at each step of a scenario, and updates the global document structure when each process is completed. When a processing unit is run, the controller transmits the required document elements and parameters to the unit. On the one hand, using a controller guarantees that all changes in a document structure are recorded and then may be utilized as a basis for building new scenarios. On the other hand, this ensures that a processing unit has no direct access to the document structure. The parts of the document structure that the unit has to access are specified by its contract.

Concerning document processing design, our contract-based approach has the advantage of being implementation independent, as users can change DPU implementations without modifying the corresponding contracts. Moreover, since the contract of each DPU is defined in a normalized way, all the platform users communicate with DPU's in the same way, especially to provide them with their parameter values.

3   The Platform Implementation

The platform implementation is based on a Java/XML architecture and relies on four major components.

The PSI Library integrates different research works of the PSI Laboratory and includes chains of processing units using statistical and/or structural approaches [5]. It is divided into three sub-libraries dedicated to image processing (mathematical morphology, blob coloring, feature extraction, etc.), classification (similarity search, model reconstruction, etc.), and XML data management. They are written in different languages (Java, C/C++, as well as XSLT stylesheets or Quilt query scripts) and can be run on Windows or Linux operating systems.

The Qgar software system[1] is developed by the same-named project for the design of document analysis applications [8] and includes three parts written in C++. QgarLib is a library of C++ classes implementing basic graphics analysis and recognition methods. QgarApps is an applicative layer, including high-level applications (text-graphics separation, thick-thin separation, vectorization, etc.). Applications may be designed and run using an interactive graphical interface called QgarGUI, that incorporates data manipulation and display capabilities. Any application, either designed apart from Qgar or not, may be integrated into the system by simply wrapping it with a predefined C++ class, without recompiling any part of the system itself.

---

[1] http://www.qgar.org/

```
<object_doc source="icdar2001.pdf" type="PdfDoc">
   <object_position h="842" w="595" x="0" y="0"/>
   <object_doc type="TextLine">
      <object_position h="17" w="309" x="144" y="104"/>
      <object_data>
         <ascii_data>Web-Based Cooperative Document Understanding</ascii_data>
      </object_data>
   </object_doc>
   <object_doc type="TextLine">
      <object_position h="12" w="225" x="62" y="267"/>
      <object_data>
         <ascii_data>This paper presents our ongoing work on the design of</ascii_data>
      </object_data>
   </object_doc>
   ...
</object_doc>
```

Fig. 2. The structure of a textual (PDF) document: Lines of text are represented by TextLine objects, provided with a location and a line content (as extra data)

xmillum (XML illuminator) is a framework for cooperative and interactive analysis of documents developed by the DIVA group at the University of Fribourg [11]. It is based on the philosophy that a document recognition system does not work in a fully automatic way, but cooperates with the user to incrementally learn from its feedback and to adapt itself to different document properties[2]. This approach implies that xmillum offers complex visualization and editing capabilities. Moreover, xmillum is independent from a particular document recognition system, as it does not require any specific language. There is a unique constraint: The original data must be represented in XML. Using an XSLT stylesheet, it is subsequently transformed into a xmillum specific structure represented with objects (defining how to visualize a data element), styles (specifying the rendering properties of the objects), handlers (encapsulating the interactions with the objects), selectors (indicating to handlers which objects are involved in an action), tools (that are specific modules extending xmillum capabilities, such as multiple views of a document), and layers (that are the data containers). The xmillum editor interprets this structure, but does not contain any implementation. It uses external modules to visualize or edit data, which makes xmillum freely extensible.

At last, the ImTrAc package, developed by the GRI Lab at France Télécom R&D Lannion, provides a processing engine, to control process running, and a scenario engine, to control scenario running, as well as tools to integrate new processing units in the system and to create scenarios.

3.1 Documents

A document is represented by an XML tree constructed according to an XML schema (Fig. 2). Basic elements are graphical objects defined by their type

---

[2] The so-called "CIDRE" (Cooperative and Interactive Document Reverse Engineering) philosophy is supported by the Swiss National Fund for Scientific Research, code 2000-059356.99-1.

(`Binary Image`, `Connected Component`, `Text Block`...), their source (the document they come from), and their location in the image. We did not try to elaborate a complete predefined taxonomy of possible types: A user can define his own graphical object types, when necessary. A graphical object includes intrinsic data describing the way the object is physically represented, using an XML schema defined from basic data types such as `Freeman Chain`, `Feature Vector`, etc. Just as previously, a user can define his own data types.

However, a document is more than a simple description in terms of graphical objects and data. Its structure also contains information (name, parameters...) about processing units that have been applied to the document and that have yielded the objects. Objects included in the document structure are visualized using xmillum, thanks to XSLT stylesheets that define which objects may be visualized, how they are visualized, and how events involving objects (mouse clicks, for example) are handled. Each object is associated to a Java class that performs the rendering.

3.2   Document Processing Units

As previously said, a DPU has no direct access to the document structure and cannot modify it unless a so-called contract, defined according to an XML schema, has been established with the document. This contract describes the unit behavior: The way the processing modifies the XML document structure (by adding, removing, or updating nodes), the kind of graphical objects it produces, as well as parameters that do not require access to the document structure. The objects that a DPU may modify or access are defined by specifying a "trigger" node (that enables the execution of the corresponding DPU) and "updated" nodes (that are modified by the DPU). This means that the node that launches a DPU is not necessarily the one that is modified by the DPU. This distinction gives more flexibility to the design of DPU's, as a user may associate conditions with launching nodes (to require the presence of a particular kind of object, for example) and updated nodes. At the present time, various separate applications from the QgarApps and PSI libraries can be run by the DocMining platform.

3.3   Scenarios

In order to achieve interpretation tasks, users can interactively construct scenarios, that are defined as structured combinations of DPU's. There are two ways of creating a scenario. One is based on the contracts: As objects input and output by units are specified in the corresponding contracts, it is possible to determine which unit can feed a given unit and then to combine them.

The other way relies on a xmillum component that has been especially developed for the DocMining platform. It provides means to interact with the processing engine (ImTrAc) and to visualize the structure of a document. For each object of the document, the engine is able to supply the list of DPU's that may be applied. Once the user has chosen a DPU, the engine supplies the parameter list of the unit to the user, so as to get the corresponding values and to be able to launch the DPU. When the DPU terminates, ImTrAc updates the document structure and the user can then interact with the newly created objects. Each user action on the document is recorded in the scenario, that may later be applied to another document.

4   A Scenario for Mixed Text/Graphics Documents

The DocMining platform has already been used to produce scenarios dedicated to various domains, like page segmentation evaluation or production of ground-truth data sets. The scenario presented here in detail performs the analysis of documents with a mixed text-graphics content and may be used for different purposes. It may become part of a more general document interpretation system, and be used to evaluate the robustness of an algorithm in case of noisy input images (leading to text-graphics separation errors). It may also be used as a benchmarking tool: When a developer implements a particular step of the scenario, he may run the different available processing units to evaluate the efficiency of his implementation.

4.1   Scenario Overview

In fact, the aim of the scenario is the separation of the graphical part of a document from its textual part, which can be briefly described as three main steps: Firstly, separate the graphical layer from the textual layer; secondly, perform a segmentation into text blocks on the textual layer, and then apply an OCR process on the resulting blocks to produce ASCII texts; finally, perform a vectorization on the graphical layer, to get graphical primitives represented in SVG or DXF format. The efficiency of such a scenario deeply depends on the efficiency of the text-graphics separation step. If some of the image components are mislabeled or not labeled during this step, further processing units cannot be correctly performed. It is therefore necessary to add an extra step dedicated to the correction of labeling errors. The final steps are ordered as follows:

1. Binarize the image.
2. Perform text-graphics separation.
3. Perform segmentation into text blocks on the textual layer.
4. Perform segmentation into connected components on the graphical layer.
5. Perform segmentation into connected components on the parts that have not been classified as graphical or textual parts.
6. Correct text-graphics separation errors by a cross-examination of the results of these three segmentations.
7. Perform OCR on the text blocks of the resulting textual layer.
8. Perform vectorization on the resulting graphical layer.

Figure 3 shows the different steps and the objects manipulated during the execution. This kind of scenario differs from classical sequential processing chains, that do not include switches like those of steps 2 and 6.

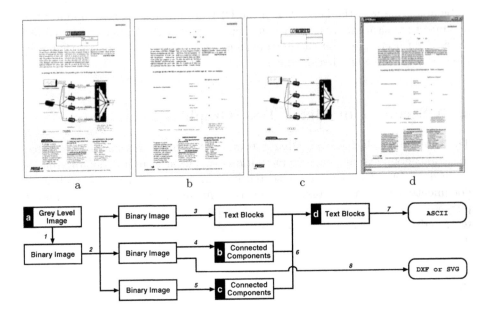

Fig. 3. The scenario for text-graphics separation. A number corresponds to a scenario step, a rectangle to the object that is produced, and a letter to an image: initial image (a), graphical (b) and textual (c) layers resulting from text-graphics separation, final text blocks visualized by xmillum (d)

4.2   The Processing Units

Processing units involved in the scenario are taken from the libraries connected to the platform. *Binarization* may be performed using one of four available units. The PSI library implements two standard algorithms for automatic computation of binarization thresholds. One is histogram-based, the other is clustering-based [12]. The QgarApps library supplies an adaptive algorithm proposed by Trier and Taxt with some minor adaptations [18]. The last processing unit implements a raw method: The binarization threshold is given by the user.

Text-graphics separation is based on a method initially proposed by Fletcher and Kasturi and implemented by the Qgar Project, with an extra absolute threshold for the size of a text component [18].

For *text block segmentation*, two processing units are available at the present time: One is based on a classical top-down approach, the other on an hybrid approach [10]. The latter works by detecting pieces of text lines in small overlapping columns. These pieces are then merged by a bottom-up algorithm to form complete text lines and blocks of text lines.

The method for *connected component segmentation* is provided by the PSI image processing (sub-)library, that includes some applications based on a standard blob coloring algorithm: Image labeling, component analysis, and occlusion extraction [5, 6].

The purpose of the last processing unit, *correction of text-graphics separation errors*, is to adequately assign mislabeled or unlabeled connected components of the graphical layer to the textual layer. Each connected component of the graphical layer located inside a text block of the textual layer is transfered to the textual layer.

4.3   Results

The execution of the scenario is partly illustrated by Figure 3. From an initial gray level image (cf. Fig. 3a), a text-graphics separation method (step 2) provides three new images representing the graphical layer (cf. Fig. 3b), the textual layer (cf. Fig. 3c), and the layer of unclassified parts (not shown here). The cross-examination of the text-blocks extracted from the textual layer and of the connected components extracted from the two other layers (step 6) allows a complete identification of the text blocks present in the initial image (cf. Fig. 3d). OCR (step 7) and vectorization (step 8) tasks are then respectively applied to the text blocks and to the graphical layer to get a full segmentation of the initial image into graphical and textual primitives.

5   Constructing the Scenario

The construction of a scenario is performed with an interactive tool called SCI (Scenario Construction Interface), that has been developed to drive the ImTrAc controller. The construction relies on a structural combination of DPU's belonging to the processing base. As explained in section 3.3, the combination is made possible by associating each DPU with a contract describing its behavior. Thanks to this very notion of contract, the elaboration of a scenario does not require any processing unit to be run.

Figure 4 shows screenshots displaying a partial view of a document tree structure: The popup menu shows authorized processing units for the currently selected node (*i.e.* the activation node). We can see that the correction of text-graphics separation errors is not possible (the corresponding processing unit does not appear in the popup menu of Fig. 4a) unless a connected component segmentation has been performed before (cf. Fig. 4b: This time, the processing unit appears in the popup menu). This implies that the coherence of a scenario is always validated during the construction itself of the scenario.

Figure 5 shows the contract defined for the DPU that performs the corrections of text-graphics separation errors. The noticeable aspects of the contract, as explained in section 3.2, can be seen: The service (tag `<service/>`), the produced objects (tag `<produced_object/>`), and the handled objects (tag `<xpath_exp/>`). The contract is not just an XML translation of a classical configuration file. In fact, it includes "processing instructions" as XPath expressions, like the one on line 8 (in italic shape), which indicates which elements the DPU needs. The ImTrAc engine interprets the Xpath expression, extracts the resulting element set from the document and transmits it to the DPU. The notion of

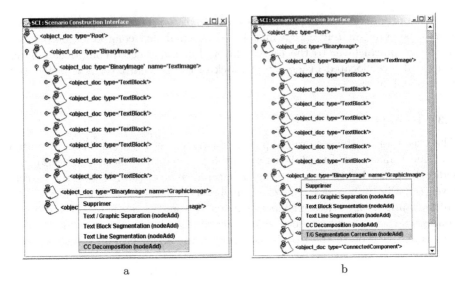

Fig. 4. The correction of text-graphics separation errors (b) is possible if and only if it is preceded by a connected component segmentation (a)

```
<process_property class_name="docmining.sox.extern.OrphanMerger">
  <service name="nodeAdd">
    <handled_object>
      <xpath_exp>./object_doc[@type="ConnectedComponent"]</xpath_exp>
      <process_config>
        <param type="Input" name="TextImage" support="ObjectDoc"
          param_value="//object_doc[@name="TextImage"]" />
        <param type="ParamIn" name="Orphans" support="ObjectDoc"
          param_value="./object_doc[@type="ConnectedComponent"]"/>
        <param type="ParamIn" name="ThreshFactor" support="Data" param_value="2"/>
      </process_config>
      <produced_object>
        <object_doc type="TextBlock">
          <object_doc type="ConnectedComponent"> <object_info type_list='yes'/> </object_doc>
          <object_info type_list='yes'/>
        </object_doc>
      </produced_object>
    </handled_object>
  </service>
</process_property>
```

Fig. 5. The contract of the processing unit that performs the corrections of the text-graphics separation errors

contract thus allows the delegation of part of a processing unit and increases the flexibility of the platform architecture. It provides a method for adapting users' data to processing units rather than adapting processing units to users' data. DPU's may be triggered from any node, may modify any node of the structure, and may take any node as a parameter, with very precise selection criteria.

The SCI tool, that drives the ImTrAc engine, has actually been integrated as a component of xmillum to be used as an interface to visualize and manipulate the document structure, as well as to construct and run scenarios. In particular, users can conveniently apply selected processing units to the document structure and, having visualized the results, tune the parameters of the units to improve the results quality. The way documents and document structures are visualized depends on styles described by XSLT scripts (cf. Fig. 3d for an example).

6   Conclusion

DocMining is not an interpretation system but a framework. It is a first step towards the definition of a flexible and reusable system to be used as a basis to develop applications related to specific domains or to design an interpretation system able to run complex scenarios requiring to combine processing units possibly coming from different sources (*e.g.* research projects). Among its main advantages, it lets users free in their choices about the information structure manipulated by the system as well as about the implementation of the processing units. These ideas has been successfully experimented and validated using scenarios to segment documents into textual and graphical parts.

Acknowledgments

The authors wish to especially thank Oliver Hitz and Rolf Ingold (DIUF Lab, Université de Fribourg), Jean-Marc Ogier (L3I Lab, Université de La Rochelle), Florent Le Dret (Université de La Rochelle), Jan Rendek (Qgar Project, LORIA, Nancy), Yves Lecourtier and Eric Trupin (PSI Lab, Université de Rouen), as well as all the other participants in the DocMining Consortium for their contribution to the work described by this paper.

References

1. J.-F. Arias, C.P. Lai, S. Surya, R. Kasturi, and A.K. Chhabra. Interpretation of telephone system manhole drawings. *Pattern Recognition Letters*, 16(1):355–359, 1995.
2. H.S. Baird. Anatomy of a versatile page reader. *Proceedings of the IEEE, Special Issue on OCR*, 80(7):1059–1065, 1992.
3. L. Boatto, V. Consorti, M. Del Buono, S. Di Zenzo, V. Eramo, A. Esposito, F. Melcarne, M. Meucci, A. Morelli, M. Mosciatti, S. Scarci, and M. Tucci. An interpretation system for land register maps. *IEEE Computer Magazine*, 25(7):25–33, 1992.
4. B. Coüasnon. DMOS: A generic document recognition method. application to an automatic generator of musical scores, mathematical formulae and table structures recognition systems. In *Proceedings of 6th International Conference on Document Analysis and Recognition, Seattle (USA)*, pages 215–220, 2001.
5. M. Delalandre, S. Nicolas, E. Trupin, and J.-M. Ogier. Symbols recognition by global-local structural approaches, based on the scenarios use, and with a XML representation of data. In *Proceedings of 7th International Conference on Document Analysis And Recognition, Edinburgh (Scotland)*, 2003.

6. M. Delalandre, Y. Saidali, J.-M. Ogier, and E. Trupin. Adaptable vectorization system based on strategic knowledge and XML representation use. In *Proceedings of 5th IAPR International Workshop on Graphics Recognition, Barcelona (Spain)*, 2003.

7. A.R. Dengel and B. Klein. smartFIX: A requirements-driven system for document analysis and understanding. In D. Lopresti, J. Hu, and R. Kashi, editors, *Proceedings of 5th IAPR International Workshop on Document Analysis Systems, Princeton (New Jersey, USA)*, volume 2423 of *Lecture Notes in Computer Science*, pages 433–444. Springer-Verlag, Berlin, 2002.

8. Ph. Dosch, C. Ah-Soon, G. Masini, G. Sánchez, and K. Tombre. Design of an integrated environment for the automated analysis of architectural drawings. In S.W. Lee and Y. Nakano, editors, *Document Analysis Systems: Theory and Practice*, volume 1655 of *Lecture Notes in Computer Science*, pages 295–309. Springer-Verlag, Berlin, 1999.

9. Ph. Dosch, K. Tombre, C. Ah-Soon, and G. Masini. A complete system for analysis of architectural drawings. *International Journal on Document Analysis and Recognition*, 3(2):102–116, 2000.

10. N. Gorski, V. Anisimov, E. Augustin, O. Baret, and S. Maximov. Industrial bank check processing: The A2iA CheckReader. *International Journal on Document Analysis and Recognition*, 3(4):196–206, 2001.

11. O. Hitz, L. Robadey, and R. Ingold. An architecture for editing document recognition results using XML. In *Proceedings of 4th IAPR International Workshop on Document Analysis Systems, Rio de Janeiro (Brazil)*, pages 385–396, 2000.

12. A. Lassaulzais, R. Mullot, J. Gardes, and Y. Lecourtier. Segmentation d'infrastructures de réseau téléphonique. In *Colloque International Francophone sur l'Écrit et le Document, Québec (Canada)*, pages 188–197, 1998.

13. D. Niyogi, S.N. Srihari, and V. Govindaraju. Analysis of printed forms. In H. Bunke and P.S.P. Wang, editors, *Handbook of character recognition and document image analysis*, pages 485–502. World Scientific, 1997.

14. B. Pasternak. *Adaptierbares Kernsystem zur Interpretation von Zeichnungen.* Dissertation zur Erlangung des akademischen Grades eines Doktors der Naturwissenschaften (Dr. rer. nat.), Universität Hamburg, 1996.

15. Y. Saidali, S. Adam, J.-M. Ogier, E. Trupin, and J. Labiche. Knowledge representation and acquisition for engineering document analysis. In *Proceedings of 5th IAPR International Workshop on Graphics Recognition, Barcelona (Spain)*, 2003.

16. H. Samet and A. Soffer. MAGELLAN: Map Acquisition of GEographic Labels by Legend ANalysis. *International Journal on Document Analysis and Recognition*, 1(2):89–101, 1998.

17. J.H. Shamilian, H.S. Baird, and T.L. Wood. A retargetable table reader. In *Proceedings of 4th International Conference on Document Analysis and Recognition, Ulm (Germany)*, pages 158–163, 1997.

18. K. Tombre, C. Ah-Soon, Ph. Dosch, A. Habed, and G. Masini. Stable, robust and off-the-shelf methods for graphics recognition. In *Proceedings of 14th International Conference on Pattern Recognition, Brisbane (Australia)*, pages 406–408, 1998.

19. Y. Yu, A. Samal, and S. C. Seth. A system for recognizing a large class of engineering drawings. *IEEE Transactions on Pattern Analysis and Machine Intelligence*, 19(8):868–890, 1997.

Knowledge Representation and Acquisition for Engineering Document Analysis

Y. Saidali[1], S. Adam[1], J. M. Ogier[2], E. Trupin[1], and J. Labiche[1]

[1] PSI Laboratory, University of Rouen, 76 821 Mont Saint Aignan, France
{first_name.last_name}@univ-rouen.fr
[2] L3I Laboratory, University of La Rochelle, 17042 La Rochelle, France
jmogier@univ-lr.fr

Abstract. This paper tackles the problem of bootstrapping engineering documents recognition systems. A user-friendly interface is presented. Its aim is to acquire knowledge concerning the graphical appearance of objects, but also to learn the best approach to use among our tools in order to recognise the learned objects.

Keywords: Technical document interpretation, knowledge representation and acquisition, XML, man-machine interaction.

1 Introduction

During the last decade, many complete line drawing understanding systems have been developed [1,2,3]. These systems aim at extracting meta-data concerning the content of documents whose structure is poor (see Fig. 1) in order to supply information systems or to index documents for example. At the present time, most of these systems are efficient but unfortunately they are always dedicated to a particular application. According to us, the main reason of this adaptability "failure" is that these systems had not been developed using a knowledge engineering perspective. More precisely, two main problems have to be emphasized. The first one is that system designers have not taken into account the fact that a great deal of knowledge has to be separated from programs if the objective is to design a generic understanding system. Beside this problem, another linked point that explains the specificity of the systems is the knowledge acquisition step, whose aim is to "configure" the system (for an adaptation to a new application). The man-machine interaction point of view has not been taken into account for this step. That's why, as far as we know, no interpretation system can neither be quickly adapted to a new application nor be initialised by a common user, that is to say a novice in document interpretation. In this paper, we present our preliminary works in order to overcome these problems. We first present, in section 2, our knowledge representation schemes for technical document understanding. Then, in section 3, we expound our accessible knowledge acquisition interfaces before showing, in 4, how the acquired knowledge is used. Finally, we conclude in 5.

J. Lladós and Y.-B. Kwon (Eds.): GREC 2003, LNCS 3088, pp. 25–37, 2004.

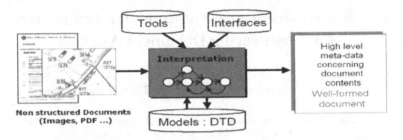

Fig. 1. Component of an engineering document analysis system

2 Knowledge Modelling and Representation

2.1 Introduction: Generalities Concerning Knowledge in Interpretation Systems

The knowledge concept covers different aspects and according to the different points of view, it can correspond to observed data, structured information, reasoning mechanisms or analysis and synthesis processes. Moreover knowledge can be acquired from human being, information systems, databases, experiments or documents for example. All these sources of knowledge are linked up together since there is not any theory without practice and there is not any inference without modelling. So the knowledge concept is not universally defined and if we only focus on computer sciences, it could be assumed that there exists three levels of representation depending on tools used to manipulate it: Data, Information and Knowledge [4]. Data are simple numerical values and can be issued from sensors. It can also be some text, images or sounds. Databases management systems or document management systems permit to store or update them and permit to extract part of them thanks to a request language. In that case, Information emerges like a data having a semantic content. For example, the numerical value D=1 becomes an information if a semantic link like "D is the distance between A and B" is attributed to D. The third level binds the knowledge to the action because knowledge does not exist if there is not any context for using information. So the knowledge is constructed from a task and it can be used to manage a decision [5]. However it remains difficult to well define the knowledge concept because there are explicit and tacit knowledge [6]. The first ones are captured and stored in archives, document management systems, databases and libraries. They are easily available, transferable and formalized. The second ones are highly personal and subjective. They involve mental schemes, expertises and habilities in specific contexts but they could not be easily formalized without a lot of difficulties in a formal language. So we focussed our knowledge modelling on the "Data – information – Knowledge".

2.2 Identification and Taxonomy of Knowledge in our Context

In our context of graphical document analysis, a process consists in a chaining of various image processing and classification tools. Each of these tools is applied to input data (images, data issued from DMS, non structured document, semi structured documents) and aim at bringing an additional structure to these data. These data are becoming information (associated to a meaning, a semantic) when they are used for a document interpretation in a considered domain. In order to manage the data structuring, the system uses it's own "knowledge" that we call a-priori knowledge and which is formalized using models. According to us, two "categories" of such knowledge can be distinguished:

- Descriptive a-priori knowledge, which concerns the document model, that is to say the document graphical entities and the relation between them.
- Strategic a-priori knowledge, which both concerns image processing tools used to construct information and chaining relations between these tools. In this category, we also consider knowledge that enables to infer a processing chain according to an intention (expressed as a request), a context and the history of the system.

In the following of this paper, we focus on the description of such a-priori knowledge, in terms of content, representation schemes, acquisition and operationalization.

2.2.1 Descriptive Knowledge

As said before, descriptive "knowledge" aims at providing a model of the content of the document that have to be interpreted. It is a set of symbolic and numeric description of the different entities manipulated by the system (semantic objects, their properties, relations binding them, image features…). In our context, it is generally admitted that descriptive knowledge can be decomposed in "professional" knowledge (we use the term "domain" knowledge in the following) and in "graphical" knowledge, what leads to a first separation of the model. This separation domain/graphic is a first step toward genericity since it is valid in all technical document production.

- Graphical descriptive knowledge concerns the set of concepts that are manipulated or generated by image processing tools. We have developed an ontology concerning these concepts. This ontology, which is strongly linked to the processing tools ontology presented in [8].
- "Domain" knowledge. To interpret a document as complex as a technical document, exploiting the relation between entities and their graphic representation is not sufficient. Indeed, concepts on such documents are respecting precise rules from the domain point of view, in term of functionality for example (for example, a room without at least one door or a network with an isolated cable are not consistent respectively on an architectural drawing and on a network map). Such knowledge has to be integrated into the system. It concerns objects of the domain, their properties, and their interactions. It is a category that has to be adapted to a given application, even if some common concepts can be distinguished. Our aim in this context is to identify these common concepts in order to help a user to adapt the system to a new application.

2.2.2 Strategic Knowledge

Concerning strategic knowledge, our problematic is based on concepts about the handling of a library of image processing tools. In this context, we deal with the strategies of graph construction, by selection and parameter setting of operators by an Image Processing (IP) expert. The so developed scenario model is thus based on the following concepts:

- Data: The data we consider are the entities that are actually handled by the operators. For example, when an expert connects IP operations, handled data can be images, which means data with file information (path, name, extension...) and information about image features (format, size, compression...). In a global point of view, by this way, we consider a major link with our descriptive knowledge model.
- Operators: According to us, the operators are the main elements of our knowledge base. One can distinguish two kinds of operators. The "singles" represent each one a library program when it is split up to the finest granularity. We can also talk about "complex" operator when it is a treatment tool made of several under-operators (example: a tool for segmentation composed of filtering operators, labelling, etc...). So in our knowledge approach, an operator is composed of several parts:

  1. A name (single) which identifies the operator eventually, eventually with a comment allowing to clarify this name and the using conditions.
  2. Comments on the functionalities of the considered operator.
  3. Input data and output data, with information on the type (Image, Float...), a name, a comment...
  4. Input parameters, their type, an interval of possible values (for the simple types), their default value (optional).
  5. A quality evaluation of results in a given context (this evaluation is given by the IP expert).

- Goal and request: In our knowledge modelling approach, we also consider the goal in IP, which is a problem specification, the expert want to solve. It includes input data, context, constraints on the output data, eventually the functionality to be reached and the operators able to solve the problem.
- History: The history represents the outline of the whole scenarios such as they were built and validated by the experts. In other words, they are chronological facts and scenarios realized by the experts in order to reach a goal in a given context.

Here are concepts the experts handle to built his strategies in image processing, and to structure strategic knowledge. So, once that knowledge identified, defined and modelled, the idea is to find formalism adapted to each one, in order to represent and formalize them. In the next section, we give an overview of different formalisms and our choices.

2.3 Formalisms and Choices

A formal language of representation permits to process these two types of knowledge. Such a language has to be defined with its own alphabet of symbols for variables, functions, predicates, and logical operators... And the best modelling has to be chosen. There are the conceptual graphs, the description logics, the frames schemes and the first order logic languages for example. For our part, and in the both cases of knowledge, we have designed a modelling and a representation scheme based on the use of graphs. These graphs are formalized using XML, in order to exploit the power of tools such as XSLT or DOM.

2.3.1 Formalism for Descriptive Knowledge

Actually, Very few systems take into account the problem of "domain" knowledge representation. Among them, one can find the different formalisms proposed by artificial intelligence, that is to say rules [1], semantic networks [2], frames network [3] or description language [9] .... We have chosen formalism close to Den Hartog's semantic networks by adding new relations. Such a network is a graph composed of nodes, representing some concepts, and of oriented edges describing the semantic relations linking these concepts. We distinguish two levels of abstraction for nodes and edges:

- The first level concerns the definition of the domain objects. The properties of these objects deal with their "domain properties" and a possible link with existing databases. At this level, two types of relations have been identified: "is a kind of" relation that corresponds in object oriented methodology to the class specialization and the "is composed of" relation to describe composition link. On such a network, we call "elementary objects" all the objects that are not "fathers" of a decomposition relation and that cannot be described by an association of others "domain". Such objects are extracted using their link with strategic knowledge.
- The second level concerns the representation types of "elementary objects". We distinguish symbols, linear shapes, polygons and text. For example, a door on architectural plan belong to the class "symbol", the quotation belong to the class "text"... Five relations can exist between these objects: neighborhoods, parallelism, inclusion, dimensions and identification.

All these concepts are grouped into the description network, which is stored as an XML file. The way this network is used with the other formalisms for document interpretation is explained in the next section.

2.3.2 Formalism for Strategic Knowledge

For strategic knowledge we use concepts defined in section 2.2.2 in order to represent and formalize our scenario model. In this perspective we use an object approach based on UML class diagram and XML. We exploit a representation in the form of a DTD (Document type definition), to validate the scenarios as they are produced by the experts in Image Processing (Fig. 2).

A scenario is thus an ordered succession of Image processing operators. This scenario spot light strategic knowledge related to the way of arranging and of using the tools to reach a goal. It looks like a process which proceeds according to a plan defined by one or several experts. In this case, a scenario such as an expert with an intention can produce it, contains:

- The context definition and categorization (using concepts defined in descriptive knowledge).
- Decomposition of the intention in sub-intentions.
- Development of a method described by steps and step chaining.
- The choice and the adjustment of parameters for each method.
- The perception and the evaluation of results.
- The taking into account of possible feedback and defects for correction.

We finally used UML class diagram to represent the existing overlapping between strategic knowledge enclosed in a scenario, when they are seen like objects handled by the users. Then this object oriented structuration enables to propose a model formalized using our XML DTD (Fig. 2).

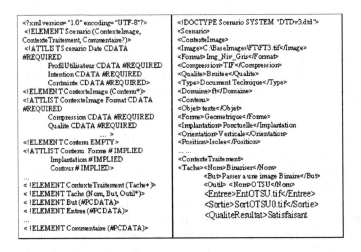

Fig. 2. DTD extract and the corresponding valid scenario

This formalization is in a rather strong relationship with the concepts hierarchisation in our ontology [8]. Concepts of this ontology have directly been translated into elements of the XML DTD.

The root element is *Scenario*. This element is splitted up into different categories on *User Profile, intentions, image context* (that include a descriptive knowledge part), *treatment context, constraints on the results,* and *eventual comments.* Then, the treatment context, for example, specializes into one or more tasks; a task being defined by its name, its goal and the tools used to achieve this goal. In the same way, a tool has a name, an input, an output, a parameter setting and a result quality (this qualification is made by the expert). For example, the user can define a filtering task, which goal is to clean the image, by choosing and parameterizing an opening and a closing on the binary image.

In other words, this model appears as a graph of actions, operators and handled objects. This graph expresses the data flow in addition of the operators order, i.e. it clarifies the order of data creation and the programs using those data. From this graph formalization, we choose tools from XML technology. Through these derived technologies (JAXB, Style sheets XSLT, DOM trees), XML is used in our approach as a switching language to structure the electronic document (Image + Scenario of treatment) and thus to standardize exchanges between various users who are the experts, the machine and the naive ones. Using these models, the next step is then to acquire knowledge.

3 Knowledge Acquisition

3.1 Introduction

After the choice of a model and a representation scheme (see 2), another key point in the design of a generic system consists in the development of interfaces to capture the different types of knowledge. In our approach, four interfaces are used:

- An interface dedicated to "graphical" (low level) descriptive knowledge acquisition (Fig. 4). This one enables a learning "from the example" of the representation of the objects in a domain. Such an approach renders the interface accessible to novices in document understanding.
- An interface dedicated to "domain" (high level) descriptive knowledge acquisition (Fig. 3). Using this one, the user creates nodes in graphs to define objects and edges to define links between the objects. A set of pre-defined relations is proposed in order to render the interface user-friendly.
- Two interfaces dedicated to "strategic" knowledge acquisition. The purpose of the first one (Fig. 5) is to construct a structured base of scenario. This interface, which is used by an expert in image processing, has been built using an original approach, taking into account both ontology and terminology in image processing. Information presented in this interface are strongly linked to the scenario model. Using the second interface (Fig. 6), the user (a novice in IP) chooses the most adapted scenario in the knowledge base to respond to a given intention.

3.2 Interfaces for Descriptive Knowledge Acquisition

3.2.1 Interface for Domain Descriptive Knowledge

The knowledge acquisition interface (see Fig. 3) we developed allows a human operator to introduce the previously presented descriptive knowledge. As said before, this interface proposes to introduce the knowledge under a network formalism, for which the user can assign any pre-defined label to the nodes and to the edges. The sets of labels that have been pre-programmed are the result of the exhaustive study concerning the objects that can be encountered on the technical documents and integrate the different categories of relations that can exist between these objects (see 2.2.1). This interface is already easy to use since user-friendly help is given but still need work. The same terminology study than in the case of strategic knowledge is considered in this context.

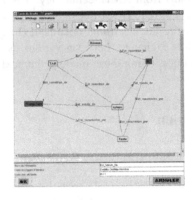

Fig. 3. Domain descriptive knowledge acquisition interface

3.2.2 Interface for Graphical Descriptive Knowledge

Following our approach, graphical knowledge acquisition is realised "from the example". The process can be decomposed into 4 steps (each step is illustrated on Fig. 4):

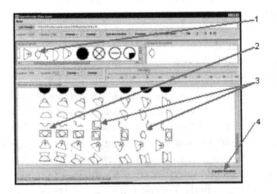

Fig. 4. Graphic descriptive knowledge acquisition interface

- The user gives an example of the object he wants the system to learn. If the object is connected, user may use a rubber to isolate it in the right window.
- A set of similar shapes is proposed, using different recognition tools (Fourier Mellin features, Zernike invariants and circular probes [10]). Each tool is characterized by a colored rectangle.

- The user corrects system's mistakes (forgotten and/or misclassified shapes). During this step, statistics concerning the different used tools are computed. These statistics are used as strategic knowledge; each object is then associated to a preferred approach.

- The user names the object with the name used during "domain" knowledge acquisition. Shapes models are stored as XML files, what enables an easy adaptation to various classifiers whose input data specifications are different. Statistics are also stored as XML files but in the strategic part of knowledge.

3.3 Interfaces for Strategic Knowledge Acquisition

3.3.1 Expert-Machine Dialogue

This interface (Fig. 5) is initially meant for expert users in image processing. With his intention, the expert has (at the very outset) a mental representation of the desired state of the system in term of chaining different treatments and their parameter settings. The idea is to make the system learn this conceptual model. Therefore, from a platform designed for document analysis, we propose a set of generic actions to an expert having expressed a particular goal in image processing. This is equivalent to interview, via a man-machine dialogue, the specialist who will put in action his plan using the control device of the proposed interface.

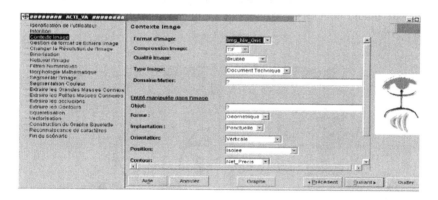

Fig. 5. Strategic knowledge acquisition interface (expert version)

This interface is based on the model of dialogue defined in section 2.3.2. It is made of windows for:

- **Intention Expression:** This first component of our Expert-Machine interface represents the main window (centre of Fig. 5). It proposes a succession of panels which contain the different tasks the expert can realize. It is thus made of several dashboards on which the expert user chooses the methods, expresses intentions and tries to achieve an expressed goal. Each method is characterized by Inputs/outputs and the externalized parameters.

- **Navigation:** This component is a navigation area presented to the user (left of Fig. 5). This traditional navigator allows having a total outline of the progress report of the scenario. The user can concretely see his position in the graph of event that is proposed to him. An action on this window enables the expert user to choose the treatment steps by which he wants realize to achieve its goal.
- **Presentation:** The main function of this last component has is the presentation of inputs, outputs, and intermediate results of actions from the running scenario. This layout is made in multi-frames windows. Using this component, the visualization of all, or a part of intermediate images, allows the expert to qualify the result of processings.

Using this interface, an image-processing expert generates new scenarios which can be stored in the history base. This base is then used during knowledge operationalization.

3.3.2 Novice-Machine Dialogue

The interaction presented in section 3.3.1, seems unadapted for managing a dialogue with a non-expert user. Indeed, we need in this case, more flexibility particularly to make easier the information extraction from the history base. That's why we have designed another interface which is dedicated to non-expert users (we call them novice in the following) (Fig. 6). The aim of this interface is to propose several tools which will enable novices to extract one or more scenarios according to different points of view.

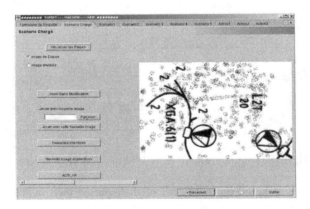

Fig. 6. Strategic knowledge acquisition interface (novice version)

In this second step of our approach, the novice will be able to exploit experts scenarios to adapt them and to solve new problems. That means that we also have in this particular use-case an evolution of our strategic knowledge base. This interface for Machine-Novice dialogue is made of three distinct modules:

- **An Image Visualizer:** This module is actually a set of Java windows which make easier the visualization of images (initial, intermediate and final) during the application of a scenario extracted from the base. Indeed, the dynamic visual perception allowed by this module facilitates the decision-making.
- **A Hyperbolic Tree:** Thanks to this module; we propose an interactive and dynamic navigation in the scenario base. This intuitive navigation is made according to points of view choosed by the user.
- **Request Form:** This method of scenarios extraction is an additional tool to the hyperbolic tree. It consists in proposing a form based on fields and buttons whose aim is to generate XLM QL requests. Generated requests are then automatically executed by an engine in order to extract appropriate scenarios.

4 Knowledge Operationalization

At the end of the acquisition process described in 3, both descriptive knowledge and strategic knowledge have been acquired and stored in DTD compliant XML files. Then, the two types of acquired knowledge are used in order to analyse documents:

- Descriptive knowledge is used in order to recognize the objects in documents and construct the network of objects.
- Strategic knowledge is used in order to execute the most adapted scenario in response to the user intention.

The knowledge operationalization relies mainly on the analysis of the data description graph that has been initialised by the user, during the knowledge acquisition stage. Indeed, as said in the knowledge acquisition part, this stage permits to the user to of the data description graph for the description of semantic, topologic, and syntactic links between graphical objects.

Actually, this operationnalization stage can be decomposed into 3 steps, which are respectively:

- Analysis of the request of the user and dynamic generation of the interpretation scenario that has to be run in order to respond to the request. During this stage, the request of the user (for instance "extract a particular object") is analysed with regard to the data description graph. This analysis permits to know how the object that has to be extracted is composed and linked with sub-objects that are described in the data description graph. Thanks to this analysis of the composition of the object to be extracted in terms of sub-objects, a dynamic scenario is constructed, allowing decomposing the request in a set of sequential operations, each operation corresponding to the extraction of a particular object in the data description graph. When the lowest part of the data description graph is reached, i.e. the frontier between domain and graphic objects has been reached, the most adapted scenario is run in order to extract the information from the image. The selection of the optimal scenario for the extraction of a graphic object is detailed in the previous section.

- Construction of the objects to be extracted, in order to answer the user request. After having "translated" the request in an adapted scenario, the extraction of the objects is processed from the image, and the required objects are progressively constructed following the generated scenario.
- Analysis of the syntactic or semantic consistency of the constructed objects, in order to eventually perform feedbacks in the processing chains, in the case of semantic ambiguities. During the construction of the objects, a consistency analysis can be performed at each stage of the scenario, in order to check if the constructed objects verify the integrity constraints that have been given by the user in the data description graph. This analysis can be syntactic and simply consists in verifying if an object has all his required attributes (in the good order), or more semantic. This analysis should permit to perform some eventual feedbacks in the processing chain in the case of ambiguity. This part has not been implemented yet in our device.

5 Conclusion and Future Works

This paper presents our preliminary results concerning the implementation of a generic interpretation/indexing device. Indeed, the approach that is proposed tries to bring some responses to the relevant question concerning the adaptability of graphic recognition systems through a complete "externalisation" of knowledge, that are generally directly disseminated in the source code, engendering thus dedicated and constrained systems. Actually, our system proposes a set of interfaces allowing to acquire interactively different knowledge categories, according to a taxonomy issuing from knowledge based systems. The considered knowledge are then operationnalized by using adapted strategies, as a function of the knowledge abstraction level. This first implementation is currently tested on a set of technical maps that are available in our laboratories. The perspectives of this work concern the testing of this system on different categories of documents (structured, handwritten...). From a pure research point of view, the perspectives of this work deal with the management of low level, syntactic, and semantic ambiguities, in order to provide autonomous and auto-learning device.

References

[1] J.M. Ogier, R. Mullot, J. Labiche, Y. Lecourtier, "Semantic coherency: the basis of an image interpretation device - application to the cadastral map interpretation", *IEEE Transactions on Systems, Man, and Cybernetics* - part B Cybernetics 30(2):322–338, 2000.

[2] J.E. Den Hartog, T. K. Ten Kates, J.J. Gerbrands, "Knowledge-based interpretation of utility maps", *Computer Vision and Image Understanding* 63(1):105–117, 1996.

[3] S.H. Joseph, T.P. Pridmore, "Knowledge-directed interpretation of mechanical engineering drawings", *IEEE Transaction on Pattern Analysis and Machine Intelligence* 14(9):928–940, 1992.

[4] F. Gandon "Ontology Engineering: a Survey and a return on Experience" INRIA Research Repport, 181 p, RR 4396, http://www.inria.fr/rrrt/rr-4396.html, 2002.

[5] R. Dieng, O. Corby, A. Giboin, M. Ribière, "Methods and Tools for Corporate Knowledge Managment", INRIA Research Repport, RR-3485, http://www.inria.fr/rapports/sophia/RR-3485.html, 2002.

[6] I. Nonak, "Dynamic theory of organisational knowledge creation", *Organizational Science* 5(1):14–37, 1994.

[7] A. Newell, "The knowledge level", *Artificial Intelligence* 19(2):87–127, 1982.

[8] Y. Saidali, N. Baudouin, E. Trupin, M. Holzem, J. Labiche, "An interactive application for knowledge acquisition in image processing", *Proc. of the second IASTED International Conference on Artificial Intelligence and Application*, Malaga, Spain, 173–177, 2002.

[9] B. Pasternak, "Processing Imprecise and Structural Distorted Line Drawings by an Adaptable Drawing Interpretation Kernel", *Proc. of the IAPR Workshop on Document Analysis Systems*, 349–365, 1994.

[10] S. Adam, J.M. Ogier, C. Cariou, R. Mullot, J. Gardes, Y. Lecourtier, "Symbol and character recognition : application to engineering drawings", *International Journal on Document Analysis and Recognition* 3(2), 2000.

Dealing with Noise in DMOS, a Generic Method for Structured Document Recognition: An Example on a Complete Grammar

Bertrand Coüasnon

IRISA / INRIA
Campus universitaire de Beaulieu
F-35042 Rennes Cedex, France
couasnon@irisa.fr

Abstract. To develop a generic method for document recognition, it is necessary to build a system with a generic approach for dealing with noise. Indeed, a lot of noise is present in an image and a recognizer needs to find the right information in the middle of noise to make a recognition. We describe in this paper the parser we develop in DMOS, a generic method for structured document recognition. This method use EPF, a grammatical language for describing documents. From an EPF description, a new recognition system is automatically build by compilation. DMOS had been successfully used for musical scores, mathematical formulae, table structure and old forms recognition (tested on 60,000 documents).

To illustrate the dealing of noise and to show how it is easy to define a grammatical description in EPF, we present in this paper a real and complete grammar defined to detect tennis court in videos. Even if this application is not directly on document, tennis court offers a good illustration example and has the same kind of problems as those found in structured documents.

Keywords: grammar, parser, generic system, structured documents, noise

1 Introduction

We presented in various papers, [2] DMOS (Description and MOdification of Segmentation) a generic recognition method for structured documents. This method is made of:

- the grammatical formalism EPF (Enhanced Position Formalism), which can be seen as a description language for structured documents. EPF makes possible at the same time a graphical, a syntactical or even a semantical description of a class of documents;
- the associated parser which is able to change the parsed structure during the parsing. This allows the system to try other segmentations with the help of context to improve recognition;

J. Lladós and Y.-B. Kwon (Eds.): GREC 2003, LNCS 3088, pp. 38–49, 2004.
© Springer-Verlag Berlin Heidelberg 2004

– the equivalent of lexical parsers to detect in the image the terminals:
  • for line segments (this extractor use a kalman filtering method),
  • for symbols which can be seen has characters (a classifier able to reject recognize those symbols).

The parsed structure is made of all the detected line segments and the connected components (for symbols) of the image (figure 2 middle right).

We have implemented this DMOS method to build an automatic generator of structured document recognition systems. Using this generator, adaptation to a new kind of document is then simply done by defining a description of the document with an EPF grammar. This grammar is then compiled to produce a new structured document recognition system. Each system can then use a classifier to recognize symbols which can be seen as characters.

By only changing the EPF grammar, and when needed by training a classifier, we produced automatically various recognition systems: one for musical scores [3], one for mathematical formulae [8], one on recursive table structures and one on military forms of the 19th century [6]. We have been able to successfully test this military forms recognition system on 60,000 pages of forms even if they were quite damaged [5].

For this generic method DMOS, we had to define a parser able to deal with noises in the parsed structure. Indeed, a classical parser usually parse a not so noisy structure but, in an image for document recognition, it is necessary that the parser can recognize as much as possible information even if the parsed structure is very noisy. The noise can come from the image itself and then be found in the parsed structure. But noise can also come from the recognition system itself: if the system is limited to a subset of a document, every information which is not part of the subset is noise for the system.

We present in this paper a way to deal with this noise. We start by a fast presentation of the EPF language, we then present the associated parser and how it can manage a very noisy environment. To illustrate this, we will give a real example of the EPF grammar which have been defined to recognize tennis court in videos. This is a good example of the recognition of a structure in a noisy environment.

Moreover, in this paper, we present a complete EPF grammar which can be directly compile to produce a new recognition system. This illustrates how it is easy to define a description with the EPF language and therefore how it is easy to produce a new recognition system.

2   DMOS Method and EPF Formalism

The EPF formalism (presented in different papers [4, 2]) can be seen as a grammatical language to describe a structured class of documents. From an EPF grammar we can automatically produce an adapted recognition system by using the automatic generator we developed.

We can find in the literature various bi-dimensional extensions of monodimensional grammars defined for object and document recognition.

Trees, Web or Plex grammars [1][10][7] offer a limited expressiveness with a too complex syntax for being used on real cases.

Graph grammars have the most important expressiveness. They have been used for example on musical scores and mathematical formulae recognition [9]. But one important problem - like others formalisms - is a complex definition of production rules as they are made with graphs. This makes difficult an implementation of a graph grammar when knowledge is quite complex.

Moreover no grammatical formalism and their associated parsers can deal with noise. All of them are used in a bottom-up way to syntactically confirm a previously made segmentation. They do not propose a solution to introduce context in segmentation.

Therefore we defined the EPF formalism and its associated parser. EPF can be seen as an adding of several operators to mono-dimensional grammars like:

Position Operator (encapsulated by `AT`):

$$\text{A \&\& AT(pos) \&\& B}$$

means A, and at the position `pos` in relation to A, we find B.

Where `&&` is the concatenation in the grammar, A and B represent a terminal or a non-terminal.

Factorization Operator (`##`, in association with the position operators):

```
A && (AT(pos1) && B ##
      AT(pos2) && C)
```

means   `A && AT(pos1) && B`   and `A && AT(pos2) && C`

With this syntax it is possible, for example, to describe a simplified beamed note (a beamed eighth note, with only one beam - a segment - that links the notes):

```
beamedNote ::= beam &&
        (AT(leftTip) && noteGr ##
         notesInBetween ##
         AT(rightTip) && noteGr)
```

Where `::=` is the constructor of a grammar rule. The writer of the grammar can define as much as necessary position operators as well as he can for non-terminals.

Save Operators (`--->` and `<---`):

```
(A ---> labelForA) &&
AT(pos1) && B && AT(pos2) &&
(A <--- labelForA)
```

These operators offer the possibility of describing a bi-directional relation between A and B. This is very important to be able to describe a document. This bi-directional relation is possible if we can use the same instance of A. Therefore we propose to save (using the operator `--->`) an instance of a terminal or a non-terminal. This backup of A gives then the possibility to refer (using the operator `<---`) to A as much as necessary.

It is then, for example, possible to describe a rectangle with the following rule:

```
rectangle ::=
   (segV ---> segLeftSide) &&
   AT(touchUp) && segH &&
   AT(touchRight) && segV &&
   AT(touchDown) && segH &&
   AT(touchLeft) &&
   (segV <--- segLeftSide).
```

Where segH and segV will match horizontal or vertical segments in the image. segLeftSide is the label to save the left vertical segment of the rectangle.

If we compare these backup operators with the position operator (@) in Prolog (used for example in [11]), they are much more powerful because:

- `--->` makes a save of the non-terminal including the attributes, as @ saves only the position in the parsing (the image). With @ it is not possible to use several times the save instance of a non-terminal as it is only the position that is checked;
- the scope of a label is limited to the static body of a grammar rule with @. Sub-rules cannot use it, or it is quite complex. In EPF, it is possible to define clearly the scope of a label.

This declaration is done in EPF with the DECLARE operator. It allows to specify the scope of this label. All the rules and sub-rules can then use this label to refer to the same non-terminal. We present here an example of a rule which describes the geometric figure of figure 1. The rule rectangle is exactly the same as before.

Declaration Operator (DECLARE):

```
exampleFig ::=
  DECLARE(segLeftSide) (
     rectangle && triangle).

triangle ::=
   (segV <--- segLeftSide) &&
   AT(touchUp) && segDiag &&
   AT(touchRight) && segDiag &&
   AT(touchLeft) &&
   (segV <--- segLeftSide).
```

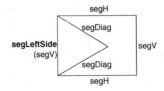

Fig. 1. Geometric figure recognized by the rule `exampleFig`

Space Reduction Operator (`IN ... DO`): EPF offers also an operator to optionally reduce the area where a rule should be applied:

```
IN(aera_definition) DO(rule).
```

This is very useful, for example, to make a recursive description of a table: a table structure is made of cells and in a cell it is possible to find a table structure:

```
tableStructure ::= ...
... insideAcell.

insideAcell ::=
    IN(cellBoundingBox)
    DO(tableStructure).
```

With this EPF formalism it is now possible to describe very different kinds of documents even if there is not a preferred reading order. Descriptions can use recursivity and bi-directional relations between objects. Moreover, as EPF is an extension of DCG (used for natural language analysis), it is possible to use its ability to define syntactical or semantical knowledge.

3   Parser and Dealing with Noise

The EPF language allows to define a description of a document. From this description, we produce by compilation, a parser with specific properties needed for parsing bi-dimensional documents. Compares to classical mono-dimensional parser the main properties of the bi-dimensional parser we develop are:

- changing the parsed structure during parsing for contextual segmentation;
- detecting of the next element to parse. Indeed, in classical parsers, the next element is simply the head of the parsed string. In two dimensions, the next element can be everywhere in the image and so everywhere in the parsed structure. The parser uses the position operators to select the next element to parse;
- dealing with noise.

We can consider that dealing with noise corresponds to find the next element to parse even when there is a lot of noise in the parsed structure. To do so we propose to work on two levels:

– The first level is for terminals. We define two terminals operators TERM_SEG and TERM_CMP (according to line segments terminal or symbols terminal) with those arguments:

```
TERM_SEG <PreCond> <PostCond> <Label> <Seg>
TERM_CMP <PreCond> <PostCond> <Label> <Comp>
```

The <PreCond> argument is a pre-condition which allows to pass elements that must not be recognized (mostly noise). The parser will search for the nearest element, in the area defined by the position operator, and with the pre-condition. The <PostCond> argument is a post-condition which must be verified by the element found with the pre-condition. <Label> is used to build the result (the terminal) found in <Seg> or <Comp>;

– The second level is for non-terminals. Normal parsing tries each rule on the current element until it applies. To deal with noise, we propose an operator FIND which transpose the parsing: a rule is tried on each element of the structure until it match or until a stop condition. The syntax of this operator is:

```
FIND(rule) UNTIL(stopCondition)
```

where rule is a terminal or a non-terminal and stopCondition is a terminal or a non-terminal which must be found to stop the FIND operator.

4   EPF Grammar for Tennis Court Detection

We propose to present the use of FIND and TERM_SEG on a real example: the EPF grammar we defined for tennis court detection in videos (figure 2). Even if a video is not a document in a classical way, we can consider that the tennis court can be seen as a structured document.

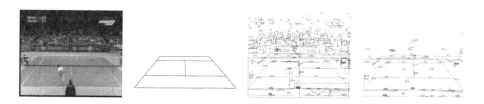

Fig. 2. DMOS: Recognition produced by tennisCourt (middle left), line segments and connected components (middle right), line segments only (right)

From the EPF grammar, we produce by compilation a parser able to detect a tennis court in an image like in (figure 2 middle left). This parser takes in input a structure made of all detected line segments and the connected components in an image (figure 2 middle right) which produces a quite noisy structure. The detected line segments are presented alone in figure 2 (right).

This grammar starts with this first rule, presented in a syntax ready to compile:

```
tennisCourt ::=
    INIT_PARSE &&
    (DECLARE(sideLineLeft) (
    (DECLARE(sideLineRight) (
    (DECLARE(serveLineH) (
        AT_ABS(middleImage) &&
        FIND(serveArea) UNTIL(noStopRule) &&
        simpleCourt
        )))))).
```

All grammar rules presented in this section are in a syntax ready to compile. For reading reasons, they are presented without the synthetic attributes used to build the result structure. The other needed attributes are still presented (identifiers starting with a capital letter).

The axiom `tennisCourt` is the description of a simple tennis court from which a recognizer will be produced by compilation.

The `INIT_PARSE` operator is needed to start the parsing at the beginning of the parsed structure. Then the description starts with the declaration of three labels: `sideLineLeft`, `sideLineRight` and `serveLineH`. An absolute position operator (`middleImage`, encapsulated by `AT_ABS`) defines the position where the serve area (figure 3, left) should be. This position operator defines a very large rectangle (almost all the image) centered in the middle of the image. The description ends with the limits of a simple court (figure 3, right).

Fig. 3. Recognition produced by `servArea` (left) and `simpleCourt` (right)

Because of noise (there is much more line segments detected than the tennis lines, see figure 2), the `FIND` rule is needed to make the parser trying the rule `serveArea` on each line segment until the serve area structure is detected. The description of the serve area is:

```
serveArea ::=
    serveMedianLine Median &&
        (AT(downTip Median) &&
            FIND(serveLineDownAndSides) UNTIL(noStopRule) ##
        AT(upTip Median) &&
            FIND(serveLineUpAndSides) UNTIL(noStopRule)).

serveMedianLine Line ::= brokenLineSegV Line.
```

```
serveLineDownAndSides ::=
      serveLineDown ServeB &&
      lineSidesD ServeB.
lineSidesD Serve ::=
      (AT(leftTip Serve)  && (sideLine SideL ---> sideLineLeft) ##
      AT(rightTip Serve) && (sideLine SideR ---> sideLineRight) ).
```

Where `serveMedianLine` (figure 4, left) has an argument (attribute) which is the detected median line. `Median` is then used by the position operators `downTip` and `upTip` to define the right position. The `FIND` operator is again used to test all the combinations to find the right structure even there is a lot of noise.

Fig. 4. Recognition produced by `serveMedianLine` (left) and `serveLineDown` (right)

The non-terminal `brokenLineSegV` describes line segments in the same axis, to find the original median line even if it is largely broken. The principle of this non-terminal is the same as `brokenLineSegH` which is completely presented further.

`serveLineDownAndSides` will detect the `serveLineDown` (figure 4, right) and the side lines (figure 5, left) which are saved by the `--->` operator.

Fig. 5. Recognition produced by `sideLine` (left) and `serveLineUp` (right)

The `serveLineUpAndSides` non-terminal describes the same way the non-terminal `serveLineDownAndSides` does. The only exception is that the side lines (figure 5, left) are the same as those described in `serveLineDownAndSides`. This is explain with the `<-+-` operator. `<-+-` is just a segment typed version of `<---`. The other typed version of `<---` is `<-=-`, for components. The `serveLineUp` (figure 5, right) is labelled by `serveLineH` because it is needed later for the description of `simpleCourt`.

```
serveLineUpAndSides ::=
     (serveLineUp ServeH --> serveLineH)&&
     lineSidesU ServeH.

lineSidesU Serve ::=
     (AT(leftTip Serve) &&
                    (sideLine SideL/SideL <-+- sideLineLeft) ##
        AT(rightTip Serve) &&
                    (sideLine SideR/SideR <-+- sideLineRight)).

serveLineDown Line ::= brokenLineSegH Line.
serveLineUp Line   ::= brokenLineSegH Line.
sideLine Side ::= brokenLineSegV Side.
```

The brokenLineSegH describes an horizontal oriented line segment ($\pm 45°$) which can be largely split into several line segments. A first line segment is detected by horizontalLineSeg and then at each tip the non-terminals leftSegH and rightSegH will detect the various part of the broken line segment. This is possible by using the TERM_SEG operator that will find the right line segment according to the pre-condition, even if the parsed structure is very noisy. cons_SegH builds only the synthetic attribute in DetectSeg.

```
brokenLineSegH DetectSeg ::=
     horizontalLineSeg Line &&
     leftSegH LeftmostSeg Line &&
     rightSegH RightmostSeg Line &&
     ''(cons_SegH serveLine Line LeftmostSeg
                    RightmostSeg DetectSeg).

horizontalLineSeg SegHor ::=
     TERM_SEG condSegH noCondS serveLine SegHor.

leftSegH LeftmostSeg Seg ::=
     AT(leftTip Seg) &&
     horizontalLineSegSameAxis Seg SegHor &&
     leftSegH LeftmostSeg SegHor.
leftSegH Seg Seg ::= ''(true).

horizontalLineSegSameAxis Seg SegHor ::=
     TERM_SEG (condSegHsameAxis Seg) noCondS serveLine SegHor.
```

The simpleCourt is just a description of the backLineUp and backLineDown using the side lines (labelled by sideLineLeft and sideLineRight) and the serve line (labelled by serveLineUp) to produce the limit of the court (figure 3, right).

```
simpleCourt ::=
      backLineUp  &&
      backLineDown.

backLineUp ::=
      (serveLineUp ServeH/ServeH <-+- serveLineH) &&
      (sideLine SideL/SideL <-+- sideLineLeft) &&
      AT(tipUp SideL) &&
              SELECT(horizontalLineSegSameDir ServeH BackLine1) &&
      (sideLine SideR/SideR <-+- sideLineRight) &&
      AT(tipUp SideR) &&
              horizontalLineSegSameAxis BackLine1 BackLineDectected.
```

The label serveLineH is used here just to get the argument ServeH which is needed in the non-terminal horizontalLineSegSameDir. The SELECT(rule) operator produces simply a parsing of rule (a terminal or a non-terminal) without changing the parsing structure. This offers a possibility of matching a rule several times.

BackLineDectected is a synthetic attribute corresponding to the detected back line, but is not used here as it is only necessary for building the result structure.

5   Examples of Tennis Court Detection

The complete grammar is made of 30 non-terminals and 10 position operators. The EPF description takes into account the noisy environment in which the tennis court must be detected with the FIND and the TERM_SEG operators. As there is also no notion of size in the grammar we presented, the same grammar can detect various tennis court, even if lines are broken, for example when they are hidden or erased by players (figure 6), even if the view angles or the playing surface are different (figure 7).

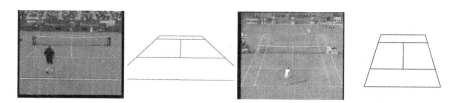

Fig. 6. DMOS: Examples of recognition of a tennis court: lines are hidden as well as part of the court, image on the right the back line is partly erased by players

Using synthetized attributes in the grammar (not presented in this paper for reading reasons), the parser produced by compilation is able to generate a recognized structure like this one:

Fig. 7. DMOS: Examples of recognition of a tennis court, with different view angles

```
(tennisCourt "/imadoc/ImagesDoc/Tennis/us_open09_ES0001.ras"
    (leftServe (coor 197 182) (coor 362 183)
               (coor 362 304) (coor 62 303))
    (rightServe (coor 362 183) (coor 525 184)
               (coor 661 305) (coor 362 304))
    (simple (coor 221 161) (coor 501 162)
            (coor 825 452) (coor -98 446)))
```

To detect a tennis court in a video image (720×576) it takes 1.4s on a Sun Sunblade 100, including image processing and parsing. This grammar has been defined (in few hours) more to illustrate, as a school example, the way EPF can be used and can deal with noise. Therefore we did not try to validate with a statistically large enough dataset. 20 images, from different match, different kind of court surface, with different view angle (some with a partly missing court), have been tested. For all of them the court was correctly detected.

6   Conclusion

This paper presents the way DMOS - a generic method for structured document recognition - deals with noise. We can consider that dealing with noise in a parser corresponds to find the next element in the parsed structure whatever noise there is in it. We propose three operators to make the parser able to deal with a very noisy parsing structure: one for non-terminals (**FIND**) and two for terminals (**TERM_SEG** and **TERM_CMP**). Those are really important in a document recognition system as noise is always found in images.

To illustrate those operators we presented an almost complete grammar to describe a tennis court. Even if tennis courts are not exactly documents, their structures can be seen as documents and they are a good example of problems in finding a structure in a noisy environment.

This grammar shows also how it is possible and fast to use the EPF language to describe a structure and then produce automatically by compilation a new recognition system. DMOS, with the EPF language have been applied on optical music recognition, on mathematical formulae, on table structure, on old forms recognition (tested on more than 60,000 images) and on tennis court detection. This proves the genericity of this method. It shows also that a generic system is a necessity to be able to build quickly a new recognition system without having to write it from scratch.

References

1. W.S. Brainerd. Tree generating regular systems. *Information and Control*, 14:217–231, 1969.
2. B. Coüasnon. Dmos: A generic document recognition method, application to an automatic generator of musical scores, mathematical formulae and table structures recognition systems. In *ICDAR, International Conference on Document Analysis and Recognition*, pages 215–220, Seattle, USA, September 2001.
3. B. Coüasnon and J. Camillerapp. Using grammars to segment and recognize music scores. In L. Spitz and A. Dengel, editors, *Document Analysis Systems*. World Scientific, 1995.
4. B. Coüasnon and J. Camillerapp. A way to separate knowledge from program in structured document analysis: application to optical music recognition. In *ICDAR, International Conference on Document Analysis and Recognition*, volume 2, pages 1092–1097, Montréal, Canada, August 1995.
5. B. Coüasnon and I. Leplumey. A generic system for making archives documents accessible to public. In *ICDAR, International Conference on Document Analysis and Recognition*, Edinburgh, UK, August 2003.
6. B. Coüasnon and L. Pasquer. A real-world evaluation of a generic document recognition method applied to a military form of the 19th century. In *ICDAR, International Conference on Document Analysis and Recognition*, pages 779–783, Seattle, USA, September 2001.
7. J. Feder. Plex languages. *Information and Science*, 3:225–241, 1971.
8. P Garcia and B. Coüasnon. Using a generic document recognition method for mathematical formulae recognition. In *GREC, IAPR International Workshop on Graphics Recognition*, Kingston, Canada, September 2001.
9. A. Grbavec and D. Blostein. Mathematics recognition using graph rewriting. In *ICDAR, International Conference on Document Analysis and Recognition*, volume 1, pages 417–421, Montréal, Canada, August 1995.
10. J.L. Pfaltz and A. Rosenfeld. Web grammars. In *Proceedings of the First International Joint Conference on Artificial Intelligence*, pages 609–619, Washington, D.C., May 1969.
11. D. B. Searls and S. L. Taylor. Document image analysis using logic-grammar-based syntactic pattern recognition. In K. Yamamoto H.S. Baird, H. Bunke, editor, *Structured Document Image Analysis*, pages 520–545. Springer-Verlag, 1992.

Raster to Vector Conversion of
Color Cartographic Maps

Serguei Levachkine

Department of Artificial Intelligence (DIA)
Centre for Computing Research (CIC) - National Polytechnic Institute (IPN)
palych@cic.ipn.mx

Abstract. An approach to automatic digitation of raster-scanned color cartographic maps is presented. This approach is concerned with three steps involved in the digitizing process: pre-processing, processing and post-
processing. Most systems for vectorization raster maps using automatic programs essentially carry out only one kind of operation: follow discrete points
along an arc (tracing, snapping) or attempt to combine automatic and interactive modes, if the tracing is met ambiguities. In our proposal, the automation
problem is approached from a unified point of view, leading to the development of *A2R2V* (Analogical-to-Raster-to-Vector) conversion system that is able
to recognize and vector a maximum number of cartographic patterns in raster
maps. We discuss some strategies for solving this hard problem and illustrate it,
briefly describing A2R2V. The place of the operator and knowledge in a raster
to vector conversion system is considered as well.

1 Introduction

The problem of automatic raster to vector (R2V) conversion is taken steadfast attention by researchers and software developers during last two decades. Numerous attempts to solve this problem have mainly originated from emerging area of automatic
Geographical Information Systems (GIS). Unfortunately, completely automatic conversion system appears unrealistic and some authors suggested putting the operator
into the loop even into the center of a conversion system. Thus, the problem of correct task division between the human and machine can be also stated [2][4].

In the present paper we discuss how to bring an automation of the single modules
of a R2V conversion system to fullest possible extent. Mainly, we focus on the case
of analytical GIS (R2V conversion for register GIS is employed in some commercial
systems [8][20]). However, our approach is effective for register GIS too. The aim is
to describe and highlight the main concepts and crucial points of our approach.

The paper is divided into two parts: 1) in Sections 1–4 we analyze the general concepts of automation of a R2V conversion system that are constituted the approach; 2)
in Section 5 we overview A2R2V conversion system in which we placed the ideas of
our approach. In Section 6 we emphasize the role of operator and knowledge in
automation of the conversion process.

J. Lladós and Y.-B. Kwon (Eds.): GREC 2003, LNCS 3088, pp. 50–62, 2004.

Two main methods are currently used for map vectorization [4]: (V1) Paper map digitation by electronic-mechanical digitizers, and (V2) Raster map (a map obtained after scanning of the paper original) digitation.

The digitizing of paper maps cannot be automated; hence the only practical approach to design R2V conversions is the development of methods and software to automate vectorization of raster maps.

Raster map digitation approaches can be divided into four intersecting groups [4]: (D1) Manual; (D2) Interactive; (D3) Semi-automated, and (D4) Automatic.

In practice, (D1) = (V1). A few examples will serve to illustrate this. In the case of "punctual" objects, the operator visually locates graphic symbols and fixes their coordinates. In the case of "linear" and polygonal objects, the operator uses rectilinear segments to approximate curvilinear contours. The manual digitation rate is one to two objects per minute.

Interactive digitation uses special programs, which, once the operator indicates the starting point on a line segment, automatically follow the contours of the line (*tracing*). These programs are capable of tracing relatively simple lines. If the program cannot solve a graphical ambiguity on the raster map, it returns a message to the operator (*alarm*). Recently, vector editors capable of carrying out this digitation process have appeared, reducing the time consumption by a factor of 1.5 to 2. These can be called semi-automated systems [1][2][4][8][20].

In theory, automatic vector editors automatically digitize all objects of a given class, leaving the operator to correct errors in the resulting vector layers. Some vector editors use this approach [8][20][23]. However, in practice, the high error level resulting from any small complication in the raster map means that alternative methods should be sought to reduce the huge volume of manual corrections. It should be noted that *the use of increasingly complex methods and algorithms for machine recognition of cartographic objects does not materially improve the results* [1]–[4] (Cf. [5][12–16] [21][23] where alternative points of view are exposed). Why?

Probably, the answer is the lack of a system approach to automatic map digitation and correct task division between human-machine. In other words, methods and software should be developed which leave to the human operator only those tasks that the computer cannot carry out. This implies a detailed analysis of all existing map digitation processes, and the development of software to automate all technological vectorization operations, based on formal, heuristic, knowledge and interactive algorithms, which can effectively be used by the computer [1]–[4]. The above thesis is especially suitable for analytical GIS in contrast to register GIS, as the former do not require an extremely high level of geometric exactness in the cartographic materials, whereas they do require fast processing of a large number of vector layers [8][20]. An example of analytical GIS is GIS developed to solve territorial planning problems, while an example of a register GIS is GIS developed for a cadastral system. Our approach is effective for both types of GIS; the reader may think on analytical GIS first.

A system approach can enhance the outcome not only of *processing* (map recognition) but also *pre-processing* (preparation of paper maps and their raster analogues) and *post-processing* (final processing of the results of automatic digitation). Thus, in the following three sections we shall consider these processing stages in the context of system approach.

2 Pre-processing

The main goal of *pre-processing* is to prepare raster cartographic images in such a way as to simplify them and increase the reliability of their recognition in the automatic system.

The proposed sequence of operations for the preparation of raster maps for automatic recognition is: **Pre-processing** = {(1) Preparation of the cartographic materials for scanning = (1.1 Restoration, 1.2 Copying, 1.3 Increasing the contrast of image objects); (2) Scanning = (2.1 Test scanning, 2.2 Definition of the optimal scanning parameters, 2.3 Final scanning, 2.4 Joining raster facets, 2.5 Correction of the raster image geometry by the reference points); (3) Preparation of the raster maps for recognition of the cartographic objects = (3.1 Edition of raster map: *3.1.1 Elimination of the map notations and map legend, 3.1.2 Elimination of the artificial objects and restoration covering by them images, 3.1.3 Restoration of the topology of cartographic images in pixel level*; 3.2 Separation of basic colors of the graphical codification on a raster map; 3.3 Restoration of the color palette of a raster map; 3.4 Stratification of raster map: *3.4.1 Stratification by reduced color palette, 3.4.2 Logical stratification of the cartographic objects)*}.

The comments on all pre-processing steps can be found in [1]–[4]. In the following, we shall discuss only most important points that highlight our approach at this stage.

Increasing the contrast of image objects. To simplify the process of vectorization, objects of the same class can be highlighted on a copy of the map using a contrasting color. Typically such marking involves enclosing linear objects such as rivers, roads or pipelines. In practice, outlines of polygonal objects, which do not have explicit borders (such as bogs, bushes, etc.), and are delineated only by dashed or patterned lines, should be drawn in. In particular, various polygonal objects may overlap, one represented by color, another outlined by a dashed line, and a third by patterned lines; in such cases, the objects should all be outlined explicitly.

Correction of the raster image geometry by the reference points. In practice, the raster image obtained after scanning is not uniformly deformed, due to printing errors, wear, scanning errors, and defects in edge-matching. Raster transformation programs exist to eliminate or at least minimize these defects. This has the direct effect of increasing the accuracy of the vectorization of the final map and the indirect effect of ultimately improving image recognition. The *general principle of raster map correction* is that of plane transformation by reference points, i.e. displacement of certain points of the raster map those coordinates are known; followed by translation of the remaining elements of the raster correspondingly. Reliability of raster map correction is maximized when geodesic reference points are used as the control points. A satisfactory correction to the raster map can be provided by a coordinate grid on the original map. In this case, if the type and parameters of the cartographic projection are known, programs can be developed which generate a theoretically exact system of the reference points used for transformation of the raster map. If neither geodesic data nor a coordinate grid are available, larger-scale or same-scale vector maps which have already been corrected, or satellite images containing the reference points can successfully be used to correct the raster map. In this case, punctual features of the cartographic objects, such as river confluences, road intersections, bridges, etc. can be chosen as control points.

Restoration of the topology of cartographic images. As a result of printing and scanning errors, graphical images of the cartographic objects on a raster map frequently have topological defects. Typical defects are breaks in thin lines, which should be continuous (such as contour lines, rivers, etc.) and the fusion of lines that logically should not intersect (e.g. contour lines). Topological errors in raster images complicate the recognition of cartographic objects, and gross errors, which can be noted by visual analysis of a raster map, should be corrected before the automatic recognition procedure is begun. The difficulty of solving this problem is increased due to the fact that such defects are often only visible, and can only be corrected at the pixel level. Nevertheless, powerful programs for correction of raster maps at pixel level currently exist, providing hope for the solution of this problem [4][5][8][20][23].

Stratification of the raster map. A raster map, considered as a unified heterogeneous graphical image, is suitable for parallel human vision. In contrast, raster images, containing homogeneous graphical information, are suited to consecutive machine vision. Two approaches can be used for the stratification of the original raster map: 1) *stratification by reduced color palette* or 2) *logical stratification of the cartographic objects.* In the first case, maps are derived from the original raster map which preserve only those pixels that have a strongly defined set of colors corresponding to the images of one class (for example, red and yellow, say, might correspond to the icons of populated places and the color of their outlines). In the second case, the map only preserves fragments of general raster image context corresponding to the locations of cartographic objects of one class (for example, railways with adjacent thin zones).

The procedure of stratification by color is clear [21], therefore let us consider here the basic features of logical stratification of a raster map. The *principle* is that the presence of a cartographic object, which should be vectored in logically separated layers, is reliably known. Thus, the only task left for the recognition program is specification of the location of the object. This simplifies the problem and increases the reliability of the solution. Logical stratification of a raster map can be done manually. The operator moves a window of given size and shape, separating the fragments of the layer formed. The efficiency of logical stratification, even when performed manually, is in that the main difficulty in vectoring raster maps is visual fixing of the coordinates of an object. In practice, this means that the operator should change the scale of the image and fix its coordinates using the cursor, perhaps two or three times, until a satisfactory result is obtained. On the other hand, defining the location of the object by specifying the size of a window is easier, especially when it is taken into consideration that the operator need not be concerned with any overlap of raster map facets, since the program can correct for this.

A typical situation that may arise is that a small-scale map already exists for a given territory. In this case, for logical stratification of a raster map, one can use methods for constructing buffer zones of the linear objects. These are already available in some vector editors [8][20][23].

3 Processing

The main goal of this principal stage of automatic vectorization of raster maps is the recognition of cartographic images, i.e. generation of vector layers and attributive information in electronic maps. From our point of view, the most promising line of R2V automation is the development of methods, algorithms and programs that focus only on locating and identifying *specific cartographic objects* that constitute the *map semantic structure*. Each cartographic image has its own graphical representation parameters, which can be used for automatic object recognition on a raster map. The particular attributes depend on the topological class of the object. Traditionally in GIS, vector map objects are divided into *three types*: points, arcs and polygons, representing respectively "punctual", "linear" and area objects. This classification can easily be extended to the analysis of cartographic images in raster maps. Objects are drawn on thematic maps in the form of graphical symbols, which are the same for all objects in a given group. Graphical images have color, geometric (location, shape), topological and attributive (quantitative and qualitative parameters, e.g. the name of object) information, which we can merge into the *concept of cartographic image.*

The classification of cartographic images is different when the vectorization of raster maps is considered. All objects on a raster map have area, and in this sense they are all polygons. It is not an easy problem to reduce the graphical coding elements of cartographic images to elements that correspond to the geometric categories "point" (a coordinate pair), "line" (a sequence of coordinate pairs) and "polygon" (a closed set of line segments which do not intersect and form the border of a geometrical figure). However, the classification of punctual, linear and polygonal objects should be preserved, because we can omit the relative stretch of the cartographic images in one or two directions (respectively lines or points) with respect to the stretch of the map field. A recognition program that recognizes, for example, punctual objects, does not have to distinguish between the punctual cartographic image itself or an element of a polygon fill pattern.

Notice that there may be other graphical objects involved in recognition of cartographic images, which are nearly always present in raster maps. Mainly, these are letters and digits (toponymic, quantitative and qualitative characteristics of objects). Additionally, there may be other graphical elements in the map (footnotes to lines, insets, etc.).

An important element of the automation of raster map vectorization is the development of an optimal sequence of steps for cartographic image recognition, successively eliminating elements already decoded from the raster map field and restoring images, which were hidden by the eliminated elements. The *basic principle* of this optimized ordering is *from simple to complex.* Nevertheless, the possibility of using information from objects already digitized (whether manually or by an automatic system) should be provided for in the development of a recognition strategy. For example, the punctual layer of hydrologic monitoring posts can be successfully used for recognition of linear elements of the river network. Moreover, the symbols of these posts generally cover images of the river, complicating automatic identification of the rivers. Taking this into account, it becomes clear that hydrologic monitoring posts should be vectored before the river network is digitized. Eliminating them from the raster map, one can use their locations and attributive data (mainly altitude marks) to aid in recognition of elements of the river network.

Further developing this approach, it is suggested to use already existing small-scale vector maps for recognition of corresponding cartographic images on large-scale maps. This strategy can also be considered as use of different sources of evidence to resolve ambiguities in a R2V conversion. An application of this strategy for toponym recognition of cartographic maps is described in [22]. The latter showed that the toponyms are excellent aids not only in processing, but also in post-processing of R2V conversion.

A small-scale map contains generalized (in a broad sense) information about a considerable proportion of the objects on the corresponding large-scale map. As a rule, the generalization involved in decreasing the map scale consists in the simplification of the geometric shape of the object and the elimination of a part of the object. For example, on a large-scale map, a river is represented by a polygon, but on the small-scale map, as a line. In general, a given object can be expected to change in topological type when the degree of generalization changes. Even if the topological type of an object is preserved after generalization, several objects on a large-scale map may correspond to a single object on a small-scale map. The use of small-scale maps solves a difficult problem in automatic digitation: the search for objects in the whole raster map field. In this case, a vectored object can be found in the nearest neighborhood of its generalized analogue, and nowhere else. We placed the proposed strategy into the *Fine-to-Coarse Scale* (F2CS) method of the recognition of cartographic objects in a large-scale map by using the information about these objects from the small-scale map. Some important steps of F2CS vectorization strategy are considered in the rest of this section; see details in [1][25].

The *search zone* for paired punctual objects can be restricted to a circle with a radius defined by the correlation between the scales of the vectored maps and the maps used. We use the *"caterpillar" algorithm* for searching for paired linear objects. The caterpillar algorithm involves the construction of a system of line segments perpendicular to the contour of their small-scale analogue, divided in half by it. The length of each segment can be chosen by the correlation between the scales of the maps used and their density, i.e. by the curvature of the generalized line. Moreover, the search object is located along segments constructed in this way. The sequence of reference points of the search curve can thus be found. The reference points obtained can be joined by straight-line segments in an interactive digitation system without any intervention by the operator.

Automatic cartographic image recognition is simplified and its reliability increased by the use of corresponding vector layers of a small-scale map for digitation of isoline and other regular systems of linear objects (such as the coordinate grid, or urban blocks with linear or radial planning). But in this case not all lines of a large-scale map have small-scale analogues. For example, the contour lines on a vectored 1:50,000 map may have 10m density while on the corresponding 1:250,000 map they have 50m density. In such a case, the contour lines that have counterparts in the generalization (0, 50, 100, etc.) are vectored first by the caterpillar algorithm. Next, the *"stairs" algorithm* is applied for the recognition of the intermediate contour lines. The stairs algorithm constructs a system of curves between each adjacent pair of already vectored contour lines, which are perpendicular to each of these contour lines. The density of these curves is defined by the curvature of the basic lines, just as in the caterpillar algorithm. Moreover, points of the adjacent contour lines to be searched for are located along the curves constructed in this way. Between two index contour lines, the number of additional lines to be found is well defined (for example, between two contour lines of 100 and 150m four additional contour lines of 110, 120, 130 and 140m always exist and can be found). Once all the required reference points have been found, it is clear that they can be joined in succession using the program tools given by the caterpillar algorithm.

The sequence of reference points of a vectored linear object can be copied from the layer, which contains the corresponding punctual objects. For example, shoreline structures (hydrometric monitoring posts, bridges, docks etc.) can be used as reference points to digitize the contours of rivers and lakes. The hydrometric monitoring posts are particularly useful here. Their coordinates and attributive data (name of the river or lake and altitude mark) can be used in automatic recognition algorithms for the elements of the hydrologic network on the raster map. Notice that in this case automatic digitizing reverses the order of operations compared to traditional techniques. Traditionally, the operator first digitized the hydrologic network manually and then vectored the location points of the shoreline structures, using vector-editing tools.

In other words, maximal use of already existing information (directly or indirectly related to the vectored objects) employed as *general principle of automatic cartographic image recognition* can increase efficiency and reliability. For example, algorithms that use digital models of a region and that are based on small-scale maps can be produced for digitation of the hydrologic network. If the layers are already vectored, this can be used to generate the sequence of reference points of the curves to be recognized; otherwise these points can be indicated manually as described above. This simplifies automatic digitation and increases its reliability.

Summarizing the processing of raster maps, we notice that the methods and algorithms used for this process should provide complete, even *redundant* cartographic image recognition (no matter a number of erroneously recognized objects), since visual control and correction of the vector layers can be carried out more quickly than manual digitation of missed objects.

To conclude the discussion in this section, the process of automatic cartographic image recognition (processing), from our point of view, should follow the scheme: **Processing** = {(1) Development of the strategy of automatic digitization of raster maps; (2) Definition of the sound matrices of raster maps = (2.1 Classification of recognized objects, 2.2 Definition of the size, form and color filling of the semantic patterns of raster maps, 2.3 Estimation of statistical weights of single elements of cartographic images; (3) Recognition of cartographic images = (3.1 Digitation of objects which have vector analogues; 3.2 Digitation of objects which have not vector analogues; 3.3 Elimination of superfluously recognized objects); (4) Recognition of attributive data of vectored objects = (4.1 Classification of attributive information carriers, 4.2 Location and identification of attributive information, 4.3 Correction of errors of attributive data recognition); (5) Elimination of recognized images from raster map = (5.1 Restoration of image covered by recognized objects, 5.2 Correction of restored image)}.

4 Post-processing

The main goal of the *post-processing* of raster maps (after cartographic image recognition) is an automatic correction of vectorization errors.

For automatic correction of digitation we suggest *three approaches*: using 1) the topological characteristics of objects in vector layers, 2) the spatial correlation (connectivity) of the corresponding vector layers, and 3) the sources of evidence (textual, spatial distribution, geographic, notational, linguistic... information).

The *first approach* is based on the fact that many cartographic objects in the map have well-defined topological characteristics, which can be used for the correction of vectorization errors. Let us give just one obvious example; more examples in [1]–[4].

Isolines. The topological characteristics of isoline systems (e.g. contour lines) are: (a) isolines are continuous, (b) they cannot intersect each other, (c) each isoline is either closed or started and finished at a domain boundary, and (d) polygons that cover the whole domain without intersections can be assembled from the arcs of the correct isoline system together with the domain boundaries. However, in a raster map these characteristics, as a rule, may be lost due to several reasons: (i) the lines are broken where a parameter value for a given isoline is written, (ii) some sections of isolines are not well drawn in high density regions, and (iii) the raster images of some isolines are merged due to defects of printing and scanning the paper maps. The "tick marks" (small segments of fixed length, which are perpendicular to the isolines and drawn in the direction of the decreasing of cartographic parameter) need special consideration. These elements of the map's graphical design, if not recognized as the parts of the isoline system, hinder the correct assembly of the polygons and either should be eliminated or (better) detached in a separate vector layer. They can be restored on the vector map and used for the automatic attribution of polygons assembled from the contour lines.

The *second approach* is newer and offers more potential. It is based on use of connectivity or spatial correlations among various vector objects to correct the results of automatic digitation and the attributes of raster map cartographic images. Let us explain this by the following examples; more examples in [1]–[4].

Hydrosphere elements. The vectored elements of the hydrosphere include objects of all three topological types: polygonal (e.g. seas, lakes, reservoirs, ponds, bogs, etc.), linear (e.g. rivers, channels, brooks) and punctual (e.g. springs, out-of-scale reservoirs). It is clear that nearly all hydrosphere elements have certain spatial relationships. For example, springs or lakes can be the sources of rivers (main hydrosphere elements). Linear river sections can connect polygonal hydrosphere elements (extended sections of riverbeds, lakes or reservoirs). Rivers discharge into seas or lakes. These spatial relationships are not only necessary for a topologically correct vector image of the hydrosphere, but can be also used to correct automatic digitation results of the river network with digitized polygonal and punctual hydrosphere elements are available.

Relief. The relief of a region on the maps is represented by objects of two topological types: (1) punctual (trigonometric points, hydrometric monitoring posts, reference points with coordinates obtained by GPS, and (2) linear (contour lines, relief features–slopes, ravines, landslides, etc.). All these objects have correlations among each other due to their location and in particular to the altitudes given as attributive information. We notice particularly the relationship between altitude and the hydrologic network; altitude decreases monotonically along a river in the direction of flow, thus each contour line intersects the river either not at all or exactly once. Due to this relationship, it is convenient to produce the vector map of the hydrologic network before digitizing the contour lines and to subsequently use the digitized hydrologic network for correction of the results of contour digitation.

The *third approach* has proven its efficiency in toponym recognition of cartographic maps and can be also used in general R2V conversion post-processing [22].

The examples presented in this section show that the characteristics of internal structure and relationships between the vector objects can be used in automatic correction of errors of the automatic vectorization of raster maps. In practice it means the development of more specific software for automatic cartographic image recognition.

Summarizing the discussion of this section, we suggest that the process of automatic correction of results of automatic cartographic image recognition (post-processing) follows the scheme: **Post-processing** = {(1) Correction of vector layers based on peculiarities of their internal topology; (2) Correction using the sources of evidence (textual, spatial distribution, geographic, notational, linguistic... information); (3) Correction of vector layers based on their spatial and logical correlation with other vector objects; (4) Final correction of vector layers in whole electronic map system}.

5   A2R2V

We are going to explain the content of the chart-flow shown in Figure 1 that summarizes our approach and introduces the methodology of A2R2V conversion; see [1]-[4][7][9][10][22][24][25] for detail description of system's modules and functioning. Due to the page limit, we should skip this description, focusing on its main concepts.

Any map interpretation system deals with the processing of alphanumeric, punctual, linear and area raster objects. Some state-of-the art systems based on the image processing and graphics recognition [11–15][21] consider the color, shape and texture components of the concept of cartographic objects, usually omitting the meaning and topology (Section 3). Of course the color, shape, etc. are important cues. However, they are *only cues*: there is no pure color in raster-scanned maps; what is the shape of raster object; what is the arc centerline; how to preserve topological "iso-structures" of map after conversion? (Cf. the discussion in Sections 2 and 4). Moreover, most

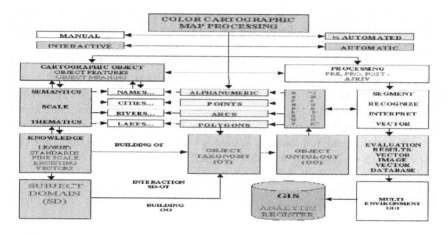

Fig. 1. A2R2V functioning (components, modules, and interaction)

systems are pixel-oriented. They are artificial and destroy a number of the essential image characteristics: general composition, object shapes, image dynamic and contextual information. All this results that increasingly complex methods and algorithms for machine recognition of cartographic objects do not materially improve the results of a R2V conversion (Cf. Section 1).

Effective image formats should preserve the natural image structure and thus provide object-oriented data integration (OODI) [22][26]. This thesis is especially true for cartographic images which being intermediate between man-made drawings and natural images provide a nearly ideal model for semantic analysis [3][7] and OODI is quite natural here in the context of GIS [1–4][22–26]. This leads to natural *taxonomic classification* of cartographic patterns, definition of the cartographic *subject domain* (SD) (a set of "names") in dependence on map thematic, scale, legend, toponyms, and a priory knowledge about the map (existing/reworked vectors in fine scale) [25]. Different sources of evidence can be also put into SD to support efficient map processing [22][25]. The interaction between SD and object taxonomy (OT) is led to the conceptual structuration of cartographic data in *hierarchical object ontology* (OO) (the nodes of OO are concepts - not words) [26]. Thus, we are looking for correct and adequate representation of raster objects as "thematic image book" *before* processing/conversion. However, the results of processing can be feedback and correct (Section 4). In Figure 1, the blocks in gray with the text in red illustrate our A2R2V system approach.

Automatic interpretation of color cartographic images as yet presents certain difficulties for state-of-the art in image processing, pattern recognition and artificial intelligence. It appears unrealistic to obtain a fully automatic computer-based interpretation system free of errors [1]. High efficiency of interpretation is required for vector map production and actualization first. It seems reasonable to obtain in both cases 90-95% successfully recognized objects. This is to avoid excessive work on corrections of errors produced by the computer system that can sometimes be greater than manual R2V conversion [16]. In the frameworks of our approach, manual, inter-active, semi-automated and automatic processing may prove useful. Our point is: Apply them application-dependently, use the sources of evidence to respond alarms [1][22][25].

We believe that only a system, semantic-based approach to the R2V problem can be fruitful. In the context of the A2R2V system, this means first, decomposition of source image by multiple hierarchical components to achieve a stable, accurate repre-sentation in the presence of degraded images. Second is segmentation with mutual recognition of appropriate primitives. Third is the development of a unified knowl-edge-based learning and self-learning system with optimal human-machine interac-tion. Our research is concerning with this approach.

6 Conclusion

The problem of automatic raster map digitation has discussed. We conjecture that the most promising line of progress toward its solution lies in successively increasing automation of the separate links of the approach considered herein. We suggest as *main principle* of such automation, maximal use of already existing and reworked vector and attributive information (sources of evidence) in the preparation, digitation and correction algorithms of each succeeding vector layer. This information can be organized and effectively used as a knowledge base in the conversion system, provid-ing object-oriented data integration to GIS. The operator should define an applica-tion-dependent subject domain for conversion and respond system's alarms in manual or interactive regimes. Thus our approach can be combined with interactive approach.

References

1. Levachkine, S.: Raster to Vector Conversion of Color Cartographic Maps for Analytical GIS. In: Llados, J. (ed.): Proc. 5th IAPR Int. Workshop on Graphics Recognition (GREC 2003) July 30–31 2003, Barcelona, Catalonia, Spain (2003) 77–91
2. Levachkine, S: System Approach to R2V Conversion for Analytical GIS. In: Levachkine, S., Serra, J., Egenhofer, M. (eds.) Proc. 2nd Int. Workshop on Semantic Processing of Spa-tial Data (GEOPRO 2003), November 4–5 2003, Mexico City, Mexico (2003) 22–33 (ISBN 970-36-0103-0)
3. Levachkine, S., Velázquez, A., Alexandrov, V., Kharinov, M.: Semantic Analysis and Recognition of Raster-scanned Color Cartographic Images. Lecture Notes in Computer Science, Vol. 2390. Springer (2002) 178–189
4. Levachkine, S., Polchkov, E.: Integrated Technique for Automated Digitation of Raster Maps. Revista Digital Universitaria (RDU). Vol. 1, No. 1 (2000). On-line: http://www. revista.unam.mx/vol.1/art4/ (ISSN 1607-6079)

5. Ablameyko, S., Pridmore, T.: Machine Interpretation of Line Drawing Images, Technical Drawings, Maps, and Diagrams. Springer (2000)
6. Doermann, D.S.: An Introduction to Vectorization and Segmentation. Lecture Notes in Computer Science, Vol. 1389. Springer (1998) 1–8
7. Levachkine, S., Alexandrov, V.: Semantic-mind Analysis of Information Flows: A Primer. In: Levachkine, S., Serra, J., Egenhofer, M. (eds.) Proc. 2nd Int. Workshop on Semantic Processing of Spatial Data (GEOPRO 2003), November 4–5 2003, Mexico City, Mexico (2003) 11–21 (ISBN 970-36-0103-0)
8. Definiens Imaging GmbH e-Cognition: *Object Oriented Image Analysis* http://www. definiens-imaging.com/ecognition/; Able Software Co.: *R2V* http://www.ablesw.com/r2v/; Resident Ltd.: *MapEdit 4.6* http://www.resident.ru/
9. Alexandrov, V., Kharinov, M., Velázquez, A. Levachkine, S.: Object-oriented Color Image Segmentation. Proc. IASTED Int. Conference on Signal Processing, Pattern Recognition, and Applications (SPPRA 2002), June 25–28 2002, Greece (2002) 493–498
10. Velázquez, A., Sossa, H., Levachkine, S.: On the Segmentation of Color Cartographic Images. Lecture Notes in Computer Science, Vol. 2396. Springer (2002) 387–395
11. Meyers G.K., Chen, C.-H.: Verification–based Approach for Automated Text and Feature Extraction from Raster-scanned Maps. Lecture Notes in Computer Science, Vol. 1072. Springer (1996) 190–203
12. Deseilligny, M.-P., Mariani, R., Labiche, J.: Topographic Maps Automatic Interpretation: Some Proposed Strategies. Lecture Notes in Computer Science, Vol. 1389. Springer (1998) 175–193
13. Dupont, F., Deseilligny, M.-P., Gonrad, M.: Automatic Interpretation of Scanned Maps: Reconstruction of Contour Lines. Lecture Notes in Computer Science, Vol. 1389. Springer (1998) 194–206
14. Frischknecht, S., Kanani, E.: Automatic Interpretation of Scanned Topographic Maps: A Raster-based Approach. Lecture Notes in Computer Science, Vol. 1389. Springer (1998) 207–220
15. Schavemaker, G.M., Reinders, M.J.T.: Information Fusion for Conflict Resolution in Map Interpretation. Lecture Notes in Computer Science, Vol. 1389. Springer (1998) 231–242
16. Parcel Mapping using GIS. A Guide to Digital Parcel Map Development for Massachusetts Office of Geography Information and Analysis (MASSGIS) (August 1999). On-line: http://umass.edu/tei/ogia/parcelguide/
17. Osamu, H., Doermann, D.S.: Quantitative Measurement of the Performance of Raster-to-vector Conversion Algorithms. Lecture Notes in Computer Science, Vol. 1072. Springer (1996) 57–68
18. Wenyin, L., Dori, D.: Genericity in Graphics Recognition Algorithms. Lecture Notes in Computer Science, Vol. 1389. Springer (1998) 9–20
19. Ishan, P., Liang Jisheng, Chhabra, A.K., Haralick, R.: A Performance Evaluation Protocol for Graphics Recognition Systems. Lecture Notes in Computer Science, Vol. 1389. Springer (1998) 372–389
20. EasyTrace: Advanced Software for Automatic R2V Conversion http://www.easytrace. com/work/english; TerraSpace: Center for Applied Informatics http://www.terraspace. ru/eng
21. Angulo, J., Serra, J.: Mathematical Morphology in Color Spaces Applied to the Analysis of Cartographic Images. In: Levachkine, S., Serra, J., Egenhofer, M. (eds.) Proc. 2nd Int. Workshop on Semantic Processing of Spatial Data (GEOPRO 2003), November 4–5 2003, Mexico City, Mexico (2003) 59–66 (ISBN 970-36-0103-0)

22. Gelbukh, A., Han SangYong, Levachkine, S.: Combining Sources of Evidence to Resolve Ambiguities in Toponym Recognition in Cartographic Maps. In: Levachkine, S., Serra, J., Egenhofer, M. (eds.) Proc. 2nd Int. Workshop on Semantic Processing of Spatial Data (GEOPRO 2003), November 4–5 2003, Mexico City, Mexico (2003) 42–51 (ISBN 970-36-0103-0)
23. Benz, U.C., Hofmann, P., Willhauck, G., Lingenfelder, I., Heynen, M.: Multi-resolution, Object-oriented Fuzzy Analysis of Remote Sensing Data for GIS Ready Information. In: Levachkine, S., Serra, J., Egenhofer, M. (eds.) Proc. 2nd Int. Workshop on Semantic Processing of Spatial Data (GEOPRO 2003), November 4–5 2003, Mexico City, Mexico (2003) 110–126 (ISBN 970-36-0103-0)
24. Levachkine, S., Torres, M., Moreno, M., Quintero, R.: Simultaneous Segmentation-Recognition-Vectorization of Meaningful Geographical Objects in Geo-images. Lecture Notes in Computer Science, Vol. 2905. Springer (2003) 635–642
25. González-Gómez, E., Levachkine, S.: Fine-to-Coarse Scale Method of Color Cartographic Images Recognition. Computación y Sistemas (to appear)
26. Torres-Ruiz, M., Levachkine, S.: Generating Spatial Ontologies based on the Spatial Semantics. In: Levachkine, S., Serra, J., Egenhofer, M. (eds.) Proc. 2nd Int. Workshop on Semantic Processing of Spatial Data (GEOPRO 2003), November 4–5 2003, Mexico City, Mexico (2003) 169–178 (ISBN 970-36-0103-0)

Text/Graphics Separation and Recognition in Raster-Scanned Color Cartographic Maps

Aurelio Velázquez[1] and Serguei Levachkine[2]

[1] Program in Applied Math and Computing - Mexican Petroleum Institute (PIMAYC - IMP)
avelaz@imp.mx
[2] Geoprocessing Laboratory (GEOLAB)
Centre for Computing Research (CIC) - National Polytechnic Institute (IPN)
palych@cic.ipn.mx

Abstract. A method to separate and recognize the touching/overlapping alphanumeric characters is proposed. The characters are processed in raster-scanned color cartographic maps. The map is segmented first to extract all text strings including those that are touching other symbols, strokes and characters. Second, OCR-based recognition with Artificial Neural Networks (ANN) is applied to define the coordinates, size and orientation of alphanumeric character strings in each case presented in the map. Third, four straight lines or a number of "curves" computed as a function of primarily recognized by ANN characters are extrapolated to separate those symbols that are attached. Finally, the separated characters input into ANN again to be finally identified. Results showed high method's rendering in the context of raster-to-vector conversion of color cartographic images.

1 Introduction

Cartographic color maps contain a lot of "punctual", "linear" and area objects. To describe these objects there can be used symbols (portrays) and labels (alphanumeric characters) presenting a great variety of features, some of them in equal shape but in different color. Different colors are used to represent different objects, including a number of character's fonts. These can be colored and following different paths in all kind of angles.

The development of a Geographical Information System (GIS) includes the selection of the paper and raster maps for vectorization Levachkine *et al.* [1]. To be included into GIS, the paper maps should be changed to a computer readable format, normally a raster format. After that, the raster maps can be converted into vector format that is most adequate to GIS. In the context of raster-to-vector conversion of graphical documents, the problem of text recognition is of special interest, because textual information can be used for verification of vectorization results (postprocessing). The retrieval of all presented elements in a map can be made manually or supported by a computer system. In the former case, the map is scanned in a raster format and then converted to vector. Before a raster-to-vector conversion a map segmentation and recognition are usually employed Levachkine [25].

J. Lladós and Y.-B. Kwon (Eds.): GREC 2003, LNCS 3088, pp. 63–74, 2004.

Some works on text processing in graphic images to be mentioned are as follows.

General frameworks. The text segmentation and its subsequent recognition in raster images are very difficult problems because, in general, there is either text embedded in graphic components, or text touching graphics Doermann [14]. These challenging problems have received numerous responses from the graphic recognition community Nagy [15]. However, there have not been developed efficient programs that solve the problem automatically. Thus, the main idea of the most works is to put the operator in the loop (even in the center of a computer system). As proposed, for example, by Ganesan [16], the operator can draw line through the text, marking it as text and revealing its orientation all in one step. Fletcher *et al.* [17] and Tan *et al.* [18] developed the algorithms to extract text strings from text/graphics images. Both methods however assume that the text does not touch or overlap with graphics. Wenyin *et al.* [7] recognized horizontal or vertical text. Luo *et al.* [3] detached characters from straight lines. For maps, the problem is much more complex since the touching or overlapping as well as many other character configurations are commonly presented in maps. Cao *et al.* [20] proposed a specific method of detecting and extracting characters that are touching graphics in raster-scanned color maps. It is based on observation that the constituent strokes of characters are usually short segments in comparison with those of graphics. It combines line continuation with the feature line width to decompose and reconstruct segments underlying the region of intersection. Experimental results showed that proposed method slightly improved the percentage of correctly detected text as well as the accuracy of character recognition with OCR.

Segmentation. Applying color and spatial attributes to segment thematic maps, Silva [2] used a 300-dpi resolution in a *RGB* color system to perform a Karhunen-Loeve transformation. Luo *et al.* [3] used the directional morphological operations. They coded images by run-length-encoded as an enchained list, deleting the text that is represented by lines, and finally subtracting the new image from the original one to obtain an image with text without lines. In [4], Li described the Comb algorithm based on the best common structure of local minima defined at the moment to search for global minima. He used the concept of maximum a posteriori (MAP) and Markov random fields (MRF) as the frameworks. To segment text from engineering drawings Adam *et al.* [11] used Fourier-Mellin transform in a five-step process. Using a heuristics, they found broken chains. In [12], Hase *et al.* described a three-step algorithm of segmentation called "multi-stage relaxation". However, they do not recognize characters. In [5], Levachkine *et al.* used false colors in a *RGB* model. They applied different combinations of basic colors to segment map objects, and then a neighborhood analysis to recover or eliminate pixels.

Extraction and recognition. In [6], Myers *et al.* described the verification-based approach for automated text and feature extraction from raster-scanned maps. They used a gazetteer (toponym dictionary) to propose a forecasting hypothesis, which characters are in labels and where is their position in the map, having the information from another map in a different scale. Character and text boxes are used in [7] by Wenyin *et al.* The authors considered only horizontal and vertical text in which a character box is a rectangle with rate sides are no larger than 10 pixels to join character boxes. Thus, they built the text box that can grow horizontally or vertically under a threshold to fit the letters. Using directional morphological operations Luo *et al.* [3] separated the text from lines but not from curves. Deseilligny *et al.* [8] proposed different knowledge levels to solve the problem. They begun with an analysis of related components (semiologic), then built the character chains (syntactic), detecting related characters (higher semiologic level) and, finally, following the natural language rules corrected the text (semantic). It seems too complex to be effective. Using templates Friscknecht *et al.* [9] linked them with symbols and characters. The approach does not require the complete template. It is pondered and hierarchically built. To retrieve street names Nagy *et al.* [10] used one of the four black layers. Taking the hue component from a *HSV* model for segmentation, they subtracted the street layer from the black layer and then made a connected component analysis to distinguish text characters. An efficient system to recognize characters by means of adaptive ANN is described in [13] by Velázquez *et al.* To train ANN, they used characters from a word processor in different fonts, sizes and inclinations by applying them to identify a great variety of characters in cartographic maps. This OCR algorithm is also used in the present paper. It is shown that using some "rules of thumb" we can obtain better results.

The rest of paper is organized as follows. In Section 2, we describe an alphanumeric segmentation-recognition system. In Section 3, we consider the touching and overlapping characters presented in raster-scanned color cartographic maps. A method. (*V-lines* and *V-curves*) to separate and further recognize such characters is described in this section as well. Section 4 contains paper's conclusion.

2   Segmentation of Overall Map Characters

A raster map has to be segmented first. All its elements should be retrieved with their coordinates and features, and then sent to the corresponding thematic layers. The layers can be symbols, landmarks, isolines, natural and artificial surroundings, words and numbers, lakes and other "punctual", "linear" and polygonal bodies. Cartographic maps are the most complex graphic documents due to the high density of information that they contain. A typical example is shown in Figure 1a (*RGB* image).

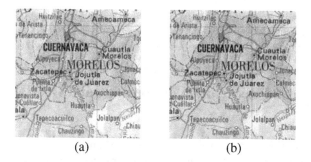

(a)   (b)

Fig. 1. (a) Example of color cartographic map with different types of characters; (b) Gray-level image (*Y*-luminance) corresponding to the image of Figure 1

To obtain a binary image from color image, the former is usually changed to a gray-level. One way to make this change is to convert the *RGB* model to the *YIQ* model, where the luminance (*Y*) is a gray-level image. Another way is to average the *R*, *G* and *B* values. Figure 1b shows the gray-level image obtained from the image of Figure 1a. In this work, we used both conversion procedures as well as their combination as described in [5] by Levachkine *et al*. The binary image can be obtained applying a threshold to the gray-level image. Usually, the threshold is selected from the histogram computed by the frequency's value that shows the pixels from the gray-level image.

The selection of the threshold is the most critical task in a transformation of the image to binary format. Figures 2a and 2b illustrate this statement: 2a (a high-value threshold) and 2b (a low-value threshold).

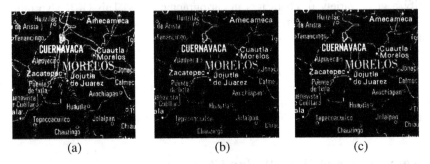

      (a)   (b)   (c)

Fig. 2. (a) Binary image of Figure 1b (a high-value threshold); (b) Binary image of Figure 1b (a low-value threshold); (c) Binary image of Figure 1b (global dynamic thresholding [5])

In Figure 2a, some "red" lines are touching the characters. In Figure 2b there are no more "red" lines, but some characters are disappeared such those that belong to the word "*Tepecoacuilco*".

In contrast, a method described in [5] uses false color combinations to obtain the binary image from a *RGB* image by applying a global dynamic thresholding. This method was primarily developed for the cartographic image subject domain. We obtained sufficiently good results in this domain [5]. Later, it was generalized to arbitrary image subject domain by Alexandrov *et al*. [21], making it application-independent. Figure 2c shows a binary image obtained with that method.

3 Separation and Recognition of Touching and Overlapping Characters

This is the main section of the paper. Based on detailed analysis of the textual characters presented in raster-scanned color cartographic maps and possible configurations of touching and/or overlapping text/graphics, we propose a simple method to separate the text from graphics component that is called *V-lines*. V-lines do work well in the case of characters with fixed inclination. However, they exhibit certain limitations in the case of curvilinear text. To partially solve the problem of curvilinear text/graphics separation, we discuss a possible generalization of V-lines method, which we call *V-curves*.

To link all characters that belong to the same (and geographically meaningful) word, it is required to select all those that are related through the spatial relationships, the average size, color similarity, trend angle, etc. Gelbukh *et al.* [22][23]. All words that have been recognized, using the gazetteer, are sent to GIS, while those that were not identified, remained in the picture matrix.

3.1 V-Lines (Horizontal Labels)

We have begun our analysis of cartographic textual characters of fixed inclination with a simple observation that such text can be accommodated between two of four (low case letters) rectilinear segments, called V-lines, while the upper case letters is considered apart as follows.

Capital letters nearly always have the same height, though some of them could be taller than the other letters that do belong to the same word such as the letter 'Q' shown in Figure 3.

Fig. 3. Capital letters forming a word, where the letter 'Q' is taller than the other letters

In this case, a recognition algorithm executed for this type of letters would has to recognize the characters touching or overlapping other objects. This sometimes reduces an efficiency of a recognition system. However, as a rule, this case is easily to maintain.

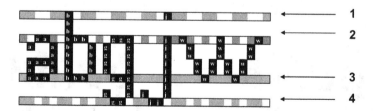

Fig. 4. Four rectilinear segments related to low case letters showing different combinations

On the other hand, low case letters are always related to two of the four imaginary lines shown in Figure 4 and ordered from the top to bottom: one, two, three and four. The possible combinations of two of these lines are *"two-three"*, *"one-three"*, *"two-four"*, and *"one-four"*.

To obtain the four V-lines, we employ the following steps:

- The imaginary lines are grouped under their position in the image matrix of map in accordance with the first and last matrix's row of each character that belongs to the cluster,
- The corresponding rows are numbered from the top to bottom,
- The row with the most bottom character's occurrences (a three-pixel tolerance is admitted) is selected as line three and an imaginary line is traced,
- The row with the most top character's occurrences is selected as imaginary line two. Thus obtained imaginary lines are the basic V-lines,
- If there is another row down the row three such that the distance (in pixels) between both is smaller than one third of the distance between row two and row three, then it is labeled as the fourth line,
- A similar process is employed to obtain the line one, at the top, if exists.

There are characters that are touching other characters (or even other objects) with the same attributes. Thus, it is impossible to make a "natural" segmentation, because the characters share similar features. Two examples of these problems are shown in Figure 5a (the character 'S' is touching a symbol) and Figure 5b (the character 'S' is overlapped two other characters 'n' and 'o'). Figure 6a shows the corresponding binary representation of Figure 5a.

(a)   (b)

Fig. 5. (a) Character touching a symbol with similar features; (b) Character overlapping two characters with identical features

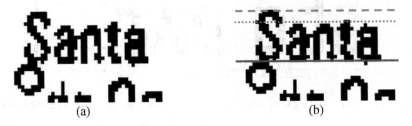

(a)   (b)

Fig. 6. (a) Binary image of Figure 5a; (b) V-lines to separate the letter 'S' from the symbol is bellow it in Figure 6a

Despite the letters 'a' and 'n' in Figure 6a are linked by a pixel, they could be moved away in the preprocessing step, under the 'neighborhood pixel analysis'. At this time, we obtain the chain "*anta*" identified by the set of ANN [13].

Extrapolating the lines shown in Figure 4, it is possible to separate the letter 'S', shown in Figure 6a from the symbol is below it, and then identified it with the set of ANN [13]. After this process is finished, it is possible to obtain the whole chain to form the word "*Santa*". The word is checked in a gazetteer to verify that it is a valid word for this geographical location [22][23]. Figure 6b shows the lines one, two and three used (line four is under the symbol touching 'S', but it is so far from line three).

3.2 Growing Rectangle (Slanted Text)

If the upper case characters are not horizontal, we can trace a "diagonal" rectangle following the same angle that those letters have. In Figure 7a, the first 'S' is touching the river's line which name is '*BALSAS*'.

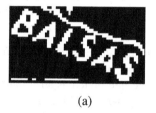 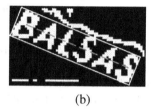

(a)   (b)

Fig. 7. (a) Label of '*BALSAS*' river is touching the line of the river at the first letter 'S'; (b) Starting with a line following the label angle, a dynamic rectangle is built

With the other five letters ('B', 'A', 'L', 'A', and 'S'); we can build a rectangle that covers all the word letters. Using the upper and lower pixels from the first and last characters of the chain, we compute their mean value obtaining two points to trace an imaginary line with them as shown in Figure 7b. Then the left or upper (if the chain is vertical) point is moved one pixel up (or right) and one left (or down) following the left (or upper) line of the rectangle so that we have two new points, the right or lower point is moved one pixel down (or left) and one right (or up) following the right (or lower) line of the rectangle so that there are four points for the first dynamic rectangle. Computing the position of each character in the largest lines, we can find if there are outside pixels. The shortest lines are used for the same purpose with the first and last characters. If there are outside pixels in a line, it is moved one pixel in corresponding direction. If more than one line has outside pixels, all those lines are moved. The process is continued until no more outside pixel are found. Now, it is possible to identify the missing letter 'S' using only the pixels inside of the rectangle box belonging to letter 'S', sending them to ANN and testing the word '*BALSAS*' in the gazetteer.

On the other hand, for upper and lower case letters, four lines should be computed. Figure 8a shows the word '*Chicayán*' touching a line of the river labeled for it. Using the procedure employed for capital letters, it is possible to construct a rectangle as shown in Figure 8b. The largest lines will be used to find the four V-lines, if they are present. Normally, three of them are present. Each line should be moved with pixel-by-pixel procedure until it is reached the next numbered level. An additional adjustment is made: each ending point is moved up three pixels and the line that better fits one of the inner lines is selected as the "leader". To the other three lines, if exist, we assign the same angle that the leader has. Figure 8c shows these lines.

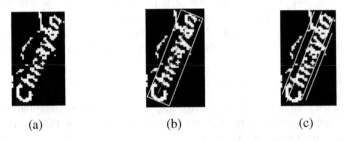

(a)   (b)   (c)

Fig. 8. (a) Label of '*Chicayán*' river is touching the line of the river with the letter '*á*'; (b) First, it is necessary to build a rectangle as it was made with capital letters; (c) Four lines to unglue letter '*a*' from the riverbed

Cutting the label with line one, the missing letter can be analyzed. It could be recognized as a letter '*d*', but the word '*Chicaydn*' does not exist in gazetteer. Thus, we attempt now with line two. Then, the letter can be interpreted as an '*a*' and the word '*Chicayan*' is already in the gazetteer and at right geographical location.

There are other manners in which objects can touch an alphanumeric character: at its left or right, at its top or bottom as in example shown in Figure 9a, where letter '*M*' is touched at its left by a state boundary.

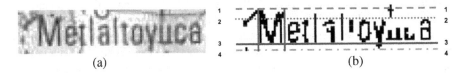

(a)   (b)

Fig. 9. (a) The word is touched at one extreme of the chain; (b) "Growing" rectangle to identify the letter 'M'

The V-lines are not helpful themselves to separate the characters. However, the V-lines are useful to build a "growing" rectangle that is fitted to the character's pixels, identifying the characters with the ANN and using the gazetteer until it matches to a correct word. The growing rectangle, around letter '*M*' is shown in Figure 9b.

To build the rectangle, we employ the following steps:

- If the character is at left of string, we start at the beginning of the first letter. At this moment, we have lines two, three and four; there is another line, the first from the top to bottom. We use a tolerance of one third of the distance (in pixels) between lines two and three. A perpendicular line, that begins at line three plus tolerance (in pixels) and ends at line two minus tolerance (in pixels) is moved left until an appropriated pixel is found,
- The line moved is the first line of the rectangle. Other is formed by copying this line two pixels left. The other lines are two and three, unless there are pixels out-

side those lines, but inside of the tolerance. The first line found is the "anchor", all others can be removed, and

- Left line is moved pixel-by-pixel. There could be a motion of upper or lower lines always inside of the tolerance. Each time the line is moved, the pixels in the rectangle are analyzed and tested by ANN, the gazetteer and the procedures described in [22][23]. The process is continued until a correct word is found or the distance between the line and the anchor is more than one and half times of the distance between upper and lower lines.

Unfortunately, there are some man-made errors on the maps and, even though our method outputs the complete chain of characters, the word can be misspelled. Figure 10a shows a word where letters '*l*' and '*n*' are touched by two lines. After the processing with V-lines shown in Figure 10b is applied the chain "*Tulacingo*" is built, but this word is not in the gazetteer, because the right word is "*Tulancingo*" in which the letter '*n*' was missing. This error can be corrected by another procedure [22][23].

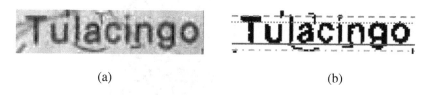

(a)   (b)

Fig. 10. (a) Original chain touching two arcs of a boundary; (b) Characters were unglued and the chain '*Tulacingo*' was build

3.3 More Difficult Cases

On the other hand, some labels are nearly impossible to detect because the background features are too close to their own features. Figure 11a shows such a label and Figure 11b shows its binary image with the damaged characters hard to identify.

(a)   (b)   (c)   (d)

Fig. 11. (a) Label overlapped by other objects with similar attributes; (b) Binary image of Figure 11a, showing distorted characters; (c) Original image; (d) Binary representation of c

Another example is shown in Figure 11c. It is impossible to detect (in automatic way) the chain of characters because all of them are touching other elements.

In last two cases the operator intervention is certainly required as by Ganesan [16] or (better) by Gelbukh *et al.* [22][23]. In the former case the computer system provides useful hints to support the operator's decisions. The operator's task is to choose the best one for the given map situation and context. For example, in [23], a set of "name placement" strategies was proposed that aim to associate the name with its correct geographic location. As we mentioned above, the name placement is based on a number of the sources of evidence that included but not limited to, textual, spatial distribution, geographic, notational, and linguistic information.

3.4   V-Curves (Curvilinear Labels)

Figure 12a displays a curvilinear text associated to a riverbed with the letter '*g*' touching the line of the river (Figure 12b shows the corresponding binary image).

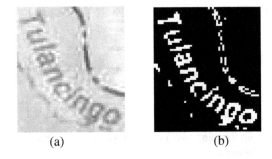

(a)   (b)

Fig. 12. (a) Color image with a curvilinear text "*Tulancingo*" (name of the river); (b) Binary image of Figure 12a

An application of V-lines method is difficult in this case. However, we can use the following procedure that we call *V-curves* to solve the problem. The text is divided into blocks of fixed (or nearly fixed) inclination by applying an algorithm similar to "growing rectangle" (Section 3.2). To each block the V-lines method is applied. Thus obtained lines are connected by a linear extrapolation, forming linear splines. These splines are V-curves. The following steps are similar to those that were used in V-lines method. To form meaningful words from disjoint text strings of each block, we use "spatial neighborhood semantic analysis" based on two sources of evidence as described in [22][23], Sections 5 and 6.

4   Conclusion

A method to separate and recognize touching and overlapping characters in raster-scanned color cartographic images has been presented. The algorithm performs the segmentation of the character layer and most valid (or "geographically meaningful") words are built. This algorithm can detach nearly all characters touching other elements in any direction. Though some words cannot be obtained complete, the system is able to suggest one word from a gazetteer to support the operator decision to resolve the ambiguous cases. OCR-based recognition procedure with ANN called ASIMILA (a modification of the backpropogation paradigm) applied to the case of study possesses some peculiarities. ANN have been trained and tested first with synthetic characters. After that the same ANN have been employed for the characters of cartographic maps on a set of 2,125 samples. The results gave 93.21% of success [13]. These results have been improved with the V-lines/V-curves to some 96.73%. Even more efficient machine recognition of toponyms is reached by applying the spatial neighborhood semantic analysis in combination with the method herein described [22][23].

Acknowledgments

The authors of this paper wish to thank the Centre for Computing Research (CIC-IPN), General Coordination of Postgraduate Study and Research (CGEPI-IPN), National Polytechnic Institute (IPN), the Program in Applied Math and Computing of the Mexican Petroleum Institute (PIMAYC-IMP), the Mexican National Council for Science and Technology (CONACYT) and National Researcher Network (SNI) for their support.

References

1. Levachkine, S., Polchkov, E.: Integrated Technique for Automated Digitation of Raster Maps. Revista Digital Universitaria (RDU). Vol. 1, No. 1 (2000). On-line: http://www.revista.unam.mx/vol.1/art4/ (ISSN 1607–6079)
2. Silva, C.J.: Segmentation of Thematic Maps using Color and Spatial Attributes. Lecture Notes in Computer Science, Vol. 1389. Springer (1998) 221–230
3. Luo, H., Rangachar, K.: Improved Directional Morphological Operations for Separation of Characters from Maps/Graphics. Lecture Notes in Computer Science, Vol. 1389. Springer (1998) 35–47
4. Li, S.Z.: Toward Global Solution to Map Image Restoration and Segmentation using Common Structure of Local Minima. Pattern Recognition. Vol. 33, No. 1 (2000) 715–723
5. Levachkine, S., Velázquez, A., Alexandrov, V., Kharinov, M.: Semantic Analysis and Recognition of Raster-scanned Color Cartographic Images. Lecture Notes in Computer Science, Vol. 2390. Springer (2002) 178–189
6. Meyers G.K., Chen, C.-H.: Verification–based Approach for Automated Text and Feature Extraction from Raster-scanned Maps. Lecture Notes in Computer Science, Vol. 1072. Springer (1996) 190–203
7. Wenyin, L., Dori, D.: Genericity in Graphics Recognition Algorithms. Lecture Notes in Computer Science, Vol. 1389. Springer (1998) 9–20
8. Deseilligny, M.-P., Mariani, R., Labiche, J.: Topographic Maps Automatic Interpretation: Some Proposed Strategies. Lecture Notes in Computer Science, Vol. 1389. Springer (1998) 175–193
9. Frischknecht, S., Kanani, E.: Automatic Interpretation of Scanned Topographic Maps: A Raster-based Approach. Lecture Notes in Computer Science, Vol. 1389. Springer (1998) 207–220

10. Nagy, G.A., Seth Samal, S., Fisher, T., Guthmann, E., Kalafala, K., Li, L., Sarkar, P., Sivasubramanian, S., Xu, Y.: A Prototype for Adaptive Association of Street Names with Streets Maps. Lecture Notes in Computer Science, Vol. 1389. Springer (1998) 302–313

11. Adam, S., Ogier, J.-M., Cariou, C., Mullot, R., Labiche, J., Gardes, J.: Symbol and Character Recognition: Application to Engineering Drawings. International Journal on Document Analysis and Recognition (IJDAR). No. 1 (2000) 89–101

12. Hase, H., Shinokawa, T., Yoneda, M., Suen, C. Y.: Character String Extraction from Color Documents. Pattern Recognition, Vol. 34, No. 1 (2001) 1349–1365

13. Velázquez, A., Sossa, J. H., Levachkine, S.: Reconocimiento Eficiente de Caracteres Alfanuméricos Provenientes de Mapas Ráster por Medio de Clasificadores Neuronales. Computación y Sistemas, Vol. 6, No. 1 (2002) 38-50 (ISSN 1405–5546)

14. Doermann, D.S.: An Introduction to Vectorization and Segmentation. Lecture Notes in Computer Science, Vol. 1389. Springer (1998) 1–8

15. Nagy, G.: Twenty Years of Document Image Analysis in PAMI. IEEE Transactions on Pattern Analysis and Machine Intelligence, Vol. 22, No. 1 (2000) 38–62

16. Ganesan, A.: Integration of Surveying and Cadastral GIS: From Field-to-fabric & Land Records-to-fabric, Proc. 22nd ESRI User Conference, 7-12 July 2002, Redlands, CA, USA (2002) on-line: http://gis.esri.com/library/userconf/proc02/abstracts/a0868.html

17. Fletcher, L.A., Kasturi, R.: A Robust Algorithm for Text String Separation from Mixed Text/Graphics Images. IEEE Transactions on Pattern Analysis and Machine Intelligence, Vol. 10, No. 6 (1988) 910–918

18. Tan, C.L., Ng, P.O.: Text Extraction using Pyramid. Pattern Recognition, Vol. 31, No. 1 (1998) 63–72

19. Velázquez, A.: Localización, Recuperación e Identificación de la Capa de Caracteres Contenida en los Planos Cartográficos. *Ph.D. Thesis*. Centre for Computing Research-IPN. Mexico City, Mexico (2002) (in Spanish)

20. Cao R., Tam, C.L.: Text/Graphics Separation in Maps. Lecture Notes in Computer Science, Vol. 2390. Springer (2002) 168–177

21. Alexandrov, V., Kharinov, M., Velázquez, A. Levachkine, S.: Object-oriented Color Image Segmentation. Proc. IASTED International Conference on Signal Processing, Pattern Recognition, and Applications (SPPRA 2002), June 25-28 2002, Crete, Greece (2002) 493–498

22. Gelbukh, A., Han SangYong, Levachkine, S.: Combining Sources of Evidence to Resolve Ambiguities in Toponym Recognition in Cartographic Maps. In: Levachkine, S., Serra, J., Egenhofer, M. (eds.) Proc. 2nd Int. Workshop on Semantic Processing of Spatial Data (GEOPRO 2003), November 4-5 2003, Mexico City, Mexico (2003) 42-51 (ISBN 970-36-0103-0)

23. Gelbukh, A., Levachkine, S.: Resolving Ambiguities in Toponym Recognition in Raster-scanned Cartographic Maps. In: Llados, J. (ed.): Proc. 5th IAPR International Workshop on Graphics Recognition (GREC 2003), July 30-31, 2003, Barcelona, Catalonia, Spain (2003) 104–112

24. Velázquez, A., Levachkine, S.: Text/Graphics Separation and Recognition in Raster-scanned Color Cartographic Maps. In: Llados, J. (ed.): Proc. 5th IAPR International Workshop on Graphics Recognition (GREC 2003), July 30-31, 2003, Barcelona, Catalonia, Spain (2003) 92–103

25. Levachkine, S.: Raster to Vector Conversion of Color Cartographic Maps for Analytical GIS. In: Llados, J. (ed.): Proc. 5th IAPR International Workshop on Graphics Recognition (GREC 2003) July 30-31, 2003, Barcelona, Catalonia, Spain (2003) 77–91

Resolving Ambiguities in
Toponym Recognition in Cartographic Maps

Alexander Gelbukh[1,3], Serguei Levachkine[2], and Sang-Yong Han[3]

[1] Natural Language Processing Lab, and [2] Image Processing and Pattern Recognition Lab
Centre for Computing Research (CIC) - National Polytechnic Institute (IPN)
{gelbukh, palych}@cic.ipn.mx
[3] Computer Science and Engineering Department,
Chung-Ang University, Korea
hansy@cau.ac.kr

Abstract. To date many methods and programs for automatic text recognition exist. However there are no effective text recognition systems for graphic documents. Graphic documents usually contain a great variety of textual information. As a rule the text appears in arbitrary spatial positions, in different fonts, sizes and colors. The text can touch and overlap graphic symbols. The text meaning is semantically much more ambiguous in comparison with standard text. To recognize a text of graphic documents, it is necessary first to separate it from linear objects, solids, and symbols and to define its orientation. Even so, the recognition programs nearly always produce errors. In the context of raster-to-vector conversion of graphic documents, the problem of text recognition is of special interest, because textual information can be used for verification of vectorization results (post-processing). In this work, we propose a method that combines OCR-based text recognition in raster-scanned maps with heuristics specially adapted for cartographic data to resolve the recognition ambiguities using, among other information sources, the spatial object relationships. Our goal is to form in the vector thematic layers geographically meaningful words correctly attached to the cartographic objects.

1 Introduction

Huge amount of geographic information collected in the last centuries is available in the form of maps printed or drawn on paper. To store, search, distribute, and view these maps in the electronic form they are to be converted in one of digital formats developed for this purpose. The simplest way of such conversion is scanning the paper map to obtain an image (a picture) stored in any of the raster graphic formats such as TIFF, GIF, etc. After that, a raster-to-vector conversion should be applied to include obtained vector maps into a Geographic Information System (GIS).

Though raster representation has important advantages in comparison with the hard copy form, it still does not allow semantic processing of the information shown in the map, for example:

J. Lladós and Y.-B. Kwon (Eds.): GREC 2003, LNCS 3088, pp. 75–86, 2004.
© Springer-Verlag Berlin Heidelberg 2004

- Search for objects: *Where is Pittsburgh? What large river is in Brazil?*
- Answering questions on the spatial relations: *Is Tibet in China? Is Nepal in Tibet? Is a part of Tibet in China?*
- Generation of specialized maps: *Generate a map of railroads and highways of France.*
- Scaling and zooming: *Generate a 1:125 000 map of Colombia. Show me more details at the point under cursor.*
- Compression: *Objects like points, arcs, or areas can be stored much more efficiently than pixels.*

Note that these are semantic tasks rather than image manipulation. E.g., when zooming in or out, objects and, most importantly, their names should appear or disappear rather than become smaller or larger. Indeed, when zooming out the area of London, the name *Greenwich* should not become small to unreadable but should disappear (and appear in an appropriate font size when zooming in).

This suggests storing and handling of a map as a database of objects (points, arcs, areas, alphanumeric, etc.)—vector database—having certain properties, such as size, color, geographic coordinates, topology, and name. Specifically, the name of the object is to be stored as a letter string rather than a set of pixels as originally scanned from the hard copy. Thus, such vector representation can solve the listed above semantic tasks, but only to some extent [1].

However, automatic recognition of such strings (toponyms) in the raster image of the map presents some particular difficulties as compared with the optical character recognition (OCR) task applied to standard texts such as books:

- The strings are out of context, which prevents from using standard spelling correction techniques based on the linguistic properties of coherent text. Moreover, often such strings are even not words of a specific modern language, which further limits applicability of the standard linguistic-based spelling correction methods.
- The background of the string in the map is very noisy since it can contain elements of geographic notation such as shading or hatching, cartographic objects such as cities or rivers, and even parts of other strings, e.g., name of a city inside of the area covered by the name of the country; see Figure 1.
- In addition, often the letters of the string are not properly aligned but instead are printed under different angles and along an arc; this happens with the names of linear and area objects, e.g., rivers or countries; see Figure 1.
- Unlike standard task, in toponym recognition it is not only required to recognize the string itself but also to associate it with a specific cartographic object, e.g., city, river, desert, etc.

On the other hand, in many cases additional information is available that can give useful cues for ambiguity resolution. One of such information sources is existing databases (usually available from the country Government, postal service, etc.) providing spatial relationships between entities (e.g., a list of cities classified by administrative units) or even exact coordinates.

In this paper we discuss how such additional information can be used to work-around the problems arising in recognition of the inscriptions in the maps, associating them with specific cartographic objects, and importing information on these objects from available databases. This paper reports work in progress. Its purpose is to iden-tify the possible pitfalls and problems in this process, which we for simplicity illus-trate on artificial examples. Discussion of real-world experimental results is beyond the scope of this paper.

First, we describe the general scheme of our method, which consists in combining the information from different sources of evidence (such as toponym databases, lin-guistic dictionaries, information on the fonts and distribution of the letters in the raster image, etc.) with subsequent verification of the obtained results. Then we dis-cuss each individual source of evidence, as well as the verification procedure. Finally, conclusions are drawn and future work directions are outlined.

2   Previous Work

The text segmentation and its subsequent recognition in raster images are very diffi-cult problems; they are complicated by the presence of the text embedded in graphic components and the text touching graphics [2]. These challenging problems have received numerous contributions from the graphic recognition community [3]. How-ever, there have not been yet developed any efficient programs to solve the task auto-matically. Thus, in the most systems human operator is involved. For example, [4] proposes that the operator draws a line through the text, marking it as text and re-vealing its orientation.

In [5] and [6], the algorithms are developed to extract text strings from text/ graphics images. However, both methods assume that the text does not touch or over-lap with graphics. For maps, the problem is much more complex, since the touching or overlapping as well as many other character configurations are commonly pre-sented in maps. That is why [7], [8], and [9] developed the methods for text/graphics separation in raster-scanned (color) cartographic maps.

In [9] a specific method of detecting and extracting characters that are touching graphics in raster-scanned color maps is proposed. It is based on observation that the constituent strokes of characters are usually short segments in comparison with those of graphics. It combines line continuation with the feature line width to decompose and reconstruct segments underlying the region of intersection. Experimental results showed that proposed method slightly improved the percentage of correctly detected text as well as the accuracy of character recognition with OCR.

In [7] and [8], the map is first segmented to extract all text strings including those that touch other symbols and strokes. Then, OCR using Artificial Neural Networks (ANN) is applied to get the coordinates, size, and orientation of alphanumeric charac-ter strings in the map. Then, four straight lines or a number of "curves" computed in function of primarily recognized by ANN characters are extrapolated to separate those symbols that are attached. Finally, the separated characters are input into ANN again for their final identification. Experimental results showed 95–97% of successfully recognized alphanumeric symbols in raster-scanned color maps.

In the present work, we use the output obtained with this method in combination with pre-existing geographical information in semantic analysis of ambiguities for "geographically meaningful" word formation. We focus on text processing rather than image processing.

The proposed system is based both on the traditional techniques used in the general-purpose OCR programs and on those we developed specifically for cartographic maps. Sections 4, 5, and 8 deal with the problems and solutions common to any OCR task. However, even in these cases there are some differences with respect to the usual OCR situation. The algorithm described in Section 4 (check against a dictionary of existing words) in our case has to deal with much more noisy strings than usual OCR programs developed for clean black-on-white running text. The same can be said of Section 5 (non-uniform spatial letter distribution): in maps the letters are often placed at significant distances one from another, cf. Figure 1; as well of Section 8 (check against the general laws of a given language): maps have many foreign or indigenous words that do not conform to the main language of the given territory.

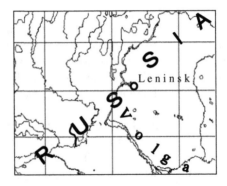

Fig. 1. Intersection of strings in a map

In contrast, Sections 6, 7, and 9 are specific for maps. In Section 6 (check against the geographic information, e.g., expected coordinates) consistency with the available information about the location of an object is used, which is obviously specific for cartographic maps. In Section 7 (check against the cartographic notation) information on the expected type of the object (river, mountain, etc.) is used. In Section 9 (global consistency check) it is verified that each object is recognized only once.

These techniques do not have direct analogs in standard OCR research and thus are contributions of our paper.

On the other hand, many techniques standard for usual text OCR use contextual information available in running text, such as morphological and syntactic analysis, semantic consistency verification [13]; paragraph layout detection, etc. These techniques are not directly applicable to recognition of toponyms in maps. However, the new techniques we introduce in the Sections 6, 7, and 9 play a similar role of verification of contextual consistency of the recognition results, but in the manner very specific to cartographic maps in contrast to the standard running text OCR.

3 Main Algorithm

We rely on a basic OCR procedure[1] (described in [1], [7], and [8]) that recognizes in the map individual letters and groups together the letters of a similar font and color located next to each other, thus forming in a hypothetical string. In this process, errors of various types can be introduced; our purpose is to detect and correct them.

The recognition algorithm for the whole map works iteratively. At each step, the basic OCR procedure selects for processing the longest clearly recognizable string s. Upon its recognition, the string is removed from the raster image so that the image becomes simpler and other strings, possibly disturbed by s, become clearly recognizable. Then the next most clearly recognizable string is selected, etc. The algorithm stops when no more letter strings can be found in the raster image.

This design allows for recognition of the names of large areas, which are usually represented by large letters scattered across the map, with many names of smaller objects between the letters of the area name. In the example shown in Figure 1, first the word *Leninsk* will be recognized and removed from the image, then the word *Volga*, and only then the letters *R-u-s-s-i-a* can be grouped together in a string.

Indeed, in the original image, the letter *L* of *Leninsk* disturbs the string *Russia* making it look like RUSLSIA or RUSLeninsk (since the direction of the string is not easy to determine). In this particular case the difference in orientation and size of the letters can be used to filter the $_L$ off the string RUS$_L$IA; however, taking into account such information would significantly complicate processing and anyway would produce unreliable results. Instead, we rely on a simpler solution: the smaller string *Leninsk*, not interleaved with any other string, is recognized first and is erased from the image. Now, the string RUSSIA is not disturbed and can be easily recognized.

The basic OCR procedure returns, for each string it recognizes, the string itself, e.g., "RUSSIA," and the geographic coordinates in the map of the frame containing each individual letter, e.g., R, U, etc. In fact, the word can be recognized with errors, e.g., "RNSoSIA," where U is erroneously recognized as N due to a nearby river, and the circle representing a city is erroneously taken for the letter o. Such errors are detected and corrected using the following algorithm.

1. The obtained string is looked for in a list (dictionary) of expected toponyms, which (if the word is found) provides the semantic information associated with it, such as the type of object (e.g., city, river), its spatial relationships (e.g., administrative unit it is in), and its geographic coordinates if available. This information is verified using different sources of evidence, such as spatial distribution of the letters in the raster image, the coordinates of the letters, etc.

---

[1] Our method does not depend on how text strings were extracted and recognized. Neither does it depend much on the type of graphic document being processed. It can be adapted to different subject domains.

2. In addition, similar strings (e.g., *RUSSIA*, *ASIA*, *Angola*, etc. for *RNSoSIA*) are looked for in the dictionary and for them, the same information is retrieved and the same check is performed, an additional source of evidence being the probability of the corresponding changes in the letters of the string.

3. The scores of all sources of evidence are multiplied to obtain the overall score of a variant. We assume that all sources of evidence give the probability of an error of the corresponding type (misrecognition of a letter, misplacing the name in the map, etc.), and that such errors are independent. Determining such probabilities is discussed in detail in [15].

4. The variant with the best score S_1 is considered.

5. If this best variant is good enough ($S_1 \geq \alpha$; α is a user-defined threshold), then:

    5.1 If the score of the best variant significantly differs from the score of the second best one ($S_1 / S_2 > \beta$, a user-defined threshold) then this variant is accepted and is added to the database together with its associated information.

    5.2 Otherwise, human intervention is requested, and the variants are presented to the operator in the order of their scores.

6. Otherwise ($S_1 < \alpha$), no correction is applied to the recognized string. It is checked against the linguistic restrictions of a given language, see Section 8.

    6.1 If no anomalies are found, it is considered a new toponym absent in our dictionary and is added to the database as is and is associated with a nearby object using an algorithm not discussed here.

    6.2 If an anomaly is found, the string is considered not recognized and human intervention is requested.

7. After all strings have been recognized, global check is performed, see Section 9.

Note that when the different sources of evidence are combined, they are taken with user-defined weights depending on the quality of the map, the reliability of the basic OCR procedure, etc. We here do not discuss the choice of these weights.

In the following sections, we will consider each source of evidence used in the presented algorithm, as well as the global check procedure.

4   Textual Information

We suppose that there is available a list (dictionary) D of toponyms that can be found in a map. The list can contain much more toponyms than the map in hand - for example, all cities of the country, all seas of the world, etc. Such a list can be compiled as a combination of different sources such as governmental statistical databases, police databases, analysis of newspapers available in Internet, etc.

For a given string s, e.g., *RNSoSIA*, a set of all strings similar to s in the dictionary D can be easily constructed [10]. By a similar string, a string s' is considered that differs from s in at most a certain number of the following disturbances: (1) substitution of a letter for another letter, (2) omission of a letter, and (3) insertion of a letter. With each such disturbance, a probability can be associated; in case of several disturbances, the corresponding probabilities are multiplied to obtain the overall probability of that s (*RNSoSIA*) was obtained from s' (say, *RUSSIA*) by this sequence of errors. For the string itself ($s' = s$ if it is present in D), the probability is 1.

The probabilities of the disturbances can depend on the specific letters involved. E.g., the probability of substitution of I for J is higher than W for L. Similarly, the probability of omission of I is higher than that of M. In a cartographic map, the probability of insertion of o is high because of the notation for cities.

We do not discuss here in detail the issue of automatically learning the corresponding probabilities. If the map is large or of standard type and quality, a statistical model can be trained by processing a part of this or another map of similar quality and manually verifying the results. Or, the iterative procedure described in Section 10 can be used to automatically adjust the model to the specific map.

5 Spatial Letter Distribution Information

As we have mentioned, the basic OCR procedure returns the coordinates of each letter. This can give us two characteristics of the recognized string:

- Whether the letters are aligned along a straight line,
- The distance between each adjacent pair of letters.

Only the names of some linear and area objects (e.g., rivers or lakes), but not punctual objects (e.g., cities), should have non-linear letter alignment. Note that the information on the type of the object for a specific variant of error correction as described in Section 4 is available from the dictionary. If the string is not found in the dictionary and is associated with a nearby object in the map (see step 6 of the algorithm, Section 3), again, the type of the object is known. Note that non-linear alignment is admitted for non-punctual objects but not required.

The distance between adjacent letters gives information on the probability of insertion or deletion-type error. Deletion-type error (a letter is to be inserted to obtain a valid word) is probable if the distance between the two neighboring letters is about twice larger than the average distance between the letters in the string (it can be the space between words, too). Similarly, insertion type error (a letter is to be deleted from the string to obtain a valid word) is probable if the mean distance between the letter in question and its neighboring letters is about twice smaller than the average. Note that in these cases the corresponding correction of the word is not only acceptable but also required: the score of a string with this type of defects is decreased.

6 Geographic Information

When the original string or a spelling correction candidate string is found in the dictionary,[2] the dictionary can provide at least two types of spatial information on the corresponding object:

---

[2] Such geographical databases are available from the corresponding governmental organizations. For example, in Mexico large geographical databases are distributed by INEGI, the National Institute for Statistics, Geography and Informatics, see www.inegi.gob.mx.

- Its inclusion in a larger area, such as province, state, etc. Areas form a hierarchy.
- Its geographic coordinates.

This information can be used to filter out the candidates that are very close as to their spelling to the original string returned by the basic OCR procedure but are not located in the area in question. E.g., suppose the OCR procedure returned the string *Xalapa* in the area of Mexican State of Oaxaca. Such a string indeed exists in the list of Mexican cities, but the corresponding city is in the state of Veracruz. On the other hand, there is a city *Jalapa* precisely in the state of Oaxaca. With this, it should be considered more probable that the string *Xalapa* was a result of a recognition error and that the correct string is a similar string *Jalapa*.

Moreover, very frequently the dictionary contains several objects with the same name, of the same or different type. When analyzing a map of Canada, the object corresponding to a recognized string *London* is to be a small Canadian city and not the large British city, so that the correct number of inhabitants for the object could be imported from the dictionary to the database being constructed. When analyzing an inscription *Moscow* in the coordinates (57° N, 35° E), its interpretation as a river rather than city is more probable.

If only the hierarchical information is available ("Jalapa city is in Oaxaca state"), it can be used to filter out undesirable variants only if the coordinates are available for one of larger areas one or more steps up the hierarchy (but small enough to serve for disambiguation). Alternatively, it might happen that the corresponding larger area has been earlier recognized in the same map. However, due to the order of recognition from smaller to larger objects (see beginning of Section 3), this is hardly probable.

The corresponding check can be performed at the post-processing stage—global verification, see Section 9, when all areas have been recognized.

In the best case, full coordinate information is available in the dictionary for the object. Then the probability for the given inscription to represent the given object can be estimated as $a \exp(-bd^2)$, where b is a coefficient depending on the scale of the map and the fonts used, a is the normalizing coefficient, and d is the distance from the inscription to the object. This distance can be heuristically defined as follows:

- For a punctual object (such as a city) represented by only one coordinate pair p, the inscription is expected to be next to the point p. Thus, we can take d as the minimum distance from the point p to any of the frames containing the individual letters of the string.
- For linear objects (such as rivers) represented by a sequence of coordinate pairs p_i, the inscription is expected to follow the shape of the arc. Thus, we can take d as the average distance from the frames containing each letter to the broken line (or otherwise interpolated arc) defined by the points p_i. To put it in a slightly simplified way, to measure the distance between a letter and the broken line, the two adjacent points p_i, p_{i+1} nearest to the letter are found and the distance from the letter to the straight line connecting the two points is determined.
- For an area object **S** (such as a province) represented by a sequence of coordinate pairs p_i corresponding to its contour, the inscription is expected to be in the middle of the area and the letters are expected to be distributed by the whole area.

Thus, we can take $d = \iint_{S'} f(x, y)\,dxdy$, where $f(x, y)$ is the minimum distance from the point (x,y) to any of the letters of the string. The integral is taken over the intersection S' of the area S and the whole area of the given map (in case a part of S proves to be out of the boundaries of the given map). Note that a similar integral along the contour would not give the desired effect. Since the number of candidates generated at the step 2 of the algorithm from Section 3 is rather small, and the area objects are much less numerous than other types of the objects in the map, we do not consider computational efficiency a major issue for our purposes. Neither precision is important for us. Thus, it is enough to compute the integral by, say, Monte-Carlo method.

In fact, the coefficient b (and thus a) in the formula above is different for these three cases. We do not discuss here selection of this scaling coefficient. More details on the quantitative evaluation of the corresponding probabilities can be found in [15].

7 Notational Information

Notation in the map can give additional information to filter out undesirable variants. In some maps, rivers are explicitly marked as "*river*" or "*r.*" and similarly mountains, peninsulas, etc. Specific font type, size, and color are usually associated with various types of objects (e.g., cities, and rivers). Though this information can provide very good filtering, it is not standard and is to be manually specified for each individual map, which limits the usefulness of such filtering capability in a practical application.

The practical system should provide the operator the means to specify such notational elements, at least the prefixes such as "*river.*" They are important for the comparison of the string with the dictionary. Indeed, for the string "*river Thames*" what is to be looked up in the dictionary is "*Thames*" and not "*river Thames*". Alternatively, such prefixes can be detected automatically in a large map:

- For each string consisting of several words, both the complete variant and the variants without the first or last word are to be tried.
- If for a specific type of objects (e.g., rivers) in most cases the string is found after taking of the word "river," then this is to be considered as notation for this type of objects.

Similarly the font features for a specific type of objects can be automatically learnt from a large map.

Finally, some precautions should be taken with such type of filters. For example, in Spanish rivers are marked as "*río*" 'river'; however the string *Río de Janeiro* should not be filtered out as a name of the city (if capital letters are not properly distinguished in the map).

8 Linguistic Information

The checks described in this Section are applied only to the strings not found in the dictionary for which the dictionary-based correction failed (no suitable similar string was found in the dictionary), see Step 6 of the algorithm from Section 3. In this case, general properties of the given language can be used to detect (though not correct) a possible recognition error.

One of simple but efficient techniques of such verification is bigram (or trigram) control [12]. In many languages, not any pair (or triplet) of letters can appear in adjacent positions of a valid word. For example, in Spanish no consonant except *r* and *l* can be repeated; after *q* no other letter than *u* can appear, etc. The statistics of such bigrams (or trigrams) is easy to learn from a large corpus of texts. The multiplication of the bigram frequencies for each adjacent pair of letters in the word (and similarly for trigrams) gives a measure of its well-formedness, which can be compared with a user-defined threshold; if a bigram not used at all in the given language appears, the word is immediately marked as probably incorrect.

Other properties of words specific to a given language can be verified: e.g., in Japanese all syllables are open.

If a recognized string for which no variants of correction by the dictionary are found does not pass any of the linguistic filters, it is presented to the human operator for possible correction.

Note that since toponyms are frequently words of another language (say, indigenous languages) or proper names of foreign origin, linguistic verification can produce a large number of false alarms.

9 Global Constraint Verification

After all inscriptions in the map have been recognized, some global constraints should be checked.

Uniqueness. To each object, only one inscription should correspond. If two inscriptions have been associated with the same object, one or both of them is to be re-assigned. Even though the information on the probability of each of the two candidates is available at this point and could allow for automatic selection of one of the candidates, we believe that such conflicts should not be arbitrated automatically but the human intervention is to be requested instead. Of course, the probability information can be used to suggest the most likely variant to the human operator.

An exception from this rule is linear objects such as long rivers. Several inscriptions can be assigned to such object provided that their text is the same, the distance between them is much larger than their lengths, and their length are much smaller than the length of the object (river).

Inclusion. The hierarchical information available from the dictionary (see Section 6) can be applied at this point. Recall that our algorithm recognizes the names of, say, cities before those of areas. So at the time of recognition of the string "*Xalapa*" the information "*Xalapa City is in Veracruz State*" could be checked since we did not know yet where Veracruz State is in the map. Now that all strings have been recognized, this information can be checked (now we know where *Veracruz* is) and the error discussed in Section 6 (*Xalapa* mistaken for *Jalapa* recognized in Oaxaca State) can be detected. In this case, again, human intervention can be requested. Alternatively, the process of error correction can be repeated for this string, and then the global verification is repeated for the objects involved in the resulting changes.

10   Conclusion

In this work we focused on maps with texts (there are many maps with numerical labels, such as elevations, geographical coordinates, and so on; see [1], [7], and [8] for discussion on this type of maps).

We have shown that the problem of recognition of inscriptions in the map, assigning them as names to specific objects (e.g., cities), and importing—using these names as keys—properties of these objects (e.g., population) from existing databases involves both traditional techniques of image recognition and methods specific for cartographic maps processing. Our algorithm combines various sources of evidence, including geographic coordinates and object inclusion hierarchy, to choose the best candidate for error detection and correction.

One obvious direction of future development is refining the heuristics used in the discussed sources of evidence and adding new sources of evidence. For example, the basic recognition procedure can return the probability (the degree of certainness) of each letter in the string, or even a list of possible letters at the given position in the string along with their respective probabilities. The idea is that if the basic recognition procedure is certain that the letter in question is exactly the one it recognized (as opposed to just looking like this), the letter should not be changed in error correction, and vice versa.

Another issue possibly to be addressed in the future is the computational complexity, especially the method used to compute the integral in Section 6.

Yet another possible modification of the algorithm is an attempt to recognize all strings before error detection and correction. In many cases this can allow to apply the hierarchical information during the main cycle of the algorithm and not at the stage of post-processing, see the discussion in the item 2 in Section 9 and [14]. This seems to be most promising in the context of our approach. In fact, the measures of similarity and dissimilarity ("distances") between hierarchical variables proposed in [14] can be used as additional source of evidence to assign correct name to the geographical location under consideration. We discuss this assignment procedure in [15].

However, the most important direction of future research is automatic training of the statistical models, automatic learning of the notational information, and automatic determination of the parameters used in various heuristics of our method.

The parameters could be adjusted by application of the algorithm iteratively while varying the parameters, say, according to the gradient descending method. For this, however, an automatically computable measure of the quality of the result is to be determined. The training of the statistical model and learning of the notation can be done using an iterative re-estimation procedure [10].

Acknowledgments

The work was partially supported by Mexican Government (CONACYT, SNI, and CGPI-IPN) and the ITRI of the Chung-Ang University. The first author is currently on Sabbatical leave at the Chung-Ang University.

References

1. Levachkine, S., Velázquez, A., Alexandrov, V., Kharinov, M.: Semantic Analysis and Recognition of Raster-scanned Color Cartographic Images. Lecture Notes in Computer Science, Vol. 2390. Springer-Verlag, Berlin Heidelberg New York (2002) 178–189
2. Doermann, D.S.: An Introduction to Vectorization and Segmentation. Lecture Notes in Computer Science, Vol. 1389. Springer-Verlag, Berlin Heidelberg New York (1998) 1–8
3. Nagy, G.: Twenty Years of Document Image Analysis in PAMI. PAMI. Vol. 22, No. 1. (2000) 38–62
4. Ganesan, A.: Integration of Surveying and Cadastral GIS: From Field-to-fabric & Land Records-to-fabric. Proc. 22nd ESRI User Conference, 7-12 July, 2002, Redlands, CA, USA (2002), see gis.esri.com/library/userconf/proc02/ abstracts/a0868.html.
5. Fletcher, L.A., Kasturi, R.: A Robust Algorithm for Text String Separation from Mixed Text/Graphics Images. PAMI. Vol. 10, No. 6. (1988) 910–918
6. Tan C.L., Ng, P.O.: Text Extraction using Pyramid. PR. Vol. 31, No. 1 (1998) 63–72
7. Velázquez, A.: Localización, Recuperación e Identificación de la Capa de Caracteres contenida en los Planos Cartográficos. *Ph.D. Thesis.* Centre for Computing Research-IPN. Mexico City, Mexico (2002) (in Spanish)
8. Velázquez, A., Levachkine, S.: Text/Graphics Separation in Raster-scanned Color Cartographic Maps. In: Levachkine, S., Serra, J., Egenhofer, M. (eds.) Proc. 2nd Int. Workshop on Semantic Processing of Spatial Data (GEOPRO 2003), November 4–5 2003, Mexico City, Mexico (2003) 34–41 (ISBN 970-36-0103-0)
9. Cao, R., Tan, C.L.: Text/Graphics Separation in Maps. Lecture Notes in Computer Science. Vol. 2390, Springer-Verlag, Berlin Heidelberg New York (2002) 168–177
10. Gelbukh, A.: Syntactic Disambiguation with Weighted Extended Subcategorization Frames. Proc. Pacific Association for Computational Linguistics (PACLING 1999), 25–28 August, 1999, Canada (1999) 244–249
11. Gelbukh, A.: Alexander Gelbukh. Exact and approximate prefix search under access locality requirements for morphological analysis and spelling correction. Computación y Sistemas, vol. 6, N 3 (2003) 167–182, see www.gelbukh.com/CV/Publications/ 2001/ CyS-2001-Morph.htm.
12. Angell, R.C., Freund, G.E., Willett, P.: Automatic Spelling Correction using a Trigram Similarity Measure. Inf. Processing & Management. Vol. 19, No. 4. (1983) 255–261
13. Hirst, G., Budanitsky, A.: Correcting Real-Word Spelling Errors by Restoring Lexical Cohesion. Natural Language Engineering, 2004 (to appear)
14. Levachkine, S., Guzman, A.: Hierarchies as a New Data Type for Qualitative Variables. Journal of Data Knowledge Engineering (DKE) (to appear)
15. Gelbukh, A., Han SangYong, Levachkine, S.: Combining Sources of Evidence to Resolve Ambiguities in Toponym Recognition in Cartographic Maps. In: Levachkine, S., Serra, J., Egenhofer, M. (eds.) Proc. 2nd Int. Workshop on Semantic Processing of Spatial Data (GEOPRO 2003), November 4–5 2003, Mexico City, Mexico (2003) 42–51 (ISBN 970-36-0103-0)

Model-Based Chart Image Recognition

Weihua Huang, Chew Lim Tan, and Wee Kheng Leow

SOC, National University of Singapore, 3 Science Drive 2, Singapore 117543
{huangwh, tancl, leowwk}@comp.nus.edu.sg

Abstract. In this paper, we introduce a system that aims at recognizing chart images using a model-based approach. First of all, basic chart models are designed for four different chart types based on their characteristics. In a chart model, basic object features and constraints between objects are defined. During the chart recognition, there are two levels of matching: feature level matching to locate basic objects and object level matching to fit in an existing chart model. After the type of a chart is determined, the next step is to do data interpretation and recover the electronic form of the chart image by examining the object attributes. Experiments were done using a set of testing images downloaded from the internet or scanned from books and papers. The results of type determination and the accuracies of the recovered data are reported.

1 Introduction

Document image analysis and recognition techniques are developed to extract both textual and graphical information from a wide range of image types, from journal papers to name cards, from forms to engineering drawings. Some common applications include image classification, content-based retrieval and data interpretation etc. Scientific charts, with very effective visual impact, are widely used in many documents to present statistical data, to analyse data trends and to compare different data series. Recently some research works have been done to analyse and recognize chart images [1–2]. However these works mainly focus on recognizing the chart types, without further interpreting the chart content and extracting the data embedded in the chart images. To achieve this task, higher-level processing and recognition methods need to be developed. Once the chart type is correctly determined and the embedded data are accurately extracted, we can convert an imaged chart into electronic form for further interpretation. For example, if we integrate this part into the traditional OCR software, then a document image containing charts can be converted to the electronic form in a more complete way.

In this paper, we introduce a system that is able to achieve both chart type recognition and chart data interpretation. The main structure of the system is shown in Figure 1. After some pre-processing to the given image, we perform raster-to-vector conversion using an algorithm similar to [3], which is computationally efficient and can detect lines and arcs that are precise enough for further processing. Based on the vectorized lines and arcs obtained, we are able to locate some higher-level shapes such as bars, pies and polylines. These shapes are then matched against the major components in each existing chart model to calculate the likelihood that the given image fits into any of the models. If all the likelihood values are very low, then the given image does not contain a chart. Otherwise the model that returns the maximum

J. Lladós and Y.-B. Kwon (Eds.): GREC 2003, LNCS 3088, pp. 87–99, 2004.

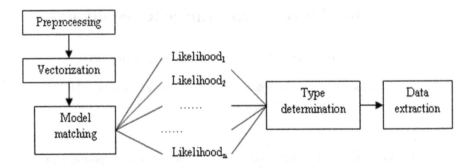

Fig. 1. Major stages in the proposed system

likelihood will indicate the chart type of the given image. In the final stage, the data values are extracted by examining the attributes of the chart components that are located. At the current stage, we concentrate on four commonly used chart types: bar chart, pie chart, line chart and high-low chart.

The remaining sections of this paper will discuss the details of the proposed system. Section 2 talks about feature extraction from a given chart image. Section 3 introduces how the chart type is determined through likelihood measure. Section 4 shows how data in the chart image is interpreted and the electronic form of the chart is recovered. Section 5 talks about experiments carried out followed by discussion of the results. Finally, section 6 concludes this paper with some future works mentioned.

2   Feature Extraction

We use a bottom-up approach for the model-based matching. In this application, the basic features, including the straight line segments and arcs, are extracted and used to match an existing model.

2.1   Text and Graphics Separation

A typical chart image contains both textual information and graphical information. Textual information includes the chart title, the name of the data series, some descriptions of the chart, and the numerical labels. On the other hand, graphical information includes the actual drawings, such as reference lines, edges and arcs. The first step in our system is to distinguish these two types of information and store them separately for further processing.

Karl Tombre et al. summarized a number of text/graphics separation techniques in their paper [4], which are very helpful for us to tackle our problem. 8-connected components are constructed, followed by a set of filters that perform thresholding based on various properties of the connected components, including height, size, black pixel density and height/width ratio. The threshold values used are determined through some training samples. Using the set of filters, most of the text and graphics can be separated. However one assumption of this approach is that the text and graphics are well separated, so more advanced technique needs to be applied to handle the case where characters are touching graphics.

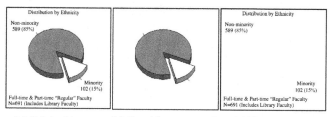

(a) Original image   (b) Graphics extracted   (c) Text extracted

Fig. 2. Example of text/graphics separation

The separated textual and graphical information are stored as two different images. One example is shown in Figure 2. Currently we focus on the graphical information only. For the image containing textual information, robust OCR technique needs to be applied to retrieve the text from it. We have tried some existing commercial OCR software, such as the ABBYY FineReader 7.0 and ReadIris Pro 9. However the results turn out to be poor. We think there are two major difficulties to be overcome here: the text size is usually very small, and the text may follow a variety of orientations. As a future work, we can design an OCR that serves our specific purpose.

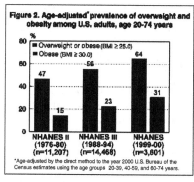
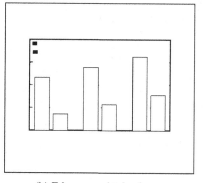

(a) Original image   (b) Edge map obtained

Fig. 3. Example of edge detection

2.2   Edge Detection

In a chart image, the colour or greyscale level within a graphical component is consistent. On the other hand, the colour difference or greyscale level difference between neighbouring graphical components is normally significant. Thus the most straightforward approach is to detect the high differential values in the pixel intensity. However by doing so, the two sides of a thick line will appear as independent lines in the edge map. So we need to set a threshold to judge how far two edge points can be to be considered as lying on the two sides of the same line. In other words, we are predicting the maximum line thickness in the given image. If the two edge points on the two sides of an area are closer than the threshold, then the pixels joining these points are all marked as edge points. An example of edge detection is in Figure 3.

After the edge detection step, only edge points are kept and passed to the next step for straight line detection, so that less information is processed and the computational efficiency is maintained.

2.3 Vectorization

Jiqiang Song et al. proposed the Line Net Global (LNG) Vectorization algorithm [3] that uses seed segments to perform directed vectorization. Here we use a similar approach: first of all, we find a straight line segment as a seed, and we try to extend it to find a complete line or arc by examining the neighboring segments. The seed segment indicates the direction of searching, thus the algorithm is computationally powerful.

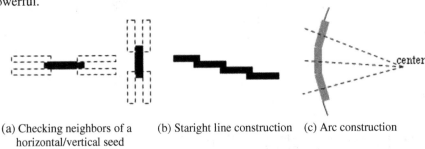

(a) Checking neighbors of a   (b) Staright line construction   (c) Arc construction
    horizontal/vertical seed
    segment

Fig. 4. Vectorization of straight lines and arcs

The search direction can be horizontal or vertical, as illustrated in Figure 4(a), thus the searching process is executed twice for both directions. As shown in Figure 4(b), to construct a straight line, the line segments should satisfy the following conditions:

- All line segments should have the same orientation, either horizontal or vertical.
- All line segments should have similar length, except for the starting segment and end segment which can be shorter.
- Along the line, the x-y coordinates should change monotonically.

As shown in Figure 4(c), to construct an arc, we need to find three consecutive line segments and check if the bisectors of these line segments converge to a common point. If so, the point becomes the estimated center for the arc and is used to find out the remaining part of the arc.

After the lines and arcs are vectorized, there is a need to refine them. The reason is that the image quality may be poor and as a result there may be broken lines and arcs. If two lines have the same orientation and the distance between their end points is smaller than certain threshold, they are merged to form a new line segment. If two arcs share the same center and similar radius, they will merge to become a new arc. Furthermore, the noise in the image becomes extra segments. So a length filter is used to remove the line segments whose length is smaller than a threshold value.

3 Chart Type Recognition

After the vectorization, we have a set of vectors representing the straight lines and arcs. We can check the following relationships among the straight lines: parallelism, perpendicular and convergence. These relationships are important to us because they are the indications of the existence of certain chart components, such as bars or pies etc. Besides these components, we are also interested in the existence of the x-y axes that is an important component for some chart types.

3.1 Calculating the Likelihood

Given the information about the existence of the basic components and the x-y axes, we can calculate the likelihood of a given image j to match a chart model i as:

$$likelihood_{ij} = \max(0, \sum_{k=0}^{n-1} W_{ik} C_{ijk} - \sum_{l=0}^{m-1} W_{jl} O_{jl}) \tag{1}$$

where W_{ik} is the weight of k_{th} component in the chart model i, W_{jl} is the weight of l_{th} unexpected object in the image j, thus $\sum W_{ik} = 1$ and $\sum W_{jl} = 1$. C_{ijk} is 1 if the k_{th} chart component from model i exists in the image j, and it is 0 otherwise. O_{jl} indicates the existence of the l_{th} object that is unexpected to appear in model i.

Different chart models have different set of basic components, resulting in different likelihood values when the formula (1) is applied to the given image. If all the likelihood values are small, then the given image is unlikely to be a chart image. If some likelihood values are sufficiently large, then we can treat the given image as a chart and pick up the model with the maximum likelihood as the type of the chart. The following subsections will talk about basic components in each chart model available.

3.2 Basic Components in the Chart Models

First of all, we need to look for the existence of x-y axes. If we assume that the given image is well positioned without too big skew angle, then the x axis should be the longest horizontal line while the y axis should be the longest vertical line, allowing some angular error. We also assume that the y axis is always at the left hand side of the image and the x axis is always at the bottom of the image. Furthermore, the space within x-y axes should contain most other objects. The x-y axes is a strong indication of the data area for bar chart, line chart and high-low chart, but is most unlikely to appear in a pie chart. Due to its distinguishing nature, the weight associated with this component is 0.5.

Data are represented by different objects in different chart types. These objects become the data components in the chart model. In a bar chart, a data component is a bar shape. In a pie chart, a data component is a pie shape. In a line chart, a data component is a vertex on the polyline. In a high-low chart, a data component is a high-low bar segment. The total weight of all the data components is 0.5 for bar chart, line chart and high-low chart, and is 1 for pie chart. Note that the number of data components in a chart model is not fixed, thus assigning equal weight to each data component is not achievable. If we denote the total weight of the data components as

W_{data}, then one approximate solution is to assign $W_{data}/2$ to the first data component, $W_{data}/4$ to the second data component, $W_{data}/8$ to the third data component etc. Generally speaking the k_{th} data component in the chart model is associated with a weight of $2^{-(k+1)} \times W_{data}$, where k ranges from 0 to $+\infty$. The effect is that the first few data components are more dominant in calculating the likelihood value, and when more data components are recognized, the summation of their weights approaches W_{data}. The following paragraphs will further explain how the data components are recognized for each chart model.

In a bar chart, the data component is a bar that consists of two vertical lines and one horizontal line on the top. There are some variations of the basic bar shape, as summarized in Figure 5. It's not difficult to find the basic shape and its variations in the given image, however some other constraints should be satisfied before we treat a shape as a bar, including:

1. Both vertical lines must touch the x-axis.
2. There should be no other object on top of a bar.
3. For all the bars, the width of a bar (the distance between two vertical lines) should be consistent.
4. In case of colour image or greyscale image, the colour of all bars should be similar (single data series is assumed here).

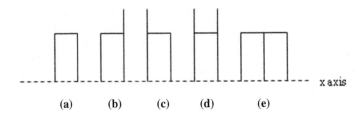

(a)   (b)   (c)   (d)   (e)

Fig. 5. Basic bar shape and its variations

In a typical pie chart, no matter 2D or 3D, the basic component is a pie, as shown in Figure 6. There are some common features for these pie shapes: the two straight line segments converge to one point, and there is an arc connecting the other endpoint of the two lines. Besides these features, there are also some constraints for the whole chart image: the converging point of all pies should be close to each other, and the summation of angles of all pies should be 360 degree or close to it.

Fig. 6. Basic pie shapes

In a typical high-low chart, the data are represented by a number of vertical line segments above the x-axis without touching it. Here we need to mention that telling whether a given chart is a high-low chart is not difficult, but we may face data loss because some high low line segments look very similar to the numeral "1", thus are treated as text and removed in the text/graphics separation stage. Such an example is shown in Figure 7.

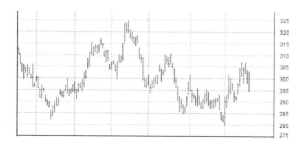

Fig. 7. A high-low chart with many high-low bars similar to "1"

In a line chart, all data points are connected from left to right in a typical line chart. After the vectorization process, a polyline is formed in the area within the x-y axes. The basic components here are the vertices along the polyline. Examples of line chart are shown in Figure 8.

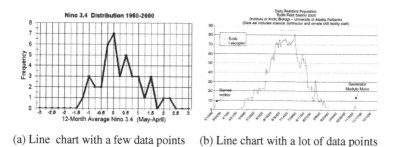

(a) Line chart with a few data points   (b) Line chart with a lot of data points

Fig. 8. Example of line charts

4 Data Interpretation

The next step is to interpret the data embedded in the chart images, where the accuracy is the major concern. When we extract data from a chart image, we need to determine the following things: the value of the data and the ordering among data. The former allows us to perform further manipulation on the data, while the latter enables us to find the correspondence between the extracted data and the original data. The basic approach here is to examine the attributes of the components found during the type determination stage and find out the relative data values. Aliasing may occur in a line chart with large amount of data points, thus another sampling-based approach is proposed to deal with this problem.

4.1 Basic Data Interpretation Process

Different chart types have different ways of representing the data values and the order among the data.

For a bar chart, the data are the set of bars that can be obtained during the type determination process. The task for restoring bar chart data is done as follows:

1. To find out the value of a bar, we calculate its height by finding the difference between the top of the bar and the x-axis.
2. To find out the relative position of a bar, we calculate the absolute position of the bar on the x-axis, and then perform a sorting and arrange the data from left to right.

One issue here is that the data values recovered can only reflect the relative values rather than the absolute values. We need help from the textual information to determine the absolute values. Since currently the textual information is not available yet, we are not able to recover the absolute values from the charts. An example of bar chart data interpretation is shown in Figure 9.

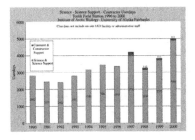 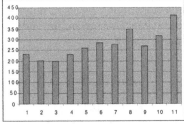

(a) Original bar chart image   (b) Bar chart generated based on data recovered

Fig. 9. Example of data interpretation for bar chart

Similar to the bar chart data interpretation, we can use the pies obtained in the previous process to recover data in a pie chart. The angle for each pie is calculated, and the percentage of each angle versus 360 degree is treated as the data for each pie. All the angles are sorted in a counter-clockwise manner to reflect the order among the data values. An example is shown in Figure 10.

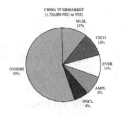 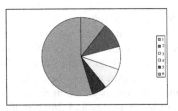

(a) Original pie chart   (b) Pie chart generated based on data recovered

Fig. 10. Example of pie chart data interpretation

For 2D pie chart, the data recovered almost truly reflect the original data except for some minor error due to discretization and imperfect line detection. However, in a 3D pie chart we are viewing an image of an ellipse instead of a circle due to the perspective distortion, thus the angle of a pie does not reflect the true percentage of data. Thus some further transformation needs to be done to remove the effect of perspective distortion, which requires more mathematical analysis.

For line chart with a few data points, we can determine the order by traversing through the vertices on the polyline from left to right, and find out the data values by calculating the distance between each vertex and the x-axis. However when the line chart contains a large number of data, such as the one in Figure 8(b), then some data are lost during the vectorization process. Thus the resulting polyline does not accurately reflect the original data values. This is known as the aliasing problem.

If all the high-low bars are found, the extraction of data from a high-low chart is straightforward. We can find out the high value and low value by calculating the distance between the two end point of a bar and the x-axis. The order among the data can be determined by sorting the high-low bars based on their x-coordinate values. However as we mentioned, many data in the high-low chart are lost due to the imperfect text/graphics separation. Currently we are still trying to improve our system on this issue. So results of data interpretation for the high-low charts are not reported.

4.2 Anti-aliasing for Line Chart Data Interpretation

To deal with the aliasing problem during the interpretation of line charts containing significantly large amount of data, we adopt another approach that is to use the polyline as a guide and sample the data points in the original image from left to right. In this way, we can collect a series of actual data points. The sampling rate affects the accuracy of the data extracted. It can be seen from Figure 11 that a smaller sampling rate returns higher precision but also means more data points to be stored. On the other hand, a larger sampling rate will reduce the precision but saves space by skipping more data points in the chart image.

5 Experimental Results

We have collected a number of testing images from various sources such as the internet or some scanned document pages. The entire test collection contains 8 bar chart images, 8 line chart images, 8 pie chart images, 3 high-low chart images and 10 engineering drawings. The charts were generated using various packages, with the Microsoft Excel as the most popular one. The chart images include most of the features that are commonly used. The resolution of the images is reasonably controlled.

Two parts of the system are evaluated using these images: the type determination and the data recovery. For the type determination, we examine the likelihood values and check the correctness of the type specified by the system. For the data recovery, we compare the extracted data with the original data to generate the accuracies.

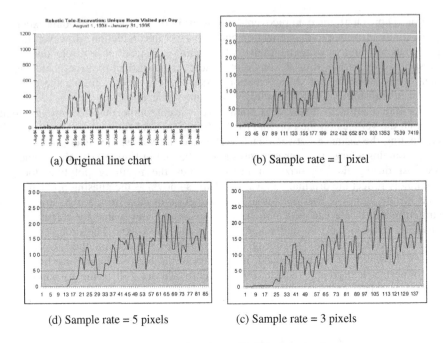

Fig. 11. Sampling line chart data with different sample rates

5.1 Type Determination and Data Accuracy

Each testing image is passed into the system. After preprocessing and vectorization, the system checks for the existence of chart components, namely the x-y axes and the data components. These components are then used to calculate the likelihood values for all the chart models based on the formula (1) in section 3.2. If the likelihood is smaller than 0.5, then the input image is not treated as a chart image. Otherwise the image is treated as a chart and the chart model returning the maximum likelihood value will be chosen as the chart type. The results of likelihood calculation and type determination are shown in Table 1. Due to the space limitation, only the average values are included in the table.

Table 1. Average likelihood for different types of images

Image Type	Average Likelihood value				Type correctly Determined
	Bar chart	Pie chart	Line chart	H-L chart	
Bar chart	**0.9374**	0	0.45	0.45	100%
Pie chart	0	**0.8473**	0	0	100%
Line chart	0.45	0	**0.8866**	0.45	100%
H-L chart	0.5	0	0.5	**0.9973**	100%
Not chart	0	0	0.0288	0.0275	100%

For the chart images with the original data known, we can calculate the error rate for the data recovered. Since the data obtained from the bar charts and the line charts are only relative values, we manually calculate the absolute values by multiplying corresponding ratio to the maximum value among the data. For bar chart and line chart, the error rate is calculated as the difference between the actual value and the recovered value divided by the actual value. For pie chart, both the actual data and the recovered data are the percentages. We can directly calculate the difference between the two and use it as the error rate. For those line charts with a large amount of data, it is difficult to measure the accuracy. Thus accuracy measure is only done to those line charts that have limited number of data points. The average error rates are summarized in Table 2 below:

Table 2. Summary of data accuracies

Type of chart	No. of images	Average error rate
Bar chart	8	0.83%
Pie chart	8	1.36%
Line chart	8	1.17%

5.2 Discussions

From the testing results obtained, we can see that the likelihood values calculated truly reflect the correct type of the input image. Thus the type determination is very successful. The likelihood values for the bar chart, the line chart and the high-low chart are correlated to some extend, because the existence of the x-y axes increases the likelihood for all of them. However, the type is still distinguishable, since the data components in one chart model become unexpected objects in another chart model.

For the data recovery, we can see that the error rates are reasonably low. There are several causes of error. Firstly, the discrete representation of the lines and arcs introduces some error that is unavoidable. Secondly, the imperfect vectorization also causes the difference between the extracted lines (arcs) and the actual lines (arcs). The third cause is the perspective distortion that occurs in 3D pie charts. In this case, the angles from the pies may not reflect the true percentages among the data since the drawing is an ellipse instead of a circle. This explains the reason why the average error rate for the pie charts is relatively higher than the other two chart types. An example, as shown in Figure 12 and Table 3, illustrates the difference between the actual data and the recovered data for 3D pie chart.

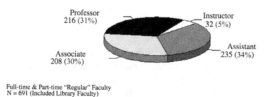

Fig. 12. The testing 3D pie chart image P4

Table 3. Difference between actual data and data recovered for the pie chart in Figure 13

	Actual data percentage	Angle measured	Percentage of angle/360 degree
Pie 1	31%	141 degree	39%
Pie 2	5%	14 degree	4%
Pie 3	34%	87 degree	24%
Pie 4	30%	118 degree	33%

There are some advantages for converting chart images into electronic forms. One of them is that much less space is required to store the data. The total size of the 37 testing images in the BMP format is about 8.32MB, while the total size of data recovered and stored as Excel Files is only about 518KB, saving more than 90% of the original space. Another advantage is that the data recovered can be further analyzed and manipulated, such as generating tables or applying other graphical representations to the data. When integrated with traditional OCR software, the recovered data from charts make the recognized document information more complete.

6   Conclusion and Future Works

In this paper, we introduce a model-based system that aims at recognizing scientific chart images and recovering their electronic forms by extracting the embedded data. The system separates text and graphics information, and then extracts lines and arcs from the graphics based on vectorization. Using the lines and arcs obtained, various objects are constructed and are used to calculate the likelihood that the input image fits into four kinds of chart models. After the type of a chart is determined, data interpretation is performed to recover the data contained in the chart. Experiments were conducted using a set of testing images and the results are encouraging.

As a new attempt, there are further works to be done, such as improving text/graphics separation, extracting the text information for more precise data interpretation, automatic locating chart images in document pages, extending the system to handle other chart models and separating multiple data series in one chart and interpret each data series independently.

We believe that the importance of information contained in chart images will attract more and more attentions from researchers. Automatic and reliable conversion from chart image to equivalent electronic form will be realized in near future as more efforts are put in and major problems are solved.

References

1. Y. P. Zhou and C. L. Tan: Hough technique for bar charts detection and recognition in document images. International Conference on Image Processing (2000) 494–497
2. Y. P. Zhou and C. L. Tan: Learning-based scientific chart recognition. 4th IAPR International Workshop on Graphics Recognition, GREC2001 482–492

3. J. Song, F. Su, J. Chen, C. L. Tai, and S. Cai: Line net global vectorization: an algorithm and its performance analysis. IEEE Conference on Computer Vision and Pattern Recognition, South Carolina (2000) 383–388
4. K. Tombre, S. Tabbone, L. Pélissier, B. Lamiroy, and P. Dosch: Text/Graphics Separation Revisited. 5th International Workshop on DAS (2002) 200–211

Extracting System-Level Understanding from Wiring Diagram Manuals[1]

Larry Baum, John Boose, Molly Boose, Carey Chaplin, and Ron Provine

Boeing Phantom Works, P.O. Box 3707 MS 7L-44, Seattle, WA 98005
{larry.baum, john.boose, molly.boose, carey.chaplin,
ronald.c.provine}@boeing.com

Abstract. In this paper we present an automatic method for recognizing the interconnections between a full set of wiring diagrams in order to derive a complete, global representation of the full set of electrical connections in an aircraft. To fully understand the nature of a link between diagrams, the system must not only parse the link itself, but also determine the surrounding graphical context and discover exactly what object in the target diagram is being referenced. This global understanding creates the potential to significantly reduce the burden of electrical troubleshooting.

1 Introduction

In Baum, et al. [1], we presented a practical application of graphics recognition and delivery technologies to support highly interactive electronic wiring diagrams to significantly improve airplane maintenance. The application automatically extracts knowledge (signal paths, behavior of electrical symbols, references, etc.) from individual wiring diagrams and transforms the diagrams into highly interactive graphical objects that dramatically improve the usability of the diagrams in online systems such as Interactive Electronic Technical Manuals [2] and portable maintenance aids. The application was limited in that it only understood the system at the individual diagram level.

This paper describes an extension of this technology to an application that integrates the knowledge extracted from individual diagrams into a global understanding of the entire electrical system of the aircraft. The system extracts the complete network of point-to-point connections between components, including complex cases that span hundreds of individual diagrams through a myriad of off-sheet references that occur in a large variety of formats. The extracted knowledge is then integrated with existing databases that support state-of-the-art online systems. As a result, we can present electrical connectivity information in much more simplified and targeted formats that significantly reduce the burden on the trouble-shooter.

Figure 1 depicts a representative signal path that starts at a battery and passes through a large number of components (connectors, circuit breakers, switches, etc.) before terminating at a ground. Tracing this circuit involves navigating through seven individual diagrams via ten references and thirty electrical components. Even with the

---

[1] Patent Pending 09/971,283.

J. Lladós and Y.-B. Kwon (Eds.): GREC 2003, LNCS 3088, pp. 100–108, 2004.

intelligent wiring diagrams discussed in [1] the burden on the trouble-shooter to traverse all of these links is significant. Once the system has automatically extracted the semantics from the diagrams, it becomes possible to provide the trouble-shooter with a simplified view (Figure 2).

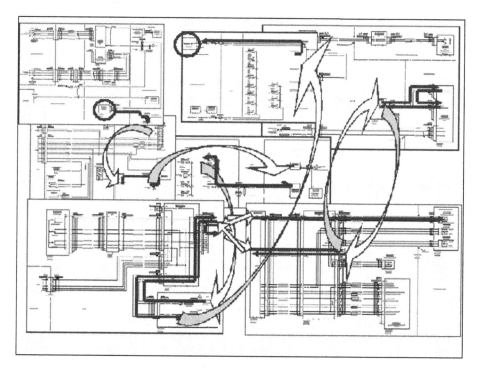

Fig. 1. A single signal path that traverses 7 wiring diagrams through 10 references and 30 components

2 Multiplicity of Link Expressions

Recognizing the link structure between all the diagrams is a major challenge because of the wide variety of link representations used by illustrators. This section catalogues some of the more common representations. This is by no means an exhaustive set, but will serve to demonstrate the complexity of the problem.

2.1 Explicit Off-sheet References

Figure 3 depicts a typical off-sheet reference to a specific diagram. In addition to recognizing the diagram (62-24-01), the recognizer must understand the context of the reference; i.e. that the target of the reference is the specific object (2151FCB2). The

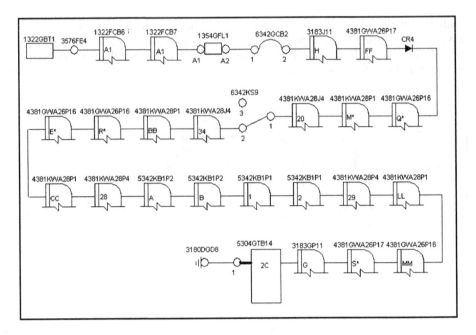

Fig. 2. Simplified view of the same signal path

goal is not simply to link to the correct diagram (Figure 4) but to the circuit breaker object (Figure 5). The recognizer must understand how the model of the circuitry in the first diagram links to the model of the circuitry in the target diagram.

As a result of understanding the links at the object level the system is able to preserve trouble-shooting state when the user exercises the link. In the left half of figure 6, the user has selected the signal path and then opened the circuit breaker, breaking the continuity. The system reflects this break by using two different colors. When the user performs the link to 62-24-01, the system automatically preserves the state, opening the target circuit breaker and using the identical color scheme.

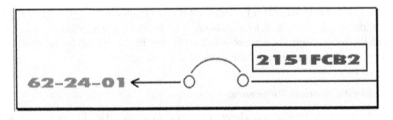

Fig. 3. The signal path continues from the circuit breaker to system 62-24-01

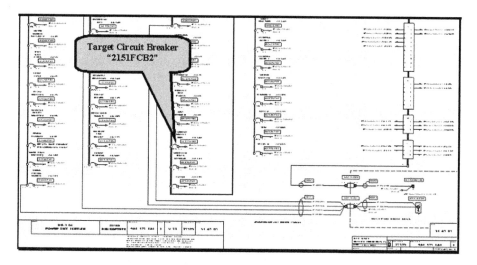

Fig. 4. The target system of the reference in figure 3

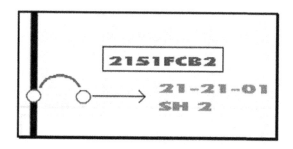

Fig. 5. The link is not just to the diagram but also to the object (2151FCB2)

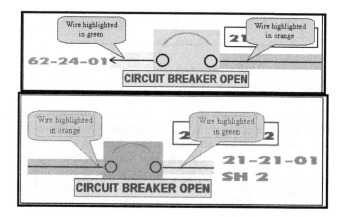

Fig. 6. Traversing the link preserves the trouble-shooting state

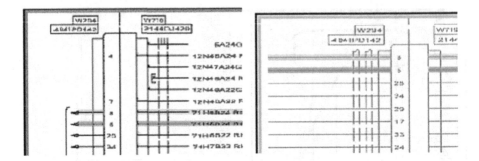

Fig. 7. Recognizing collections

Figure 7 depicts another explicit off-sheet reference; however in this case the context of the reference is a collection of wires connected to the same connector. The recognizer understands that the off-sheet reference applies only those wires delimited by the brace. Furthermore, the system understands which two of the bracketed wires have been highlighted and correctly highlights just those wires in the target diagram.

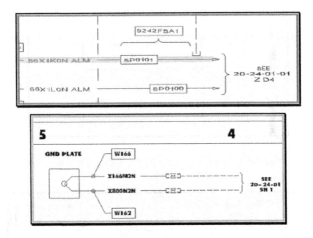

Fig. 8. Off-sheet reference to a zone

In the left half of Figure 8, we see that we have another off-sheet reference but the illustrator has specified a specific zone within the sheet. This allows the system to conclude that the selected wire does terminate in the depicted ground plate. However, because the illustrator neglected to label the two splices in the target drawing, the system cannot determine which of the two wires is the one in question. It is probably the top wire, since the highlighted wire is on top in the left diagram, but this is not a reliable heuristic. It is a limitation of our system that it is unable to compensate for this sort of omission by the illustrator.

2.2 Implicit Links

In order to fully comprehend the wiring network, the recognizer must also find links that are implied by symbology and other link metaphors. The terminal block symbol labeled 1Y in the left of Figure 9 is typical. Note that the target diagram is not specified. The system knows, however, that this should link to pin Y of block 1 of ground bus 2943FTB1. Because the system understands the diagrams at the object level, it knows what diagram contains that object and can complete the link.

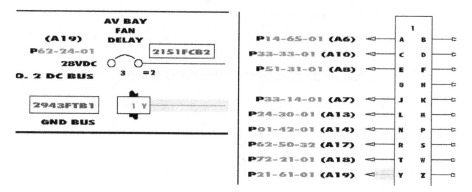

Fig. 9. Implicit link to a terminal block

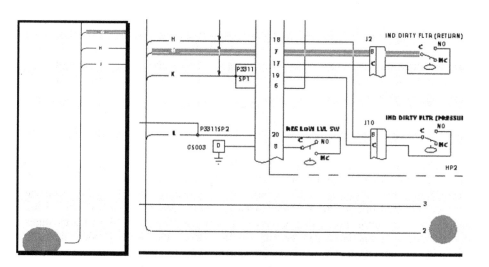

Fig. 10. Wire highways

Airplane wiring is installed with wire bundles often containing hundreds of wires. Illustrators often show the wire bundle architecture using "wire highways" as in figure 10. In this case, the illustrator simply employs a gray circle to depict the link. The recognizer must determine that the circle is in fact a link, associate with the proper highway and understand which wires flow into the highway. As a result it can discover on which drawing the selected wire re-emerges from the highway, as shown on the right.

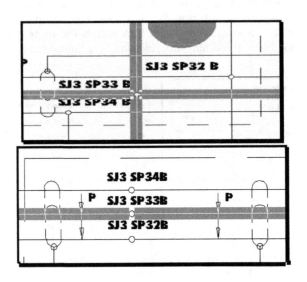

Fig. 11. Implicit links through splices

Figure 11 depicts a link implied by the symbology for a splice. The left-hand drawing shows four wires connected at SJ3 SP33B; the gray circle provides a link to a different drawing where two other wires connect to the same splice. The system is thus able to integrate all of its knowledge of the function of SJ3 SP33B into its unified model of that splice.

3 Recognition

The link recognition algorithms are a natural extension of the work described in [1]. Accordingly, the recognizer starts from a comprehensive model of the electrical network depicted in a single diagram. That model already represents all the wiring and electrical components in the diagram, including constructs for the various states that electrical components can be in. With that as the starting point the link recognition occurs thus:

3.1 Pattern Recognition

As illustrated above, many of the links emanate from text elements that conform to predictable patterns such as System-Subsystem-Subject ("62-24-01"), sheet references ("SH 2"), and zone indicators ("Z D4"). The patterns of interest vary from customer to customer. Determining the specific patterns to use for a customer's data set is one of the principal tasks in defining system requirements. The application reads the patterns from a configuration file, making it easy to control without re-building the application.

3.2 Symbol Recognition

As the example of the ground terminal bus (Figure 9) indicates, certain patterns ("1Y") should be interpreted as links only when in the context of an associated graphical symbol. Similarly the splice links in figure 11 consist of three separate items of art: the text string ("SJ3 SP33B"), the small circle where the wires connect, and the large gray circle that the user clicks to operate the link. The bracket in figure 7 is not an electrical symbol, but it plays a critical role in defining the link and consequently is another symbol to be recognized. Again, it is a principal requirement definition task to identify all such 'link symbology'.

3.3 Proximity Analysis

The recognizer uses proximity analysis to determine link context. It must decide whether a given a link expression ("62-24-01") and a bracket should be paired. It is common to have several brackets and link expressions fairly close together and the recognizer must find which of the possible such pairings is optimal. Similarly, proximity analysis determines which wires a bracket encompasses and which splices are close enough to a gray circle to be within the context of that link.

4 Simplifying the View

The examples above describe interactions that can be provided by an intelligent graphic viewer such as that described in [1]. That is the systems renders the diagrams, allows the user to select wire nets, pull circuit breakers, operate switches and traverse links interactively. This allows users to work much more effectively with the diagrams. Nevertheless, the fact remains that traditional wiring diagrams are extremely complex and difficult to comprehend, even with these advanced capabilities. An important benefit of our work is that the software can automatically extract the complete model of the wiring network into a wiring database that contains the to/from connections of every wire in the vehicle. This enables the dynamic generation of much more simplified, more comprehensible views such as that in Figure 2. That is the subject of additional research and outside the scope of this paper.

Often, wiring databases with to/from information already exist. In that case, the results of the recognition can be used to automatically validate the data. Aerospace vehicles have very long life spans and undergo considerable modifications. Discrepancies between product databases and illustrations are a real problem. By extracting the continuity model of the wiring system from the illustrations, our system can provide reports of those discrepancies. Especially for older models, this has proven to be an extremely important benefit of our approach.

References

1. L. Baum, J. Boose, M. Boose, M. Post, K. Spietz, B. Johnson, D. Shema, S. Chew, E. Hall. "Interpretation of Wiring Diagrams for Aerospace Information Systems". *Third International Workshop GREC'99*, Jaipur, India, September 1999
2. Manuals, Interactive Electronic Technical: General Content, Style, Format, and User-Interaction Requirements, Revision A, MIL-PRF-87268A, 1 October 1995

Automatic Generation of Layered Illustrated Parts Drawings for Advanced Technical Data Systems[1]

Molly L. Boose, David B. Shema, and Lawrence S. Baum

Boeing Phantom Works, P.O. Box 3707 MS 7L-44, Seattle, WA 98005
{Molly.Boose, David.Shema, Larry.Baum}@boeing.com

Abstract. Illustrated Parts drawings are used extensively in the maintenance and repair of commercial and military aircraft. The Boeing Company has hundreds of thousands of illustrated parts drawings that must be transformed into richer, more intelligent formats for use in advanced technical data systems. Because manually re-authoring the drawings is prohibitively expensive, our solution is to provide a batch-processing system that automatically transforms **raster** illustrated parts drawings into intelligent, interactive, layered **vector** graphic files.

A typical aircraft may have thousands of illustrated parts drawings that identify hierarchies of assemblies and parts. These assemblies and parts are labeled to show how they fit together. Reference labels and arrows are used to identify specific parts. Supporting parts information is stored in a database and is indexed by the reference labels on the drawings. There are cross-references among the different detail pictures, within a single raster file and across different raster files.

1 Approach

A typical aircraft has thousands of illustrated parts drawings that identify hierarchies of assemblies and parts. These assemblies and parts are labeled to show how they fit together (Figure 1). Reference labels and arrows are used to identify specific parts. Supporting parts information is stored in a database and is indexed by the reference labels on the illustrated parts drawings. The drawings were typically authored for paper usage and thus the authors reduced printing costs by filling the pages with multiple detail pictures. Figure 1 shows 3 details G, H and J. There are cross-references among the different detail pictures, within a single raster file and across different raster files.

In the paper world, using illustrated parts catalog to perform maintenance operations is tedious and error-prone. Illustrations can cover dozens of sheets, each more detailed than the previous. As Figure 1 shows, there can be dozens of reference labels that cross-reference other pictures or link to a database with additional parts information. There are often multiple pictures within an illustration, but only one of the pictures is relevant during a particular step of a maintenance task. These problems persist in an electronic manual and limited screen real estate and screen resolution can make the problems even worse.

---

[1] Patent Pending, U.S. Application No. 10/318,921. Dec 13, 2002.

J. Lladós and Y.-B. Kwon (Eds.): GREC 2003, LNCS 3088, pp. 109–115, 2004.
© Springer-Verlag Berlin Heidelberg 2004

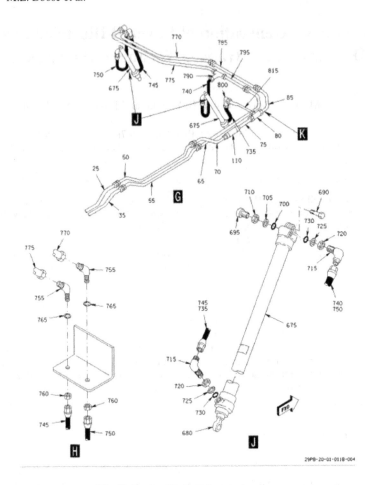

Fig. 1. Raster illustrated parts drawing

Our solution aims to eliminate these problems and make the technical information more useable in an electronic environment. Figure 2 shows an advanced technical data system that describes a procedure for the technician. The associated drawing only shows the reference labels at the top of the drawing that are relevant to this procedure, while the reference labels at the bottom are not relevant and are thus not shown.

There are two major parts to our solution. First, we recognize objects of interest and discover the individual pictures that appear on an illustration. Figure 1 has three separate pictures and has dozens of references and arrows that we will recognize. Second, we create a new set of illustrations that are vector files. Each new vector file contains a single embedded raster base graphic and a vector layer for each of the reference labels and their associated arrows. A base graphic is an individual picture from the original illustration with text and arrows erased.

We describe the software algorithms we have developed to solve this problem. We discuss our accuracies over large collections of illustrated parts drawings and the measured cost-savings over various other methods for similarly transforming the

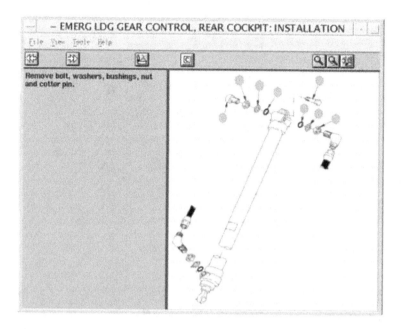

Fig. 2. An intelligent, interactive, layered vector graphic. Of the 17 original reference arrows, only 8 are visible for this particular step in the procedure. The other 9 are not relevant, so we do not want to distract the user by showing them. Also note that the other pictures originally grouped with this picture are not shown as they are not relevant to the current step

drawings. We will conclude with a discussion of our current results using this system in a production environment and our plans for future work.

2 Recognition

The three primary recognition tasks are: (1) recognizing reference labels, (2) recognizing individual detail pictures, and (3) recognizing arrows.

2.1 Recognizing Reference Labels

Our first recognition task is to find all of the reference labels. To recognize reference labels, the software first identifies blobs, or connected groups of pixels. By defining the range of valid sizes for reference labels, most blobs are eliminated from consideration. A commercially available character recognizer[2] locates characters, using a character set built especially for these drawings. Our raster text recognizer uses the output from the character recognizer to categorize the reference labels as item numbers, detail labels or callout labels. The detail labels and callout labels look identical on the drawing. The recognizer has to figure out the difference by looking for possible arrows emanating from the label. If a potential arrow is found (i.e. there

---

[2] We are using an OCR library from RAF Technologies, Inc.

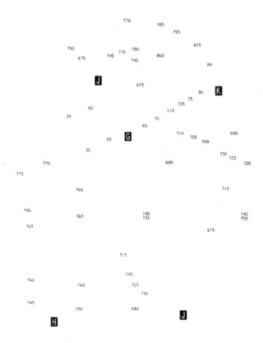

Fig. 3. Recognized reference labels

is artwork very close to the label), the label is categorized as a callout label. Figure 3 shows all of the identified reference labels from our drawing in Figure 1.

2.2 Recognizing Individual Detail Pictures

Using the detail labels that appear beneath their associated picture, we use proximity reasoning and heuristics to group art. The software iteratively applies a "closeness test" that initially requires that "blobs" (i.e. collections of connected pixels) be extremely close to a reference label if they are to be associated with that label (and thus that picture). As the individual picture grows in size, we can relax the closeness test and rely on art being *closer* to one individual picture than another. This is how we create the separated pictures that are shown in Figure 4.

Now that we have three individual pictures, we are ready to recognize the arrows. During the process of separating the original drawing into three drawings, we identified 3 reference labels as the picture labels (G, H and J). All remaining labels are now expected to have an arrow emanating from them.

2.3 Recognizing Arrows

Using the bounding region of each reference label, we begin sweeping outward looking for a close-by pixel that may be the start of an arrow. We follow connected

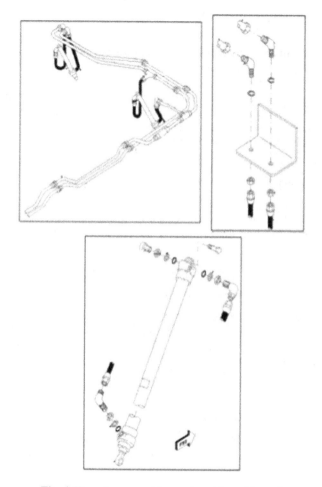

Fig. 4. Three *base graphics* produced from Figure 1

pixels, moving away from our reference label. We iteratively collect pixels and analyze our collection to ensure we have a straight line. When we can find no more valid pixels to add, we apply tests to determine if we have found an arrow.

The first test we apply is to determine if the length of the arrow is valid (i.e. neither too long nor too short). We then test that the arrow has an arrowhead at the end farthest from the reference label. If our arrowhead test fails, we back up towards the reference label, retesting for an arrowhead. This is necessary because often the arrow will overlay part of our base graphic, which causes "non-arrow" pixels to erroneously be added to our collection. We can simply remove pixels from our collection and see if the adjusted collection is valid. This method produces a fairly accurate identification of arrows, but a small percentage of arrows require manual clean up because they were either too short or they overlay surrounding art in such a way that the algorithms failed. Currently, in the production system, about 10% of arrows must be manually corrected.

3   Creating New Graphic Files

Now that our recognition is complete, we can create our new intelligent, interactive, layered vector graphic files. The four primary tasks in creating the new graphic files are: (1) separating each detail picture into a separate raster image file, (2) erasing all reference labels and arrows from the individual detail raster image files (i.e. producing a stripped raster image), (3) producing a vector graphic with an embedded bitmap of the stripped raster image, (4) generating intelligent vector layers for each of the reference labels and its associated arrows.

3.1   Separating Each Detail Picture

For each individual picture that was identified during recognition, we generate a raster file containing all of the art that was not identified as part of a reference label or an arrow. We call this resulting image the new *base graphic*. Figure 4 shows the three resulting base graphics for Figure 1.

3.2   Erasing Reference Labels and Arrows

As we recognize reference labels and arrows, we separate the pixels that were part of the labels and arrows so that they are no longer considered part of the base graphic. Thus when we create our base graphic, we effectively erase reference labels and arrows – simply by *not* writing out those pixels. The base graphics in Figure 4 do not include the text or the arrows.

3.3   Producing the Vector Graphic

A commercial application embeds the raster version of the base graphic in a vector file to which we can add layers. This greatly simplifies the process of embedding vector layers for the reference labels and arrows.

3.4   Generating the Vector Layers

Finally, we iterate over each reference label, creating a single, unique layer for each one. For each reference label, we add any arrows that are associated with the label into that label's layer. This enables downstream processes to make layers visible or invisible based on applications' specific requirements. This supports the authoring communities, by allowing authors to identify which labels and arrows should be shown to the user. The users benefit by having only relevant information displayed when they are performing maintenance tasks.

4   Conclusion

This system has been put into production use and has processed several thousand illustrated parts drawings to date. There is a manual authoring process that cleans up erroneous results. We are working with illustrators and authors of the drawings to improve the software accuracies and further reduce the manual labor required to migrate these drawings to advanced technical data systems. The system is successfully separating about 70% of the multi-picture illustrations into individual base graphics. The system is finding about 99% of the reference labels. About 75% of the associated arrows are correctly found, while an additional 15% of the remaining arrows are only partially found (i.e. the system finds what it thinks is an arrowhead prematurely). The remaining 5% of arrows are completely missed by the software.

Boeing has millions of legacy technical illustrations that are used across the company in engineering, manufacturing and design processes, as well as in support systems development. We want to identify applications for this technology that will reduce internal costs and improve our support products. We are eager to explore variations of this software that will enable efficient, cost-effective transformation of legacy data sources.

References

1. DoD Interactive Electronic Technical Manuals, http://www.ietm.net/DoD.html.
2. Interactive Electronic Technical Manuals: General Content, Style, Format, and User-Interaction Requirements, Revision A, MIL-PRF-87268A, October 1, 1995.
3. Dov Dori, David Doerman, Christian Shin, Robert Haralick, Ihisin Phillips, Mitchell Buchman, and David Ross. Handbook on Optical Character Recognition and Document Image Analysis, chapter The Representation of Document Structure: a Generic Object-Process Analysis. World Scientific Publishing Company, 1996.
4. David S. Doermann. An Introduction to Vectorization and Segmentation. In Proceedings of the International Workshop on Graphics Recognition, pages 1–5, 1997.
5. Computer Graphics Metafile (CGM), Version 4, International Standards Organization IS 8632: 1992

Main Wall Recognition of Architectural Drawings Using Dimension Extension Line

Jaehwa Park and Young-Bin Kwon

Dept. of Computer Engineering, Chung-Ang University
{jaehwa, ybkwon}@cau.ac.kr

Abstract. This paper deals with plain figures on the architectural drawings of apartment. This kind of architectural drawings consist of main walls represented by two parallel bold lines, symbols (door, window, tile...), dimension line, extension line, and dimensions represent various numerical values and characters. This paper suggests a method for recognizing main wall which is a backbone of apartment in an architectural drawing. In this thesis, the following modules are realized: an efficient image binarization, a removal of thin lines, a vectorization of detected lines, a region bounding for main walls, a calculation of extension lines, a finding main walls based on extension line, and a field expansion by searching other main walls which are linked with the detected main walls. Although the windows between main walls are not represented as main walls, a detection module for the windows is considered during the recognition period. So the windows are found as a part of main wall. An experimental result on 9 different architectural drawings shows 96.5% recognition of main walls and windows, which is about 5.8% higher than that of Karl Tombre.

Keywords: Architectural drawings, recognition, main wall, dimension line

1 Introduction

Recognizing architectural drawings is an important step in processing architectural information. Architectural drawings are produced and stored using CAD which makes the storage, editing and processing of the data easier than before. However, for buildings that have been build before the introduction of CAD tools, the architectural drawings exist in paper forms that have been manually drawn. Also with the increase in the number of architectures, much heavier facilities are required both in physical facilities and in equipments for maintaining such large storage facilities. More effort is required in acquiring such stored information and when an enhancement is necessary, the drawings must be redrawn manually which is a time and effort-consuming process. To effectively manage architectural drawings, we suggest a method of scanning the architectural drawings for recognition which makes the storage, maintenance, and processing of the drawings much easier and more effective than before.

J. Lladós and Y.-B. Kwon (Eds.): GREC 2003, LNCS 3088, pp. 116–127, 2004.

Optical filing, which is a method of simply scanning and storing the data as pictures, has been used up to now. A simple index (name of the building or a number) has been attached to each drawing for an easier search and location of the scanned data. However, users are only able to view the data on the screen and not able to modify parts of the drawing. It is also inefficient in the search of information since only a simple index is provided for the search. The method of recognizing the architectural drawings is much more effective in producing and maintaining the information by extracting the information from the drawings and storing it after vectorizing the information for each layer.

The topic of recognizing architectural drawings is an issue that is associated with two different areas of architecture and computer science and has not been a popular topic of research. It has been studied in the US, Europe, Israel, and Singapore as a part of a research for constructing spacial database. The INRIA of France is the institute that shows the most interest in this area through research on architectural drawings by the Tombre research center [1][2][3][4][5].

We used the architectural drawings of an apartment for the research. Architectural drawings of an apartment show a general form and it is an area that requires providing service to a large number of residents which makes it a suitable choice for research. Architectural drawings of an apartment consist of a main wall expressed using two thick perpendicular lines, symbols (door, window, etc), dimension lines, auxiliary dimension lines, numbers indicating various figures and characters. In our research, we suggest a method of recognizing the main wall of the apartment which is the backbone of the overall building. For the recognition of main walls, a binarization process of removing the thin lines, as well as vectorizing the lines and limiting the location of the main wall are suggested in this study. The windows between the main walls, expressed using a symbol, have to be recognized as a main wall by searching for the window symbols between the recognized the main walls.

This paper consists of the following parts. In the following chapter, we take a look at the characteristics of an architectural drawing of an apartment. In chapter 3, the related studies on binarization and recognition of the surrounding environment are introduced before taking a look at the methods used in our study.

2   Characteristics of the Architectural Drawings

There are various types of architectural drawings by the point of view and the characteristics of each expression. The architectural drawings used in this study are the architectural drawing of an apartment that has been reduced by a 1/150 ratio. The method used to express each architectural drawing differs for each architect. The thickness of the line, the size of the character or number used to express the size may differ for each architect. However, they are only given a meaning when they are within a general rule applied to architectural drawings. If there were no general rule applied for designing architectural drawings, each drawing would become worthless to others than the designer himself/herself. There is a common rule for expression applied to architectural drawings that can be understood by every architect and constructor. Therefore, we need to understand these rules in order to analyze and understand the architectural drawings. Figure 1 in the following page is the architectural drawing of the apartment used in this study.

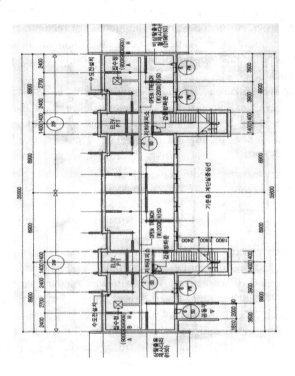

Fig. 1. An Example of Architectural Drawing

3   The Recognition Method of the Architectural Drawings

3.1   Related Studies on Recognition of the Main Wall

The researchers of the Karl Tombre research team have been working on a study on 3-dimensionally reconstructing a 2-dimensional architectural drawing [3]. When a drawing is input, the overall structure is analysed to locate the wall to limit the location of the windows and doors on the drawing. The rooms and kitchen is separated through a spatial analysis before recognizing the architectural symbols used to express a window. Finally, the 3D image of a building is constructed using this drawing.

3.2   Parts of the Architectural Drawing

The architectural drawing shown in Figure 1 consists of the following parts shown in Figure 3-1, when analysed element by element. Therefore, we need to recognize each element that forms the drawing in order to recognize the whole architectural drawing.

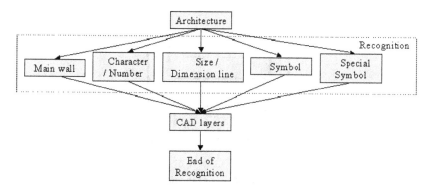

Fig. 2. Overall procedure of architectural drawings recognition

We first need to recognize the main walls of the architecture. We are able to recognize the structure of the building by recognizing the overall structure through the main wall recognition. Then the characters and symbols used in the drawings must be recognized. The information on the drawing is acquired through these steps. Then the dimension line and size used to express the size of the architecture must be recognized. The relative location of al the lines in the drawing can be obtained by recognizing the dimension line and size. After that, the symbols indicating the windows and doors are recognized before the special characters used to indicate the stairways and veranda are recognized.

All the recognized elements of the architectural drawings are transformed into CAD data as the final step. We perform a research on the first step of these procedures of recognizing architectural drawings.

4   Overall Process of Main Wall Recognition

4.1   Characteristics of the Main Wall

The main wall consists of a horizontal and vertical main wall components connected together as shown in Figure 2.The line indicating a main wall appears thicker than the other components on the architectural drawing and contains an auxiliary dimension line inside it. Also, these lines express the outer lines of the main wall and therefore form a closed space, which in turn are all connected together.

In our study, we have implemented a main wall recognition method based on the auxiliary dimension line. The main wall components exist in the form, which enables us to confirm the other main wall components when one of the auxiliary dimension lines has been located. When one of the main wall components is found using the auxiliary dimension line, one of the main wall components form a closed space and all the other main wall lines can be located using the characteristics that they are all connected together.

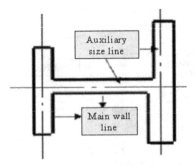

Fig. 3. Characteristics of the main wall

4.2 Proposed Recognition Process

The main wall recognition process proposed in our study is shown in Figure 4.

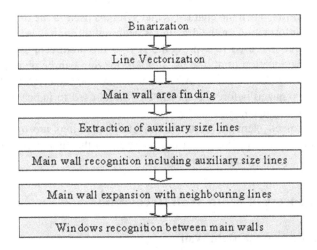

Fig. 4. Main wall recognition process

In the binarisation process, the thin lines are removed during the process. The thick lines remaining are vectorised after the binarisation process. During the vectorisation process, the lines shorter than the threshold run length are left out of the process to remove noise. The areas where the lines that are longer than the threshold value exist are located to limit the area where a main wall can be located. The area where a main wall may exist is expressed using a maximum outbounding rectangle, which is used to locate the auxiliary dimension line. After the auxiliary dimension lines have been located, the main walls containing these auxiliary dimension lines are recognized from outside to inside. Therefore, the main walls connected to the main walls recognized during the previous process have to be located as well to complete this procedure. After all the main wall components have been located, the windows between the main walls are recognized.

4.3 Main Wall Recognition

Vectorisation of the Line. By using the image from which the thin horizontal/vertical lines have been removed, the vectorisation of the line is processed [3][4]. This image contains not only the thick lines, but also some of the thin lines that have not been removed during the binarization process, as well as some characters and numbers. Such data needs to be removed since they are only noise. A threshold value is given during the vectorization process to remove these lines.

Main Wall Area Finding Using Maximum Outbound Rectangle. The auxiliary dimension line is used to indicate the dimension of the drawing and therefore exists in a larger area than the main wall. The main wall exists in an arbitrary rectangular shaped space. By limiting the main wall, the area is reduced for the search which makes the main wall extraction an easier task. By locating the rectangular area where the main wall may exist, the lines outside this area are treated as lines that cannot become main walls. This fact is also used to extract the auxiliary dimension lines.

Extracting the Auxiliary Dimension Lines. An auxiliary dimension lines intersects the inside of the main wall in an architectural drawing. When a rectangle that limits the main walls has been drawn as shown in Figure 5, any line outside the area has a high probability of being a auxiliary lines for dimension. The lines on the rectangular shaped area are compared against the threshold value to extract the auxiliary dimension lines.

Main Wall Recognition Using the Auxiliary Dimension Lines. Since an auxiliary dimension lines crosses the main wall, it can be used to recognize the main wall. An auxiliary dimension lines may cross more than just on main wall. Therefore, the y-coordinate region of a horizontal auxiliary dimension lines are all investigated for the main wall recognition. The lines that are perpendicular are found within a certain distance around the auxiliary dimension lines. There are five different cases when two lines are parallel to each other.

Recognition of the Connected Main Wall. The lines expressing the main wall components are all connected to each other. Therefore, all the main wall lines in the component can be found by locating a single line of the main wall components. During the process of recognizing the main wall using the auxiliary dimension lines, we can find some of the lines in the component. Using the line found during this process, we can find the lines connected to this line. If it begins from a horizontal line, a vertical line will be connected next to it, and vice versa.

5 Results and Discussions

5.1 Auxiliary Dimension Line Extraction by Area Outbounding

Figure 7 shows the result of limiting the main wall area and the result of extracting the auxiliary dimension line using this fact. The auxiliary dimension line found during this process is indicated using a thick line on the outside of the rectangle. The lines of the vertical auxiliary dimension line are all connected to the edge the rectangle and can easily be found.

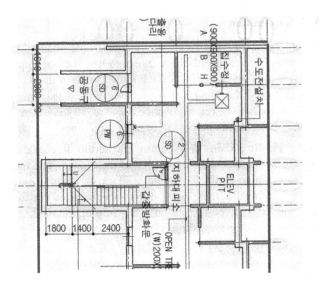

Fig. 5. Auxiliary dimension lines from bounded rectangular area

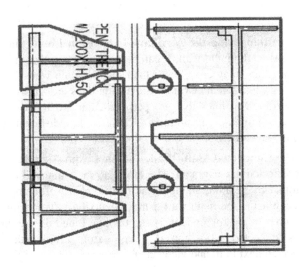

Fig. 6. 6 connected components

5.2 Main Wall Recognition

Main Wall Recognition Using the Auxiliary Dimension Line. As shown in Figure 7, more than one auxiliary dimension line can be drawn within a single main wall component. However, they are not really lines that express the main wall but just satisfy the requirements of an auxiliary dimension line and therefore are mis-recognized as one. The main wall recognized is only a part of the main wall on the

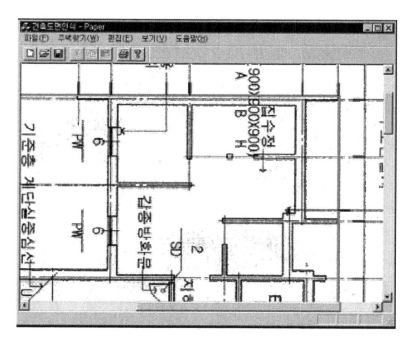

Fig. 7. Result of extracting the auxiliary dimension line using the area bounding

drawing and some of the connected parts may be left out. Therefore, we need to recognize these missed out parts of the drawing, as well as the windows on the recognized main wall.

Recognition of the Connected Main Wall. Figure 8 shows the result of the recognized main wall that is connected to the main wall lines found in Figure 7. All main wall has been recognized and the mis-recognized lines from Figure 8 have been removed effectively.

5.3 Performance Measure by Components

Although some of the methods used may be different, we thought that it would be adequate to compare our method to that of Karl Tombre. The horizontal and vertical main walls are connected in an architectural drawing. Therefore, the main walls have to be separated into horizontal and vertical components before counting their number. As for Figure 9(a), there is a single horizontal main wall component and another vertical main wall component. In Figure 9(b), there is a rectangular shaped main wall with a horizontal auxiliary dimension lines crossing inside, which is therefore recognized as a horizontal component. When the thickness of the main wall line changes and the auxiliary dimension lines crossing the inside is the same line, it is recognized as a single main wall component. Therefore, (b) can be divided into 3 horizontal main wall component and 2 vertical main wall components.

The non-recognition rate is lower in Karl Tombre's method than in our method as shown in Table 1 This is because our method uses the auxiliary dimension lines and

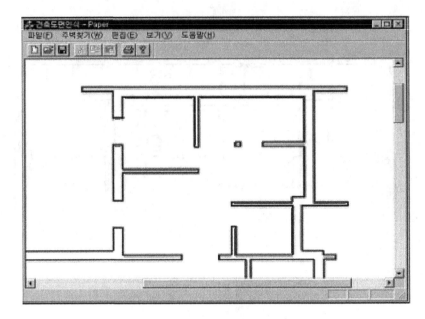

Fig. 8. Result of recognizing the connected main wall

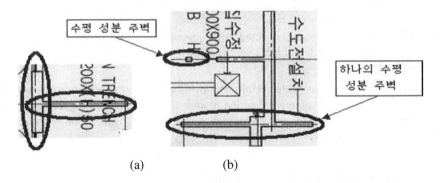

(a)   (b)

Fig. 9. Separation of horizontal and vertical components

therefore is not able to recognize the main walls whose auxiliary dimension line has not been recognized. On the other hand, Karl Tombre's method recognizes all the thick lines as a main wall. As shown in the result, our method showed a 96.5% recognition rate which is higher than the result of Karl Tombre's method of 90.7%. However, a 3.5% recognition error rate has occurred in our study because the method is based on using the auxiliary dimension lines for the recognition.

6   Conclusion

We performed binarization before the recognition of the main wall. Vectorization has been performed to remove the thick lines remaining after the binarization process.

Table 1. Result of the main wall recognition using two different methods

Method	Main wall		Correct		Non		Miss		Rec. rate (%)	Windows	Miss	Rec. rate (%)	Overall rec. rate (%)
	H	V	H	V	H	V	H	V					
Karl Tombre	246	304	245	303	1	1	23	31	90.7	-	-	-	90.7
Proposed	246	304	239	303	6	0	6	7	96.6	70	3	95.7	96.5

H: Horizontal, V: Vertical

Vectorization has been performed on the lines on the drawings both horizontally and vertically. Also, the lines shorter than the threshold are left out of the vectorization process to remove the noise.

The main wall area has been limited using the vectorized lines. The main wall lines that fit the structure. This limitation can be used to recognize the main wall. In other words, the lines outside the area cannot be main walls. The auxiliary size lines can also be found using this area. The lines outside the rectangular area with a run length longer than the threshold value are categorized as auxiliary size lines. More research is needed on the extraction of the auxiliary size lines.

Since most of the main walls contain an auxiliary size line, we can extract the main wall using this characteristic. However, not all the auxiliary size lines are found using this process since not all the main walls contain an auxiliary size line. Therefore, the fact that all the main walls form a closed space and are connected to each other has been used. In other words, when the main wall has been recognized using the auxiliary size lines, the main wall connected to this wall are found to recognized the other main walls. After all the main walls have been recognized, the windows that exist between these main walls can also be recognized.

We have implemented the main wall recognition method proposed by Karl Tombre for comparison. The fact that the drawings used for the study are different has been taken into account. However, it does not have a big effect on the comparison itself. The recognition rate of our proposed method was 96.5% which is higher than the 90.7% accuracy acquired through Karl Tombre's method. However, our method had more mis-recognised cases than Tombre's method. This is because our method applied the auxiliary size lines which can become a liability in some cases.

The main wall recognition method proposed in out study is based on the auxiliary size lines. Therefore, if we do not find more than one auxiliary size line contained in the main wall component, the component itself will not be recognized. Therefore, we need to find a more effective method for extracting the auxiliary size lines. Also, a method for recognizing the size, symbols and characters on the drawing for a more complete recognition of the drawing itself is required.

Acknowledgement

This work is supported by ITRI, Chung-Ang University.

References

[1] Karl Tombre, "Analysis of Engineering Drawings: State of the Art and Challenges". Graphics Recognition Algorithms and Systems, Lecture Notes in Computer Science, Vol. 1389, pp. 257–264, 1998.

[2] Christian Ah-Soon, "Symbol Detection in Architectural Drawings", *GREC*, pp. 280–286, 1997.

[3] Christian Ah-Soon and Karl Tombre, "Variations on the Analysis of Architectural Drawings", *ICDAR97*, pp. 347–351, 1997.

[4] Karl Tombre, Christian Ah-Soon, Philippe Dosch, Adlane Habed, Gérald Masini, "Stable, Robust and Off-the-Shelf Methods for Graphics Recognition", *ICPR*, Vol. 1, pp. 406–408, 1998.

[5] Christian Ah-Soon and Karl Tombre, "Network-Based Recognition of Architectural Symbols", *In Advances in Pattern Recognition (Proceedings of Joint IAPR Workshops SSPR'98 and SPR'98)*, Lecture Notes in Computer Science, Vol. 1451, pp. 252–261, 1998.

[6] Due Trier and Torfinn Taxt, "Improvement of "Integrated Functioin Algorithm: for Binarization of Document Image", *Pattern Recognition Letters*, Vol. 16, pp. 277–283, March 1995.

[7] J. M. White and G. D. Rohrer, "Image thresholding for optical character recognition and other applications requiring character image extraction", *IBM Journal of Research and Development*, Vol. 27, no. 4 pp. 400–411, 1983.

[8] A. K. Chhabra, V. Misra and J. Arias, "Detection of Horizontal Lines in Noisy Run Length Encoded Images: The FST Method", *Graphics Recognition Methods and Applications, Lecture Note in Computer Science* Vol. 1072, pp. 35–48, 1995.

[9] M. Röösli and G. Monagan, "Adding Geometric Constraints to the Vectorization of Line Drawings", *Graphics Recognition Methods and Applications, Lecture Note in Computer Science* Vol. 1072, pp. 49–56, 1995.

[10] Quantitative Measurement of the Performance of Raster-to-Vector Conversion Algorithms", *Graphics Recognition Methods and Applications, Lecture Note in Computer Science* Vol. 1072, pp. 57–68, 1995.

[11] E. Turolla, Y. Belaïd and A. Belaïd, "Form Item Extraction Based on Line Searching", *Graphics Recognition Methods and Applications, Lecture Note in Computer Science* Vol. 1072, pp. 69–79, 1995.

[12] G. Agam, H. Luo and I. Dinstein, "Morphological Approach for Dashed Lines Detection", *Graphics Recognition Methods and Applications, Lecture Note in Computer Science* Vol. 1072, pp. 92–105, 1995.

[13] D. Dori, L. Wenyin and M. Peleg, "How to Win a Dashed Line Detection Contest", *Graphics Recognition Methods and Applications, Lecture Note in Computer Science* Vol. 1072, pp. 186–300, 1995.

[14] B. T. Messmer and H. Bunke, "Automatic Learning and Recognition of Graphical Symbols in Engineering Drawings", *Graphics Recognition Methods and Applications, Lecture Note in Computer Science* Vol. 1072, pp. 123–134, 1995.

[15] F. Cesarini, M. Gori, S. Marinai and G. Soda, "A Hybrid Systems for Locating and Recognizing Low Level Graphic Items", *Graphics Recognition Methods and Applications, Lecture Note in Computer Science* Vol. 1072, pp. 135–147, 1995.

[16] Henning Bässmann and Philipp W. Besslich, "Ad Oculos Digital Image Processing", *Professional Version 2.0, ITP,* 1995.

Interactive Recognition of Graphic Objects in Engineering Drawings

Yan Luo and Wenyin Liu

Department of Computer Science, City University of Hong Kong
83, Tat Chee Avenue, Kowloon Tong, Kowloon, Hong Kong SAR, China
luoyan@cs.cityu.edu.hk, csliuwy@cityu.edu.hk

Abstract. In this paper, an interactive approach to recognition of graphic objects in engineering drawings is proposed. Interactively, the user provides an example of one type of graphic object by selecting it in an engineering drawing, and then the system learns its graphical knowledge and uses this learnt knowledge to recognize or search for other similar graphic objects. For improving the recognition accuracy of the system, we also propose a user feedback scheme based on multiple examples from both positive and negative aspects. We summarized four types of geometric constraints to represent the generic graphical knowledge of graphic objects. We also developed two algorithms for case-based graphical knowledge acquisition and knowledge-based graphics recognition, respectively. For the user feedback scheme, we adjust our original knowledge representation by associating a few types of tolerances to every piece of graphical knowledge and use different tolerances for recognizing different graphical objects. Experiments have shown that our proposed framework is both efficient and effective for recognizing various types of graphic objects in engineering drawings.

Keywords: Graphics Recognition, Engineering Drawings, Interactive System

1 Introduction

Conversion from paper-formed engineering drawings to CAD drawings is in great demands in many engineering domains. However, such conversion used to be done manually by redrawing the paper engineering drawings in CAD tools, which obviously requires considerable human involvement and leads to low efficiency. A promising way to improve the efficiency of this task is the automatic interpretation of engineering drawings by computers. In general, a significant part of many engineering drawings is made of entities that can be classified as graphic objects. Therefore, graphics recognition is becoming to act as the kernel problem for automatic interpretation of engineering drawings.

Actually, graphics recognition has received and continues to receive much attention by many researchers. In a sense, graphic objects are simpler than those arbitrary-shaped patterns, such as face and fingerprint. However, it seems that the completely graphics recognition has not been done satisfactorily, as Tombre commented [1], "None of these methods works. ... Actually, the methods do work, but none of them is perfect." Existing graphics recognition techniques can be classified into statistical-based method and knowledge-based method according to their paradigms. The former class uses statistical methods to extract various features

J. Lladós and Y.-B. Kwon (Eds.): GREC 2003, LNCS 3088, pp. 128–141, 2004.
© Springer-Verlag Berlin Heidelberg 2004

from enormous samples to train the models, and then recognizes graphic objects by comparison to the existing models. While the latter class first defines the knowledge of particular graphic objects, and then employs some knowledge-based recognition algorithms to produce the final recognition results. Both classes claim that they overcome the difficulties of the other class; however, they also suffer from their own unsolved difficulties. Actually, both classes do have made significant progress in recent years; therefore, the most promising way is perhaps to explore a new paradigm which well integrates their advantages and avoids their weaknesses.

In Section 2, we first review the popular methods of both statistical-based paradigm and knowledge-based paradigm to realize their advantages and disadvantages. In Section 3, a new integrated paradigm will be proposed and the sub modules of the system are described in detail in Section 4, 5, and 6 respectively. In Section 7, we explore an interactive user feedback scheme based on multiple examples from both positive and negative to improve the system's learning ability and recognition accuracy. Finally, experiments and concluding remarks are presented.

2   Reviews

A number of good review papers on graphics recognition have been published in the literature (e.g., [2], [3], and [4]). In this section, we only discuss the representative methods of statistical-based paradigm and knowledge-based paradigm.

2.1   Statistical-Based Methods

In most statistical-based recognition methods, the graphic object features are first defined, and then the decision boundaries in the feature space are determined. Trier described many such features in [5]. Many methods based on statistical techniques have been developed and proved to be effective. A representative of these methods is Template Matching (e.g. [6] and [7]). This method is that the system recognizes graphic objects by comparing them to the stored standard templates. Usually, the system carries around a vast storehouse of templates that can be compared with the input. Neural Network (NN) is another classical representative of statistical-based recognition methods, which can be effectively used to extract or cluster the features of graphic objects. A successful NN-based graphics recognition system, the Necognitron [8], is an attempted to imitate the human visual system for pattern recognition. All these statistical-based recognition systems need a large number of training samples to extract or cluster the features. If the features are not selected (or extracted) properly the graphic object feature space regions will be overlapped and there will be many mis-recognized results in the overlapped regions. Generally, each statistical-based recognition system is developed for a certain application and cannot learn new graphic objects easily. If the system is required to add one or more new graphic objects representing, then the system should be retrained with the whole training data (old and new samples). Another drawback of statistical-based recognition methods is the computation complexity is particularly high and the memory usage is tremendous, since these methods use a lot of samples to extract or cluster features for training models and seek to apply geometric information to the pixel analysis directly.

2.2 Knowledge-Based Methods

In knowledge-based graphics recognition, the graphic objects are represented by some knowledge, such as rules and grammars, as shown by Fu in [9]. One of the representative methods of this class is structure and syntactic method, which has been used in many systems for various practical applications (e.g., [10] and [11]). In these systems, the particular graphic object is represented in logical description before recognition phase. Based on the pre-defined knowledge, the system applies some AI algorithms, such as Syntactic Parse, Graph Matching, Interpretation Tree, etc., to produce the recognition results. Knowledge-based methods generally seek to capture the information of graphic objects from vector level, much higher than pixel level, which have lower computation complexity and memory usage. However, they actually need much human involvement to pre-define the knowledge of particular graphic objects. These tasks presently not only require professional knowledge but also are quite time-consuming and labor-intensive. It is also true that the rules, syntaxes, and other knowledge about the graphic object are usually hard-coded in the recognition system. Hence, the current knowledge-based graphic object recognition system can deal with only a limited set of specific and known graphic objects. In order to recognize new classes of graphic objects, the same analysis-design process needs to be repeated.

3 The Integrated Paradigm

From above reviews, the two main classes of graphics recognition methods have both advantages and disadvantages. In engineering drawings, there are enormous types of graphic objects, thus producing templates or defining knowledge for each type of graphic object is nearly impossible and unacceptable. Hence, an incrementally learning strategy is strongly desired. That is, the system can automatically learn the knowledge of graphic objects; when a new sample of same graphic object is input, the system can incrementally update the leaned knowledge and provide information with highest possible quality for recognition. We proposed a new set of features for representing the knowledge of graphic objects using geometric constraints and developed two algorithms for learning graphical knowledge and recognizing graphic objects based on this knowledge representation, respectively.

Fig. 1 is the architecture diagram of our system. The system is divided into four parts, a pre-processing part, a knowledge acquisition part, a run-time recognition part, and a knowledge maintaining part. The pre-processing part deals with converting a raster image to a vector form graphics and applying some refinements to produce a possible high quality vectorization result. After pre-processing, the user can interactively select a desired graphic object, which the system first uses existing graphical knowledge to attempt to recognize. If succeeds, the system outputs a recognition result to the user. The user can give a feedback to tell the system whether the recognition result is correct or wrong. Based on the user feedback, the system automatically updates the old knowledge in the database for future recognition. If the recognition fails, the system treats this graphic object as a new type and learns its knowledge at the knowledge acquisition part. The user can also select a particular graphic object type in the knowledge database, and the system uses its knowledge to search the engineering drawings for recognizing all the same type of graphic objects.

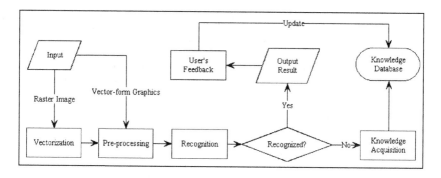

Fig. 1. The architecture diagram of the system

4   Knowledge Representation

We have proposed an original basic knowledge representation for linear graphic objects in our last paper [12] in detail. In this paper, we only describe our new graphical knowledge representation briefly. We analyzed more than 300 types of different common graphic objects and summarized four types of geometric constraints, Intersection, Parallelism, Perpendicularity, which three are for linear vectors, and another geometric constraint for circles and arcs (actually, a circle is a special kind of arc, so only one geometric constraint is enough).

Before defining the graphical knowledge, we first define the primitive components of a graphic object: *Line* and *Arc*. A Line has two endpoints: P_1, P_2, and an *Arc* has four attributes: *Center, Radius, Start-Angle,* and *End-Angle.* In the following sub-sections, four basic geometric constraints will be described in detail, respectively.

4.1   Intersection

We first decompose the lines by their points of intersection. After decomposition, the points of intersection are all at the end of lines. Thus two lines are intersected only in four types, as illustrated in Fig. 2. We use a parameter type to represent this information and use another parameter angle to store the angle between them: $angle = \cos(\alpha) = L_1 \bullet L_2 /(|L_1| \| L_2|)$.

In this definition, the parameter angle itself is not sufficient to fully specify the spatial relationship of two intersected lines since the angle has a direction. Thus, we use another parameter *direction* to describe this information. Consider $L_1(x_1,y_1,0)$ and $L_2(x_2,y_2,0)$, which are 2D vectors in 3D space, their cross product

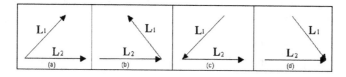

Fig. 2. Four types of Intersection

$$L = L_1 \times L_2 = \left(\begin{vmatrix} y_1 & 0 \\ y_2 & 0 \end{vmatrix}, \begin{vmatrix} 0 & x_1 \\ 0 & x_2 \end{vmatrix}, \begin{vmatrix} x_1 & y_1 \\ x_2 & y_2 \end{vmatrix} \right) = (0,0,L_z) \quad L_z = \begin{vmatrix} x_1 & y_1 \\ x_2 & y_2 \end{vmatrix} = x_1 y_2 - x_2 y_1$$

L is perpendicular to the plane formed by L_1 and L_2, and its direction complies with the *Right Hand Rule*. Thus we can determine the direction only by calculating $L_z > 0$ (or <0, $=0$). In addition, we use a parameter *length* to describe the relative length of L_2 to L_1 (*length* = $|L_2|/|L_1|$).

4.2 Parallelism

Similar to Intersection, we also use four parameters to describe Parallelism geometric constraint. The first one is *distance* = $D(L_1,L_2)/|L_1|$, in which $D(L_1,L_2)$ denotes the real distance between line L_1 and L_2. The second one, *direction*, is used to describe whether L_2 is on the left or right to L_1 and the computing method is similar to the definition in Intersection. We use two other parameters, Q_1 and Q_2, to specify their relative position and length, which are described by a common concept, *Cross Ratio*. *Cross Ratio* is a geometric invariant. That is, for any three distinct, collinear points A, B, and C, the value $(B–C)/(A–C)$, where $B–C$ denotes the distance from B to C with direction, is unchanged by a geometric transformation, such as scaling, translation, and rotation, or by any composition of these geometric transformations. In Fig. 3, L_1 and L_2 are parallel to each other; *sp* and *ep* are the projections of the endpoints of L_2 on L_1. We set:

$$Q_1 = \frac{sp - L_1.P_2}{L_1.P_1 - L_1.P_2} \qquad Q_2 = \frac{ep - L_1.P_2}{L_1.P_1 - L_1.P_2}$$

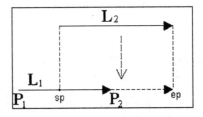

Fig. 3. Start-point and end-point

4.3 Perpendicularity

For Perpendicularity which two lines are intersected, we use Intersection to represent it. Here, we only define the Perpendicularity in which two lines are not intersected:

- Length = $| L_2 | / | L_1 |$
- Per-point is the perpendicular point of L_2 on L_1
- Start-point = $|$ per - point, $L_2.P_1 | / | L_2 |$
- End-point = $|$ per - point, $L_2.P_2 | / | L_2 |$

When we calculate start-point and end-point, we set a sign to the value of them. We set it positive if the point is on the left-hand side of L_i and negative on the right-hand side. The computing method is similar to computing direction in Intersection and Parallelism. In Fig. 4, the values of start-point and end-point are both positive.

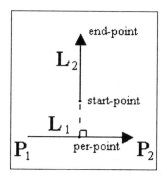

Fig. 4. Perpendicularity

4.4 Arcs and Circles

We use the following six parameters to represent an arc (A) constrained with a line (L) as illustrated in Fig. 5. A circle is a special kind of an arc.

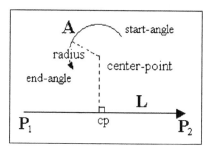

Fig. 5. Arcs and Circles

- Center $-$ point $= (cp - L.P_2)/(L.P_1 - L.P_2)$
- Distance $= D(\text{center - point}, cp)/|L|$
- Direction : center - point is on the left or the right to L
- Radius $= radius |/|L|$
- Start - angle : start - angle of A
- End - angle : end - angle of A

5 Knowledge Acquisition

In this section, we introduce the Case-based Knowledge Acquisition Algorithm (CKAA). For easy understanding, we use a graph $G(V,E)$ to represent the graphical knowledge in which the vertexes are the vectors' sequence numbers and the edges are the geometric constraints between the vectors. In our algorithm, we first extract the Intersection geometric constraints since its frequency in graphic objects is the highest and its computation is easier than others. For example, in Fig. 6, (a) is a is a raster image of a graphic object, (b) is its vector-form graphics after vectorization and refinement, (c) is the result of basic $G(V,E)$ after extracting all the Intersection geometric constraints. Sometimes only Intersection geometric constraints cannot connect all vector components of a graphic object, and an unconnected graph $G(V,E)$, e.g. Fig. 6(c), should be resulted. Therefore, our algorithm searches for this unconnected-ness in graph $G(V,E)$ and tries to use the Parallelism or the Perpendicularity geometric constraint to connect all vertexes. For instance, Fig. 6(d) is a connected graph after adding a Parallelism geometric constraint between *Vector 0* and *Vector 2*. If all attempts are failed, the knowledge of the graphic object cannot be represented by our defined geometric constraints. In fact the probability of this instance is really very low since most graphic object are regular and we have also done some refinement in pre-processing step to adjust their directions to either horizontal or vertical, even parallel or perpendicular.

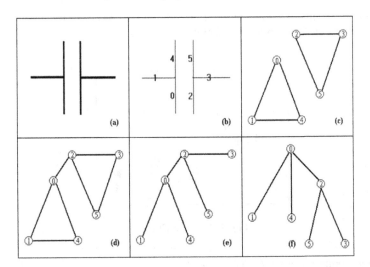

Fig. 6. Intermediate results of CKAA

Although a connected $G(V,E)$ is complete for the graphical knowledge representation, it is not concise and convenient for the reasoning recognition procedure. Hence, we propose a reduction procedure on $G(V,E)$ using the Spanning Tree. After reduction, all the edges are necessary for graphical knowledge representation, e.g. Fig. 6(e), (Fig. 6(f) is the same as Fig. 6(e), but it only looks more like a tree). Finally, if the graphic object contains circles or arcs, we add necessary geometric constraints for them. The following is the detail of CKAA:

Input: the set of vectors, which compose the graphic object
Output: the graphical knowledge, $K(c_1, c_2, ..., c_n)$, a set of geometric constraints
1. Extract all the Intersection geometric constraints and construct $G(V,E)$
2. If $G(V,E)$ is connected then goto Step 5
3. Divide $G(V,E)$ into a few sub graphs, $G_1, G_2, ..., G_n$, each of them is a connected graph, but any two of them are not connected each other
4. Search for any Parallelism or Perpendicularity that can connect the sub graphs. If found then add it to $G(V,E)$ and goto Step 2. If not, stop (failure)
5. Construct a spanning tree (ST) on $G(V,E)$
6. Add geometric constraints for circles and arcs
7. Stop (success) and store $K(c_1, c_2, ..., c_n)$ as this type graphical knowledge

6 Recognition

As discussed in Section 5, our acquired knowledge is essentially a tree containing all necessary geometric constraints of a graphic object. If another graphic object can be represented as the same tree, it can be classified in the same class. However, we cannot use the matching method for recognition since there is not only one Spanning Tree for the same graph. That means even for the same graphic object, the knowledge representation for it can be in different forms, not to say other similar graphic objects. Therefore, we propose a new scheme for recognizing graphic objects based on the knowledge learnt previously. Our basic scheme is like a reasoning method. Because we focus on the geometric constraints among the vector components of a graphic object in our defined representation, the edges of the knowledge tree store the details of the geometric constraints but the vertexes contain only a label without any specifications. However, the specification of a vector component at a vertex of the tree can be calculated (or reasoned) from its parent's specification and the edge's geometric constraint. Using this method, we can reconstruct the similar graphic object based on the knowledge tree. Thus if a graphic object contains all constructed vectors, it is (or contains) the graphic object of the same class as specified by the knowledge tree. Suppose a graphic object is composed of a set of vectors SV and we want to know whether it belongs to the class represented by a knowledge tree K. We randomly select a vector V from SV as the root to start the reasoning procedure. Based on the Breadth First Searching (BFS) scheme, we select the first edge E from K. Since E is a geometric constraint between V and its child, we can use V and E to calculate the child of V, which is denoted as V'. Then, we search for a vector V'' in SV, which is the most similar to V'. If V'' is found, we set V'' as the child of V and continue tracing other edges in K; if it is not found, we select another vector in SV as the root to restart reasoning procedure. If all edges in K have been traced and all similar vectors have been found in SV, then SV is (or contains) a graphic object of the class specified by K. The algorithm presented above deals with ideal situations, in practice there are still some problems. First, the directions of vectors are stochastic. Thus, when selecting a vector to start reasoning procedure or searching for a similar vector, we all test two directions. We also set some tolerances for matching vectors. For the case of absence or redundancy of some vectors according to the graphical knowledge, we set a tolerance range in recognizing. The following is the detail of KGRA.

Input:	*SV*:	the set of vectors, which compose the graphic object
	KD:	the knowledge database consists of graphical knowledge
	TL:	the tolerances, e.g., length tolerance and number tolerance
Variables:	*CT*:	the temporary constructed tree for reasoning procedure
	SM:	the set of marks to indicate which vector has been used
Output:	*RR*:	the recognition result, which type the graphic object is

1. Select a knowledge tree *K* from *KD*. If all trees have been tried, then stop (failure)
2. Set *CT* empty and initialize *SM*
3. Select the next vector *V* from *SV*, which has not been marked in *SM*. Add it into *CT* as the root, and mark it in *SM* to indicate this vector has been used in the reasoning procedure
4. Select the next edge *E* from *K*. If all edges have been traced and the number of redundant vectors does not exceed the tolerant range then stop (success) and *RR* is specified by the current *K*
5. Calculate the new vector *V'* using *V* and *E*
6. Search for a *V''* in *SV*, which is similar to *V'* using the tolerances in *TL*. Test both directions of *V''*
7. If *V''* is found then set it as a child of *V* in *CT* and mark in *SM* to indicate *V''* has been used and goto Step 4
8. If *V''* is not found and the number of the absent vectors exceeds the tolerant range, then goto Step 2. Otherwise, goto Step 4

7 The User Feedback Scheme

Using the above two algorithms, CKAA and KGRA, the computer can easily learn the graphical knowledge of the specified graphic object at run time and apply the learnt knowledge to recognize similar graphic objects immediately. However, the recognition results are usually not 100% correct. In general, the recognition errors can be classified into two main classes:

- Mis-recognition, which means some graphic objects not belonging to this type are recognized as this type
- Missing recognition, which means some graphic objects belonging to this type are not recognized successfully

These incorrect recognition results, as well as the correct recognition results, contain much useful and important knowledge for future recognition. We proposed an interactive user feedback scheme to provide the system with an incremental learning ability and much higher recognition accuracy. The basic procedure of the scheme is that, the user first gives an example of the graphic object to the system, which can be done by inputting a single graphic object to the system or selecting a region in an engineering drawing. The system then learns its graphical knowledge at run time and stores this graphical knowledge into the knowledge database. Using the learnt graphical knowledge, the system can recognize other similar graphic objects immediately. For many cases, the recognition results are not 100% correct since the system only learnt the graphical knowledge form one single example. In the next step, we collect the user feedback about the current recognition results. The user can give the feedback to the system by marking the results as correct, wrong, or missing.

- Correct results, that the user expects, or denoted as positive examples
- Wrong results, that the user does not expect, or denoted as negative examples
- Missing results, those the user expects but the system does not recognize, or denoted as additional positive examples.

We explore a new simple method to implementing the above interactive user feedback scheme based on multiple examples. Our original graphical knowledge representation is a precise and invariable specification of the primitive components' attributes and their relationships. In order to make the system update the graphical knowledge, we must use another ambiguous and tolerant representation for the graphical knowledge. Thus, we consider the tolerances (e.g., length tolerance, angle tolerance, and the number of vectors tolerance), which are used in the recognition procedure in our algorithms. In our original recognition algorithm, KGRA, we use the same and invariant tolerances to recognize different graphic objects. Actually, different graphic objects have different level of tolerances. For a simple example, a rectangle should have exactly four edges and four right angles, so the tolerance for number of vectors and the tolerance for angle should be strict, while the tolerance for edges' length may be loose. Hence, the tolerance is a very important knowledge for graphics representation and recognition. We proposed three basic types of tolerances for length, angle, and the number of vectors respectively and associate them to every piece of graphical knowledge. That is, every piece of graphical knowledge has a few tolerances for length and angle and the whole graphical knowledge of a graphic object has a tolerance for the number of vectors. The system uses different tolerances to recognize different graphic objects. When the user gives the feedback, the system can also update the old graphical knowledge by adjusting particular tolerances to obtain a more accurate knowledge representation and achieve higher recognition accuracy.

At first, a set of default tolerances is assigned to every piece of graphical knowledge. When the user gives the feedback to the system about recognition results, the system first detects the difference of the old knowledge and the new knowledge, and then adjusts particular tolerances as the new graphical knowledge of this type of graphic object. With this interactive user feedback scheme based on multiple examples, the graphical knowledge representation can be more thorough and more accurate and the system's learning and recognition ability can also be more powerful and incremental.

8 Experimental Results

We have implemented a prototype system based on our proposed case-based interactive paradigm. The architecture of the system is shown in Fig. 1. In the pre-processing module, a freeware (*Ras2Vec* [13]) is selected to finish the vectorization task. However, the vectorization result is usually not very good and regular. For refining the basic vectorization result of *Ras2Vec*, we also proposed some post-processing procedures including removing trivial vectors, connecting adjacent points, straightening vectors, and adjusting horizontal and vertical vectors.

8.1 Single Graphic Objects Recognition

We have done experiments on a collection of 325 graphic objects, which are selected from an online graphic objects database [14] and *GREC'03* symbol recognition contest sample images [15], to test our prototype system. Fig. 7 is some graphic object examples in this collection.

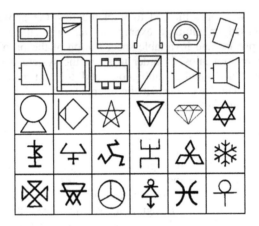

Fig. 7. Examples of single graphic objects

We first let the system learn the knowledge of every graphic object and establish an original knowledge database. The average knowledge acquisition time for each object is 42.81 10^{-6}s (on a PC with P-II 450MHz CPU and 128M SDRAM) and the knowledge acquisition rate is 99.38% since there are 2 graphic objects that the system cannot learn their knowledge successfully from the examples. Then we input the graphic objects into the system for recognition. Experimental results show that the recognition rate is 100% for the original graphic objects and the average recognition time is 74.32 10^{-3}s. We also add some basic geometric transformations and common noises (e.g. scaling, rotation, Gaussian random noise, etc.) on the original graphic objects and the recognition rate is still as high as 98.45%.

8.2 Recognition in Engineering Drawings

With promising experimental results on recognition of single graphic objects, we also test our prototype system on real engineering drawings. The following are some examples of our experiments. First, the user interactively specifies a graphic object example by selecting a region in the engineering drawing, as shown in the dashed line rectangle in the engineering drawing of Fig. 8. Then the system learns its knowledge at run time and uses this learnt knowledge to recognize other similar graphic objects immediately.

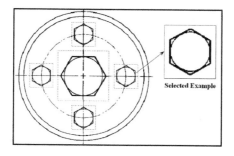

Fig. 8. A mechanical drawing

Fig. 8 is a mechanical engineering drawing containing three concentric circles and five similar graphic objects. In the experiment, the user specifies one (the right most one) of the five similar graphic objects. The system learns its knowledge and successfully recognizes all five similar graphic objects (including the selected example), with translation, scaling, and rotation geometric transforms. Fig. 9 is a circuit diagram consists of several basic electronic components. From the experimental results, we can see the system can successfully recognize almost all of these components by learning their graphical knowledge at run time. However, there are also some graphic objects that the system cannot recognize successfully by learning its knowledge from only one example. For instance, in Fig. 9, the graphic object labelled as 'A' is an example specified by the user for the first time, the knowledge learnt from which can recognize only the four similar graphic objects marked as '#' and misses the other three graphic objects of the same type. For this case, the user randomly selects another graphic object from the three missed objects, such as the one labelled as 'B' and tells the system to do recognition again. The system learns the knowledge of 'B' and compares it to the existing knowledge learnt from of 'A'. By adjusting the particular tolerances, the system updates the graphical knowledge of this type of graphic object. Using the updated knowledge, the system then successfully recognizes all graphic objects of this type, including the three missed ones, marked as '+'. The following table shows the change of the graphical knowledge before and after the user feedback, in which *C#* is the constraint number,

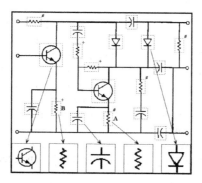

Fig. 9. An Electronic Drawing

V_1 and V_2 is the vector number, T is type, D is direction, $A(A)$ and $A(B)$ is $cos(Angle)$ in A and B, $L(A)$ and $L(B)$ is relative length in A and B, ΔA is angle tolerance, ΔL is length tolerance. For ΔA and ΔL values, the left is the old value and the right is the updated value. In this example, the tolerance for the number of vectors remains 0.

C#	V_1	V_2	T	D	A(A)	A(B)	L(A)	L(B)	ΔA	ΔL
1	0	1	3	−1	−0.54	−0.48	1.88	2.10	0.05 I 0.06	10% I 12%
2	1	2	3	1	−0.63	−0.70	0.93	0.83	0.05 I 0.07	10% I 11%
3	2	3	3	−1	−0.57	−0.72	1.00	1.08	0.05 I 0.15	10% I 10%
4	3	4	3	1	−0.50	−0.49	1.07	1.11	0.05 I 0.05	10% I 10%
5	4	5	3	−1	−0.61	−0.68	1.00	0.76	0.05 I 0.07	10% I 24%
6	5	6	3	1	−0.58	−0.60	0.51	0.52	0.05 I 0.05	10% I 10%

The right table shows the statistical data of the objects in our experiments, in which L is the number of lines, and A is the number of arcs in the graphic object specified by the user, GC is the number of geometric constraints generated by $CKAA$, RN is the number of recognized objects, AT is the knowledge acquisition time in microsecond (10^{-6}s), and RT is the recognition time in millisecond (10^{-3}s). This should be sufficiently fast for interactive recognition systems.

Object		L	A	GC	RN	AT	RT
1	◯	6	1	6	5	32	15
2	◉	7	1	7	2	53	37
3	朩	4	1	4	7	28	32
4	ξ	7	0	6	7	57	35
5	♀	8	0	7	2	58	28

9   Conclusions and Future Work

In this paper we proposed a new interactive approach to recognition of graphics objects in engineering drawings. We summarized four geometric constraints to represent generic graphical knowledge. We also developed two algorithms for knowledge acquisition and graphics recognition, respectively. For improving the recognition accuracy, we explored a new user feedback scheme based on multiple examples from both positive and negative aspects. Experimental results have shown that our proposed scheme is both efficient and effective for recognizing various graphic objects in engineering drawings. However, there is still much work to do to enhance and enrich this framework. For example, in this paper, the method for implementing the user feedback scheme and the incremental learning strategy is very simple. In the future, we will do deeper research on representing graphical knowledge in a more effective way, which can capture the essential information of graphic objects more accurately. We will also consider adding more information (e.g., line style and width) for representing graphical knowledge and recognizing more complex graphic objects.

Acknowledgements

The work described in this paper was fully supported by a grant from the Research Grants Council of the Hong Kong Special Administrative Region, China [Project No. CityU 1073/02E]

References

[1] K. Tombre, "Analysis of Engineering Drawings: State of the Art and Challenges", *Graphics Recognition – Algorithms and Systems, LNCS*, 1389, 257–264, 1998

[2] J.F. Arias and R. Kasturi, "Recognition of Graphical Objects for Intelligent Interpretation of Line Drawings", *Aspects of Visual Form Processing*, eds, World Scientific, 11–31, 1994

[3] T. Kanungo, R. Haralick and D. Dori, "Understanding Engineering Drawings: A Survey", *GREC'95*, 119–130, 1995

[4] K. Tombre, C. Ah-Soon, P. Dosch, A. Habed and G. Masini, "Stable, Robust and Off-the-Shelf Methods for Graphics Recognition", *Proc. ICPR'98*, 406–408, 1998

[5] O.D. Trier, A.K. Jain and T. Taxt, "Feature Extraction Methods for Character Recognition - A Survey", *Pattern Recognition*, 29, 641–662, 1996

[6] D.M. Gavrila, "Multi-feature Hierarchical Template Matching Using Distance Transforms", *Proc. ICPR'98*, 1, 439–444, 1998

[7] S. Belongie, J. Puzicha and J. Malik, "Matching Shapes", *Proc. ICCV'2001*, 454–461, 2001

[8] K. Fukushima, "Necognitron: A Hierarchical Neural Network Capable of Visual Pattern Recognition", *Neural Networks*, 1(2), 119–130, 1988

[9] K.S. Fu, "Syntactic Pattern Recognition and Applications", *Prentice-Hall*, Englewood cliffs, 1982

[10] D. Dori, "A Syntactic/Geometric Approach to Recognition of Dimensions in Engineering Drawings", *Computer Vision, Graphics and Image Processing*, 47, 271–291, 1989

[11] S. Collin and D. Colnet, "Syntactic Analysis of Technical Drawing Dimensions", *Int. Journal of Pattern Recognition & Artificial Intelligence*, 8(5), 1131–1148, 1994

[12] Y. Luo and W.Y. Liu, "Engineering Drawings Recognition Using a Case-based Approach", *Proc. of ICDAR*, 190–194, 2003

[13] D. Libenzi, "Ras2Vec 1.2 freeware", http://xmailserver.org/davide.html

[14] "http://www.symbols.com", the largest online encyclopedia of graphic symbols

[15] "http://www.cvc.uab.es/grec2003/SymRecContest/images.htm", sample images of GREC'03 Symbol Recognition Contest, 2003

Skewed Mirror Symmetry for Depth Estimation in 3D Line-Drawings

Ana Piquer[1], Ralph Martin[2], and Pedro Company[1]

[1] Department of Technology, Universitat Jaume I, Castellon, Spain
Ana.Piquer@uji.es, pcompany@tec.uji.es
[2] Department of Computer Science, Cardiff University, Cardiff, UK
Ralph.Martin@cs.cf.ac.uk

Abstract. We aim to reconstruct three-dimensional polyhedral solids from axonometric-like line drawings. A new approach is proposed to make use of planes of mirror symmetry detected in such sketches. Taking account of mirror symmetry of such polyhedra can significantly improve the reconstruction process. Applying symmetry as a regularity in optimisation-based reconstruction is shown to be adequate by itself, without the need for other inflation techniques or regularities. Furthermore, symmetry can be used to reduce the size of the reconstruction problem, leading to a reduction in computing time.

1 Introduction

Sketch input-based geometric modellers have been investigated during the last decade [1, 2, 3, 4, 5, 6], providing a very intuitive and easy to use interface to 3D reconstruction engines. Optimisation has been used with some success in this sketch-based modelling approach. One of the main challenges in optimisation-based 3D reconstruction is the mathematical formulation of perceptual cues, also called artefacts, or regularities [6]. At present, they lead to poorly defined objective functions, and hence the success rate is below the expectations of users. In addition, optimisation processes are bottlenecks for an interactive session, with clearly unacceptable calculation times (typically up to several minutes).

Using symmetry improves the results, since it is a fundamental concept utilized by human visual perception [7]. Furthermore, many man-made objects are symmetric, both because this makes them easier to interpret and manufacture, and because of functional and aesthetic requirements. Studies have shown that a large proportion of industrial components have some symmetry [8].

In a previous paper, we presented a novel method for determining skewed planes of symmetry of polyhedral objects, starting with a two-dimensional axonometric-like view [9]. This algorithm is intended for *single* view reconstruction: 3D reconstruction from *multiple* orthographic views requires a radically different approach. The nature of shapes that can be reconstructed with this optimisation-based approach extends, at present, to polyhedral blocks (manifolds), origami objects (sheet metal) and wire frame models (non-manifold objects).

J. Lladós and Y.-B. Kwon (Eds.): GREC 2003, LNCS 3088, pp. 142–154, 2004.
© Springer-Verlag Berlin Heidelberg 2004

In this paper, we present a new optimisation regularity based on a novel formulation of model symmetry. Its advantages in improving the success rate of optimisation-based model building are discussed. We also examine the advantages of dealing with model symmetries as constraints, rather than regularities, which significantly reduces the calculation time required for optimisation-based 3D reconstruction.

2 Related Work

Various research has focused on using freehand drawings and sketches as a way to obtain 3D geometric models using input devices like graphic tablets and tablet PCs. *Gestural modelling* systems are one approach. Predefined gestures encode a set of geometric manipulation operations [10, 11, 12, 13]. Reconstructive modelling is an alternative, where geometric reconstruction techniques build the object's geometry from a sketch representing a projection of the object [14, 15, 16, 17, 18, 19].

Optimisation-based 3D reconstruction is discussed in [20, 21, 22, 23, 24, 25, 26, 27]. We simply note that coordinates are related to a so-called inflation-coordinate-system, where the xy coordinate plane is the drawing plane and the infinite set of three-dimensional objects whose orthogonal projection matches the given line drawing (i.e. the *orthographic extension*) is defined by the set of z coordinates of all model vertices: $z = (z_1, z_2, ..., z_n)$. A psychologically plausible model is selected by *optimising* a figure of merit, or objective function, defined as a weighted sum of contributions from perceptual cues, as suggested by Eqn 1.

$$F(z) = \sum \alpha_j R_j(z). \tag{1}$$

Various researchers have studied such *perceptual cues* or *regularities* [22, 24, 28, 29]. Currently, inflation approaches succeed in 3D reconstruction whenever the input drawings are *geometrically correct*, i.e. they correspond to an orthogonal projection of a real shape. However, if input drawings are approximate sketches, with imprecise coordinates, inflation gives distorted or even *tangled* shapes. Sketching interfaces typically convert sketches to line drawings online. Inaccuracies in the initial sketch can influence the detection of regularities, but such low-level considerations are outside the scope of this paper.

We are concerned with the particular regularity of *mirror symmetry*, which is often an explicit design intent. Previous work exists on the detection and application of symmetry to object modelling and recognition [30].

In our approach, a symmetry plane is obtained from a set of symmetry lines. Finding model symmetry planes requires the prior detection of axes of skewed facial symmetry, which, in turn, requires edges bounding faces to be recognised in the two-dimensional image [9]. We need to search for 2-D circuits representing intersections of the model with a symmetry plane. Each skewed plane of symmetry is made up of skewed axes of symmetry and edges of various faces. A closed sequence of axes and edges that meet each other must be found, forming a planar polygon. The plane that contains that *polygon of symmetry* represents a plane of symmetry (Fig. 1). We perform our computation in 2D, so the resulting

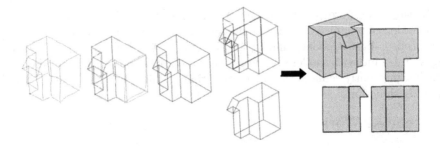

Fig. 1. Input sketch, a wire-frame line drawing, and symmetry plane, represented as a 2-D circuit (left); the final reconstructed 3-D model (right)

output comprises *skewed planes of symmetry*: real planes of symmetry viewed from some (unknown) viewing direction [9].

3   Overview of Our New Approach

Once the symmetry planes have been determined [9], in order to deal with symmetry, it is convenient to introduce a new coordinate system, a so-called *symmetry system*, as explained in the next Section. This allows the symmetry condition to be formulated in a compact and convenient way.

To do this, symmetric vertices have to be properly paired or *matched*. This is simple whenever a vertex in one half is connected to its pair through an edge that crosses the symmetry plane, with midpoint on the plane, as for example in e_1, e_2 and e_3 in Fig. 2a, or e_4 and e_5 in Fig. 2b.

However, the general matching problem is more difficult (see Section 5), and needs to be solved for a practical formulation of *bilateral symmetry regularity*.

Note that the presence of a symmetry plane can be used to reduce the size of the inflation problem. Because of the symmetry, only one half of the object needs to be inflated. When multiple symmetry planes exist, further reductions of problem size can be obtained. Overall, a much smaller problem may be result.

4   Symmetry Coordinate System and
Symmetry Condition

We introduce a different *symmetry coordinate system* for each symmetry plane, in which the symmetry plane is the XY plane. One such system $(O_{S1}X_{S1}Y_{S1}Z_{S1})$, together with the inflation coordinate system $(O_I X_I Y_I Z_I)$ and the model coordinate system $(O_M X_M Y_M Z_M)$, is illustrated in Fig. 3. The origin is placed at the centroid of the planar symmetry polygon, which is invariant and so ensures that the origin of all symmetry systems is the same. X_{S1} and Y_{S1} are aligned with two model coordinate system axes, whenever such a system has already been determined (this problem is related to detecting main directions,

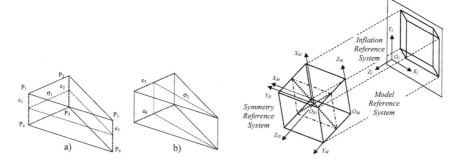

Fig. 2.   Determination of subsets of
symmetric vertices

Fig. 3. Inflation, model and symmetry
reference systems

and is beyond the scope of this paper [24]). Z_{S1} is chosen to give a right hand
system.

The coefficients A, B, C and D in the equation $Ax + By + Cz + D = 0$
of the best-fit plane defined by all vertices of the symmetry polygon is initially
calculated by computing the respective areas of the projection of the virtual face
in the yz plane (for A), xz plane (for B), and xy plane (for C). D is estimated
by simply substituting the coordinates of one of the vertices into the equation.

Let (x_c, y_c, z_c) be the coordinates of the centroid of the symmetry polygon.
Let (u_1, u_2, u_3) be a unit vector normal to the symmetry plane, and let R be
defined by: $R = \sqrt{u_2^2 + u_3^2}$. We denote the coordinates of a vertex P in the
model by (x_p, y_p, z_p) when they are in the inflation coordinate system, and by
(x_p', y_p', z_p') when they are in the symmetry coordinate system. Then, the homogeneous transformation between these systems is:

$$\left(x_p'\ y_p'\ z_p'\ 1 \right) = \tag{2}$$

$$\left(x_p\ y_p\ z_p\ 1 \right) \begin{bmatrix} R & 0 & u_1 & 0 \\ -u_1 u_2/R & u_3/R & u_2 & 0 \\ -u_1 u_3/R & -u_2/R & u_3 & 0 \\ -x_c R + \frac{u_1 u_2 y_c}{R} + \frac{u_1 u_3 z_c}{R} & \frac{u_3 y_c}{R} + \frac{u_2 z_c}{R} & -u_1 x_c - u_2 y_c - u_3 z_c & 1 \end{bmatrix}.$$

To formulate the symmetry condition we need to renumber the set of n
vertices of the model. If m points lie on one side of the symmetry plane, then m
points lie on the opposite side, and $n - 2m$ points are contained in the symmetry
plane (m may be 0). The vertices are renumbered so that vertex 1 corresponds
to vertex $m + 1$ and so on. This gives the following conditions:

$$x_1' = x_{m+1}', \quad \dots, \quad x_m' = x_{2m}',$$
$$y_1' = y_{m+1}', \quad \dots, \quad y_m' = y_{2m}',$$
$$z_1' = -z_{m+1}', \quad \dots, \quad z_m' = -z_{2m}'. \tag{3}$$

This is the simplest formulation of the symmetry condition for vertices, and
is the basic formulation of our *bilateral symmetry regularity*.

5   Matching Symmetric Vertices

Once the symmetry plane has been detected, if a full symmetry formulation is
desired, a matching vertex must be located for each vertex. Our algorithm fills
the elements of a $2 \times n$ matrix V (Fig. 4). In $V(1,i)$ the vertex symmetric to
vertex i (its match) is stored. The second row $V(2,i)$ stores a label indicating
which subset vertex i belongs to. The label $+1$ is assigned to vertices on one side
of the symmetry plane, label -1 is assigned to those on the other side, and label
0 corresponds to vertices on the symmetry plane.

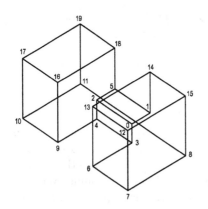

Face No.	Vertices on faces
Face 0	0, 2, 5, 1
Face 1	2, 0, 3, 4
Face 2	18, 16, 17, 19
Face 3	6, 13, 12, 7
Face 4	7, 12, 15, 8
Face 5	0, 1, 14, 13, 6, 3
Face 6	12, 13, 14, 15
Face 7	17, 16, 9, 10
Face 8	5, 2, 4, 9, 16, 18
Face 9	17, 10, 11, 19
Face 10	15, 14, 1, 5, 18, 19, 11, 8
Face 11	11, 8, 7, 6, 3, 4, 9, 10

$$V = \begin{pmatrix} 2 & 5 & 0 & 4 & 3 & 1 & 9 & 10 & 11 & 6 & 7 & 8 & 17 & 16 & 18 & 19 & 13 & 12 & 14 & 15 \\ +1 & +1 & -1 & +1 & -1 & -1 & +1 & +1 & +1 & -1 & -1 & -1 & +1 & +1 & +1 & +1 & -1 & -1 & -1 & -1 \end{pmatrix}.$$

Fig. 4. Matching symmetric vertices

5.1   Identification of the Two Sides of a Symmetric Model

Identification starts at one of the faces divided by the symmetry plane. One of the
sides of the symmetry plane is arbitrarily assigned $+1$ without loss of generality.
Next, adjacent faces that are also cut by the symmetry plane are evaluated
in turn. In this way, common vertices can be used to guarantee consistency in
labelling propagation.

In a third step, the process is consistently extended to remaining faces. All
vertices in such faces are assigned the same label as the one assigned to previously
labelled vertices of the face. Vertices belonging to the symmetry polygon are
finally visited and labelled 0.

5.2   Matching Vertices

Next, symmetry axes are considered in turn, and the vertices of the faces they
belong to are explored. Their vertices are matched through a simultaneous
clockwise-anticlockwise scan. For instance, in face 11 (Fig. 5), if evaluation starts
at the a axis, which cuts the mid-point of edge 11-8, it is easy to fix vertices 11

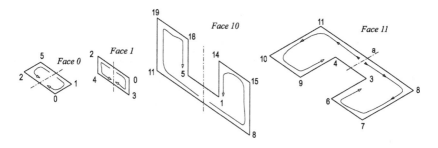

Fig. 5. Faces with axis belonging to the polygon of symmetry

and 8 as a pair of symmetric vertices. The vertices of one half of the face starting at this edge are scanned clockwise (8-7-6-3) and the other half anticlockwise (11-10-9-4), and the two resulting lists are paired to match all the vertices in the face. The same procedure is applied to each face sharing a line with the symmetry polygon. See Fig. 5.

Once all such faces have been evaluated, we continue with the remaining faces. In that case, symmetry between vertices involves vertices of different faces. Thus, the objective is to find symmetric faces.

The list of such unprocessed faces is scanned by searching for a face F_m with at least three vertices already labelled ($v_i, v_j, v_k \subset F_m$); two of these (at least) must be at the ends of an edge shared with an already-processed face. Three non-collinear points determine a plane, so the vertices symmetric to (v_i, v_j, v_k) must determine a symmetric face ($v'_i, v'_j, v'_k \subset F'_m$). The correspondence between the vertices must still be found; this is done by considering the vertices at the ends of the edges shared with already processed faces. (see Fig. 6: for example 6-7 in face 3, and 9-10 in face 7). The relative ordering of vertices around the faces may be the same or opposite, and must be determined. For instance, the correspondence between faces 3 and 7 has oppositely ordered vertices (9-10-17-16) and (6-7-12-13). However, faces 9 and 4 have a correspondence (19-17-10-11) and (15-12-7-8) with vertices arranged in the same order.

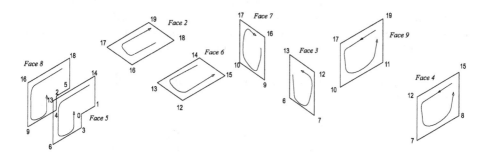

Fig. 6. Faces without axis belonging to the polygon of symmetry

6   Symmetry as Regularity

Once the symmetry polygon has been detected and matching of vertices completed, the symmetry regularity is easy to formulate. In reconstruction by optimisation, every regularity has a cost, and the objective is to minimize the sum of costs. A cost is chosen to be zero when the desired condition is achieved, and differs from zero as we go away from this ideal. Hence, the bilateral symmetry condition for a single plane j formulated in Eqn 3 can be reformulated as the standard deviation (σ) of the difference of coordinates of all pairs of symmetric vertices:

$$\mathrm{Cost}_j = \sigma^2(\Delta(x')) + \sigma^2(\Delta(y')) + \sigma^2(\Lambda(z')) \tag{4}$$

where for every vertex $i = 1, ..., m$:

$$\Delta(x') = x'_i - x'_{m+i}, \quad \Delta(y') = y'_i - y'_{m+i}, \quad \Lambda(z') = z'_i + z'_{m+i},$$

and for every vertex $i = 2m + 1, ..., n$:

$$\Delta(x') = \Delta(y') = 0, \quad \Lambda(z') = z_i.$$

The standard deviations are calculated with an assumed mean equal to zero. Using the real mean does not improve reconstruction results and the objective of the function is distorted. The real objective is to find variables in which the mean of every summand is also zero. When every pair of vertices fulfils the condition, the cost of the regularity reaches the minimum.

The total cost for a model with r planes of symmetry is defined as:

$$\text{Cost of Symmetry} = \frac{1}{r}\sum_{j=1}^{r} \mathrm{Cost}_j. \tag{5}$$

7   Model Rebuilding from a Half

Faster reconstruction can be obtained using the idea that, knowing the symmetric pairs of vertices, we need only reconstruct one half of the model in the drawing, and from this half model, symmetry can be applied to obtain the rebuilt complete model. This reduces the number of vertices, edges and faces in the sketch graph, thus reducing calculation times for reconstruction. This idea can be extended to divide the model size by 2 again for each further plane of symmetry.

Symmetry in 3-D space can be obtained by composition of transformations of the form:

$$S = \begin{bmatrix} 1 - 2u_1^2 & -2u_1u_2 & -2u_1u_3 & 0 \\ -2u_1u_2 & 1 - 2u_2^2 & -2u_2u_3 & 0 \\ -2u_1u_3 & -2u_2u_3 & 1 - 2u_3^2 & 0 \\ -2Du_1 & -2Du_2 & -2Du_3 & 1 \end{bmatrix} \tag{6}$$

where (u_1, u_2, u_3) is the unit normal vector of the symmetry plane $(Ax + By + Cz + D = 0)$.

Having found a plane of symmetry and a half 3-D model, applying S to its vertices allows the complete 3-D model to be obtained. Actually, as the final model retains x and y vertex coordinates from the original drawing, only the computation of z' coordinates for reflected vertices is required. If (x, y, z) are the coordinates of a vertex in the reconstructed half, z' for the reflected vertex is given by:

$$z' = -2u_1u_3 \cdot x - 2u_2u_3 \cdot y + (1 - 2u_3^2) \cdot z - 2Du_3. \tag{7}$$

Note that information is used from the whole object even when we eliminate half of the figure. The planes of symmetry [9] are found from points situated at the midpoints of edges (and vertices). Thus, 3-D object reconstruction is based on information averaged from both halves.

8   Results

A sketch with a single symmetry plane is used to illustrate the results. Initially, a tidied line drawing and symmetry polygon were obtained using previously reported methods (see Fig. 7).

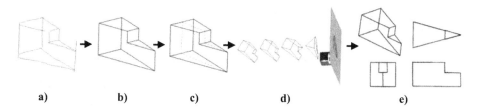

a)   b)   c)   d)   e)

Fig. 7. a) Input sketch, b) line drawing, c) symmetry polygon, d) reconstruction process, e) final model obtained using the bilateral symmetry regularity

Using the bilateral symmetry regularity described in Section 6, a good final model was obtained (see Fig. 7). Additionally, no initial inflation method was required, since the symmetric-model regularity is not trivially satisfied in the input image. The regularity is formulated as a quadric function (see Equations 5-6), which provides quicker convergence than a linear function. In Table 1, four examples are shown as they appeared after the symmetry regularity was applied as the sole inflation mechanism.

This regularity is a *true regularity*. Its use only depends on the detection of characteristic clues in the input drawing. It can be applied alone for converting sketches to 3D models, without any other inflation method, and without the use of other, possibly conflicting, regularities. Thus, this regularity can be considered as a new inflation method by itself. It solves reconstruction for every symmetric sketch for which the planes of symmetry have been detected.

Table 1. Examples and Performance

Line drawing	3D model	Line drawing	3D model
19 edges 12 vertices	9 faces 1 plane of symmetry. Inflation time: less than 1sec.	33 edges 22 vertices	13 faces, 1 plane of symmetry. Inflation time: 1 sec.
24 edges 16 vertices	10 faces, 1 plane of symmetry. Inflation time: less than 1 sec.	46 edges 30 vertices	18 faces, 1 plane of symmetry. Inflation time: 2 sec.

Finally, we give some examples of more complex shapes (Fig. 8–11) which illustrate the benefits of half-part reduction. Fig. 9 shows a shape with three planes of symmetry. Two of them are used to reduce the problem size, then the last one is used as a regularity to reconstruct a partial model. Finally, the complete model is restored. In this example, computation times are reduced from 3 seconds for reconstruction of the complete drawing to less than 1 second using the reduced model (on a Pentium III 1GHz, with 256 Mb RAM).

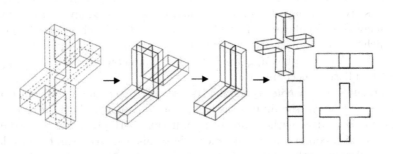

Fig. 8. Model with three planes of symmetry

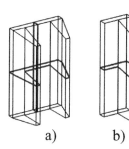
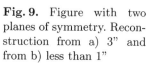
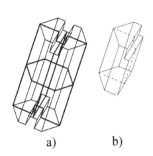
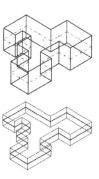

Fig. 9. Figure with two planes of symmetry. Reconstruction from a) 3" and from b) less than 1"

Fig. 10. Figure with two planes of symmetry. Reconstruction from a) 6" and from b) less than 1"

Fig. 11. Detection of symmetry planes in extruded shapes

Our new approach simplifies the process of reconstruction by diminishing the number of variables used in the main computation, leading to a reduction of time in the whole process. Extruded models are an exception to this observation. They have (at least) one plane of symmetry (orthogonal to the extrusion direction), but a half part of such an object has exactly the same number of vertices, edges and faces as the original figure (see Fig. 11). Furthermore, after this simplification, a new plane of symmetry with the same shape as the first is found. An additional test must be done for extrusions to prevent this *false simplification*.

9 Summary

This paper considers the three-dimensional reconstruction of polyhedral solids from planar sketches. A new approach has been presented which makes use of planes of mirror symmetry detected in sketches (using methods from [8]). The approach is based on identification of the two symmetric sides in the 2D representation and the matching of corresponding vertices.

Two novel ideas for reconstruction have been presented. The first is to apply symmetry as a regularity in optimisation-based reconstruction. In fact, symmetry is shown to be adequate by itself, without the need for other inflation techniques or regularities. Good qualitative results and acceptable computing times are provided by this method.

The second idea is to eliminate the duplicated information in symmetric models before reconstruction. After elimination of half of the drawing, reconstruction of the simplified drawing can be made by any of the methods already known (and indeed using the first idea above). The aim of this technique is to decrease computing time. This objective is achieved in most examples, although not for extrusions.

Overall, use of symmetry is a powerful method, since it allows complex shapes to be inflated without introducing a large set of potentially conflicting heterogeneous regularities (face planarity, orthogonality, and so on), and it does not require initial estimates for inflation. Moreover, it has been successfully employed to recursively reduce the problem size.

Acknowledgements

This work was partially supported by Fundació Caixa Castelló-Bancaixa - Universitat Jaume I (Project P1-1B2002-08, titled *From Sketch to Model*), and by facilities provided by Cardiff University School of Computer Science.

References

1. Ullman, D.G., Wood S., Craig D.: The Importance of Drawing in the Mechanical Design Process. Computers and Graphics, **14**:2 (1990) 263–274
2. Cugini, U.: The problem of user interface in geometric modelling. Computers in Industry, **17** (1991) 335–339
3. Dori, D.: From engineering drawings to 3D CAD models: are we ready now? Computer Aided Design, **27**:4 (1995) 243–254
4. Lipson, H., Shpitalni, M.A.: New Interface of Conceptual Design Based on Object Reconstruction From a Single Freehand Sketch. Ann. CIRP. **44**:1 (1995) 133–136
5. Ullman, D.G.: Toward the ideal mechanical engineering design support system. Research in Engineering Design. **13** (2002) 55–64
6. Company, P., Contero, M., Conesa, J., Piquer, A.: An Optimisation-Based Reconstruction Engine to Model by sketching. Computers and Graphics (2004)
7. Palmer, S. E.: Vision Science. Photons to Phenomenology. The MIT Press. (1999)
8. Langbein, F.C., Mills, B.I., Marshall, A.D., Martin, R.R.: Recognizing Geometric Patterns for Beautification of Reconstructed Solid Models. Proc. Int. Conf. on Shape Modelling and Applications, Genova (2001)
9. Piquer, A., Company, P., Martin, R.R.: Skewed mirror symmetry in the 3D reconstruction of polyhedral models. J. of WSCG. **11**:3 (2003) 504–511
10. Zeleznik, R.C., Herndon, K.P., Hughes, J.F.: SKETCH: An interface for sketching 3D scenes. SIGGRAPH'96 Proc., **1** (1996) 163–170
11. Eggli, L., Hsu, C.-Y., Bruederlin, B. D., Elber, G.: Inferring 3D Models from Freehand Sketches and Constraints. Computer-Aided Design, **29**:2 (1997) 101–112
12. Bloomenthal, K., Zeleznik, R.C. et al.: SKETCH-N-MAKE: Automated machining of CAD sketches. Proc. of ASME DETC'98, **1** (1998) 1–11
13. Pereira, J., Jorge, J., Branco, V., Nunes, F.: Towards calligraphic interfaces: sketching 3D scenes with gestures and context icons. WSCG'2000. Proc., Prague, (2000)
14. Jenkins, D.L., Martin, R.R.: Applying constraints to enforce users' intentions in free-hand 2-D sketches. Intelligent Systems Engineering, **1** (1992) 31–49
15. Igarashi, T., Matsuoka, S., Kawachiya, S., Tanaka, H.: Interactive Beautification: A Technique for Rapid Geometric Design. Proc. ACM Symposium on User Interface Software and Technology UIST'97, **1** (1997) 105–114
16. Schweikardt, E., Gross, M.D.: Digital Clay: deriving digital models from freehand sketches. ACADIA '98, Quebec City, Canada, **1** (1998) 202–211
17. Oh, B.S., Kim, C.H.: Progressive 3D reconstruction from a sketch drawing. Proc. 9th Pacific Conference on Computer Graphics and Applications, **1** (2001) 108–117

18. Naya, F., Jorge, J., Conesa, J., Contero, M., Gomis J.M.: Direct modeling: from sketches to 3D models. Proc. 1st Ibero-American Symposium in Computer Graphics SIACG, Guimraes, Portugal, **1** (2002) 109–117

19. Naya, F., Conesa, J., Contero, M., Company, P., Jorge, J.: Smart Sketch System for 3D Reconstruction Based Modeling. Lecture Notes in Computer Science, Vol. 2733 (2003) 58–68

20. Marill, T.: Emulating the Human Interpretation of Line-Drawings as Three-Dimensional Objects. Int. J. Computer Vision, **6**:2 (1991) 147–161

21. Baird, L., Wang, P.: 3D object recognition using Gradient descent and the Universal 3-D array grammar. Proc. SPIE. Conf. on Intelligent Robots and Computer Vision X: Algorithms and Techniques, Vol. 1607 (1991) 711–718

22. Leclerc, Y., Fischler, M.: An Optimization-Based Approach to the Interpretation of Single Line Drawings as 3D Wire Frames. Int. J. Computer Vision, **9**:2 (1992) 113–136

23. Baird, L., Wang, P.: 3D Object Perception Using Gradient Descent. Int. J. Mathematical Imaging and Vision, **5** (1995) 111-117

24. Lipson, H., Shpitalni, M.: Optimization-Based Reconstruction of a 3D Object from a Single Freehand Line Drawing. Computer-Aided Design, **28**:8 (1996) 651–663

25. Brown, E.W., Wang, P.S.: Three-dimensional object recovery from two-dimensional images: A new approach. Proc. SPIE. Intelligent Robots and Computer Vision, Vol.2904 (1996) 138–147

26. Company, P., Gomis, J.M., Contero, M.: Geometrical Reconstruction from Single Line Drawings Using Optimization-Based Approaches. WSCG'99, **2** (1999) 361–368

27. Lipson, H., Shpitalni, M.: Correlation-Based Reconstruction of a 3D Object From a Single Freehand Sketch. AAAI Spring Sym. Series- Sketch Understanding (2002)

28. Grimstead, I.J., Martin, R.R.: Creating solid models from single 2D sketches. Proc. Sym. on Solid Modeling and Applications, ACM Siggraph, **1** (1995) 323–337

29. Varley, P. A. C., Martin, R. R.: Constructing Boundary Representation Solid Models from a Two-Dimensional Sketch – Frontal Geometry and Sketch Categorisation. Proc. UK-Korea Workshop on Geometric Modeling and Computer Graphics, Kyung Moon Publishers, **1** (2000) 113–128

30. Tate, S.J., Jared, G.E.M.: Recognising symmetry in solid models. Computer-Aided Design, **35** (2003) 673–692

Vectorial Signatures for Symbol Discrimination

Philippe Dosch[1] and Josep Lladós[2]

[1] LORIA, 615, rue du jardin botanique,
B.P. 101, 54602 Villers-lès-Nancy Cedex, France
Philippe.Dosch@loria.fr
[2] Centre de Visió per Computador, Edifici O, Campus UAB,
08193 Bellaterra (Cerdanyola), Barcelona, Spain
josep@cvc.uab.es

Abstract. In this paper, we present a method based on vectorial signatures, which aims at discriminating, by a fast technique, symbols represented within technical documents. Considering a raw vectorial description of the graphical layer of a technical document, we have based our approach on a method proposed by Etemadi et al. The signature of all models of symbols that could be found in a given document are computed and matched against the signature of the document, in order to determine what symbols the document is likely to contain. A quality factor associated with each relation is used to prune relations whose quality factor is too low. We present the first tests obtained with this method, and we discuss the improvements we plan to do.

Keywords: symbol discrimination, symbol recognition, vectorial signatures, technical drawings

1 Introduction and Related Works

In this paper, we present a method based on vectorial signatures, which aims at discriminating symbols represented in technical documents. Within the field of pattern recognition, signatures belong to the large family of pattern numerical descriptors. These descriptors are often used on bitmap images to efficiently analyze some structural features, allowing a statistical classification.

Among the global descriptors, some descriptors like moments invariants [1] or Zernike moments are useful to describe the global shape of a pre-segmented pattern. Some comparative studies of these moments can be found in [2] and [3]. To the opposite of these approaches, a geometrical invariant description can be computed by using some primitives, which are locally very informative. These local descriptors appear to be easy to use and relatively robust, in particular to handle occlusions, junctions, etc. [4]

In graphics recognition, high level processes for the analysis and recognition of the document components are usually formulated in terms of vectorial representations. Thus, signatures in terms of raw images as described above are not suitable, but vectorial signatures are required. However, the literature seems to

J. Lladós and Y.-B. Kwon (Eds.): GREC 2003, LNCS 3088, pp. 154–165, 2004.
© Springer-Verlag Berlin Heidelberg 2004

be a bit poor in the field of vectorial signatures, although the use of signatures on this kind of document has an obvious interest. Indeed, systems based on signature techniques are generally fast, as they rely on relatively basic computations. Considering a raw vectorial description of the graphical layer of a technical document (e.g. a set of arcs and segments), signatures can be used to perform a pre-processing step before a "traditional" graphics recognition processing, this kind of methods being very time and CPU consuming in some cases. They can also be used to establish a classification that can be sufficient to feed a further indexation step.

In our knowledge, few papers present the use of vectorial signatures for recognition or discrimination needs. Approaches for iconic indexing in image databases in terms of a 2D string encoding can inspire the statement of vectorial signatures. It is the case in particular for the system of Huang[5] which improves the indexation of some large databases with this kind of techniques. These databases contain several thousands of pictures, composed of several basic distinct objects. One the one hand, each picture is indexed according to an object-oriented image knowledge structure called 2D C^+-string, which is computed with respect to 13 defined spatial relations between the objects of the images. The retrieval of a picture with this structure is then computed by a strings subsequence matching. However, this matching is time consuming as the retrieval involves the check of the string representing the query with each of the strings representing the pictures. So, on the other hand, some of the basic objects are chosen to be the keys used to build some signatures. The choice of these keys depends of the frequency of the objects occurrence in the database pictures. When a query occurs, the signature of the query is matched with the image signatures, which are then mapped to the corresponding 2D C^+-strings. This allows to decrease the complexity of the retrieval with respect to the straight retrieval based on 2D C^+-strings.

Ventura and Schettini [6] use vectorial signatures to directly recognize symbols. They work on technical documents created with CAD software. These documents are binarized, segmented (text/graphic and thick/thin lines), skeletonized and vectorized. From the thin segments resulting from the vectorization, they extract some features as the number of segments intersecting in one point, the acute angles between segments, the length... From the thick segments, they extract the area, the orientation and second order moments. All these features are combined to create symbols signatures. Signatures are then organized into a structured filter used for the recognition task. Two values are associated with each features of the signature: a tolerance threshold and a weight. A candidate symbol is then analyzed in the same way. Its signature is compared with the signatures of the symbols library. For each feature of the signatures, its value must be lower than the associated tolerance threshold. Then, each parameter is normalized using the weight, and the sum is compared to a global threshold. If the sum is lower than this threshold, the candidate matches the symbol.

Thus, even if few methods deal with vectorial signatures, it appears that they can be employed both for optimization and recognition purposes. The remainder of this paper is organized as follows. Section 2 presents the objectives of our method, the framework and the assumptions made. Section 3 describes how the vectorial signatures are computed from the vectorial description of an image. The implementation side of this method, giving some optimization tips, is studied in section 4. In section 5, we present how these signatures are used to discriminate symbols. Finally, results and perspectives are discussed in section 6.

2   Objectives and Framework

By considering vectorial signatures, our intention is not to deal with the hard problem of symbol recognition. It is essentially to discriminate symbols by a fast technique, rather than to recognize them, as this latter task can be approached by some well-known techniques in document analysis. The advantages of using vectorial signatures in the context of symbol recognition are twofold. First, it allows to reduce the computation time of the symbol recognition stage that usually is a time-consuming process. Second, it solves the symbol segmentation problem, i.e. sometimes the type of documents does not allow to segment symbols to their recognition because they appear embedded in the document. The vectorial signature allows to define regions of interest likely to be a given prototype symbol.

Few assumptions have been made, as our method intends to be as generic as possible. We consider the family of technical documents, which are essentially composed of graphical information. We especially work on a raw vectorial description of these documents, that is supposed to be a set of arcs and segments. It is also assumed that these documents usually include several representations of a predefined number of symbols, whose construction follows some structural rules. However, no assumption is made about possible transformations (rotation, scaling) between the symbols models and their instances in a document. Note that, as this paper describes a work in progress, the segments alone are considered in this paper.

3   Toward Vectorial Signatures

3.1   Introduction

A signature of an entity may be defined as a set of elementary features, containing intrinsically a discrimination potential. In some cases, this allows several entities to share the same signature, even if a unique signature for each entity is desirable. In the particular context of graphics recognition, a symbol signature is computed from the primitives composing the symbol (some pixels if one works on a bitmap image, or some vectorial primitives if the input data is a vectorial image). In our case, we work on the vectorial description of technical documents.

To compute vectorial signatures, we have based our approach on the method proposed by Etemadi et al. [7], who study spatial relations between primitives to solve a vision problem. The method starts by a study of basic relationship between pairs of lines. Several main relations are thus enumerated: collinearity, parallelism and intersections. For each of these relations, some extensions are considered, like overlapping for parallelism, or the kind of intersection point (lying on either, both or only one segment). By grouping these basic relations, the authors compute some higher level relations, expressing more symbolic relations between sets of segments. Thus, the approach is clearly hierarchical. The relations are associated with a quality factor, computed as a comparison between a given pair of segments and their grouping in an ideal case, and the method is invariant to affine transformations, like rotation, scaling or translation.

So, even if the method is designed for a computer vision purpose, a few assumptions are made on the segments and this method seems to be suitable for our needs.

3.2   Basic Features Computation

Our current work is based on this method. Of the seven proposed relations of the article, we consider only five (see the "Junction detection" section). These five types of relations express relationship between neighboring segments, and are computable with low requirements: parallelism with or without overlapping, collinearity, L junctions and V junctions, described below. These relations are successively studied in a way presented by the figure 1.

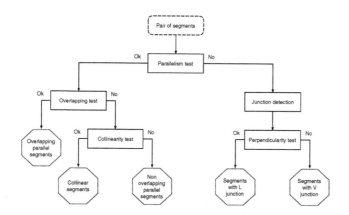

Fig. 1. Determination of the relationship between a pair of segments

Some of them require some thresholds, which are presented below:

– σ^θ is the threshold used to determine whether two segments are considered parallel (as well as not parallel). Thus, if the acute angle θ between two segments satisfies: $|\theta| < \sigma^\theta$, the two segments are considered as parallel. Note that, as mentioned by Etemadi et al. [7], there is no restriction for the choice of the threshold. Indeed, whatever the value, the parallelism relation, as it is defined, is consistent. This allows to tune this value, according to the quality of input graphical primitives, as well as the expected quality of the signatures.

- $\sigma_i^{\parallel}$, as introduced by Etemadi et al. is called the *standard deviation of the position of the end points of a segment S_i along its direction*. It allows to take into account the location uncertainties associated with the segment extraction process. In our case, this process is the vectorization, which delivers segments provided with their thickness (let T_i be this thickness for the segment S_i). As the vectorization step may cause junction misplacements, proportional to the thickness of the strokes, $\sigma_i^{\parallel}$ is defined as: $\sigma_i^{\parallel} = \left\lceil \frac{T_i}{2} + 1 \right\rceil$, where $\lceil \rceil$ expresses the rounded up notation.
- $\sigma_i^{\perp}$, as introduced by Etemadi et al. is called the *standard deviation of the position of the end points of a segment S_i perpendicular to its direction*. It corresponds to the maximum perpendicular distance allowed between S_i and another segment collinear to S_i. In this case, the tolerance has to be greater than in the precedent case, and $\sigma_i^{\perp}$ is defined as: $\sigma_i^{\perp} = \left\lceil \frac{T_i}{2} + 3 \right\rceil$.

Let us further describe the different types of relationships between pairs of segments. But before presenting them, we want to point out some useful remarks about the segments. In our analysis, segments result from a vectorization step[8] which delivers sometimes spurious short segments, especially whenever thick lines are present in the original document. These artifacts, as all short segments, are not considered in our method, as their consistency is very low. So we consider only segments larger than a given threshold (experimentally fixed to 10 pixels in our case) as input data of figure 1.

Parallelism Test. As said previously, if the acute angle between two segments is below the chosen threshold σ^{θ}, the segments are considered as *parallel*. Note that if this property is fulfilled, it does not ensure that a relation will be created between the segments. Indeed, according to the figure 1, some other tests have to be performed to determine what is the exact type of the relation, which will be finally created if the segments satisfy some quality requirements.

Overlapping Test. To perform this test between two segment S_1 and S_2, we first determine the virtual line VL lying between the two considered segments. Let L_i and θ_i be respectively the length and the orientation angle of S_i. The orientation angle θ_{VL} of the virtual line is computed as the weighted mean of the orientation of the two segments, as:

$$\theta_{VL} = \frac{L_1 \times \theta_1 + L_2 \times \theta_2}{L_1 + L_2}.$$

Let $M_i(x_i, y_i)$ be the midpoint of the segment S_i. The point $P(x_{VL}, y_{VL})$ through which the virtual line passes is defined by (see figure 2):

$$x_{VL} = \frac{L_1 \times x_1 + L_2 \times x_2}{L_1 + L_2} \quad \text{and} \quad y_{VL} = \frac{L_1 \times y_1 + L_2 \times y_2}{L_1 + L_2}.$$

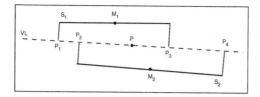

Fig. 2. Representation of the overlapping relation

Once the virtual line is computed, the points P_1, P_2, P_3 and P_4 can be computed by a perpendicular projection of the endpoints of S_1 and S_2 on the virtual line. From the virtual line, a virtual segment VS is defined as the longest segment that it is possible to define with the points P_1, P_2, P_3 and P_4 (which is $[P_1, P_4]$ on figure 2). Let L_{VS} be the length of the virtual segment VS, and L_{P_i} the projected length of the segment S_i on the virtual segment. Now, the two segments S_1 and S_2 are considered as *overlapping* segments if:

$$L_{VS} \le L_{P_1} + L_{P_2} + \sigma_1^{\|} + \sigma_2^{\|}.$$

The quality factor Q_{OVP} of the overlapping relation is obtained by computing:

$$Q_{OVP} = \frac{L_{P_1} + L_{P_2} - \sigma_1^{\|} - \sigma_2^{\|}}{2 \times L_{VS}}.$$

Thus, a perfect quality factor of 1 is obtained if the sum of the two projected length is equal to the double of the length of the virtual segment.

Collinearity Test. If a pair of segments are parallel without overlapping, these segments can be classified as non-overlapping parallel segments or collinear segments. According to the definition of $\sigma_i^{\perp}$, if the perpendicular distance between two segments S_1 and S_2 is greater than $\sigma_1^{\perp} + \sigma_2^{\perp}$, the segments are classified as non-overlapping parallel segments. Otherwise, they are classified as *collinear* segments. In both cases, the quality factor Q_{NOVP} is defined as:

$$Q_{NOVP} = \frac{L_{P_1} + L_{P_2} - \sigma_1^{\|} - \sigma_2^{\|}}{L_{VS}}.$$

Thus, a perfect quality factor of 1 for either a non-overlapping parallel or a collinear relation is obtained if the sum of the two projected length is equal to the length of the virtual segments.

Junction Detection. From a mathematical point of view, a pair of non-parallel segments is a pair of segments that intersect. In our case, we consider that a pair of segments intersect if the acute angle between them is equal to or greater than σ^{θ}. This threshold is the same as the one used to test the parallelism, in order to ensure the consistency between the different relationships.

As noticed previously, short segments are not considered in our analysis. But it appears that junctions are often represented after the vectorization step by a short segment joining 2 other segments. By choosing to not consider short segments, the junction between two segments may be lost, as well as the associated symbolic information. So, our approach is to make no difference between segments that really intersect (that share an endpoint) and segments that *virtually* intersect, even if we test the existence of a possible shared point in order to avoid useless computations. If no shared point is found, we compute the intersection point of the segments by extending the segments as shown on figure 3.

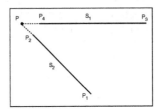

Fig. 2. Representation of the overlapping relation

We call P the intersection point between the two (virtually extended) segments. The quality factor Q_J is computed as follows:

$$Q_J = \frac{L_1 - \sigma_1^{\parallel} - \sigma_2^{\perp}}{L_{VL1}} \times \frac{L_2 - \sigma_2^{\parallel} - \sigma_1^{\perp}}{L_{VL2}}.$$

Thus, the more the segments are virtually extended, the more Q_V decreases. If only one segment (say L_1) has to be extended in order to find the intersection point, the quality factor Q_J is computed as:

$$Q_J = \frac{L_1 - \sigma_1^{\parallel} - \sigma_2^{\perp}}{L_{VL1}}.$$

This special case of intersection could produce some new types of relations. In particular, Etemadi et al. define two relations called λ and T junctions. But it appears that these relations do not represent relevant information when dealing with technical documents. Indeed, these relations are usually detected on special cases, corresponding to vectorization artifacts. Thus, for our needs, no discrimination potential is expressed by using them with technical documents. This is probably related to the processing chain which is different between computer vision and technical document analysis, and in particular to the way the chaining process deals with junction points. And anyway, even for Etemadi et al. few relations of these two types are found on their examples.

Perpendicular Test. Once the junction is computed, we classify it according to the acute angle between the two segments. If this angle is close to $\frac{\pi}{2}$, more or less σ^θ, we consider that the junction is perpendicular (*L junction*). Otherwise, the junction is classified as non-perpendicular (*V junction*).

Quality Factor. For each relation among the 5 types defined above (parallelism with or without overlapping, collinearity, L junctions and V junctions), a quality factor has been defined to express the pertinence of the relation (e.g. perfect overlapping for parallelism with overlapping). In order to keep only a set of relevant relations for the next steps, non-relevant relations, that is to say the relations whose the quality factor is lower than a fixed threshold Q_F, have to be pruned. The value of Q_F has to be fixed with care: choosing a too high value will result in few produced relations and choosing a too low value will result in too many produced relations. In both cases, the set of produced relations is not suitable enough to be used as a signature.

3.3   Clustering

Even if these basic relationships represent interesting discrimination features, more interesting ones can be computed by clustering the relations. Indeed, a cluster of relations of the same type is more symbolic and relevant than the same set of individual relations. So, once all the basic relations are computed, and are pruned using the quality factor, a simple clustering is performed. The *signature* of an entity is then defined as the set of clustered features and unclustered relations found in that entity. For the purpose of symbol discrimination, two kinds of entities are handled: the references symbols, cropped directly from an image (see section 5 for details) and the buckets of a test image (see section 4 for more explanations about buckets). Briefly, these buckets can be defined as small rectangular parts of the test image.

Considering all the relations of an entity, the relations of the same type are incrementally clustered. Starting from a relation of a type $\mathcal{T}$, containing two segments S_1 and S_2, we search for the relations where either S_1 or S_2 is a part of another relation of the same type $\mathcal{T}$. All the relations satisfying this constraint are then merged into a new cluster. The process is iterated, considering the new set of relations of the current cluster, until no more relation can be added to this cluster. No new quality factor is computed for the clusters, as the relations of the clusters have already been filtered using a quality factor, and as the matching step essentially lies in an inclusion test (see section 5).

4   Implementation Side

In our case, implementation is very important as the method has to be very time-efficient in order to be as interesting as possible. Remember that one of the main application is to constitute a pre-processing step before a "traditional" recognition step. In this case, the time spent with the signature system must be less important than the same recognition system without signatures.

So, if the method and the algorithms are naturally important, so is the implementation. We have chosen to implement the signature system with C++ and the STL, known to be very efficient development tools. One of the most time expensive step in the method described above is the computation of neighboring relations. Without any particular data structure, this computation for n segments leads to $\frac{n^2-3n-2}{2}$ computations. To reduce the complexity, we use a bucket structure, which allows just to locally study the relationship between pairs of segments. This kind of technique is used for example in [9].

This technique, very basic, consists in a decomposition of the image in several non overlapping tiles. The graphical primitives are then stored in these buckets, and relationships are only computed between the primitives of a bucket and the primitives of its neighboring buckets. As the objective of signature is to discriminate symbols, the size of the buckets can be based on the size of the biggest symbol available. Let m be the number of buckets. Depending on the repartition of the graphical primitives on the image, the complexity can be reduced to $\frac{n^2-mn-m^2}{2}$ computations (considering an homogeneous distribution). As a typical example, a bitmap image of 1685×1583 pixels is converted into 450 segments and is decomposed with 256 buckets, decreasing the number of computations by a factor of 10.

We plan to use a more sophisticated bucket structure, as the ones described in [10] for example, in order to decrease the complexity more significantly.

5   Discrimination Using Symbol Signatures

These signatures are used in the following way. Using the method described above, we compute the signature of all symbols we can find in a given document. The resulting signatures are stored in a symbol library. The representation of each symbol is actually directly cropped from an original document – that is to say we do not use ideal models for symbol representation (see figure 4 for examples). The underlying idea is to allow a user to select an area from a document including a symbol, from which all symbols having the same representation are found. Also, the vectorized representations of the reference symbols have to be built with the same processes as the test images, in order to reproduce the same

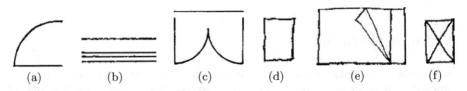

(a)   (b)   (c)   (d)   (e)   (f)

Fig. 4. Examples of reference symbols, cropped directly from an architectural drawing. (a) A door. (b) A window. (c) A French window. (d) A table. (e) A bed. (f) Another kind of table

artifacts, and then similar signatures. The number and the type of the relations found for each symbols of figure 4 are presented in table 1.

Table 1. Number of relations found per type from the symbols of figure 4, using a quality factor equal to 0.5. Note that the symbols have been vectorized before the computation of the relations

Symbol	Overlap. Paral.	Non overlap. paral.	Collinear	L junction	V junction
(a)	1	0	0	0	4
(b)	6	0	0	0	0
(c)	3	1	0	8	10
(d)	2	0	0	4	0
(e)	6	4	2	10	15
(f)	2	3	0	4	12

Then, considering the vectorial representation of a test image, the corresponding graphical primitives (segments) are stored in buckets, whose size is set to half the size of the biggest symbol available. The signature of each bucket is computed, determined by the set of relations found in it. As for the symbols signatures, a quality factor is used to prune the relations whose relevance is too low. The signatures of the buckets are then matched against the symbols signatures to determine what kind of symbols a bucket is likely to contain.

The matching is implemented as an inclusion test. For the signature of a given bucket, the signature of each reference symbol is considered. The signature of a reference symbol S is included in the signature of the bucket B if:

- Each basic (individual) relation of S matches a distinct basic relation of B of the same type.
- Each clustered relation $\mathcal{R}_S$ of S matches a distinct clustered relation $\mathcal{R}_B$ of B of the same type, containing *at least* as much relations as in $\mathcal{R}_S$.

In these rules, "distinct" means that a given relation of the bucket can be matched with at most one relation of the studied symbol. If this inclusion test succeeds, the signature of the bucket contains the signature of the symbol, and thus the bucket is likely to contain the symbol.

The first tests are encouraging, even if we consider only a minimal set of features to compute the signatures. The figure 5 presents results obtained from a vectorial representation of an architectural drawing, with a symbol library containing symbols (a), (b) and (c) of the figure 4. In this figure, the areas of interest (buckets), determining the potential presence of architectural symbols (doors, windows...), are presented by a box containing the name of the symbol(s) detected. Some comments about these results are:

- All symbols are detected with the good type, except a window at the bottom right.

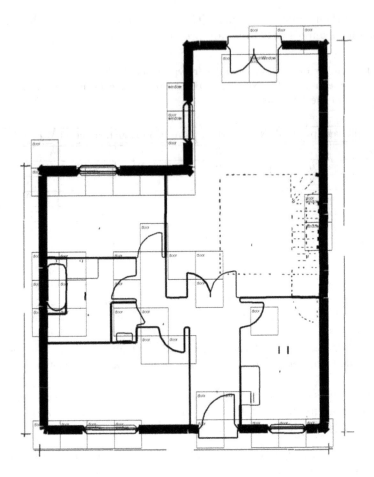

Fig. 5. Some results obtained by vectorial signatures computation on an architectural drawing. The areas of interest, determining the potential presence of architectural symbols (doors, windows...), are presented by a box containing the name of the symbol(s) detected

- A lot of false alarms are present, especially with symbols not present in the library (like the bathtub) and with corners that, after the vectorization, have a representation close to the representation of the doors.
- Symbols containing some arcs (typically, doors) often lead to non relevant signatures, depending on the way the arcs are approximated during the vectorization step.
- Since reference symbols have small dimensions, the length of some segments resulting from the vectorization is lower than 10 pixels. It distorts the resulting set of relations.

6 Conclusion and Further Work

As said previously, this paper describes a work in progress, and a lot of improvements can be done. We plan to improve the management of neighboring relations, in particular the definition and the use of buckets, as the speed is a critical aspect of the process. It appears also obvious that arcs have to be taken into account to avoid some of these false alarms and that we have to work with a vectorization which delivers segments with more accurate locations. We also work on a better definition of the relations, including width of primitives, arity of primitives, more sophisticated possibilities of clustering... Few symbols have been considered during our tests. If the number of symbols grows, it may also be interesting to "organize" the symbols signatures, e.g. in a hierarchical way, in order to optimize the matching step.

We wish to point out that most of the work needed to compute the relations could be done in a previous process (e.g. vectorization step), making this method even faster. Finally, as claimed in the introduction of this paper, we have to measure the potential use of this method to improve a technical document recognition chain. All implementations have been realized using the Qgar software package, available at http://www.qgar.org.

References

1. Rothe, I., Susse, H., Voss, K.: The Method of Normalization to Determine Invariants. IEEE Transactions on PAMI **18** (1996) 366–379.
2. Teh, C., Chin, R.T.: On Image analysis by the method of Moments. IEEE Transactions on PAMI **10** (1988) 496–513.
3. Belkasim, S.O., Shridar, M.Ahmadi, M.: Pattern Recognition with Moment Invariants: A Comparative Study and New Results. Pattern Recognition **24** (1991) 1117–1138.
4. Taxt, T., Olafsdottir, J.B., Daehlen, M.: Recognition of Handwritten Symbols. Pattern Recognition **23** (1990) 1155–1166.
5. Huang, P.: Indexing Picture by Key Objects for Large-Scale Image Databases.Pattern Recognition **30** (1997) 1229–1237.
6. Ventura, A.D., Schettini, R.: Graphic Symbol Recognition using a Signature Technique. In: Proceedings of the 12th International Confrence on Pattern Recognition, Jerusalem(Israek). Volume 2 (1994) 533–535.
7. Etemadi, A., Schmidt, J.P., Matas, G., Illingworth, J., Kittler, J.: Lowlevel Grouping of Straight Line Segments. In: Proceedings of Second British Machine Vision Confrence, Glasgow, Scotland. (1991) 118–126.
8. Tombre, K., Ah-Soon, C., Dosch, P., Masini, G., Tabbone, S.: Stable and Robust Vectorization: How to Make the Right Choices. In Chhabra, A.K., Dori, D., eds.: Graphics Recognition—Recent Advances.Volume 1941 of Lecture Notes in Computer Science. Springer-Verlag (2000) 3–18.
9. Bolles, R.C., Cain, R.A.: Recognising and Locating Partially Visible Objects: the Local-Feature-Focus Method. In Pugh, A., ed.: Robot Vision. Springer-Verlag, Berlin (1983) 43–82.
10. Samet, H.: The Design and Analysis of Spatial Data Structures. Addison-Wesley, Reading, MA (1990).

Syntactic Models to Represent Perceptually Regular Repetitive Patterns in Graphic Documents

Gemma Sánchez and Josep Lladós

Computer Vision Center, Dept. Informàtica. Universitat Autònoma de Barcelona,
08193 Bellaterra (Barcelona), Spain
{gemma, josep}@cvc.uab.es
http://www.cvc.uab.es

Abstract. In this paper we propose syntactical models to represent repetitive regular structures in graphical documents. We refer to these structures as texture symbols and they usually contain hatched or tiled patterns. Our grammar-based models can be automatically inferred from the document and used as signatures to describe salient features consisting of regular repetitions of primitives. These signatures compactly describe texture symbols and its primitives can be used for indexing purposes. We describe different models suitable for a number of patterns. Particularly, a linear grammar to describe hatched patterns and a plex grammar and a graph grammar for different types of tiled patterns.

1 Introduction

Symbol recognition is a classical activity in the field of graphics recognition. From a general point of view symbol recognition aims to identify and localize graphical structures with a particular meaning in the domain where they appear. We can distinguish two major research trends in the symbol recognition problem. The first one consists in solving the usual classification problem, i.e. classifying an unknown pattern in a class by comparing it with a set of prototype symbols from a library. A literature review of symbol recognition methods can be found in [1]. The second trend focuses on a more novel paradigm, indexing in graphic documents. Retrieval from document databases has used to be formulated in terms of textual information. On the other hand, in Computer Vision, the task of retrieving images by content from databases is formulated in terms of visual cues such as color, shape or texture. If we try to translate these ideas to the Graphics Recognition world, symbol recognition plays an important role. Thus, indexing in documents by graphical content, either for retrieving or browsing purposes, requires to deal with graphic signatures. Symbol signatures are used to formulate graphical queries to index in a document database. However, other scenarios does not require previously defined symbol descriptors but they are directly inferred from unstructured documents. An example is a service for browsing large graphical documents in terms of graphical structures present in it. In this kind of applications, symbol signatures are computed

J. Lladós and Y.-B. Kwon (Eds.): GREC 2003, LNCS 3088, pp. 166–175, 2004.

from low level document primitives, building a higher level semantical layer that describes common substructures. It can be seen as a coarse-to-fine structuring hierarchy from lower level primitives (pixels, lines, arcs, regions) to higher level structures (symbol signatures).To see a recent survey of such a paradigm see [2].

This paper is concerned on the symbol indexing paradigm. We propose syntactical models that can be used as signatures for a particular class of symbols that consist of regular repetitive patterns. Our framework deals with line drawings represented according to a vectorial format. Indexing and browsing such type of documents requires the definition of signatures formulated in terms of geometric and relational information among primitives. In the formulation of our syntactical models for symbol description Perceptual Organization (PO) plays an important role. PO operates at the intermediate vision level to identify some particular emergent patterns that are used in end tasks as indexing and recognition. Recently, Saund et al. [3] studied the application of the PO framework to the field of Graphics Recognition. In this work they noticed that PO allows to extract salient patterns with weak prior models and also to represent them compactly making explicit many of their features. The syntactic models presented in this paper pursue these goals.

Symbol signatures can be formulated in terms of *proximity, continuation*, and *parallelism* of primitives [4]. In this work, we focus on repetitive regular structures, i.e. structured textures, as salient patterns to be identified in a graphic document. It would allow to browse from a database those documents containing for example a *hatching* or a *tiled* pattern. Since a structured texture can be described as a set of primitives regularly arranged following some placement rules, we use a syntactic formalism as signature. Grammars are a suitable tool to represent repetitive structures in graphic documents, either linear structures, as dashed lines [5], or bi-dimensional structures, as tiled patterns [6, 7]. In this paper we describe different grammatical models at different levels of complexity as signatures of bi-dimensional repetitive structures. We will refer to these structures as *texture symbols*. All proposed models are formulated in terms of the primitives that are repeated and the placement rules that define their regular repetition.

Assuming that documents have been vectorized, we use a two-level attributed graph representation. In the first level, graph nodes represent characteristic points and graph edges represent lines after being them polygonally approximated. The second level graph is computed from the former one and is a Region Adjacency Graph (RAG) in which RAG nodes represent closed loops (regions) of the first level graphs and graph edges represent neighboring relationships between regions. Starting from a graph representation, a graph clustering approach allows to find classes of primitives candidate to belong to a structured texture. Afterwards, for those primitives in the same class, regular structural relationships are also found. It means that the detection of a regular repetitive structure actually involves two clustering processes depending whether the elements that are clustered are document primitives or relationships. In our models we use two kind of primitives: straight lines (first level graph edges) are used as salient features for hatched patterns, and regions (second level graph nodes) are considered as primitives for tiled patterns. Once structured texture patterns have been detected, a grammar-based representation is inferred to compactly represent and recognize them in terms of a parsing process.

The remainder of this paper is organized as follows. First we describe syntactic models to represent repetitive structures. Particularly, we describe a simple linear grammar to describe hatched patterns (section 2). Afterwards we propose two types of grammars to represent bi-dimensional repetitive structures, namely a plex grammar (section 3.1) and a graph grammar (section 3.2). To illustrate the suitability of these models in retrieving and browsing frameworks, we briefly describe in section 4 how grammars can be inferred from a given document or drive an indexing process. Finally, section 5 is devoted to conclusions.

2   A Linear Grammar for Hatched Patterns

Hatched patterns are usual structures in graphic documents. A hatched pattern can be defined as a sequence of straight lines placed at regular intervals. In [8] we proposed a Hough based approach applied on an attributed graph that segments hatched regions from the input document. The main idea is to map each pair of parallel straight edges to a parameter space defined in terms of edge orientation and distance between them. Peaks in the parameter space characterize hatched patterns. Once hatched patterns have been detected, they can be represented by a string consisting of straight lines and concatenation operations. The model for valid strings can be formulated in terms of a linear grammar $G = (S, N, T, P)$ where N is the nonterminal alphabet $N = \{S, H_1, H_2, H_3, H_4, H_5\}$, T is the terminal alphabet $T = \{l, +, <, (,)\}$, and P is the set of productions:

$$S \rightarrow H_1,$$
$$H_1 \rightarrow H_2 H_3,$$
$$H_3 \rightarrow \text{`` + ''} H_2 H_3 | \lambda$$
$$H_2 \rightarrow H_4 H_5$$
$$H_5 \rightarrow \text{`` < ''} H_4 H_5 | \lambda$$
$$H_4 \rightarrow l | \text{``(''} H_1 \text{'')''}$$

The terminal symbols $<, + \in T$ represent concatenation operators in the following way: The symbol $<$ concatenates either two consecutive lines or two hatched patterns of the same class. The symbol $+$ concatenates either two colinear lines or two hatched patterns of the same class. Figure 1 shows a hatched pattern and its corresponding string defined in terms of concatenating lines and hatched substructures according to the above operators.

3   Grammars to Represent Tiled Patterns

A tiled pattern is formed by one or several kinds of shapes, called primitives, placed following a placement rule. This structure can be represented by a grammar. In this section we describe a plex grammar and a graph grammar as models to represent tiled patterns.

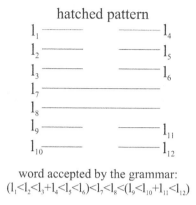

word accepted by the grammar:
$(l_1<l_2<l_3+l_4<l_5<l_6)<l_7<l_8<(l_9<l_{10}+l_{11}<l_{12})$

Fig. 1. A hatched pattern and the corresponding string

3.1   Plex Grammar

Plex grammars are a class of one-dimensional grammars that allow to represent bidimensional structures [9]. The main idea is to define a terminal alphabet consisting of a set of primitives that have n connection points. Thus, plex productions define how to combine these primitives through the corresponding connection points. The structure generated by applying a plex rule is called *plex structure* and the production also involves the definition of connecting points for this structure through which it can be connected to other ones. We propose a plex grammar as first approach to modelize tiled patterns. The main idea is that a plex structure is a set of primitives (tiles) already connected and the plex productions define how a new primitive can be connected to the plex structure through the corresponding boundary edges. This idea does not completely fit with the basic plex grammar definition. Thus, a standard plex grammar considers a fixed number of connecting points for each plex structure. We modify the standard plex grammar definition by adding the possibility of defining an incremental set of connection points in each new generated plex structure. The ordered list of connection points of the generated structure is created by deleting from the plex substructure the points used to connect with the new primitive and adding to the list the points of the primitive which are not connected. This process generates as connection points of the plex structure the list of points of its periphery.

An illustrative example of our plex grammar model is shown in Figs. 2 and 3. Figure 2, presents a texture symbol formed by squares. Let A be the primitive element forming a texture symbol. It can be connected to another one by one of its edges. Then the list $a_1, \ldots, a_n$ represents the sequence of connecting points of A, where a_i are its edges in clockwise sense. A plex structure is described as $R(r_1, \ldots, r_m)$, where R is an identifier and $r_1, \ldots, r_m$ is the list of connection points defined as the edges in its periphery. The grammar defines the productions to generate plex structures by connecting substructures and primitives. A production describes how to concatenate a given plex structure Q and a primitive A to generate a new plex structure R. It is represented as

Fig. 2. Texture symbol formed by squares

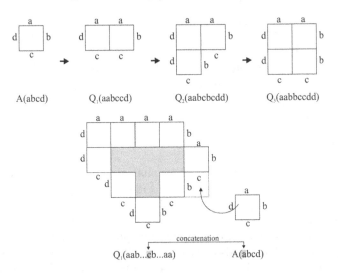

Fig. 3. Creation of the texture symbol of Fig. 2 by concatenation of plex structures

$R(w_1^Q, w_2^A, w_1^A, w_2^Q) \rightarrow Q(w_1^Q, q, w_2^Q)A(w_1^A, a, w_2^A)$, where q and a are the edges connecting Q and A respectively, and w_1^Q, w_2^Q, w_1^A and w_2^A are the sublists of connecting points of Q and A respectively which are not used in the connection.

Given a primitive shape A with n connection points, the plex grammar has one production for each configuration that allows to connect A to one existing plex substructure. So it is necessary one production for each edge forming A. The context where a connection point appears has to be taken into account, that is the predecessors and successors in the connection list. For example, Fig. 3 presents a general case where the plex structure Q by the edge c is connected to the primitive shape A by the point a. The local configuration of c in Q makes that when it is connected to A, the successor of c in Q, i.e. b, must be connected to the predecessor of a in A, i.e. d. In general, for each edge a_i, $i = 1, ..., n$, of a primitive A, the following productions are defined:

- $R(w_1^Q, w_2^A, w_1^A, w_2^Q) \rightarrow Q(w_1^Q, a_i, w_2^Q)A(w_1^A, \overline{a_i}, w_2^A)$
- $R(w_1^Q, w_2^A, w_1^A, w_2^Q) \rightarrow Q(w_1^Q, a_{i+1}, a_i, w_2^Q)A(w_1^A, \overline{a_i}, \overline{a_{i+1}}, w_2^A)$
- $R(w_1^Q, w_2^A, w_1^A, w_2^Q) \rightarrow Q(w_1^Q, a_i, a_{i-1}, w_2^Q)A(w_1^A, \overline{a_{i-1}}, \overline{a_i}, w_2^A)$
- $R(w_1^Q, w_2^A, w_1^A, w_2^Q) \rightarrow Q(w_1^Q, a_{i+1}, a_i, a_{i-1}, w_2^Q)A(w_1^A, \overline{a_{i-1}}, \overline{a_i}, \overline{a_{i+1}}, w_2^A)$

where $\overline{a_i}$ represents the complementary edge of a_i, i.e. the edge to which a_i can be connected. The four rules are graphically presented in Fig. 4. This example shows four possibilities of connection for the primitive A by the edge a to a plex substructure Q by the edge c. They are derived by taking into account whether the previous or the following point in the list are connected or not. The grammar can be generalized to any texture symbol generated by connecting regular polygonal shapes.

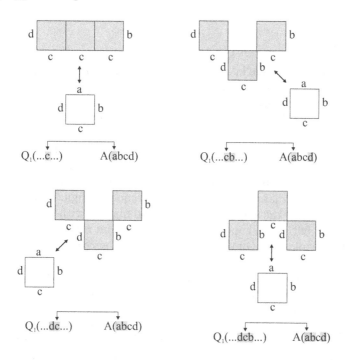

Fig. 4. Generation of a texture symbol by connecting plex structures

3.2   Graph Grammar

As it is explained in section 1 a document is represented by a graph whose nodes are regions and its edges relations among them. A texture symbol is defined by one or more kind of regions with certain neighborhoods. Then a texture symbol is represented by a graph grammar that represent all the graphs that follow this structure, and thus all the possible occurrences of this symbol. This grammar defines which kind of shapes are forming the symbol and also which kind of relations exist among them. The relations are defined by the segments connecting the centroids of two neighboring shapes.

Let us explain the model of a graph grammar $G(\Sigma, \Delta, \Omega, P, S)$ following the inference and parsing processes of the grammar presented in Fig. 6, that corresponds to the texture symbol in Fig. 5. The process starts defining the sets of terminal Σ and non-terminal node labels Δ, defining one terminal node label and one non-terminal node label for each kind of primitive shape forming the symbol. For the sake of simplicity, in this example we have only rectangles. Then

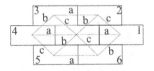

Fig. 5. Texture symbol

the sets are defined as $\Sigma = \{r\}$ and $\Delta = \{R, S'\}$, that has also the start symbol S'. The set of terminal edge labels Ω is constructed generating one for each kind of neighborhood, $\Omega = \{a, b, c\}$. One production $P = (h_l, h_r, T)$, is defined with its left and right subgraphs, h_l and h_r respectively, and its embedding rule T. The idea is to start the generation or recognition of a texture symbol with one node representing one of the primitives forming the symbol. Then to apply the start production associated with this primitive and to mark its neighbors with the non-terminal labels associated with the shape they are representing. The process continues by applying, to each node marked with a non-terminal label, the production that matches with its neighborhood configuration. At the end, all the nodes forming the symbol are visited and marked with the terminal node label associated with the shape it is representing, and the process stops. For a more extended explanation of the definition and inference of this graph grammar for texture symbols see [7].

In the example of Fig. 5 the start production I is defined with its h_l having one node, node 1, labeled as S'. Its h_r is a subgraph having one node, node $1'$, in the middle labeled with r, and having all its six neighbors around labeled as R. For each neighbor we have all the closed cycles starting in r and their edges labeled with their terminal labels a, b, c. Then we define the different sets of productions, from II to IV, from V to VII, from VIII to X, from XI to XIII, and from XIV to XVI, considering R to have 1, 2, 3 and 4 terminal neighbors respectively. To define the first set, we generate one rule for each kind of neighboring that R can have. For example in production II we consider the two relations a, in III the $b's$ and in IV the $c's$. The production II is defined having as h_l a graph with the node 1, labeled as R, then a terminal neighbor, node 7, following the neighborhood a, is defined with the neighbors it shared with R, that is the nodes 2, and 6, and labeled as non-terminals, and then all the edges connecting nodes 1, 2, 6 and 7. Then h_r is defined by copying h_l and substituting the numbers q over the nodes by q', then we have the embedding defined as $\{(1, 1'), (2, 2'), (6, 6'), (7, 7')\}$, then we copy all the edges defined in h_l, and we change the label R from node $1'$ by the terminal label r, and we add all the neighbors of $1'$ that are missed in the subgraph h_l, that is the nodes $3', 4'$, and $5'$, and the edges connecting them. In that way we generate productions from II to IV. Then in production V we consider the same kind of neighborhood as in production II, i.e. a, but now instead of having only one terminal node 7 we have also the next one, that is the node 2 and the neighbors that both shared with node 1, that is the nodes 3 and 6. The rest of the process is as before, and in that way we generate the rest of the sets considering from two to six

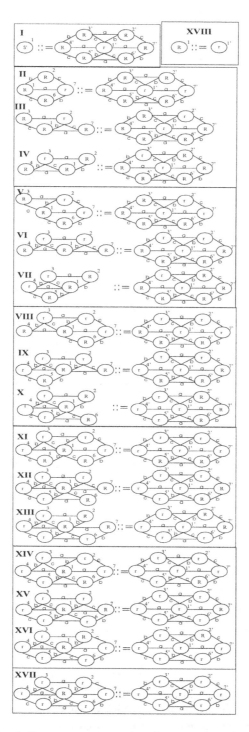

Fig. 6. Graph Grammar representing the texture symbol of Fig. 5

terminal neighbors. At the end we define the production XVII having all the six neighbors labeled as terminal nodes, and the last production XVIII having one node labeled as R in h_l, and changing R by r in h_r.

4 Using Grammars for Browsing and Retrieving

In the above sections we have proposed different grammatical models as signatures to compactly represent texture symbols. Nevertheless those modelizations are the focus of this paper, in this section we will overview the framework in which such grammatical models are useful as symbol signatures.

Some information systems do not require a matching between a library of model symbols and the document but to add a layer of knowledge to unstructured documents. This layer can then be used to build indexes for browsing or organizing these documents in large document databases. The grammatical models proposed in this paper can represent part of such knowledge layer and the task of building it involves a grammatical inference from low level primitives. In [7] we proposed an inference strategy to build graph grammars from regular repetitive structures.

Once they are inferred, grammars can also be used in an indexing process. This process should follow a parsing procedure. However a parsing procedure directly applied on a large graphic document is a computationally hard process. For that reason, we extract indices from the document, seen as hashing structures, that allow the parsing to focus only on certain primitives. Given a query texture symbol, a coarse-to-fine approach is performed to index into graphic documents. First, given a graphic document represented as a graph structure, descriptors consisting in graphic primitives that are likely to produce texture symbols are extracted and used as indices. Thus, straight lines are clustered in terms of orientation and proximity and graph regions are clustered in terms of area and shape. Each class of similar primitives is represented by a representative. See [8] and [10] respectively for further details on these processes. We have to notice that this process is made off-line, i.e. clusters of similar primitives are extracted prior to the parsing. Given a texture symbol to recognize, its constituent primitives are compared with representatives of primitive classes of the document. Only those primitives of the input document similar to constituent primitives of the query texture symbol remain in the graph that is used for the second step. Afterwards, in a second step, the remaining primitive descriptors are parsed using the grammar that defines the query texture symbol.

5 Conclusions and Discussion

Indexing in graphic documents requires the use of features in terms of which formulate queries. These features are usually associated to different types of emergent patterns consisting of colinearities, parallelisms, symmetries, repetitions, etc. In this paper we have focused on texture symbols, defined as regular repetitions of primitives that are used as indices. We have proposed different grammars to represent texture symbols. First, a linear grammar have been described to modelize hatched patterns. Second, two types of grammars, a plex and a graph grammar, have been proposed for tiled patterns. The main advantage of such models is that they can be automatically inferred and they can represent a wide range of patterns in a compact way. The three proposed grammars are at increasing levels of complexity but also of representational power. Thus, a graph grammar allows to represent the patterns accepted by the other two but it is at the highest level of complexity. For that reason, we have proposed an indexing schema that allows to reduce the parsing space to which the grammar is applied. However, in [10] we demonstrated that, with some constraints, the inference and the parsing processes for such a grammar con be computed in a near polynomial time.

Acknowledgements

This work has been partially supported by the spanish projects CICYT TIC2000-0382 and TIC2003-09291.

References

1. Lladós, J., Valveny, E., Sánchez, G., Martí, E.: Symbol recognition: Current advances and perspectives. In Blostein, D., Kwon, Y., eds.: Graphics Recognition: Algorithms and Applications. Springer, Berlin (2002) 104–127 Vol. 2390 of LNCS.
2. Tombre, K., Lamiroy, B.: Graphics recognition: from re-engineering to retrieval. In: Proceedings of 7th Int. Conf. on Document Analysis and Recognition. (2003) 148–155 Edinburgh, Scotland.
3. Saund, E., Mahoney, J., Fleet, D., Larner, D.: Perceptual organization as a foundation for graphics recognition. In Blostein, D., Kwon, Y., eds.: Graphics Recognition: Algorithms and Applications. Springer, Berlin (2002) 139–147 Vol. 2390 of LNCS.
4. Lorenz, O., Monagan, G.: Automatic indexing for storage and retrieval of line drawings. In: Storage and Retrieval for Image and Video Databases (SPIE). (1995) 216–227
5. Jonk, A., van den Boomgaard, Smeulders, A.: Grammatical inference of dashed lines. Computer Vision and Image Understanding **74** (1999) 212–226
6. Matsuyama, T., Saburi, K., Nagao, M.: A structural analyzer for regularly arranged textures. Computer Graphics and Image Processing **18** (1982) 259–278
7. Sánchez, G., Lladós, J.: A graph grammar to recognize textured symbols. In: Proceedings of 6th Int. Conf. on Document Analysis and Recognition. (2001) 465–469 Seattle, USA.
8. Lladós, J., Martí, E., López-Krahe, J.: A Hough-based method for hatched pattern detection in maps and diagrams. In: Proceedings of 5th Int. Conf. on Document Analysis and Recognition. (1999) 479–482 Bangalore, India.
9. Bunke, H.: String grammars for syntactic pattern recognition. In Bunke, H., Sanfeliu, A., eds.: Syntactic and Structural Pattern Recognition. Theory and Applications. World Scientific Publishing Company (1990) 29–54
10. Sánchez, G.: Un modelo sintáctico para la representación, segmentación y reconocimiento de símbolos texturados en documentos gráficos. PhD thesis, Universitat Autònoma de Barcelona and Université Henri Poincaré - Nancy 1 (2001)

Indexing Technical Symbols Using Ridgelets Transform

Oriol Ramos Terrades* and Ernest Valveny**

Computer Vision Center
Dept. Informàtica, Universitat Autònoma de Barcelona,
EdificiO - Campus UAB,
08193 Bellaterra, Spain
{oriolrt, ernest}@cvc.uab.es

Abstract. This paper presents a new use of the Ridgelets Transform as a multiscale method for indexing linear symbols in graphic documents. The Ridgelets Transform is useful to detect linear singularities in images. Therefore, it can be used to get a good representation of linear symbols. Moreover, as it belongs to the Wavelet family, this representation can be useful at several scales of detail. Thus, the proposed scheme targets to detect linear singularities at different scales, using the Ridgelets properties to group similar symbols at rough scales. In this way, we can use Ridgelets representation when searching in large symbol databases by finding similar symbols at rough scales and discriminating them at finer scales.

Keywords: Graphics Recognition, Indexing Technical Drawings, Ridgelets Transform

1 Introduction

In this paper, we present the ridgelets transform, belonging to the wavelets transform family, as a useful technic for indexing linear symbols in graphic documents. Some properties of this transform, such as coefficient sparsity, distinguish it from usual separate wavelets (Haar, Daubechies, Meyer,...) [9]. Roughly speaking, the ridgelets transform is an usual wavelet transform, using Meyer and Meyer-Lemarié basis, but applied to a Radon image of the symbol. Existing theory [4] assure us the completeness of this representation, i.e. any intensity image can be decomposed uniquely in an orthonormal ridgelets basis. In addition, due to the coefficients sparsity, images with singularities along straight lines provoke high coefficients around line parameters (θ, t) while far from these points, the ridgelets response is lower (near 0) giving us a good representation scheme and a high discrimination power between symbols, in particular when symbols are essentially composed of straight lines, as is the case of graphic documents.

This transform offers a mathematical background where Hough-Radon based technics, used in several approaches for symbol indexing and retrieval [5,11],

---

* Supported by DURSI. Generalitat de Catalunya.
** Partially supported by CICYT TIC2000-0382, Spain.

J. Lladós and Y.-B. Kwon (Eds.): GREC 2003, LNCS 3088, pp. 176–187, 2004.

fusion with the wavelet theory. In addition, the ridgelets transform introduces a multiresolution representation for symbols by decomposing the Radon space into separate subspaces corresponding to different scales, or resolutions. In figure 1 we can see two different symbols and their ridgelets decomposition at three different scales. We can observe how almost all image is white (corresponding to 0) while in angles 0, $\pi/2$, π, $3/2\pi$, 2π radians, we have high response of ridgelets transform, corresponding to line contour localization. At the finest scale we can distinguish different coefficients for all contour lines, whereas at coarsest scales, coefficients corresponding to nearby lines collapse to a single point.

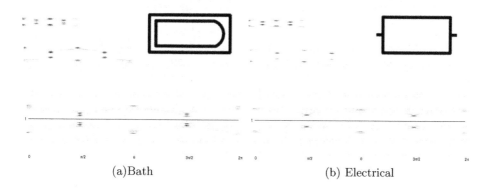

(a)Bath   (b) Electrical

Fig. 1. Symbols and their Ridgelets Coefficients

We can use this multiresolution representation in order to reduce data size and to save time derived from computing distance measures between symbols. Coarsest scales may allow us to unify different models' representations in a same cluster. Then, we propose to use coarsest scales to filter out similar symbols in large symbol databases, while discrimination will be carried out using the representation at finer scales depending on the desired detail level. In such way, we propose a classification algorithm which takes advantage of ridgelets decomposition into different detail levels, by grouping similar symbols at each level.

This paper is structured as follows. In section 2, we briefly summarize the ridgelets transform, its properties and some implementation details. For then, in section 3 we will explain how we have structured ridgelets coefficients in order to make the representation invariant to similarities and facilitate the design of a multiscale clustering algorithm, in section 4. Finally, in sections 5 and 6, we discuss some experiments and state some conclusions.

2   The Ridgelets Transform

The Ridgelets transform was first defined by Candès [3]. It is a family of non-separated wavelets defined as follows. Let ψ be a wavelet. For each positive a, any $t \in \mathbb{R}$ and $\theta \in [0, 2\pi)$, we define $\psi_{a,t,\theta} : \mathbb{R}^2 \to \mathbb{R}^2$ as:

$$\psi_{a,t,\theta}(x, y) = a^{-1/2}\psi((x \cos\theta + y \sin\theta - t)/a).$$

This function is constant along lines $x\cos\theta + y\sin\theta = t$ and transverse to the "ridges" - lines -, it is a wavelet. Then, the continuous Ridgelets transform of a function f is defined as:

$$\mathcal{R}f_\psi(a,t,\theta) = \int f(x,y)\bar{\psi}_{a,t,\theta}(x,y)dxdy \tag{1}$$

This transform has good properties such as the existence of orthonormal basis [4] and coefficient sparsity. In relation to this, higher coefficients will be concentrated around the parameters θ and t corresponding to longer lines. Thus, sparsity permits us to localize and to separate line singularities into the parameter space. This is the main property that distinguish this wavelet from usual separate wavelets (Haar, Daubechies, Meyer,...) [9].

Thanks to the algorithm developed by Flesia et al. [6], we can decompose any intensity image, f, in its ridgelets coefficients, computing it in a fast way. First we compute the Radon transform of f, using a modified version of Fast Slant Stack algorithm, FSS [8]. The FSS, introduced by Averbuch, is based on the Slice Projection theorem and it is computed using essentially fourier transforms. Then, considering Meyer and Lemarié-Meyer wavelets in slice and angular parameters, respectively, we decompose the Radon transform of f in its wavelets coefficients. In such way, we have obtained a four indexed family of ridgelets, $WRf_{j,k}[n,m]$.

3   Symbol Representation

By $WRf_{j,k}[n,m]$ we denote the ridgelets coefficients, where each couple (j,k) corresponds to different scale parameters in the standard two dimensional discrete wavelet transform. Thus, $WRf_{j,k}$ is a matrix of coefficients. We will use all these matrix of coefficients for all pairs (j,k) to get a multiscale representation of a symbol.

First of all, let's recall that there is a relationship between the size of an image and the number of couples (j,k). Each time the size of an image is doubled a new range of couples (j,k), like the shaded band in figure 2, appears. Therefore, any representation and classification scheme must be consistent with these ranges. We bunch couples (j,k) in sets, $\{I_s\}_{s=0,...,\infty}$, indexed from 0 to infinity. We will refer to each of these sets by the term "level". In this way, in figure 2, when we say: "Coefficients corresponding to level $s = 2$"; we mean the set composed of the image coefficients ranged from $7 = (s+1)s+1$ to $12 = 7+2(s+1)-1$. At each "level", we will take coefficients in all pairs (j,k) in it as the representation of the symbol at this "level".

We want our representation to be invariant to affine transformations (translation, rotation and scaling). Therefore, we must normalize our representation in some way. Before computing the ridgelets coefficients, we find the minimal enclosing circle [10] and we center the image at the center of the circle, and scale it to the nearest dyadic radius. In such way, we get a ridgelets representation invariant to shifts and scale. Regarding rotation invariance, we have tested different strategies, before and after application of ridgelets transform, with poor

0	1	2	5	10	17	
1	3	4	6	11	18	
2	7	8	9	12	19	
3	13	14	15	16		

Fig. 2. Indexes of couples (j, k). Shaded band corresponds to indexes in level 2

results. However, thanks to the invariance to scale and shifts, discrete orthogonal ridgelets have a rotation property similar to that of the Radon transform.

$$WR(f \circ G_\alpha)_{(j,k)}[n, m] \approx WRf_{(j,k)}[n, m + \alpha_{(j,k)}]. \tag{2}$$

This expression means that the rotation of a symbol provokes horizontal circular shifts in the ridgelets coefficients. This effect is inherited from the Radon transform, losing equality because the wavelet transform is not invariant to shifts in finest scales. Hence, using this fact, we will get rotation invariance when we compare the symbols, by the definition of a circular distance [5] in expression (6).

Before defining a rotation invariant distance, we should relax ridgelets description if we want our symbol recognition system to be robust to noise and to some distortions and some kind of image degradations. We must permit some variability in the representation of a symbol. We will achieve it by taking each image coefficient, $WRf_{(j,k)}$ as a random variable $X_{(j,k)}$. This way, each line of a symbol hasn't to be in an exact location in the image, but it can be in the area of influence around the location of the coefficients of the symbol model, defined by this random variable. The density of this random variable $X_{(j,k)}$ is defined by the following expression:

$$X \sim f_X = \frac{|WRf|}{\|WRf\|_{L^1}}, \tag{3}$$

in which we have omitted the scale parameter to simplify our notation. We relax the description of a symbol by adding to X, a gaussian distribution, centered at 0, W_Σ: $Y = X + W_\Sigma$. It is known that Y's density is obtained by the X's and W_Σ's convolution, i.e:

$$f_Y = f_X(x) * \frac{1}{K_\Sigma} \exp\left[-\frac{x^t \Sigma^{-1} x}{2}\right], \tag{4}$$

being K_Σ the normalization constant. Therefore, we can construct a feature vector, robust to noise and symbol distortions, by smoothing our original ridgelets coefficients of the symbol model with a gaussian distribution whose covariance matrix, Σ, will be related to the degree of distortion allowed to the symbol.

4   Indexing of Symbols

Classification tends to be an expensive process as several factors may affect. The definition of the distance and the size of the symbol database are two of the main shortcomings. In our case, the distance defined in (6) has a quadratic complexity, and we would like to apply our method to large symbol databases. Hence, to reduce the number of comparisons between symbols is vital. In this section, we propose a clustering algorithm to minimize the number of comparisons. We want to group similar symbols at each level, so that comparisons can be done between the image and the representant of the groups instead of between the image and all the symbols in the database. Grouping will be done using the similarity measure defined in expression (6).

Once we have a representation of the symbols tolerant to distortion, we must define a distance which combines, at each decomposition level, ridgelets coefficients. Following ridgelets theory, we use the inner product defined in [4]:

$$[F_1, F_2] = \frac{1}{4\pi} \int_0^{2\pi} \int_{-\infty}^{\infty} F_1(t, \theta)\bar{F}_2(t, \theta) dt d\theta, \qquad (5)$$

F_1 and F_2 are in the Radon space – referring to the Radon transforms of symbol f_1 and f_2, respectively –, and we use the associated norm, $\|\cdot, \cdot\|$, to measure the distance between ridgelets coefficients. As we normalize each symbol to norm 1, at each scale, computing distances between symbols is equivalent to computing the inner product:

$$[F_1, F_2] = 1 - \frac{\|F_1 - F_2\|^2}{2}.$$

Hence, using this definition of distance, we can define a circular similarity measure which, as we have explained in section 3, will allow to achieve rotation invariance:

$$d(F_1, F_2) = \max_{\alpha \in [0, 2\pi)} \frac{[F_1, F_2 \circ G_\alpha]}{\|F_1\| \|F_2\|}, \qquad (6)$$

where we denote by $F_2 \circ G_\alpha$ the rotation of symbol f_2 by an angle α. d can be seen as a kind of correlation measure: $d(F, F) = 1$. Similar symbols will return values near to 1. Fixing a level s, we define the distance between two symbols $S^{(1)}$ and $S^{(2)}$ at level s, as the average of the similarity measure d between both symbols for all pairs of scales (j, k), belonging to level s:

$$\bar{d}_s(S^{(1)}, S^{(2)}) = \frac{1}{|I_s|} \sum_{(j,k) \in I_s} d(Y_{j,k}^{(1)}, Y_{j,k}^{(2)}), \qquad (7)$$

where d is the distance defined in (6) and by $S^{(p)} = \left\{ Y_{j,k}^{(p)} \right\}_{j,k=1,2,\ldots}$ we refer to the feature vector. By construction, $\bar{d}_s$ is in the interval $[0, 1]$.

Now, we have a similarity measure between two symbols at each level s. Using this measure we can think of grouping similar symbols at each level to get an indexing scheme at each level. We are going to group symbols with a $\bar{d}_s$ value grater than a fixed parameter $T \in [0,1)$ – let us consider we have an indexed database symbol $\{S^{(1)}, S^{(2)}, \ldots, S^{(L)}\}$ –. For each level s, we can define an adjacency matrix, giving us the relationships between symbols with $\bar{d}_s$ greater than the threshold T:

$$Adj_s(p, q) = \bar{d}_s(S^{(p)}, S^{(q)}) > T, \qquad (8)$$

that expression defines a graph, $\mathcal{G}$. Symbol groups will be composed of the maximal cliques in $\mathcal{G}$. Each clique gives us a symbol list composed of those symbols that are into a boule of radius $\sqrt{2(1-T)}$. In such way, we have built a set of "non-separate classes"' that will form the symbol groups. With this grouping scheme, it is possible that some symbols belong to several groups. However, we see this fact, more than a deficiency, an aid to our classification algorithm. Each class representant is the average over all the symbols belonging to the same class. Hence, $\mathcal{G}$ and, in particular, its cliques, depends on T choice. In our experiments, we have taken two values for T, $1/\sqrt{2}$ and 0.9, naming $\mathcal{G}1$ and $\mathcal{G}2$ for $T = .9$ and $T = 1/\sqrt{2}$, respectively.

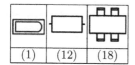 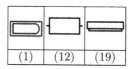

Fig. 3. Some samples of classes at 2nd level of decomposition taking $T = 1/\sqrt{2}$

Figure 3 shows an exemple of symbols belonging to two different classes at second level of decomposition. This figure shows the superposition degree of some classes when we use a low T parameter in the clustering step. However, considering $T = 0.9$ these four symbols define their own class, i.e. we can not group any symbol if we use high values of T. We have to work more in the clustering procedure to obtain classes where we are able to control the overlapping degree between symbols.

5   Experiments and Discussion

To test our approach, we will use the symbol database proposed for the symbol recognition contest held during the GREC'03 workshop – figure 4 –. It is composed of 256×256 binary images. After applying the ridgelets transform to these images, we have a 512×512 array broken in 42 sub-matrices. From these we have used the first 20, indexed as explained in section 3. The size of the smallest matrix of ridgelets coefficients is 32×64 while the biggest one is 128×256. Our purpose is to state whether it is possible to use only some of these arrays or whether we must use all matrices of coefficients to discriminate symbols.

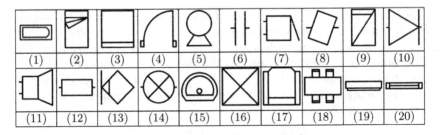

Fig. 4. Symbol Database to be used in the GREC 2003 symbol recognition contest

First, to validate if our similarity measure (6) is robust to symbol rotation, we have rotated each symbol by increments of 8 degrees and we have verified if the best match with all symbols corresponds to the original one. For each symbol we have obtained a 4×5 array where each component of the array corresponds to one of the selected pairs (j, k). For each component in the array, its value is the ratio of the correct matches over the total number of rotations. Averaging over all symbols we obtain the left table in figure 5, where we can observe the distance robustness. We can see how for some pairs (j, k), some ratios are extremely low. This value is understandable after visual examination of the ridgelets coefficients – right image in figure 5 –. The reason is that almost all symbols have high coefficients value near angles 0, π and 2π with independence of symbol rotation. In consequence, those coefficients should not be considered in a symbol recognition system.

	1	2	3	4	5
1	0.91	0.20	0.19	0.20	0.20
2	1.00	0.99	0.72	0.15	0.15
3	0.98	0.96	0.96	0.91	0.18
4	0.99	0.99	0.99	0.97	0.80

0   π   2π

Fig. 5. Average of recognition hits, over all GREC03 symbol database. Ridgelets coefficients of symbol 4 rotated $256°$

As we want to work using the multiscale representation explained in section 3, we need some method to combine all distances at each pair (j, k) belonging to a given level s. To combine the distances, we have defined four different combination schemes, giving place to four different classifiers: $C1, C2, C3, C4$. $C1$ corresponds to the formula (7) and it is defined as the average of distances for all pairs (j, k) belonging to s. We define: Combine$(d(S^{(1)}, S^{(2)})) = \frac{1}{|I_s|} \sum_{(j,k) \in I_s} d(S^{(1)}, S^{(2)})_{j,k}$; $C2$ is defined as follows: From $d(S^{(1)}, S^{(2)})$ we keep the symbol with the best match at each scale (j, k), then we sum over all scales and return the symbol with the biggest number of hits. Finally, $C3$ and $C4$ are defined as $C1$ and $C2$ respectively but working only with scales in $I'_s = \{(s+1)s+1, \ldots, (s+1)s+(s+1)\} \subset I_s$. These sets correspond to those scales where values in figure 5 are higher than 0.95.

Now, we present a classification algorithm which takes advantage of the ridgelets multiscale representation and the indexing scheme described in the previous section. This algorithm starts working with the coarsest scales, i.e, the first level going up to the higher level. At each level, we combine all distances using one of the four classifiers defined before, and we only need to compute the distance between the image and the representant of every group obtained after application of the indexing scheme. We keep the N groups with the best matches and then we take those models belonging to these groups (*groups2models*) and repeat the computation of the distance but now between the image and all selected models. In the next iteration we will only consider those groups at level $s+1$ containing models which have been selected at level s in the best matches (*models2groups*). We have thought of this algorithm to be used for large symbols database. First we select groups where we might find our query symbol. Then, we refine the search among symbols belonging to those groups. We reduce time complexity when total comparisons in both steps (*symbol query - groups* and *symbol query - models*) are highly lower than symbols database size.

In table 1 we summarize the performance of this classification algorithm for all four classifiers and for the two indexing schemes described in the previous section. We can see how the worst performance corresponds to the first classifier whereas the third, using the second clustering graph, is the best.

Procedure Classification.

- **Input**: Symbol, Models, Groups.
- **Output**: distances, position.

begin:

      L_groups ← initialize groups' list;
      $N \leftarrow 3$;
      for each level: $s \leftarrow 0, 1 \ldots$
          for each group in L_groups,
              compute distance between symbol and Groups;
              Combine distances at level s using function *Combine*;
          end for
          L_models← *groups2models*(L groups,N,s) ;
          for each group in L_models,
              compute distance between symbol and Models;
              Combine distances at level s using function *Combine*;
          end for
          L_groups← *models2groups*(L models,s+1) ;
      end for
end:
return distances and Models' position sorted in decreasing order;

Fig. 6. Classification Procedure

Table 1. Classifiers' hits percentage. Rows correspond to different clustering graphs. We set $T = 1/\sqrt{2}$ ($\mathcal{G}1$) and T=0.9 ($\mathcal{G}2$). We have broken down results in different columns to see the performance at each decomposition level

	Level 0	Level 1	Level 2	Level 3
graphs $\mathcal{G}1$	53.00	70.00	67.78	70.89
graphs $\mathcal{G}2$	49.33	92.78	88.00	89.67

Classifier $C1$

	Level 0	Level 1	Level 2	Level 3
graphs $\mathcal{G}1$	46.78	96.22	97.78	97.78
graphs $\mathcal{G}2$	51.44	97.11	97.44	97.89

Classifier $C2$

	Level 0	Level 1	Level 2	Level 3
graphs $\mathcal{G}1$	92.00	99.89	98.56	99.89
graphs $\mathcal{G}2$	82.67	99.89	98.44	99.89

Classifier $C3$

	Level 0	Level 1	Level 2	Level 3
graphs $\mathcal{G}1$	95.22	95.78	98.44	98.67
graphs $\mathcal{G}2$	90.89	97.11	97.11	98.89

Classifier $C4$

We have observed that misclassification comes from the first level. i.e. when a symbol does not belong to the N nearest groups, misclassification in higher levels is assured. For instance, symbol 9 using classifier $C1$ and graph $\mathcal{G}1$ is misclassified. However, we can not assure that this misplacement is the only reason for misclassification with the same classifier. In $\mathcal{G}2$, also, low classification hits in levels 3 and 4 can not be attributed to misclassification in level 1 because classification at level 2 is 0.93 – table 2–.

Table 2. Classifiers' hits percentage for symbol 9 at each level. Each row corresponds to a different classifier

	Level 0	Level 1	Level 2	Level 3
C1	0.13	0.16	0.16	0.16
C2	0.31	1.00	1.00	1.00
C3	1.00	1.00	1.00	1.00
C4	1.00	1.00	1.00	1.00

Graph $\mathcal{G}1$

	Level 0	Level 1	Level 2	Level 3
C1	0.16	0.93	0.71	0.51
C2	0.42	1.00	1.00	0.98
C3	1.00	1.00	1.00	1.00
C4	0.84	1.00	1.00	1.00

Graph $\mathcal{G}2$

We have tested the robustness of similarity measure in respect to symbol rotation and we have seen the slight differences performance of our grouping and classification algorithms, when we choose different values of T and *Combine* functions. Now, it is time to validate the ridgelets description of symbols when they are affected by several kind of transformations, noise and distortion. In such way, we have considered some tests from the GREC'03 graphic recognition contest in order to obtain results we can compare our method with. The tests considered and discussed are: rotation, scale, rotation and scale, degradation (from model 1 to 9) and distortion (levels 1, 2 and 3). Moreover, the symbol database is that composed of the twenty images in figure 4 and the variability, Σ, permitted in distortions correspons to five pixels and 1 degree in slice and angular parameters, respectively. All the experiments we have carried out have taken $T = 1/\sqrt{2}$ and the third classifier $C3$, i.e. a distance average using only the first scales at each decomposition level, because these are the parameter T and the classifier which have done the best results in previous experiments.

First, we have tested our method against rotation, against scale and combining both rotation and scale. In most cases, hits are higher than 90% – table 3 on the left – observing a slight decreasing tendency when decomposition levels increase. That is a surprising effect and it is making us considering other grouping and classification algorithms which could take advantage of different decomposition levels. Thus classification rates could be enhanced by refining symbol description and adding more details at each decomposition level. On the other hand, the worst results, as could be expected, have been achieved when we have combined both geometrical transforms: rotation and scale. The apparent stability in recognition rates, in comparison to other tests, makes us remain optimists when we will consider the most realistic cases, i.e. when all kinds of similarity transforms, degradations and distortions will be found in the image.

Table 3. Results of tests: Scale, rotation, rotation-scale and distortion (considering 3 different distortion degree) from set 2 of GREC'03 contest

	0	1	2	3
Scale	0,98	0,98	0,97	0,98
Rotation	1,00	0,91	0,92	0,94
Rotation-Scale	1,00	0,87	0,94	0,93

	0	1	2	3
distortion 1	1,00	0,88	0,97	1,00
distortion 2	0,97	0,92	0,95	0,95
distortion 3	0,95	0,75	0,88	0,85

Relating to distortion, GREC'03 symbol database proposes three different degrees of vectorial distortion, sorted from lower to higher degree. The symbol database is composed of seventy-five images for each distortion degree. Due to the database design and generation, it only contains fifteen of twenty symbols. However, we have used all twenty models in the recognition procedure. The results (table 3) are similar to those obtained in previous tests. Performance decreases when the decomposition level increases. Nevertheless, hits' rates are quite stable in all decomposition levels. On the other hand, as could be imagined, when distortion degree increases the recognition rates worsen. It could be interesting to establish some kind of relationship between the parameters used for generating the distortion of symbols and Σ. In such way, Σ could be chosen depending on the distortion degree applied. In that direction more experiments and studies should be done.

Finally, we have tested the ridgelets robustness using the degraded symbols from the GREC'03 contest database. There are nine different degradation levels – figure 7 shows some of them –. We have launched the classifier with a global performance of 80%. However, if we look separately at the result in each degradation level, we state that the worst results correspond to degradation levels 3, 4 and 5, which is easily understandable after visual inspection. These symbols are heavily noised over all the image and, consequently, minimal enclosing circle is bigger than what it should theoretically be. This fact affects to the scale normalization, pointing at the importance of the pre-processing step to obtain comparable ridgelets descriptors. De-noising techniques, such as gaussian convolution, combined with an algorithm to compute the enclosing circle more robust to noise should solve this lack. Without considering the results corresponding

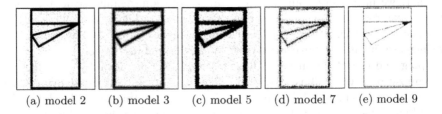

(a) model 2   (b) model 3   (c) model 5   (d) model 7   (e) model 9

Fig. 7. Some examples of degraded images. (a) Local noise. (b) Local & global noise. (c) Thickening. (d) Broken lines. (e) Thinning

Table 4. Correct classification ratio for each symbol at levels 0, 1, 2 and 3

	level 0	level 1	level 2	level 3
degrad 1	0,86	0,82	0,91	0,93
degrad 2	0,79	0,73	0,93	0,89
degrad 3	0,42	0,66	0,68	0,41
degrad 4	0,43	0,66	0,74	0,46
degrad 5	0,42	0,66	0,70	0,55
degrad 6	1,00	0,99	1,00	0,98
degrad 7	1,00	0,91	0,91	0,90
degrad 8	1,00	0,90	0,94	1,00
degrad 9	0,99	0,95	0,94	0,99
Average	0,77	0,81	0,86	0,79
Average (without symbols 3,4,5)	0,94	0,88	0,94	0,95

to degradations 3,4 and 5, hits percentage grows to 100% in almost all cases – table 4 –. Obviously, more experiments are required.

6   Conclusion and Future Work

Having a good representation of images able to capture the most relevant information is the basis for any application concerning matching, retrieval, browsing or recognition. In addition, many applications works with large symbol databases. Therefore, a good indexing method is needed to reduce the number of comparisons and to target the correct model in the classification problem. In this work we have explored the ridgelets transform possibilities to represent linear symbols and to index large databases, using its multiscale property.

Ridgelets transform shows to be well-suited to represent linear symbols, as higher response corresponds to the location of lines in the image. Moreover, only a few pre-preprocessing work is needed in order to have scale and shift invariant multiscale descriptors. Rotation invariance can be achieved by defining a circular similarity measure.

We have proposed a multiscale representation for symbols taking advantage of the decomposition at different scales of the ridgelets transform. We have also introduced a probabilistic theoretical framework to handle some level of symbol distortions in our representation and classification scheme through matrix Σ – see section 3 –. We have grouped scales in levels of details, and we have defined an indexing scheme by grouping similar symbols at each level. In this way, in our classification scheme, we only need to compare with the representant of each group and then perform a more detailed search only in the best groups, reducing computation time and reducing, also, the number of symbols to be considered at higher levels of detail.

These results must be taken as a preliminary study in the way of getting a general representation and indexing scheme for lineal symbols. The algorithms proposed have still some lacks and must be improved. In our probabilistic scheme, we must deeply study the covariance matrix Σ. The clustering parameter T must be a soft threshold, i.e. two symbols must be grouped according to Σ parameter, not T. Moreover, we should improve the indexing and classification scheme in order to avoid classification errors due to misclassification at coarsest levels.

References

1. A. Averbuch, R. Coifman, D. Donoho, M. Israeli, and W. J. Fast slant stack: A notion of radon transform for data in a cartesian grid which is rapidly computible, algebraically exact, geometrically faithful and invertible. *tech. report 2001*.
2. E. J. Candès. *Ridgelets: Theory and Applications*. Technical report, Standford University, September 1998.
3. E. J. Candès and D. L. Donoho. Ridgelets: a key to higher-dimensional intermittency? *Phil. Trans. R. Soc. Lond. A*, 357:2495–2509, 1999.
4. D. L. Donoho. Orthonormal ridgelets and linear singularities. *Tech. report 2001*.
5. P. Fränti, A. Mednonogov, V. Kyrki, and H. Kalviainen. Content-based matching of line-drawing images using the hough transform. *IJDAR*, 3:117–124, 2000.
6. Flesia. A. G., Hel-Or H., Averbuch A., Candès. E.J., Coifman. R.R., and Donoho. D.L. Digital implementation of ridgelet packets. *Beyond Wavelets*, pages 1–33, 2001.
7. J. Lladós. *Combining Graph Matching and Hough Transform for Hand-Drawn Graphical Document Analysis. Application to Architectural Drawings*. Thesis, Universitat Autònoma de Barcelona, September 1997.
8. O. R. Terrades and E. Valveny. Radon Transform for Lineal Symbol Representation. In *Proceedings of the 7th International Conference on Document Analisys and Recognition*, volume 1, pages 195–199, August 2003. Edimburg, Scotland.
9. S. Mallat. *A Wavelet Tour of Signal Processing*. Academic Press, 1999.
10. S. Skyun. A simple algorithm for computing the smallest enclosing circle. *Information Processing Letters*, 37:121–125, 1991.
11. S. Tabbone and L. Wendling. Technical symbols recognition using the two-dimensional radon transform. In *Proceedings of the 16th International Conference on Pattern Recognition*, volume 3, pages 200–203, August 2002. Montreal, Canada.

Automatic Measuring
the Local Thickness of Raster Lines

Alexander Gribov and Eugene Bodansky

Environmental System Research Institute (ESRI)
380 New York St., Redlands, CA 92373-8100, USA
{agribov, ebodansky}@esri.com

Abstract. This paper describes a procedure for measuring the local thickness of raster lines. The operator has only to place the cursor near the point where measuring needs to be done. The suggested algorithm is designed only for black and white raster images.

Keywords: Vectorization, raster line, local thickness.

1 Introduction

Users of vectorization systems and raster and vector editors usually look for the system that produces acceptable results with the least operator time [1]. The time an operator takes depends on the number of the automatic and interactive functions implemented in the system, on the degree of automatization of these functions, and on the precision of the results.

Sometimes, when working with raster images obtained by scanning line drawings, the operator has to measure the local thickness of raster lines either to make some decision, or to evaluate thresholds (minimum and maximum thickness of raster lines) used by algorithms of automatic and semi-automatic vectorization.

Almost any vector and raster editor has a tool that can be used for measuring distance. To measure a local thickness with a measure tool, it is necessary to put the cursor on the opposite edges of the raster line. This can be done only if this part of the raster line is shown on a fairly large scale. Therefore, an operator who wants to measure the local thickness in several places has to zoom in and out of an image several times and put the cursor on the edges of the raster line over and over again.

The suggested algorithm does this job for black and white raster images of line drawings with high accuracy, regardless of the scale of the image. The operator has only to place the cursor near the point where measuring needs to be done.

The algorithm was used in the raster-vector conversion system, ArcScan.

2 Local Thickness of Raster Lines Measuring

We will explain only the main concept and illustrate it with some figures.

The thickness of a smooth line can be defined as the length of the segment AB that is perpendicular to the centerline $a - a$ of the line (see figure 1). We will

J. Lladós and Y.-B. Kwon (Eds.): GREC 2003, LNCS 3088, pp. 188–192, 2004.
© Springer-Verlag Berlin Heidelberg 2004

call such a segment the shortest cross-section. The place where the thickness of the line has to be measured is defined by the operator with the cursor (point C).

If the scale is small, the cursor may hit the line or miss it. First, the closest point of the raster line border (point A) will be found. Then we build a fan of rays coming from this point and find segments appeared as intersections of the rays with the raster line. The shortest of them with some degree of approximation can be accepted as the shortest cross-section. Therefore, the local thickness of the raster line at point C will be measured as the length of the segment AB.

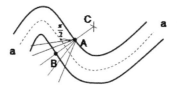

Fig. 1. Local thickness of a line

Because of the finite number of rays, the shortest segment could differ from the shortest cross-section, but an error of measuring of the local thickness of the raster line caused by this reason should be not more than $W \left/ \left(\dfrac{1}{\cos(\alpha/2)} - 1 \right) \right.$, where W is the real thickness of the line and α is an angle between adjacent rays. If the number of rays equals 16 and α equals 22.5 degrees, the error will be less than 2%.

However, there are cases when this simple algorithm can give the wrong result. Figure 2 shows raster lines. If the scale were enlarged, we could see that the borders of the lines not are smooth.

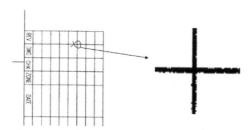

Fig. 2. Noise because of scanning, binarization, and discretization

"Outgrowths" of "thick" line can be thin lines. In this case, the result of vectorization should be as shown on figure 3a. If outgrowths are noise caused by scanning, binarization, and discretization, the result of vectorization should be as shown on figure 3b.

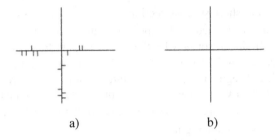

a)   b)

Fig. 3. Dependence the result of vectorization on the interpretation of the raster image (noise vs. desired signal)

If the cursor is located close to such outgrowth, our simple algorithm can measure its thickness (see figure 4). If it is a line the result is correct, but if it is a noise the result is wrong. So we have the problem of dividing the noise from the desired signal. As we saw above (figures 2 and 3), the same problem has to be resolved during building centerlines.

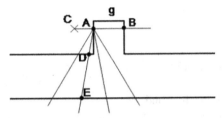

Fig. 4. Rejecting the shortest line

In signal processing, this problem often is solved with statistical methods. Unfortunately, we usually do not have any information about the characteristics of the noise and the desired signal of the images being processed. If the operator performs vectorization manually, he makes the decision using his knowledge of the domain. Automatic vectorization methods use thresholds.

We solved this problem with the parameter β, which is the value of the ratio of the cross-section length (segment AB on figure 4) to the minimum distance between its ends measured along the border (the length of AgB on figure 4). A similar parameter was used in [2] for cleaning the result of automatic vectorization from small spurs and spurious vectors. The threshold β_{max} is the maximum value of the parameter when the outgrowth is interpreted as a line. This parameter defines the distance from the cross-section to the line end. If $\beta_{max} = 0.25$ the outgrowth will be interpreted as a line when this distance is more than $1.5 * W$, where W is the thickness of the outgrowth. The algorithm is looking for the shortest cross-section satisfying the condition $\beta \le \beta_{max}$. For example, on figure 4, it will be cross-section DE but not AB. Note that the measurement error does not depend on the value of β_{max}.

To use the suggested algorithm, it is first necessary to build the borders of the raster objects. This task, in contrast to building centerlines, has a unique solution and is solved with relatively simple algorithms (see for example [3]).

The size of the source raster image can be too large. Borders of raster objects are built not for the full image, but only for some part of it, because measuring a line thickness is an interactive procedure and so has to be done in real time.

To define the local thickness of the line, it is enough to build the borders of the raster objects which contain the shortest cross-section of the line being processed. This part of the image can be defined by the cursor position and the search radius. In commercial vector and raster editors, the operator assigns the search radius. The error does not depend on the search radius. If the search radius is too small, the algorithm will not find the line thickness, if the search radius is too big, the task may be resolved with too long a delay.

Smoothing of the borders reduces the influence of noise and improves the precision. For smoothing, we use an algorithm described in [4].

In our implementation, we show on the screen not only a thickness of line, but the segment that was used as the shortest cross-section of the line as well. This way, the operator can see the thickness of what line was measured, and in what place. If the line and the place are correct, the operator can use the obtained value because the error does not depend on the threshold and search radius.

So for measuring the local thickness of the line, it is enough to select the search radius and to put the cursor near the place of the interest. Obviously, it is much simpler than placing the cursor on the opposite edges of the line, especially if the source image is big and it is shown on the screen at a small scale.

Figure 5 shows the result of measuring a local thickness of the line with ArcScan, an extension of ArcGis. More detailed description of the algorithm can be found in [5].

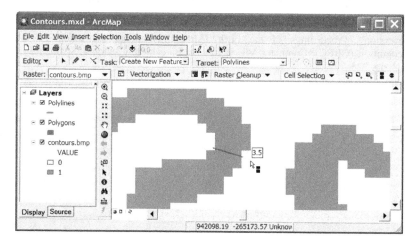

Fig. 5. Measuring the local thickness of a raster line (ArcScan)

3 Conclusion

There was described an algorithm that automatically measures the local thickness of a raster line as the length of its shortest cross-section. First, there are built the borders of some part of the source raster image. Then, the algorithm looks for the shortest cross-section of the line. The error caused by raster noise is reduced by border smoothing.

The algorithm uses one threshold to distinguish noise from a desired signal, or the line from the "outgrowth" caused by the noise. If the line was found correctly, the error does not overdraw several percent. Because the noise of scanning, binarization, and discretization are usually not more than 1 - 2 pixels and the threshold is dimensionless, it is possible to select a default value of the threshold that will provide high accuracy.

This algorithm is implemented in the vectorization system ArcScan. The operator watches not only the value of the line thickness but the cross-section used for measuring as well. It helps him to verify the result.

References

1. Bodansky E. (2002) "System approach to a raster-to-vector conversion: from research to conversion system". In: S.Levachkin, E.Bodansky, A.Ruas (eds), e-Proceedings of International Workshop on Semantic Processing of Spatial Data (GEOPRO2002), 3-4 December 2002, Mexico City, Mexico (CD ISBN: 970-18-8521-X).
2. Elliman D. (1999) "A Really Useful Vectorization Algorithm", Lecture Notes in Computer Science (LNCS 1941), pp. 19–27.
3. Quek F.K.H. (2000) "An algorithm of the rapid computation of boundaries of run-length encoded regions", Pattern recognition, pp. 1637–1649.
4. Bodansky E., Gribov A., Pilouk M. (2002) "Smoothing and Compression of Lines Obtained by Raster-to-Vector Conversion", Lecture Notes in Computer Science (LNCS 2390), Springer, pp. 256–265.
5. Gribov A., Bodansky E. (2003) "How to increase the efficiency of raster-to-vector conversion", Proceedings of the Fifth IAPR International Workshop on Graphics Recognition (GREC), Computer Vision Center, Barcelona, Catalonia, Spain, July 30–31, 2003, pp. 225–232.

Approximation of Polylines with Circular Arcs

Eugene Bodansky and Alexander Gribov

Environmental System Research Institute (ESRI)
380 New York St., Redlands, CA 92373-8100, USA
{ebodansky, agribov}@esri.com

Abstract. Approximation of piecewise linear polylines with circle arcs is an important problem. The approximation is used for polyline compression, noise filtering, feature detection, and inspection of mechanical parts [1–5]. A new accurate and fast iterative method of polyline approximation with a circle arc is described in the paper.

1 Introduction

Usually, methods of describing polylines with circle arcs consist of two steps. The first step is building the fitting circle. The second step is finding an arc of the circle that is "the best" (in some sense) approximation of the source polyline.

There are several methods of building a fitting circle.

Papers [1–3] describe explicit methods of building fitting circles.

Let (x_i, y_i), $i = 1, 2, ..., n$ be the consecutive vertices of a source polyline.

These methods give explicit expressions for a center (x_c, y_c) and radius R of the circle. These expressions are a solution of systems of two (in paper [2]) and three (in paper [3]) linear equations. The methods provide the same result because they minimize the same functional.

The systems were derived by minimization of the functional

$$F(x_c, y_c, R) = \sum_{i=1}^{N} e_i^2 \text{, where } e_i = \pi\{(x_i - x_c)^2 + (y_i - y_c)^2\} - \pi R^2 . \qquad (1)$$

Minimization of this functional leads to a bias result [2]. The less the angle of the arc, the bigger the bias of estimated parameters are.

Robinson S.M. [6] suggests minimization of the least square error criterion:

$$F(x_c, y_c, R) = \sum_{i=1}^{N} e_i^2 \text{, where } e_i = \sqrt{(x_i - x_c)^2 + (y_i - y_c)^2} - R . \qquad (2)$$

Minimization of this criterion produces a better precision than minimization of the functional (1).

Berman M. [7] analyzed the dependence of the mean value of the bias on a statistical model for noise. He shows "the need for a careful consideration of the appropriate error structure allied with the use of a suitable estimation procedure when large samples are used to obtain accurate and precise estimates of circle parameters".

J. Lladós and Y.-B. Kwon (Eds.): GREC 2003, LNCS 3088, pp. 193–198, 2004.
© Springer-Verlag Berlin Heidelberg 2004

Landau U.M. [4] developed an iterative method minimizing the functional (2). To use this method it is necessary to know an initial estimation of a circle center. The estimation is used to evaluate a radius, then the radius and center are used to calculate a new iteration of the circle center, and so on. The method is converged even when the initial estimation of the center is bad. Unfortunately the speed of the method convergence is too slow.

Rosin P. and West A.W. [5] simplified the task of approximation by requiring that the circle passes through the ends of the source polyline. Two points of the circle define a line where the center of the circle is located. A recursive algorithm calculates estimations of the center and the radius, which minimize the least square error criterion (2).

Because of the constraint, the method is less accurate and more sensitive to the noise than the method suggested by Landau [4]. But this constraint simplifies conjugation of adjacent parts of polyline, which is required for approximation polylines with straight segments and arcs.

After estimating the center and the radius of the circle it is necessary to perform the second step: to find the arc of this circle that approximates the source polyline. This task is not as simple as it might seem, because a polyline cannot always be approximated with an arc even if the maximum deviations of its vertices from the circle is small. A small deviation of polyline vertices from the circle is only one of the necessary conditions. To be approximated with a circle arc, a source polyline should not contain any critical points. This is an additional condition.

A critical vertex divides the polyline into separate geometrical primitives. On fig. 1, one vertex of the polyline, point A, is critical. One circular arc cannot approximate such a polyline.

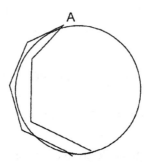

Fig. 1. Example of a good approximation of a set of points but a bad approximation of a polyline

Ichoku Ch. *et al.* [3] suggest several criteria for establishing a fact of presence of a critical point but this part of the article looks like a general discussion rather than a description of the method.

2   A New Iterative Approximation Method

We suggest a new iterative method of minimizing the least square error criterion (2) used by Landau [4] and Robinson [6]. Our method converges very fast, but in contrast to Landau's method, requires a good initial estimation of the center and radius of the circle.

Let

$$x_c = x_0 + \delta_x,$$
$$y_c = y_0 + \delta_y, \qquad (3)$$
$$R = R_0 + \delta_R,$$

where x_0, y_0, and R_0 are initial estimations; x_c, y_c, and R are the true values; and δ_x, δ_y, and δ_R are errors of the center coordinates and the radius.

Let initial estimations x_0, y_0, and R_0 of x_c, y_c, and R be known with enough precision to neglect the second order of the errors in comparison with R.

Present $e_i = \sqrt{(x_i - x_c)^2 + (y_i - y_c)^2} - R$, $i = 1, 2, \ldots, n$, as the series of powers of δ_x, δ_y, and δ_R. Neglecting the second powers of δ_x, δ_y, and δ_R, we obtain:

$$e \approx z - M \cdot \delta, \qquad (4)$$

where $e = \begin{pmatrix} e_1 \\ e_2 \\ \vdots \\ e_n \end{pmatrix}$, $z = \begin{pmatrix} z_1 \\ z_2 \\ \vdots \\ z_n \end{pmatrix}$, $z_i = r_i - R_0$, $M = \begin{pmatrix} \dfrac{r_{1x}}{r_1} & \dfrac{r_{1y}}{r_1} & 1 \\ \dfrac{r_{2x}}{r_2} & \dfrac{r_{2y}}{r_2} & 1 \\ \vdots & \vdots & \vdots \\ \dfrac{r_{nx}}{r_n} & \dfrac{r_{ny}}{r_n} & 1 \end{pmatrix}$, $\delta = \begin{pmatrix} \delta_x \\ \delta_y \\ \delta_R \end{pmatrix}$,

$r_{ix} = x_i - x_0$, $r_{iy} = y_i - y_0$, $r_i = \sqrt{r_{ix}^2 + r_{iy}^2}$.

Now the expression $(z - M \cdot \delta)^T \cdot (z - M \cdot \delta)$ can approximate the functional (2). This expression reaches the minimum when

$$\delta = M^+ \cdot z, \qquad (5)$$

where $M^+ = (M^T \cdot M)^{-1} \cdot M^T$ and superscript "T" designates transposition.

The new values of the coordinates of the center and the radius are equal to

$$x_1 = x_0 + \delta_x,$$
$$y_1 = y_0 + \delta_y, \qquad (6)$$
$$R_1 = R_0 + \delta_R,$$

The calculated values can be used as the initial estimations for the next iteration. This iteration process minimizes functional (2). The iteration process will end when the change in the functional (2) or center location becomes less than a given threshold.

Figure 2 shows the graph illustrating the speed of convergence for suggested method. For comparison, the figure also shows the graph illustrating the speed of convergence of the Landau method.

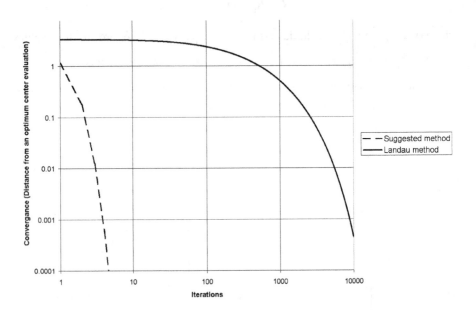

Fig. 2. Convergence of a circle center to its optimal value. Arc = 60°, radius = 10, a radial model of noise [7], a uniform noise from +0.5 till -0.5, initial estimations x_0, y_0, and R_0 were calculated with the method suggested in [3]

3   Fitting Circular Arc

After evaluating the circle it is necessary to obtain an arc that approximates the source polyline. Our task could have a solution only if the maximum deviation of the source polyline is less than a given threshold. The ends of the fitting arc, points a and b, can be calculated as projections of the first and last ends, points, A and B, of the polyline. Two arcs with such ends exist. A fitting arc is the one that crosses the ray passing from the center O of the circle through the middle point of the polyline, point C (see fig. 3).

Let $\bar{r}_i$ be a vector with the origin at the center of the circle, the end at the i-th polyline vertex, and α_i be the angle between $\bar{r}_1$ and $\bar{r}_i$, where $i = 1,...,n$.

Define the direction of rotation from $\bar{r}_1$ to $\bar{r}_n$ as positive. Then the angle α_n between $\bar{r}_1$ and $\bar{r}_n$ always will be positive. In fig. 3, the positive direction of rotation is clockwise.

Let the current vector be $\bar{r}_k$, $1 \le k \le n$, and α_m, be the maximum angle of the sequence α_i ($1 \le i \le k$). Then the difference $\alpha_m - \alpha_k$ is the current reverse motion.

Define the maximum reverse motion as α_{rv}^{max}.

The maximum reverse motion, α_{rv}^{max}, has to be less than some threshold. If this constraint is not satisfied, the polyline will contain at least one critical point and cannot be approximated with one circular arc. The polyline has to be divided into several polylines.

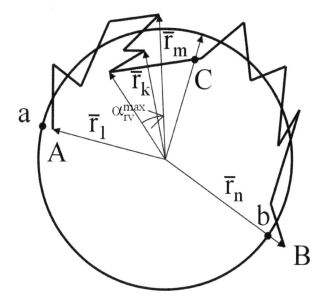

Fig. 3. Calculation of a maximum reverse motion

The procedure has a computational complexity equals $O(n)$, where n is the number of vertices of the source polyline.

4 Conclusion

An iterative method of approximation of a polyline with a circle arc suggested in this paper has the same asymptotic accuracy as the approximation method from [4], but the new method converges to the optimum much faster. This conclusion was conformed to the result of simulation (see. fig. 2).

A new method for detection of critical vertices of polylines was also suggested.

References

1. Fred Bookstein, "Fitting conic sections to scattered data", Computer Graphics and Image Processing, V. 9, pp. 56–71, 1979.
2. Thomas S.M., Chan Y.T., "A Simple Approach for the Estimation of Circular Arc Center and Its Radius" (Note), Computer Vision, Graphics, and Image Processing, Vol. 45, pp. 362–370, 1989.
3. Ichoku Ch., Deffontaines B., Chorowicz J., "Segmentation of Digital Plain Curves: A Dynamic Focusing Approach", Pattern Recognition Letters, Vol. 17, pp. 741–750, 1996.
4. Landau U.M.,"Estimation of a Circular Arc Center and Its Radius", Computer Vision, Graphics, and Image Processing, Vol. 38, pp. 317–326, 1987.
5. Rosin P., West A.W., "Segmentation of Edges into Lines and Arcs", Image and Vision Computing, 7(2), pp. 109–114, 1989.
6. Robinson S.M., "Fitting Spheres by the Method of Least Squares", Commun. Assoc. Comput. Mach., 4, 1961, 491.
7. Berman M., "Large Sample Bias in the Least Squares Estimators of a Circular Arc Center and Its Radius", Computer Vision, Graphics, and Image Processing, 45, 126–128, 1989.

Adaptable Vectorisation System Based on Strategic Knowledge and XML Representation Use

Mathieu Delalandre[1], Youssouf Saidali[1], Eric Trupin[1], and Jean-Marc Ogier[2]

[1] Laboratory PSI, University of Rouen, 76 821 Mont Saint Aignan, France
{first_name.last_name}@univ-rouen.fr
[2] Laboratory L3I, University of La Rochelle, 17042 La Rochelle, France
jmogier@univ-lr.fr

Abstract. This paper presents a vectorisation system based on the use of *strategic knowledge*. This one is composed of two parts: a processing library and a graphic user interface. Our processing library is composed of image pre-processing and vectorisation tools. Our graphic user interface is used for the *strategic knowledge* acquisition and operationalisation. It allows to construct and to execute scenarios, exploiting any processing of our library, according to documents' contexts and users' adopted strategies. A XML data representation is used, allowing an easy data manipulation. A scenario example is presented for graphics recognition on utility maps.

1 Introduction

Vectorisation is used for different purposes like: graphic document recognition, handwriting recognition, and so on. Vectorisation systems use two main types of knowledge: *descriptive knowledge* and *strategic knowledge*. The first one concerns descriptions of documents' objects, and the second one concerns chaining links between image processing tools. The *descriptive knowledge* is usually employed, but not the *strategic knowledge*. This paper presents a vectorisation system based on the use of *strategic knowledge*. We present here our first advancements concerning the experimentation of this system. This one is composed of two parts: a processing library and a graphic user interface. Our processing library is composed of image pre-processing and vectorisation tools. Our pre-processing tools allow to deal with noisy images. Our vectorisation processing tools are of high granularity level in order to use them within a strategic approach. Our graphic user interface is used for *strategic knowledge* acquisition and operationalisation. This graphic user interface allows to construct and to execute scenarios, exploiting any processing of our library. A XML data representation is used in the system, allowing an easy data manipulation. In the paper's follow-up, we present in section (2), an overview on knowledge based vectorisation systems. In section (3) and (4), we present our image processing library and our graphic user interface. In section (5), we present the XML use in the system. In section (6), we present a scenario example for graphics recognition on utility maps. Finally, in section (7), we conclude.

J. Lladós and Y.-B. Kwon (Eds.): GREC 2003, LNCS 3088, pp. 199–210, 2004.
© Springer-Verlag Berlin Heidelberg 2004

2 Overview on Knowledge Based Vectorisation Systems

Vectorisation is a stage of document interpretation problem that is used for different purposes like: graphic document recognition (technical document [1], map [16] symbol [13], and so on.), handwriting recognition (especially Chinese handwriting [7]), and so on. It is a well-known problem and many commercial applications exist [14]. A vectorisation system can be decomposed into two parts: a processing part (vectorisation) and a system part (the control).

Vectorisation extracts vector data from document images [1]. These vector data correspond to mathematical object graphs composed of: vectors, circles, and curves. Vectorisation is a complex process that may rely on many different methods [5]. Some of them perform vectorisation in two steps [26]. The first one extracts pixel chain graphs. Various approaches may be used [5] like: contouring, skeletonisation, and run decomposition. The second one transforms pixel chains into mathematical object lists [21] (vectors, arcs, curves). Some other methods perform directly vectorisation like: tracking methods, object segmentation methods, and meshes based methods. Several overviews on vectorisation can be found in [1], [5], and [26].

The control system may use various approaches in order to supervise the vectorisation process. These approaches come from pattern recognition and artificial intelligence domains. Among them, let's cite: the knowledge based systems [8], the multi-agent systems [9], blackboard based systems [1], and so on. These systems are generally used for recognition and interpretation, but can have other applications like: learning, indexing, structuring data, and so on. So, systems deal with two main properties: knowledge use [8] and automatic control of processings [9]. The last ones deal currently with the both. Several overviews on vectorisation systems can be found in [1], [16], and [25].

Like document interpretation systems, vectorisation systems use two main types of knowledge: *descriptive knowledge* and *strategic knowledge* [22]. The first one concerns documents' objects and links between them. The second one concerns image processing tools that are used to construct documents' objects and chaining links between these tools. The descriptive knowledge is usually employed in vectorisation systems [1]. At the opposite, the strategic knowledge is less used, whereas many common steps exist among vectorisation process [5]. In the paper's follow-up, we propose a vectorisation system based on strategic knowledge use. It is composed of a processing library and a graphic user interface for scenarios construction and their executions.

3 Image Processing Library

3.1 Introduction

All our image processings are included in the PSI[1] Image Processing Library, which is composed of image pre-processings and vectorisation processings. This library is included in a complete document image recognition library, the PSI Library. A description of some library's processings can be found in [4]. Image pre-processings

---

[1] Perception Systems Information Laboratory: http://www.univ-rouen.fr/psi/

can be used on grey-level and binary images. We develop its content in section (3.2). Vectorisation processings are based on various approaches (skeletonisation, contouring, region and run decomposition, direct vectorisation). We have decomposed the classical vectorisation chain into granular processings (Table 1) in order to use them within a strategic approach. Our vectorisation processings are decomposed according to three data levels: an image level, a structured data level, and a boundary level between the image data and the structured data levels. We present each level in sections (3.3), (3.4), and (3.5).

Table 1. Data levels of vectorisation processings

Image	Skeletonisation Adaptation, Contouring, Skeletonisation
Boundary	Progressive Object Simplification, Pixel List Extraction, Direct Vectorisation, Direct Contouring, Run Decomposition, Region Decomposition
Structured Data	Interiority Degree Segmentation, Junction Reconstruction, Graph Construction, Polygonisation, Curve and circle fitting, Pruning, Merging, Smoothing, List Filtering

3.2 Image Pre-processing

The image pre-processing level is composed of different methods for the processing of noisy images. Firstly, we use grey-level filtering methods on scanned images like median filter and mean filter [18]. Next, we binarise our images. We use two standard algorithms for the automatic computation of binarisation thresholds: the Otsu's method [17] and the Kittler's method [10]. The first one is a histogram based method and the second one a clustering based method. These two methods have been used for map pre-processing [11], in order to segment the network part from the cadastral part, according to parts' grey-levels. Then, we can use two methods families for noise reduction on obtained binary images. The first ones are connected components and loops filtering methods, based on a "classical" blob coloring algorithm. They use automatic or pre-defined user surface threshold, the automatic threshold computation is based on maximum proportional ratio search of connected components' surfaces. The second ones are mathematical morphology operations like dilatation, erosion, opening, and closing. These operations use classical masks 3*3 sized and of "+" "×" type.

3.3 Vectorisation's Image Level

The vectorisation's image level uses classical image processings for the contouring and the skeletonisation. For the skeletonisation, we use two standard algorithms: Di Baja [6] and Taconet [24]. These skeletonisation algorithms are based on the medial axis transform [1]. For the contouring, we use a classical neighbouring test method with classical masks 3*3 sized and of "+" "×" type. These contours are then processed in order to obtain 2-connected contour lists. The Fig. 1 (a) illustrates overlapped results of skeletonisation and contouring. The main problem of the skeletonisation is the noise which depends on lines' thickness of images. In order to adapt images for the skeletonisation, we use the 3-4 distance transform of Di Baja [6] in combination with a classical image reducing tool. The Fig. 1 (b) gives an example of the skeletonisation's impact without any reduction (middle) and with a reduction (right).

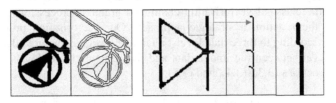

Fig. 1. (a) Skeletonisation and contouring (b) skeletonisation adaptation

3.4 Vectorisation's Boundary Level

Our vectorisation's boundary level uses different methods in order to extract structured data from images. We present each method in the six next paragraphs.

We use a contouring method based on a classical blob coloring algorithm. During the connected components labelling, the internal and external shapes' contours are extracted. Then, the contours' pixels are structured into chains. In a following step, the inclusion links between connected components are searched. With this application, we extract inclusion graphs which contain the external and the internal contour chains, and the inclusion links between the connected components. This method gives global/local descriptions of image's shapes [5]. The Fig. 2 (a) gives an example of raster representation of extracted external contours.

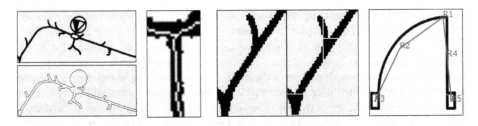

Fig. 2. (a) Contouring (b) direct vectorisation (c) run (d) region

We use a direct vectorisation method. This method has been used for roads extraction on cadastral maps [15]. Firstly, image is analyzed to find an entry point. The following tracking process is two types: line tracking and junction tracking [5]. The line tracking uses a point element, which advances into line's middle according to contours follow-up. The displacement's length is proportional to line's thickness. The junction tracking analyses connection breaks of contours follow-up. In this case, a circle including the junction is used to find the other junction's starting lines. The crossings between the lines and the circle are searched. From these data, a image's graph is updated and used to start the tracking of new lines. The Fig. 2 (b) gives an example of raster representation of line and junction extraction.

We use a run decomposition method. This method is under construction. In a first step the image is encoded into runs. Then, runs are structured into run graphs [3]. In these graphs, the successive runs are represented by run chains and the 3-connected runs (or more) by junctions. The encoded runs can be horizontal and/or vertical. From these run graphs, contours and skeleton can be extracted. The Fig. 2 (c) gives an example of mixed raster representation of a horizontal and vertical run graph (the junction nodes are represented in white).

We use region decomposition method based on a wave aggregation. Firstly, the image is analyzed to find an entry point. Then, the method searches the neighbouring points. These points are labelled, aggregated, and stored into a wave object. Successively, the previous waves are used for new aggregation processes. The wave breaking and stopping cases define the regions' boundaries. The boundaries are next used in order to create entry waves for the new region search. From the labelled region map, a primary region graph is created. In a following step, this primary region graph is analysed in order to construct the line and junction regions. From these region graphs, contours and skeletons can be extracted. Also, graphs' regions can be processed by statistical recognition methods [2]. The Fig. 2 (d) gives an example of constructed primary region graph from a labelled region map.

We use a pixel list extraction method to convert skeleton and contour images into structured data. This method is based on the connected pixel destruction. Firstly, all 3-connected pixels are destroyed. After, we chain connected pixels into pixel list. Each list is composed of 1-connected pixel (extremity) and 2-connected pixel. The Fig. 3 (a) gives an example of extracted pixel lists.

We use a last object simplification method. This one allows to exploit structured data on images. We use this approach to simplify processed images during vectorisation scenarios [23]. Currently, this tool can process only circle objects. The Fig. 3 (b) gives an example of circle erasing result.

Fig. 3. (a) Pixel list extraction (b) Object simplification

3.5 Vectorisation's Structured Data Level

The structured data level is the central part of vectorisation scenario. Indeed, all the processings use the same input/output data format. Our data format represents a graph base of geometrical objects like: circles, curves, polylines, pixel lists, and junctions. In practice, we can call any processing in any order, but in theory, some processings depend on a minimum structuring level of data (for example the circle fitting depends on polygonisation results). All boundary level's processings (see section 3.4) export their data in this format. The goal of structured data level's processings is to add semantic information to basic lists obtained by the boundary level's processings. For that, we use different granular processings (see Table 1). We can decompose these processings in two types: lists processing and graphs processing. We present these two types in the two following sections.

3.5.1 Lists Processing

The lists processings are used for different purposes like the interiority degree segmentation and the mathematical approximation (vectors, circles, and curves).

For the interiority degree segmentation, we apply a thickness segmentation threshold based on a simple test of thickness' variation. Information about pixels' interiority degrees is obtained by the successive calls of skeletonisation/pixel list extraction tools. The Fig. 4 (a) gives an example of interiority degree segmentation, with the original image (high), the graphic representation of pixel lists before segmentation (middle) and after segmentation (low).

For the polygonisation (transformation of pixel lists into vector lists "polylines"), we use the "standard" Ramer's method [20], with the "standard" split & merge Pavlidis' method [19]. For each polyline, we compute some attributes, like the vectors' thickness (from original pixel lists), vectors' lengths, and angular links between two consecutive vectors according to the polyline tracing. Our circle fitting algorithm is a basic tool only based on the test of angular and length links inside a polyline. We use here a standard geometrical property: a circle can be approximated by a regular polygon (in length and angle). The Fig. 4 (b left) gives an example of polygonisation and circles fittings applied on a contours image. Recently, we have extended the geometrical object extraction with the standard Bernstein's curve approximation [12] of pixel lists. The Fig. 4 (b right) gives an example of Bernstein's curve approximation.

Furthermore, we use some post-correction processings on lists. In one hand we use a list filtering processing. The Fig. 4 (c left-middle) gives an example of list filtering. The used threshold can be automatically computed, or pre-defined by the user. The automatic computation is based on maximum proportional ratio search of lists' lengths. This processing decreases the complexity of the junction detection method (section 3.5.2). On the other hand we use a list smoothing algorithm. The Fig. 4 (c middle-right) gives an example of list smoothing. It is based on variations analysis of Freeman directions into pixel lists. This processing increases data qualities for the polygonisation and curve fitting.

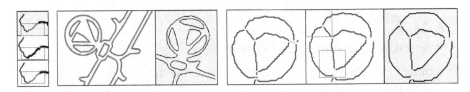

Fig. 4. (a) Interiority segmentation (b) mathematical approximation (c) list correction

3.5.2 Graphs Processing

An important processing of structured data level is the junction detection. We base our approach on a junction reconstruction algorithm. This algorithm constructs all the connections between the objects' extremities according to a distance threshold. During this construction, the algorithm forbids the connections between extremities of same objects. The distance threshold can be defined by the user or automatically computed. This automatic computation is based on maximum proportional ratio search of connections' lengths. Next, the algorithm analyzes all the connections to find the inter-connections (group of joined extremities). Each inter-connection constitutes a junction. With information about junctions, we use a graph construction algorithm in order to obtain the geometrical object graphs composed of pixels, circles, curves, and polylines. We exploit information about junctions for two standard processings in the vectorisation process: pruning and merging [1]. The Fig. 5 gives a reconstruction example (a, b) with the successive pruning (b, c) and merging (c, d).

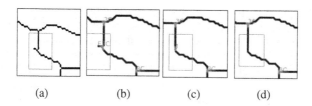

(a)   (b)   (c)   (d)

Fig. 5. (a-b) Junction reconstruction (b-c) pruning (c-d) merging

4 Vectorisation Scenarios Construction

We use a graphic user interface for strategic knowledge acquisition and operationalisation: ACTI_VA[2] [22]. It enables to construct scenarios for document image recognition according to documents' contexts (recognition goal, document type, and so on.), and users' adopted strategies. In a first step, the user defines the context of the analyzed image (quality, type, and so on.) (Fig. 6 (a)). The PSI library's processings (see section 3) are then proposed to the user. Each processing is realized

Fig. 6. (a) Document's context acquisition (b) state viewer

from its dashboard "or processing panel" representing a scenario stage. The user oversees the scenario's construction, following permanently the results' evolutions. So, a state viewer shows the data's intermediate graphic representations (image and/or structured data results) between each scenario's stage (Fig. 6 (b)). For an adaptable and evolving assistance, the user can at any time return to any previous stage in order

---

[2] In French: "Acquisition de Connaissances Traiteur d'Images pour leur VAlorisation".

to, modify the parameters setting, change the processing stage, seek a textual help, or display use examples. When the user reaches his purpose, he saves its scenario in a scenario base. During the scenario's construction, the user can search similar scenario examples in the scenario base with two research tools: a query language allowing to request the scenario base, and a graph-matching tool allowing to compare the scenarios' structures.

5   XML Use in System

Our two system's parts (processing library and graphic user interface) use the XML language for the data representation. The use of this data representation language offers several possibilities and as much as enhancement for our system. XML is a meta-language because it is defined as a root language, what enables to define specialized sub-languages. We use SVG[3] in the system for our data's graphic representations. We also use XGMML[4] for the graphs' description provided by some PSI Library's processings. XML allows to use transforming processors. These processors easily transform the XML data streams with the help of XSLT[5] scripts. This enables easy data communications between the processings, and between processings and our graphic user interface. XML enables to request XML file bases with XML-QL[6]. We use the candidate languages for XML-QL: Quilt[7]. We use Quilt for management of scenarios bases and reconstruction of final XML documents (see section 6.5). The use of Quilt with XSLT enables to transform scenarios into graphs base for the structural classifiers of the PSI Library [4] (see section 4).

6   Scenario Example

6.1   Introduction

We present here our first advancements concerning the experimentation of this system, through a scenario example on FT's utility maps[8]. We have two main components on these utility maps (Fig. 7 (a)): the characters, and the graphic parts. We present here the graphic parts recognition. We suggest the reader to consult [2] for the description of the character recognition. Also, we have two main components on these graphic parts (Fig. 7 (a)): the symbols and the network. The symbols represent technical equipments allowing connections on the network. We have three symbols' classes (Fig. 7 (a)): room, CP1[9] and CP2. Our graphics recognition scenario may be decomposed into four main steps: noise pre-processing and characters segmentation, network's   contours   vectorisation,   characters   detection,   and   XML   object reconstruction. We present each scenario's step in the four next sections.

---

[3] Scalable Vector Graphics.
[4] eXtensible Graph Markup and Modelling Language.
[5] eXtensible Stylesheet Transform Language.
[6] XML Query Language.
[7] http://www.almaden.ibm.com/cs/people/chamberlin/quilt.html
[8] French Telecommunication operator: http://www.rd.francetelecom.fr/
[9] Concentration Point 1.

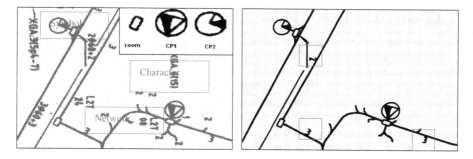

Fig. 7. (a) FT's utility map (b) clean map

6.2 Noise Pre-processing and Characters Segmentation

In a first step, we use a pre-processing scenario (see section (3.2)) on scanned images in order to reduce the result noise of the acquisition stage, and to segment the characters and the graphic parts. We have applied successively a median filtering, an Otsu's binarisation, an automatic connected component filtering, and an opening. Thus, we have obtained clean network images (Fig. 7 (b)). However, this pre-processing step cannot deal with the connected characters to the network (Fig. 7 (b)'s rectangles).

6.3 Network's Contours Vectorisation

Next, we use a vectorisation scenario in order to extract vector data corresponding to graphic parts (see sections (3.3), (3.4), and (3.5)). Successively, we have applied a contouring, a pixel list extraction, a smoothing, a polygonisation, a split and merge method, and a circle fitting. The Fig. 8 (a, and b) gives an example of graphic parts' vectorisation. Following the vectorisation, a vector data reconstruction tool is used. Firstly, this one links internal contours with circles, according to their inclusion links. Indeed, the symbols' internal contour numbers define their classes: 4 for CP1, 2 for CP2, and 1 for room. These numbers are next used during the XML object reconstruction step to give the symbols' labels (see section 6.5). Secondly, the vector data reconstruction tool matches contours in order to reconstruct network parts' vectors. For example, on the Fig. 8 (a) we have three network's parts. Thus in the data's graphic representation, the internal contours and the circle correspond to symbols (Fig. 8 (b)), and the other vectors correspond to the different network's parts (Fig. 8 (a)).

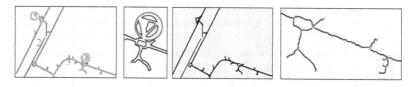

Fig. 8. (a) Network's vectorisation (b) symbol's vectorisation (c) circle simplification (d) interest zone research

6.4 Connected Characters Detection

In a third step, we use another vectorisation scenario in order to deal with the connected characters detection. Firstly, we use vector data of the last step in order to reduce complexity of processed images (Fig. 7 (b)). We apply a circle object simplification (see section 3.4) with an automatic connected component filtering (see section (3.2)). The automatic connected component filtering erases the possible small connected components obtained after the circle simplification. The Fig. 8 (c) gives an example of result after circle simplification. Next, we use a skeleton graph in order to research the zones of interest for connected characters. We have applied successively a skeletonisation adaptation, a skeletonisation, a pixel list extraction, a junction detection, a graph construction, and a pruning and a merging. Finally, we use a graph tool [4] in order to search the graphs' parts corresponding to zones of interest. We construct graphs with length information of pixel lists (two node labels: *short* and *long*), and search into the image's graphs groups of connected nodes, which are labelled *short*. The Fig. 8 (d) gives an example of result, with the detection of "3" connected character. Thereafter, these zones of interest can be exploited by statistical filtering methods [2].

6.5 XML Object Reconstruction

The two last steps give recognition results into XML format, stored into different XML files. These XML data are weakly structured: there are no links between them. In order to solve this problem, we use an XML object reconstruction step. This step organizes the different XML streams of the two last steps, in order to reconstruct the document's objects. This reconstruction allows to structure the symbols and connected characters with their network's parts. During this step, the internal contours numbers are used to give the symbols' labels. We use for that a reconstruction scenario based on XSLT and Quilt (see section 5).

7 Conclusion

In this paper we have presented a vectorisation system based on strategic knowledge use. This system is under experimentation, but allows first uses. Our processing library is composed of image pre-processing and vectorisation tools. Our pre-processing tools allow to deal with noisy images. Our vectorisation tools are of high granularity level in order to use them within a strategic approach. In both case, several different processings can be used for a same recognition goal. The graphic user interface is used to construct and execute vectorisation scenarios. Scenarios are stored in a database and then can be replayed partially or totally. In both system's parts, a XML data representation is used allowing an easy data manipulation. So, this system allows to construct several vectorisation scenarios, to test different strategies according to the recognition goals, and can be easily adapted to new applications.

For the perspectives, currently the system does not analyze the consistency of scenario's results. For that, we plan to use RuleML[10], which will allow to use domain knowledge [22], stored in rules base, and depending on processed document's type.

---

[10] Rule Markup Language.

Next we will extend our graphic user interface for the scenario construction of symbol recognition [4]. Finally, we will plan to use RDF[11] in order to structure the knowledge provided scenarios' results with the strategic knowledge provided by the graphic user interface.

References

1. S. Ablameyko, T.P. Pridmore. Machine Interpretation of Line Drawing Images. Springer-Verlag, 2000.
2. S. Adam, J.M. Ogier, C. Cariou, J. Gardes, Y. Lecourtier. Combination of Invariant Pattern Recognition Primitive on Technical Documents. Graphics Recognition (GREC), 1999.
3. M. Burge, W.G. Kropatsh. A Minimal Line Property Preserving Representation of Line Images. Structural and Syntactical Pattern Recognition (SSPR), 1998.
4. M. Delalandre, S. Nicolas, E. Trupin, J.M. Ogier. Symbols Recognition by Global-Local Structural Approaches, Based on the Scenarios Use, and with a XML Representation of Data. International Conference on Document Analysis And Recognition (ICDAR), 2003.
5. M. Delalandre, E. Trupin, J.M, Ogier. Local Structural Analysis: A Primer. Graphics Recognition (GREC), 2003.
6. G.B Di Baja. Well shaped, Stable, and Reversible Skeletons from the 3-4 Distance Transform. Journal of Visual Communication and Image Representation, 5(1): 107–115, 1992.
7. J. Fan. Off-line Optical Character Recognition for Printed Chinese Character-A Survey. Technical Report, University of Colombia, USA, 2002.
8. J.E. Den Hartog. Knowledge Based Interpretation of Utility Maps. Computer Vision and Image Understanding (CVIU), 63(1): 105–117, 1996.
9. T.C. Henderson, L. Swaminathan. Agent Based Engineering Drawing Analysis. Symposium on Document Image Understanding Technology (SDIUT), 2003.
10. J. Kittler, J. Illingworth. Minimum Error Thresholding. Pattern Recognition (PR), 19(1): 41–47, 1986.
11. A. Lassaulzais, R. Mullot, J. Gardes, Y. Lecourtier. Segmentation d'Infrastructures de Réseau Téléphonique. Colloque International Francophone sur l'Ecrit et le Document (CIFED), 1998.
12. C. W Liao, J. S. Huang. Stroke Segmentation by Bernstein-Bezier Curve Fitting. Pattern Recognition (PR), 23(5): 475–484, 1990.
13. J. Lladós, E. Valveny, G. Sánchez, E. Martí. Symbol Recognition: Current Advances an Perspectives. Graphics Recognition (GREC), 2001.
14. E.F El-Mejbri, H. Grabowski, H. Kunze, R.S. Lossack, A. Michelis. A Contribution to the Reconstruction Process of Article Based Assembly Drawings. Graphics Recognition (GREC), 2001.
15. J.M. Ogier, C. Olivier, Y. Lecourtier. Extraction of Roads from Digitized Maps. European Signal Processing Conference (EUSIPCO), 1992.
16. J.M. Ogier, S. Adam, A. Bessaid, H. Bechar. Automatic Topographic Color Map Analysis. System. Graphics Recognition (GREC), 2001.
17. N. Otsu. A Threshold Selection Method from Gray-Level Histograms. Transactions on Systems, Man and Cybernetics (TSMC), 9(1): 62–66, 1979.
18. J.R. Parker. Algorithms for Image Processing and Computer Vision. Paperback editions, 1996.

---

[11] Resource Description Framework.

19. T. Pavlidis, S. L. Horowitz. Segmentation of Plane Curves. Transactions on Computers (TC), 23: 860–870, 1974.
20. V. Ramer. An Iterative Procedure for the Polygonal Approximation of Plane Curves. Computer Vision Graphics and Image Processing, 1(3): 244–246, 1972.
21. P.L. Rosin, A.W. West. Nonparametric Segmentation of Curves Into Various Representations. Pattern Analysis and Machine Intelligence (PAMI), 17(12): 1140–1153, 1995.
22. Y. Saidali, S. Adam, J.M. Ogier, E. Trupin, J. Labiche. Knowledge Representation and Acquisition for Engineering Document Analysis. Graphics Recognition (GREC), 2003.
23. J. Song, F. Su, C. Tai, S. Cai. An Object-Oriented Progressive-Simplification based Vectorisation System for Engineering Drawings: Model, Algorithm and Performance. Pattern Analysis and Machine Intelligence (PAMI), 24(8): 1048–1060, 2002.
24. B. Taconet, A. Zahour, S. Zhang, A. Faure. Deux Algorithmes de Squelettisation. Reconnaissance Automatique de l'Ecriture (RAE), 1990.
25. K. Tombre. Ten Years of Research in the Analysis of Graphics Documents, Achievements and Open Problems. Image Processing and Image Understanding, 1998.
26. K. Tombre, C. Ah-Soon, P. Dosch, G. Masini, S.Tabbone. Stable and Robust Vectorisation: How to Make the Right Choices. Graphics Recognition (GREC), 1999.

Image Quality Measure Using Sliced Block Distance as a Graphical Element

Jaehwa Park and Young-Bin Kwon

Dept. of Computer Engineering, Chung-Ang University
{jaehwa, ybkwon}@cau.ac.kr

Abstract. This paper deals with the quality of the image itself as well as the algorithm used for evaluating the quality of the fingerprints to construct an effective algorithm for evaluating the quality of the fingerprints. The quality of the fingerprint is acquired by taking the regional quality of each fingerprint image. The regional quality is acquired by measuring the quality of the fingerprint in blocks in the enrollment stage. The amount of fingerprint varies according to the size of each block which makes the result unsteady. We concentrated on finding the right size for the block used to acquire the fingerprint image as a graphical element. Also, the quality distribution included in the fingerprint image was acquired when the optimal block size was adopted. The threshold value of this distribution rate is expected to be used to acquire a high classification.

Keywords: image quality measure, Fingerprint, sliced block, block size optimisation

1 Introduction

In the age of information, the need for a personal authentication system has increased more than ever. With the spread of the internet, the use of e-commerce and electronic cash has become a general trend. These techniques require biometrics for the authentication process. The advantages of biometrics are that samples can be easily acquired from individuals and that they are hard to forge or modulate. These samples are unique in its form and therefore can be used for identification and authentication of individuals [1].

After various researches have been done on this area, the algorithm for fingerprint recognition has reached a certain level nowadays. However, such systems rely on the FAR (False Acceptance Rate) and FRR (False Reject Rate), which makes the accuracy lower when the quality of the image itself is below a certain level [2]. If the acquired fingerprint is contaminated in any way such as by a cut or through an incomplete contact, a recognition error occurs and the fingerprint is misread [3].

A sample with bad quality becomes one of the main causes of a mismatch for the fingerprint recognition system. Therefore, measuring the quality of the fingerprint sample becomes an important factor in acquiring a high-quality fingerprint. The system provides the user with a chance to self-correct the fingerprint that the user had input. Also, by classifying the qualities of the fingerprint from a large database of

J. Lladós and Y.-B. Kwon (Eds.): GREC 2003, LNCS 3088, pp. 211–222, 2004.
© Springer-Verlag Berlin Heidelberg 2004

fingerprints using a classification algorithm using a dynamic threshold, set by the quality of each print, the recognition rate can further be improved [4][5].

It has only been a few years since research has been done in the area of measuring the quality of fingerprints. The quality evaluation system in most fingerprint recognition systems had been adopted to acquire a quality fingerprint by detecting the relative amount of area for the fingerprint compared to the location of the finger. This could only be used to notify the user whether the location of the finger was sufficient to acquire the fingerprint but not the quality of the fingerprint itself. Current systems relied on human heuristic to evaluate the quality of the fingerprint image. Therefore, it relied too much on human-decision which dropped its reliability. Some researched have recently begun in the area of evaluating the quality of the fingerprint images [2][6]. We will talk about the quality of the image itself as well as the algorithm used for evaluating the quality of the fingerprints to construct an effective algorithm for evaluating the quality of the fingerprints.

2   Necessity of Quality Measure

Measuring the quality of the fingerprints is required to measure the quality of the fingerprint image used for the AFIS. We can acquire a higher quality image by taking the quality of the image in the post-processing stage of the authentication and matching process. Also, by rejecting a low quality image and making user to input the fingerprint, we can guarantee better image quality. The bifurcation and the ridges become unclear if there is too much or less pressure on the finger in the input process. If the quality of fingerprints is poor (bad), we can find out three cases: false minutiae finding, omission of minutiae, and error occurrence in the position of minutiae. In order to solve these problems, the enrol stage must have a measure to select the good quality of fingerprint images. In this paper, we defined the area where the boundary is clear as a good quality region and the contaminated area and the area that cannot be recovered as a poor quality region. The region where the disconnection of the ridge occurs frequently is defined weak, and where the fingerprint is printed firmly is defined strong in a bad quality region.

3   Proposed Image Quality Measurement Method

3.1   Pre-requisite Condition of Quality Measure Samples

The samples used for the quality measurement were acquired using the fingerprint input sensor from Huno System. The image should not contain any rotating fingerprints or falsely input in any way. It means that the quality measurement was performed on images that passed the minimum satisfactory level of quality. Also, the samples should be taken from different levels respectively, because it is difficult to classify images of similar quality. The pre-processing steps such as the enhancement of the input image should not be processed before the quality measurement. Through pre-processing the images, some of the original information may be lost from the image [13].

3.2 Definition of the Quality Features of the Fingerprint Image

The standard for classifying the quality of the fingerprint image was set by experts in the field of fingerprint classification. However, it still remains objective and is prone to differences made by different experts, and therefore it was necessary to set a generalized standard for classifying the images in this paper. We have classified the images as Good Quality and Poor Quality in our study.

Even images that have been classified as poor quality images contain both good quality and poor quality image blocks. The following shows an example of such case. Figure 1 shows a good quality image. The ridge and the valley are clearly separated but the block indicated using dotted lines are of poor quality.

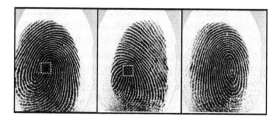

Fig. 1. Poor quality block within good quality

Fig. 2. Good quality block within poor quality

Figure 2 shows a poor quality image. The ridge and the valley are not clearly separated due to factors such as sweat and high pressure. However, locally there are some blocks which could be classified as good quality. The area shown with the dotted line in Figure 2 shows such example.

3.3 Proposed Classification Method for Fingerprint Images

3.3.1 Choosing the Optimal Block Size

The existing methods based on the grey-level change showed low performance because they did not take the structure of the ridge and the occurrence factor into account. A solution to this problem would be to divide the image into block sizes sufficient to take the local features of the fingerprint into account. Better quality can be obtained by including sufficient amount of ridge and valley in the block, when measuring the grey-level value for the pixels in each direction. Therefore, the size of the block is defined while changing the occurrence of the ridge to find the sufficient size for the block to measure the quality.

3.3.1.1 Definition by Size of Good and Poor Quality Blocks. Good and poor quality blocks are extracted from images classified by human experts. The quality pattern shown on the fingerprint image can be defined as the following few patterns. The size of the block was decided based on the number of ridge. The following is an example of a quality pattern extracted for each block size. The fingerprints used in the experiment were acquired from adults in the age between 20 and 30. Therefore, fingerprints obtained from minors can show the following difference. We were able to find out that there were 1 or 2 ridges in a 12*12 block. There were 2 or 3 ridges in a 16*16 block, 3 or 4 in a 24*24 block and 4 or 5 in a 36*36 block. In the example of a good quality image shown in Figure 3, the ridge and the valley are clearly shown within the block. However, in a poor quality image, they did not show up clearly. Poor quality image, as shown in Figure 3 [A](b), the ridge and valley were merged together or had many disconnected areas.

3.3.1.2 Applying the Directional Slot for Each Block Size. 8 directional slots out of the 16 chain codes were used for each block. Directions of the same index are defined for each 25° [12]. Each directional slot is formed to contain odd number of pixels to make it cross the centre of the block. Also, it is calculated for all direction to include specific information about the block. The slot applied for each block only differs in its size and not in its application and calculation method. Therefore, we will only give a single example using a 12*12 block.

The directional slot from Figure 4 is applied on the 12*12 pixel block. The pixel for each direction in the figure has been indicated with numbers from 0 to 7. The pixels indicated with the alphabet are the pixels calculated more than once. The sum of the grey level for each direction is shown in Figure 5. Dd indicates the sum of all directions. Direction d is defined for 8 directions from 0 to 7. From the expression pdi, p indicates the pixel, d the direction index and i represents the order number of the pixel. In Figure 4, the pixels surrounding the centre pixel E are the pixels that are calculated redundantly. They are expressed with alphabet. After adding all the grey level value for the pixels in each direction, the average is calculated. Each average value is defined as Dm (Direction mean). m (mean) indicates the 8 directions 0, 1, ...6, 7. The following equation is used to get the average value.

$$Dm = Dd / \text{directional pixel number} \qquad \text{(Eq. 1)}$$

The average values are compared to get the Max and Min value in order to get their difference. They are each defined as DMax and DMin, and their difference is defined as QB (Quality Block).

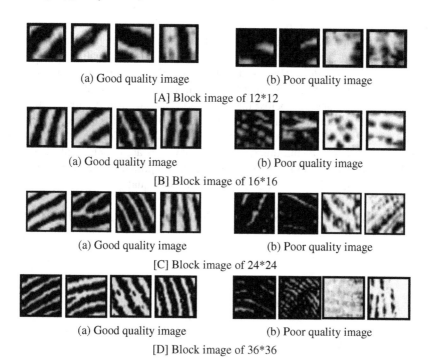

(a) Good quality image   (b) Poor quality image

[A] Block image of 12*12

(a) Good quality image   (b) Poor quality image

[B] Block image of 16*16

(a) Good quality image   (b) Poor quality image

[C] Block image of 24*24

(a) Good quality image   (b) Poor quality image

[D] Block image of 36*36

Fig. 3. Quality examples by block size

$p2_0$	$p3_0$		$p4_0$		$p5_7$	$p6_7$					
	$p2_1$	$p3_1$	$p4_1$	$p5_6$	$p6_6$						
$p1_0$	$p2_2$	$p3_2$	$p4_2$	$p5_5$	$p6_5$		$p7_7$				
	$p1_1$	$p1_2$	$p2_3$ $p3_3$	$p4_3$	$p5_4$	$p6_4$	$p7_5$	$p7_6$			
			$p1_3$	A	B	C	$p7_4$				
$p0_0$	$p0_1$	$p0_2$	$p0_3$	D	E	F	$p0_4$	$p0_5$	$p0_6$	$p0_7$	
		$p7_2$	$p7_3$	G	H	I	$p1_4$	$p1_5$			
$P7_0$	$p7_1$		$p6_3$	$p5_3$	$p4_4$	$p3_4$	$p2_4$		$p1_6$	$p1_7$	
		$p6_2$		$p5_2$	$p4_5$	$p3_5$		$p2_5$			
	$p6_1$		$p5_1$	$p4_6$		$p3_6$		$p2_6$			
$P6_0$			$p5_0$	$p4_7$		$p3_7$					$p2_7$

Fig. 4. Directional slit on 12*12 block

The above equation is each applied on a good and poor quality block to acquire QB. A high value is obtained for a good quality block and vice versa. However, there are some cases where a poor quality block shows a high QB value, as well as good quality blocks with a low QB value. This is the disadvantage of using the change in the grey level for the quality classification, which occurs when the grey level is not properly taken into account due to the directional slot. This can be corrected using the following method. The QB value of both the good and poor quality block are compared to the Quality Block Threshold value within the range from 0 to the maximum QB value. A block with a QB value larger than the threshold value is classified as a good quality block and that below the threshold as a poor quality block. The preciseness of the classification depends on the size of the threshold. The preciseness is calculated using (Eq. 2), by dividing the number of values under the QBT by the total number of QB values of the image. Redundant values are counted only once within the QB values that are under the QBT value. The optimal threshold value is set by comparing the classification rate of the good and poor quality images.

Classification Rate = number of values under the QBT / total number of QB value * 100   (Eq. 2)

$$D_0 = \sum_{\delta=0}^{7} p0_i + D + E + F, \qquad D_4 = \sum_{\delta=0}^{7} p4_i + B + E + H$$

$$D_1 = \sum_{\delta=0}^{7} p1_i + A + E + F, \qquad D_5 = \sum_{\delta=0}^{7} p5_i + C + E + H$$

$$D_2 = \sum_{\delta=0}^{7} p2_i + A + E + I, \qquad D_6 = \sum_{\delta=0}^{7} p6_i + C + E + G,$$

$$D_3 = \sum_{\delta=0}^{7} p3_i + A + E + H, \qquad D_7 = \sum_{\delta=0}^{7} p7_i + C + E + D$$

Fig. 5. An example of gray level value calculation for each direction (based on Figure 4)

3.3.2 Measuring the QB for Each Region of the Fingerprint Image

3.3.2.1 Applying the QBT. The quality of the fingerprint image can be analyzed by applying the QBT on each block size. There are more poor quality blocks than good quality blocks in a poor quality image. On the other hand, there are more good quality blocks than poor quality blocks in a good quality image. The ratio for both a good quality image and a poor quality image can be obtained by analyzing the ration of poor quality blocks in a poor quality image and good quality blocks in a good quality image.

First of all, the image is divided into blocks to acquire the QB. The quality of the block is decided by comparing the QB value with the threshold value. The background region and the fingerprint region are separated to obtain the QB from only the fingerprint region to reduce the amount of calculation and increase the accuracy. The segmentation of the fingerprint region is processed through the following method.

3.3.2.2   Segmentation of the Fingerprint image. A background region is formed around the actual fingerprint image when the fingerprint has been input. The analysis should be performed on only the fingerprint image itself. The blocks in the background image do not contain a ridge, which results in a higher grey level value. The QB value also shows up low due to the grey level value. The process for segmenting the fingerprint image is as follows:

1. Calculate the GM (Global Mean) of the whole image.
2. Divide the whole image into blocks to get the BM (Block Mean).
3. Calculate the QB (Quality Block) for each block.
4. If GM is greater than BM and QB is greater than QBT, it is defined as a background region. The region that does not fit into these categories is defined as the fingerprint region.

Blocks that include only parts of the fingerprint occur on the blocks that are on the border of the image. These blocks were not included in the quality measurement process because of the background region. Blocks that partially include the fingerprints were classified as background regions.

(a) before (bn: 278)   (b) after (bn: 332)

Fig. 6. Block segmentation of 12*12

The following figure shows an example of the image before and after the segmentation rules have been applied. Figure 6 shows an example when segmentation has been applied for each block size (12*12 to 32*32). Only the blocks within the fingerprint area are marked as a fingerprint block when classification is applied. Therefore, the number of background blocks increases after the classification.

3.3.3 Configuration of Quality Classification System

The overall system configuration of quality classification is shown in Figure 7.

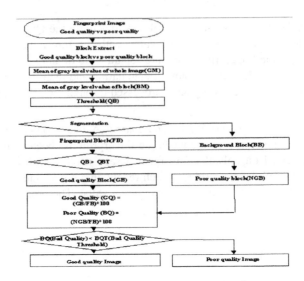

Fig. 7. Configuration of Quality Classification System

4   Results and Discussions

4.1   Block Size Optimization

It is important to set the block to an appropriate size to apply the quality classification method explained in chapter 3. The ridge and valley would not be properly expressed if the block was too small, an unnecessary value would be acquired. Therefore, we have made the block size appropriate to take the ridge and valley information into account. The fingerprint image for the sensor used in this study is 500dpi, from which the ridge took 3-7pixel and the valley 2-7. Therefore, the block size should be larger than the ridge. The quality classification method has been applied on blocks with the size of 12*12 pixel, 16*16 pixel, 24*24 pixel, and 36*36 pixel each. We were able to find the appropriate block size that showed the highest accuracy in its threshold value.

a. Experiments on 12*12 block size

Figure 8 shows the result of the classification rate found within the quality group when the QBT value has been applied as a graph. The x-axis indicates the QBT threshold value and the y-axis indicates the classification rate when a threshold was given. 'Good' indicates the rate that a block is classified as a good quality block, and 'bad' indicates the rate that a block is classified as a bad quality block when the QBT was given. For example, when the threshold value was 0, the QB of the good quality blocks would be 100% and the QB of bad quality blocks would be 0%. The point where the graph for the good and bad quality blocks cross is set as the QBT. The classification rate was 80% when the QBT value was set to 61 and a 12*12 block was used.

b. Experiments on 16*16 block size

The result after being applied on a 16*16 block is represented as a graph in the following figure. If the resulting QBT is 49 on a 16*16 size image, the classification rate is 82 shown in Figure 9.

c. Experiments on 24*24 block size

The result of applying it on a 24*24 block showed a 79% classification rate when the threshold was 44 as shown in the graph. This is worse than the result of the 16*16 block.

d. Experiments on 32*32 block size

The classification rate was 59% when a threshold of 48 was given for a 32*32 block, which is worse than the 24*24 block.

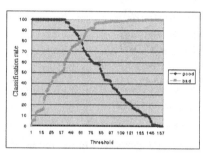   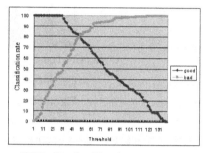

(QBT: 61, classification rate: 80%)   (QBT: 49, classification rate: 82%)

Fig. 8. Result on 12*12 block size   **Fig. 9.** Result on 16*16 block size

e. Analysis on block size optimization

As shown in the experiments above, any blocks larger than or smaller than the 16*16 block showed a lower classification rate. This means that the classification rate is best expressed using the 16*16 block. Therefore, it can be assumed that the classification would become most accurate when a 16*16 block was used. The threshold value to be applied will be discussed.

4.2 Quality Distribution of Block Images

The quality distribution of the good and bad quality images is acquired by applying the threshold for each block size on the fingerprint area acquired through the segmentation. The ratio of the good quality block is higher in a good quality image. The optimal classification rate when the threshold has been applied is as follows.

A block whose QB is higher than the QBT is classified as a good quality block. If the QB is lower than the QBT, the conditions of a bad quality block are applied to figure out the number of blocks for both quality. Then the following equation is applied to calculate the ration of each quality blocks in every region.

-Ratio of good quality blocks = 100 * Number of good quality block / Total number of blocks   (Eq. 3)

-Ratio of poor quality block = 100 – Ratio of good quality block   (Eq. 4)

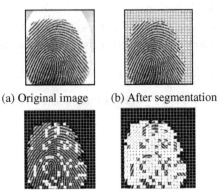

(a) Original image   (b) After segmentation

(c) Good quality block (d) Good quality block
  (poor blocks: 296)   (poor blocks: 73)

Fig. 10. Block thresholding on 12*12

Figure 10 shows a good quality image. Figure 10(a) is the original image and (b) is the segmented image used for the experiment. In Figure (c), the good quality blocks are indicated using white-colored blocks. Therefore, the number of bad quality blocks in Figure (c) is the rest of the blocks not including the white-colored blocks. The same coloring is applied for Figure (d). The following graph shows the ratio of good quality blocks in a good quality image. In our experiment using 12*12 blocks, the classification rate was 63% when the ratio of the bad quality blocks was 71%. Therefore, the optimal threshold value is 71.

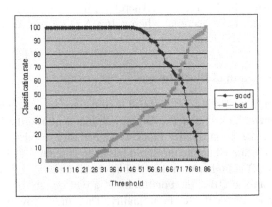

Fig. 11. Block thresholding on 12*12

The 16*16 block showed a 92% classification rate. A good quality block contains clear ridge and valley information. A bad quality block has the following two problems. First of all is the effect of the ridge and valley being merged together into an unclear shape. The second problem is the disconnection of the ridge. A 16*16 block, shows the best performance, for the quality classification that defines a bad case only when the ridge and valley are mashed together. The threshold is nearly identical to the quality classification threshold from the previous section. Therefore, the method used in our experiment showed a high classification rate when the bad quality blocks were strong types.

5 Conclusion and Future Works

Classification of the fingerprints by humans may vary according to the person appointed to do the job and the threshold would change if the person is replaced with another human expert. This study aims at providing a subjective method for classification that is similar to the human expert. Various methods have been proposed before, but they were not able to provide a method that considers the areal characteristics of the fingerprints.

Therefore, we proposed a method that changes the block size to find the optimal threshold value for the classification. Through experiments, the optimal block size to be used for the classification has been measured, which is useful when the resolution changes by using a different sensor to acquire the fingerprint image. The method proposed in this paper estimates the area quality of the fingerprints to decide the quality distribution. The threshold value changes for different block sizes. The accuracy was the highest when the optimal threshold value acquired through this method was applied on the whole area. The grey-level value for each direction was measure for the regional characteristics which could not take the overall structure of the image into account. This could cause a problem when the valley and boundary were merged together and unclear. It also presented a problem when the ridge was disconnected in the image. Future works should provide a method to overcome such adversities that could affect the overall performance of the classification.

Acknowledgement

This work is supported by ITRI, Chung-Ang University.

References

[1] L. C. Jain, U. Halici, I. Hayashi, S. B. Lee, S. Tsutsui, *Intelligent Biometric Techiques in Fingerprint and Face Recognition*, CRC Press LLC, pp. 3–21, 1999.

[2] M. Y. Yao, S. Pankanti, N. Haas, N. K. Ratha, R. M. Bolle, "Quantifying Quality: A Case Study in Fingerprints", http://www.research.ibm.com/ecvg/pubs/sharat-qqual. html, 2002.

[3] L. Hong, A. K. Jain, S. Pankanti, and R. M. Bolle, "Fingerprint Enhancement". Proc. 1st IEEE Workshop on the Application of Computer Vision, pp. 202–207, Sarasota, FL, 1996.

[4] L. L. Shen, A. Kot and W. M. Koo, "Quality Measures of Fingerprint Images", Proceedings of the Third International Conference on Audio and Video Based Biometric Person Authentication 2001, pp. 266–271, Halmstad, Sweden, 2001.

[5] N. K. Ratha, R. M. Bolle, "Fingerprint Image Quality Estimation", IBM Computer Science Research Report RC 21622, 1999   http://www.research.ibm.com/ecvg/pubs/ratha-qual.html

[6] W. Jang et al., "Quality Check for fingerprint Recognition", CVPR Spring Workshop, KISS, pp. 69–72, 2001.

[7] L. Coetzee and E. C. Botha. "Fingerprint Recognition In Low Quality Images", Pattern Recognition, vol. 26, no. 10, pp. 1441–1460, 1993.

[8] A. L. Jain And S. Pankanti, "Automated Fingerprint Identification and Imaging Systems", *Advances in Fingerprint Technology*, 2nd Ed. (H. C.   Lee and R. E. Gaensslen), CRC Press, 2001

[9] Q. Zhang, K. Huang, H. Yan, "Fingerprint Classification Based on Extraction and Analysis of Singularities and Pseudo-ridges, http://www.jrpit.flinders.edu.au/confpapers/CRPITV11Zhang1.pdf, 2001.

[10] H. Kim, D. S. Ahn, "Statistical Fingerprint Recognition using Block-FFT", Proceedings of First Asian Conference on Control, pp. 953–956, 1994.

[11] L. Hong, Y. Wan, A. Jain, "Fingerprint Image Enhancement:" Algorithm and Performance Evaluation", IEEE Trans. on Pattern Analysis and Machine Intelligence, vol. 20, no. 8, pp. 777–789, 1998.

[12] Y. Hamamoto, S. Uchimura, M. Watanabe, "A Gabor filter-based method for recognizing handwritten numerals", Pattern Recognition, vol. 21, no. 4, pp. 395–400, 1998.

[13] Fingerprint Quality, http://www.hbs-jena.com/Dummy/QualityCheck/qualitycheck.html.

Local Structural Analysis: A Primer

Mathieu Delalandre[1], Eric Trupin[1], and Jean-Marc Ogier[2]

[1] Laboratory PSI, University of Rouen, 76 821 Mont Saint Aignan, France
{mathieu.delalandre, eric.trupin}@univ-rouen.fr
[2] Laboratory L3I, University of La Rochelle, 17042 La Rochelle, France
jmogier@univ-lr.fr

Abstract. The structural analysis is a processing step during which graphs are extracted from binary images. We can decompose the structural analysis into local and global approaches. The local approach decomposes the connected components, and the global approach groups them together. This paper deals especially with the local structural analysis. The local structural analysis is employed for different applications like symbol recognition, line drawing interpretation, and character recognition. We propose here a primer on the local structural analysis. First, we propose a general decomposition of the local structural analysis into four steps: object graph extraction, mathematical approximation, high-level object construction, and object graph correction. Then, we present some considerations on the method comparison and combination.

1 Introduction

The problem of document image interpretation is a vast field gathering three main applications: handwriting [58], graphic documents (technical documents [51], maps [43], symbols [32], and so on.), and structured documents [39]. Document image interpretation is an artificial intelligence problem based on three entities: a control system, a pattern recognition process for document images[1], and a knowledge base. Several common works on this problem have been realized during the last fifteen years [12].

This paper deals with the pattern recognition process. Classically, a pattern recognition process is decomposed into two main steps [25]. The first one is an image processing step which has two goals: the image pre-processing allowing to enhance the image's conditions, and the feature extraction for the description of image's shapes. In the following of this paper, as [34], we simply call the feature extraction step "analysis". The second one is the recognition step. This step exploits the extracted features by the analysis step for different purposes like recognition [33], learning [37], indexing [15], data structuring [59], interest zone search [13], and so on. Two main approaches for the pattern recognition process exist: statistical &

---

[1] In the following, we talk about "recognition process" for "recognition process for document images".

J. Lladós and Y.-B. Kwon (Eds.): GREC 2003, LNCS 3088, pp. 223–234, 2004.
© Springer-Verlag Berlin Heidelberg 2004

connexionnist [24], and structural & syntactic[2] [53]. This paper deals especially with the structural approach. In this approach, the image-processing step extracts graphs from images and the recognition step exploits them. In these graphs, nodes represent images' objects, and edges represent structural links between these objects. Many different shapes could be described by graphs in document image interpretation such as forms [39], oriental characters [18], and graphic parts [51].

The structural recognition step is a graph exploitation problem, which uses two main approaches: graph-matching [19] and grammar [4]. The first one matches extracted graphs with model graphs. The second one applies different rules to transform extracted graphs into model graphs. A graph problem depends on two criteria: graph/subgraph, and exact-inexact. A subgraph is a subset of node and edge of a larger graph. The subgraph problem is to recognize a model subgraph into a candidate graph. If extracted graphs correspond exactly to model graphs, the problem is known as exact. Unfortunately, in image applications, graphic parts are often connected to other parts, and extracted graphs are noisy and large sized. So, it is an inexact subgraph problem, into candidate graphs of large size.

The analysis step extracts (or constructs) graphs from images. For the purpose of this paper, we simply call it "structural analysis". We can decompose the structural analysis into local and global approaches[3]. The boundary between these two approaches is the connected component. The local approach decomposes a connected component into basic object, and the global approach groups together connected components according to some closeness and connection constraints. The Fig. 1 gives an example of global/local analysis results, with graphic representations and graph visualisations. The local approach (b) decomposes the connected component (a) into arc, junction, and polyline objects. The global approach (c) groups together three connected components (a) according to some neighboring constraints.

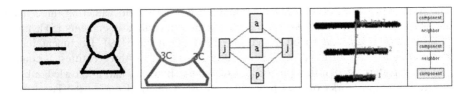

Fig. 1. (a) Symbols (b) local structural analysis (c) global structural analysis

This paper especially deals with the local structural analysis. We propose here a primer on the local structural analysis. In section 2, we give a general decomposition of the local structural analysis into four steps. Then, in section 3, we present a comparison study of methods. In section 4, we present some considerations on the method combination. Finally in section 5, we conclude.

---

[2] In the following, we talk about "structural" for "structural & syntactic".
[3] This classification also exists in statistical analysis [41].

2   General Decomposition

The local analysis employs different approaches from character recognition (latin [55], oriental [18]), and graphics recognition (technical documents [51], maps [43], symbols [32], and so on.). It extracts different objects from documents according to the exploration granularity. The smallest objects are the pixels and the biggest objects are the connected components. We propose here a general decomposition of the local structural analysis into four steps: object graph extraction, mathematical approximation, high-level object construction, and object graph correction. We present each step in sections 2.1, 2.2, 2.3, and 2.4.

2.1   Object Graph Extraction

This step decomposes the connected component into an object graph. We have listed seven method families as shown in the Fig. 2. The methods are based on skeletonisation (a), contouring (b), tracking (c), run decomposition (d), region decomposition (e), mesh decomposition (f), and object segmentation (g). We present each method family in the next subsections.

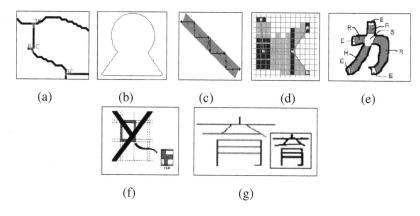

(a)   (b)   (c)   (d)   (e)

(f)   (g)

Fig. 2. (a) Skeletonisation (b) contouring (c) tracking (d) run decomposition (e) region decomposition (f) mesh decomposition (g) object segmentation

2.1.1   Skeletonisation Based Methods

The skeletonisation based methods are the most commonly used. They involve two steps. The first one extracts the skeleton images [26]. Two main families exist, by distance transform and by iterative thinning [1]. The second one analyses skeleton images in order to extract pixel graphs. In these pixel graphs, nodes represent the skeleton' junctions and chains (pixels lists), and edges represent connection links between these two object types. The junctions detection is based on different methods: the connectivity analysis [54] [44], or the 3-connected pixel destruction [14] [27]. The Fig. 2 (a) gives an example of an extracted pixel graph [14].

2.1.2 Contouring Based Methods

The contouring based methods are often used. Two methods families exist [56]. The first ones use contour images like intermediate representations. They are based on mathematical morphology [20] or on neighbouring tests [14]. Similar to skeletonisation based methods, they involve a second step to extract the contours' pixel chains. The second ones directly extract the contours' pixel chains without any intermediate image representation. They use line following methods [1], or blob coloring methods [14]. Their advantages rely on the fact that they provide the inclusion links between chains, and they permit the selection of internal or external contours [14]. So, it is possible to construct contour graphs in which, nodes represent chains (pixels lists), and edges represent inclusion links between these chains. The Fig. 2 (b) gives an example of external contours' pixel chains of the Fig. 1 [14].

2.1.3 Tracking Based Methods

The tracking based methods directly analyse the images without any intermediate representation. They are based on the structuring elements use in order to track the shapes, of pixel type [16] [48], or area type (circle [11], gaussian bead [61]). They produce pixel graphs [11], or geometric object graphs (arc and vector [48]). In these geometric object graphs, nodes represent geometric objects, and edges connection links between these geometrical objects. The produced graph types depend on the adopted tracking model (linear [16], circular [48]), and on the structuring element's progression into the shape (continuous [11], by jump [16]). The tracking process may be of two types: line tracking and junction tracking. In both cases, the employed structuring element can be of "pixel type" [11] [16], of "area type" [11] [61], or even both [42]. The Fig. 2 (c) gives an example of pixel tracking [16].

2.1.4 Run Decomposition Based Methods

The run decomposition based methods are used for line drawing interpretation [6] and handwriting recognition [17] [60]. A run is a maximal sequence of black pixel in a column or a row of the image. The run graph is constructed with vertical and horizontal runs according to construction rules. In these run graphs, nodes represents runs chains (1-2 connected runs) and run junctions (3-n connected run), and edges represent the connection links between these runs. From this definition, [6] constructs the MRG "Mixed Run Graph", a vertical and horizontal run graph (Fig. 2 (d)). In this MRG, vertical and horizontal runs are merged into junction and line nodes.

2.1.5 Region Decomposition Based Methods

The region decomposition based methods are less used in the literature. They decompose a connected component into different regions in order to construct region graphs. In these region graphs, nodes represent regions, and edges connection links between these regions. [7] [9] compute orientations data of each image's pixel with its contour pixels. Then, they search the majority directions for each pixel, and construct like this the line, extremity, and junction regions (Fig. 2 (e)). In [14], we propose region decomposition method based on a wave aggregation. The wave breaking and stopping cases define the regions' boundaries. In the following step, the region graph is analysed to construct the line or junction regions.

2.1.6 Meshes Decomposition Based Methods

The mesh decomposition based methods have been used for vectorisation applications [29] [57]. Image is firstly split up into meshes. Then, the meshes are recognized according to a mesh library (Fig. 2 (f)) [57]. So, the result mesh map is analysed to construct the mesh graphs. In these mesh graphs, nodes represent the different meshes' objects (vector, arc, symbols, and so on.), and edges the structural links between theses objects (connections, parallelism, and so on.).

2.1.7 Segmented Object Based Methods

The segmented object based methods are often used in vision [38] and in document image interpretation [52]. The segmented object methods directly extract the objects such as lines, arcs, ellipsis, and junctions. These methods employ mathematical transforms in order to change the image's representation space. This representation space is used to find the objects according to their mathematical models. [52] extracts like this the vertical, diagonal, and horizontal lines for Chinese handwriting recognition (Fig. 2 (g)). Some works deal with the junction segmentation [10] ('T' junction, 'X' junction, and so on.), in order to construct geometrical object graphs. Different techniques exist like the Hough transform [38] or the Gabor filters [10]. If the system does not deal with the junction segmentation, the mathematical objects' crossings [36] and the connections between mathematical objects' extremities [52] are searched to construct the structural links between these objects.

2.2 Mathematical Approximation

During this step, the step 1's result objects (graphs' nodes) are approximated by mathematical objects like vectors, arcs, elliptical arcs, and curves (Fig. 1 (a)). The mathematical approximation functions can exploit various entry data like pixels, vectors, curves, and circles. In fact, we can approximate vectors into circles, curves into circles, and so on. The pixel and vector graphs (Fig. 2 (a), (b), (c)) are often used. The region and run graphs (Fig. 2 (d), (e)) are also used after their skeletons and contours extractions [17] [14]. The mesh and segmented object graphs (Fig. 2 (f), (g)) are not used because their objects are enough approximated. So in practice, pixels graphs are the most commonly used for the vectorisation step [31] [54]. An overview and an algorithm permitting a combination of mathematical object approximation can be found in [46]. Also, an algorithm to extract contextual information on the data quality (in order to control a system in the approximation algorithm choice) can be found in [47].

2.3 High-Level Object Construction

After the mathematical approximation step, some systems construct from low-level objects (vectors, arcs, curves) higher level objects like circles, parallelograms, triangles, and so on. These objects are constructed from skeletonisation based process [23] or contouring based process [28] [8] [62] (we talk about contour matching). The contour matching is generally used to rebuild the shapes' junctions [28]. Position constraints of mathematical objects are tested during this high-level object construction. So, this construction is not only a graph factorisation step. After this construction, new structural representations can be created, describing the structural links between the high-level objects [45]. The Fig. 3 (a) gives a use-case for circle reconstruction from skeletonisation based process [23]. The Fig. 3 (b) gives an example of contour matching into triangle graph [62].

2.4 Object Graph Correction

Some systems analyse the extracted object graphs to correct the structural descriptions. [50] distinguishes systems with corrections (two steps) and without correction (one step). Some corrections add or delete some nodes and edges into object graphs. Other corrections compute new edges or nodes' attributes. These correction processings use image processing steps, so they are not only graph correction processings. These corrections can be used on different data types in (or between) each of steps 1, 2, and 3 (sections 2.1, 2.2, and 2.3).

On the pixel graphs different correction types can be used like pruning and merging [14] (Fig. 3 (c)), and the correction of junctions' distortions [30] (Fig. 3 (d)). These correction methods can be also used on vector graphs [16], but in this case the junction correction by vector crossing search is also used [22] (Fig. 3 (e)). [57] corrects its mesh graphs by a splitting/merging processing. [17] corrects its run graphs with merging/deleting processings of segmented/isolated runs. [45] corrects its high-level object graphs with a merging processing.

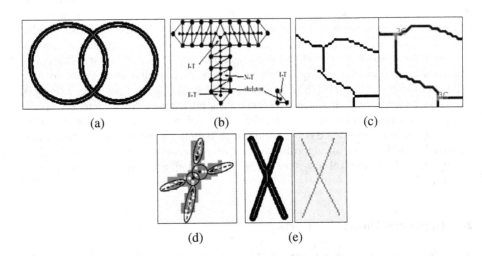

(a)   (b)   (c)

(d)   (e)

Fig. 3. (a) Circle construction case (b) contour matching (c) (d) skeleton correction (e) vectorial correction

3   Method Comparison

We compare in the Table 1 advantages and drawbacks of the object graph extraction step's methods (section 2.1). The comparisons concerning mathematical approximation step's methods (section 2.2), high-level object construction step's methods (section 2.3), and object graph correction step's methods (section 2.4), that are not detailed in this paper and can be found in [46], [40], and [5]. We compare the object graph extraction methods according to seven criteria which are respectively named "Junction", "Morphology", "Invariance", "Sensitivity", "Semantic", "Reversibility", and "Complexity". "Junction" criterion specifies the methods' ability to detect the shapes' junctions. "Morphology" criterion specifies the methods' ability to analyse heterogeneous shapes. "Invariance" criterion specifies the methods' ability to analyse multiple scales and orientations of shapes. "Sensitivity" criterion specifies the methods' distortion noise resistance. "Semantic" criterion specifies the methods' information adding for the shapes' descriptions. "Reversibility" criterion specifies the methods' ability to restore the raster data. "Complexity" criterion specifies the methods' algorithmic complexity. This comparison study is only based on a set of significant experiments performed in our laboratories [14].

Table 1. Method comparison

	Advantages	Drawbacks
Skeleton	Invariance	Morphology, Sensitivity, Complexity
Contouring	Morphology, Invariance, Reversibility	Junction
Tracking	Junction, Semantic, Complexity	Morphology
Run	Junction, Morphology, Reversibility	Invariance, Complexity
Region	Junction, Morphology, Reversibility	Semantic, Complexity
Mesh	Junction, Semantic, Complexity	Morphology, Invariance, Sensitivity, Reversibility
Segmentation	Sensitivity, Semantic	Junction, Morphology, Invariance, Reversibility, Complexity

The skeletonisation based methods are invariant [54], but they only permit the linear shape analysis [45], and are noise sensitive (especially for the junction zone analysis [54]).

The contouring based methods permit to analyse all the shape types, and are reversible [20]. Their drawback is the no detection of junctions that must rebuilt with a high-level object construction step [28].

The tracking based methods permit a good junction detection. Beside, they export vectorial data, and are of low complexity [49]. However, they have some difficulties with shapes' thickness variation [42].

The run decomposition based methods [6] permit a good junction detection, any analysis of shape type, and a raster restoration. However, they are sensitive to orientation (because of vertical and horizontal run types) and complex (because of runs encoding and structuring).

The region decomposition based methods also permit a good junction detection, allow to analyse all the shape types, and permit a raster restoration. However, the regions give few information like representation object (analysis must be completed [13] [14]), and have a high memory cost of manipulation.

The mesh decomposition based methods permit a good junction detection, a complex object export, and are of low complexity. However, these methods are very sensitive to the initial positions of considered meshes [57] (invariance, sensitivity) and strongly depend on mesh library / shapes types adequacy.

The segmented object based methods are noise resistant [50], and export geometrical objects [50]. However, the mathematical transforms used are complex [38], based on the known model search [50] (reversible, morphology), limited to some orientations [52] (invariance), and have some difficulties with the junction segmentation [10].

4   Method Combination

Several research perspectives exist on the subject dealing with the local structural analysis. Some works use recognition step in order to control the graphs' constructions with knowledge bases. These controls can be used for all analysis levels and approaches (sections 2.1, 2.2, 2.3, and 2.4) [2] [52] [59] [6]. Other works deal with the segmentation/recognition problem by utilization of "system approaches", like the perceptive approaches [61] for instance, or multi-agent approaches [21]. Finally, some works use strategic approaches in order to combine the methods [14]. We develop this last perspective in this section.

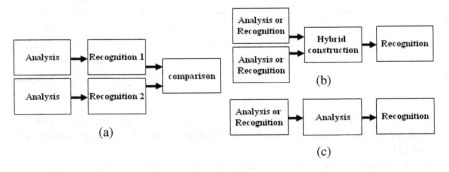

Fig. 4. (a) Comparative combination (b) hybrid combination (c) cooperative combination

We propose here a combinations' classification into three categories: comparative, hybrid, and cooperative (Fig. 4). These combinations are essentially local, but some of them deal with the local/global aspects [13] [3]. The comparative combinations (Fig. 4 (a)) analyze the shapes in order to extract different graphs from different methods. These graphs are then compared during the recognition step. [40] compares vector graphs obtained from contour and skeleton images. In [13] we compare loop graphs (global) with skeleton graphs (local). The hybrid combinations (Fig. 4 (b)) analyze the shapes in order to extract hybrid graphs. These graphs are the combinations of two (or several) analysis methods. Besides, the global methods [13] and local [6] [7] [14] exploiting the region objects permit to use a statistico-structural approach [13] [14]. [3] extracts connected component graphs, and completes these graphs with the concavity local information for each connected component. In [13] and [14], we use statistico-structural approaches for the recognition of local/global region graphs. The cooperative combinations (Fig. 4 (c)) exploit the analysis methods in order to simplify the recognition process' complexity. [49] uses an object progressive simplification process. In [13] we simplify our global analysis by the use of a local analysis.

The comparative and hybrid combinations permit the multi-models representations of shapes (or adopted graph model). The multi-model representation's possibilities are obtained by the combinations local, local/global, and statistico-structural. The works on the construction and exploitation of the multi-model representation certainly constitute an important research perspective of the local structural analysis.

5   Conclusion

In this paper, we propose a primer on the local structural analysis. This analysis decomposes the connected components into graph of basic object. Then, these graphs are exploited during the recognition step. This analysis declines itself according to different construction levels, using different methods. Each method presents some advantages and drawbacks. All these methods can be combined, for especially the multi-model representation. These multi-models representations certainly constitute an important research perspective of the local structural analysis.

Acknowledgement

The authors wish to thank Noorazrim Zakaria (L3I Laboratory, La Rochelle University, France) and Jean-Yves Ramel (LI Laboratory, Tours University, France) for their contribution to this work. Also, the authors wish to thank the reviewers for their comments and remarks about this work.

References

1. S. Ablameyko, T.P. Pridmore. Machine Interpretation of Line Drawing Images. Springer-Verlag, 2000.

2. M. Ahmed, R. Ward. A Rotation Invariant Rule Based Thinning Algorithm for Character Recognition. Pattern Analysis and Machine Intelligence (PAMI), 24(12): 1672–1678, 2002.
3. O. El Badawy, M. Kamel. Shape Representation using Concavity Graphs. International Conference on Pattern Recognition (ICPR), 2002.
4. D. Blostein, H. Fahmy, A. Grbavec. Issues in the Practical Use of Graph Rewriting. Lecture Notes in Computer Sciences (LNCS), 1073: 38–55, 1996.
5. E. Bodansky, A. Gribov, M. Pilouk. Post-processing of Lines Obtained by Raster-to-Vector Conversion. Graphics Recognition (GREC), 2001.
6. M. Burge, W.G. Kropatsh. A Minimal Line Property Preserving Representation of Line Images. Structural and Syntactical Pattern Recognition (SSPR), 1998.
7. R. Cao, C.L. Tan. A Model of Stroke Extraction from Chinese Character Images. International Conference on Pattern Recognition (ICPR), 2000.
8. F. Chang, Y.C. Lu, T. Palvidis. Feature Analysis Using Line Sweep Thinning Algorithm. Pattern Analysis and Machine Intelligence (PAMI), 21(2): 145–158, 1999.
9. Y.S. Chen. Segmentation and Association Among Lines and Junctions for a Line Image. Pattern Recognition (PR), 27(9): 1135–1157, 1994.
10. J. Chen, Y. Sato, S. Tamura. Orientation Space Filtering for Multiple Orientation Line Segmentation. Pattern Analysis and Machine Intelligence (PAMI), 22(5): 417–429, 2000.
11. J. Chiang, S. Tue. A New Algorithm for Line Image Vectorization. Pattern Recognition (PR), 31(10): 1541–1549, 1998.
12. D. Crevier, R. Lepage. Knowledge-Based Image Understanding Systems: A Survey. Computer Vision and Image Understanding (CVIU), 67(2): 161–185, 1997.
13. M. Delalandre, S. Nicolas, E. Trupin, J.M. Ogier. Symbols Recognition by Global-Local Structural Approaches, Based on the Scenarios Use, and with a XML Representation of Data. International Conference on Document Analysis And Recognition (ICDAR), 2003.
14. M. Delalandre, Y. Saidali, J.M. Ogier, E. Trupin. Adaptable Vectorisation System Based on Strategic Knowledge and XML Representation Use. Graphics Recognition (GREC), 2003.
15. D. Doermann. The Indexing and Retrieval Document, a Survey. Technical Report CS-TR-3876, University of Maryland Computer Science Department, USA, 1998.
16. D. Dori. Sparse Pixel Vectorisation: An Algorithm and its Performance Evaluation. Pattern Analysis and Machine Intelligence (PAMI), 21(3): 202–215, 1999.
17. K.C. Fan, W.H. Wu. A Run Length Coding Based Approach to Stroke Extraction of Chinese Characters. Pattern Recognition (PR), 33(11): 1881–1895, 2000.
18. J. Fan. Off-line Optical Character Recognition for Printed Chinese Character-A Survey. Technical Report, University of Colombia, USA, 2002.
19. E. Hancock, R. Wilson. Graph-Based Methods for Vision: A Yorkist Manifesto. Structural and Syntactical Pattern Recognition (SSPR), 2002.
20. Y.M.Y Hasan, L.J Karan. Morphological Reversible Contour Representation. Pattern Analysis and Machine Intelligence (PAMI), 22(3): 227–239, 2000.
21. T.C. Henderson, L. Swaminathan. Agent Based Engineering Drawing Analysis. Symposium on Document Image Understanding Technology (SDIUT), 2003.
22. X. Hilaire and K. Tombre. Improving the Accuracy of Skeleton-Based Vectorisation. Graphics Recognition (GREC), 2001.
23. X. Hilaire. Ranvec and the Arc Segmentation Contest. Graphics Recognition (GREC), 2001.
24. A.K. Jain, R.P.W. Duin, J. Mao. Statistical Pattern Recognition: a Review. Pattern Analysis and Machine Intelligence (PAMI), 22(1): 4–37, 2000.
25. R. Kasturi, L. O'Gorman, V. Govindaraju. Document Image Analysis: A Primer. Sadhana, 27(1): 3–22, 2002.
26. L. Lam, C.Y. Suen. An Evaluation of Parallel Thinning Algorithms for Character Recognition. Pattern Analysis and Machine Intelligence (PAMI), 17(9): 914–919, 1995.

27. K.K. Lau, P.C. Yuen, Y.Y. Tang. Stroke Extraction and Stroke Sequence Estimation On Signatures. International Conference on Pattern Recognition (ICDAR), 2002.
28. C. Lee, B. Wu. A Chinese Character Stroke Extraction Algorithm Based on Contour Information. Pattern Recognition (PR), 31(6): 651–653, 1998.
29. X. Lin, S. Shimotsuji, M. Mihoh, T. Sakai. Efficient Diagram Understanding with Characteristic Pattern Detection. Computer Vision Graphics and Image Processing, 30: 84–106, 1985.
30. F. Lin, X. Tang. Off-line Handwritten Chinese Character Stroke Extraction. International Conference on Pattern Recognition (ICPR), 2002.
31. W. Liu, D. Dori. From Raster to Vectors: Extracting Visual Information from Line Drawings. Pattern Analysis and Applications (PAA), 2(2): 10–21, 1999.
32. J. Lladós, E. Valveny, G. Sánchez, E. Martí. Symbol Recognition: Current Advances an Perspectives. Graphics Recognition (GREC), 2001.
33. J. Llados, E. Marti, J.J. Villuanueva. Symbol Recognition by Error Subgraph Matching Between Region Adjacency Graphs. Pattern Analysis and Machine Intelligence (PAMI), 23(10): 1137–1143, 2001.
34. S. Locarnic. A Survey of Shape Analysis Techniques. Pattern Recognition (PR), 31(8): 983–1001, 1998.
35. P.K. Loo, C.L. Tan. Detection of Word Group Based on Irregular Pyramid. International Conference on Document Analysis And Recognition (ICDAR), 2001.
36. K. Loudon. Mastering Algorithms with C. O'Reilly Editions, 2000.
37. Y. Luo, W. Liu. Engineering Drawings Recognition Using a Case-based Approach. International Conference on Document Analysis And Recognition (ICDAR), 2003.
38. J. Matas, C. Galambos, J. Kittler. Progressive Probabilistic Hough Transform for Line Detection. Computer Vision and Pattern Recognition (CVPR), 1999.
39. G. Nagy. Twenty Years of Document Image Analysis in PAMI. Pattern Analysis and Machine Intelligence (PAMI), 22(1): 38–62, 2000.
40. Y. Nakajima, S. Mori, S. Takegami, S. Sato. Global Methods for Stroke Segmentation. International Journal Document Analysis and Recognition (IJDAR), 2: 19–23, 1999.
41. J. Neumann, H. Samet, A. Soffer. Integration of Local and Global Shape Analysis for Logo Classification. International Workshop on Visual Form (IWVF), 2001.
42. J.M. Ogier, C. Olivier, Y. Lecourtier. Extraction of Roads from Digitized Maps. European Signal Processing Conference (EUSIPCO), 1992.
43. J.M. Ogier, S. Adam, A. Bessaid, H. Bechar. Automatic Topographic Color Map Analysis System. Graphics Recognition (GREC), 2001.
44. D.V. Popel. Compact Graph Model of Handwritten Images: Integration into Authentification and Recognition. Structural and Syntactical Pattern Recognition (SSPR), 2002.
45. J.Y. Ramel, N. Vincent, H. Emptoz. A Structural Representation for Understanding Line-Drawing Images. International Journal on Document Analysis And Recognition (IJDAR), 3: 58–66, 2000.
46. P.L. Rosin, A.W. West. Nonparametric Segmentation of Curves Into Various Representations. Pattern Analysis and Machine Intelligence (PAMI), 17(12): 1140–1153, 1995.
47. P.L. Rosin. Techniques for Assessing Polygonal Approximation of Curves. Pattern Analysis and Machine Intelligence (PAMI), 19(6): 659–666, 1997.
48. J. Song, F. Su, C. Tai, S. Cai. An Object-Oriented Progressive-Simplification based Vectorisation System for Engineering Drawings: Model, Algorithm and Performance. Pattern Analysis and Machine Intelligence (PAMI), 24(8): 1048–1060, 2002.
49. J. Song, M. Cai, M.R. Lyu, S. Cai. Graphics Recognition from Binary Images: One Step or Two Steps. International Conference on Pattern Recognition (ICPR), 2002.

50. J. Song, M. Cai, M.R. Lyu, S. Cai. A New Approach for Line Recognition in Large-Size Images Using Hough Transform. International Conference on Pattern Recognition (ICPR), 2002.

51. J. Song, M.R. Lyu, M. Cai, and S. Cai. Graphic Object Recognition from Binary Images: a Survey and an Integrated Paradigm. Transactions on Systems, Man and Cybernetics, part C: Applications and Reviews (TSMCC), under review.

52. Y.M. Su, J.F Wang. A Learning Process to the Identification of Feature Points on Chinese Characters. International Conference on Pattern Recognition (ICPR), 2002.

53. K. Tombre. Structural and Syntactic Methods in Line Drawing Analysis: To Which Extent do they Work? Structural and Syntactical Pattern Recognition (SSPR), 1996.

54. K. Tombre, C. Ah-Soon, P. Dosch, G. Masini, S.Tabbone. Stable and Robust Vectorization: How to Make the Right Choices. Graphics Recognition (GREC), 1999.

55. O. D. Trier, A. K. Jain, T. Taxt. Features Extraction Methods for Character Recognition – A Survey. Pattern Recognition (PR), 29(4): 641–662, 1996.

56. M.J. Turner, N.E. Wiseman. Efficient Lossless Image Contour Coding. Computer Graphics Forum, 15(2): 107–118, 1996.

57. P. Vaxivière, K. Tombre. Subsampling: A Structural Approach to Technical Document Vectorisation. Syntactic and Structural Pattern Recognition (SSPR), 1995.

58. A. Vinciarelli. A Survey on Off-Line Cursive Word Recognition. Pattern Recognition (PR), 35(7): 1443–1446, 2002.

59. M. Weindorf. Structure Based Interpretation of Unstructured Vector Maps. Graphics Recognition (GREC), 2001.

60. H. Xue. Building Skeletal Graphs for Structural Feature Extraction on Handwriting Images. International Conference on Document Analysis And Recognition (ICDAR), 2001.

61. S. Yoon, G. Kim, Y. Choi, Y. Lee. New Paradigm for Segmentation and Recognition. Graphics Recognition (GREC), 2001.

62. J.J. Zou, H. Yan. Vectorization of Cartoon Drawings. Visual Information, 2000.

Recognition of Target Graphs from Images Using a Genetic Algorithm with Hill Climbing Searching

Jien Kato[1], Takeyuki Suzuki[2], and Toyohide Watanabe[1]

[1] Dept. of Systems and Social Informatics
Graduate School of Information Science, Nagoya University
Furo-cho, Chikusa-ku, Nagoya 464-8603, Japan
{jien, watanabe}@is.nagoya-u.ac.jp
[2] Dept. of Information Engineering
Graduate School of Engineering, Nagoya University

Abstract. We are developing a recognition system which aims to convert a sequence of illustrations in origami drill books into a 3D animation, with a view to providing an easy way for learning and enjoying origami art. As a part of this work, this paper proposes a method that recognizes a target graph corresponding to an origami shape from an origami illustration image. The target graph, called ISG (Ideal Shape Graphs), generated from an internal model that maintains 3D information about changes of origami states during the interpretation for the whole folding process. In order to understand the folding operation applied to the origami at each step, an ISG of the origami generated at current step has to be matched with the image of the origami illustration at the next step, to find whether there exists a similar graph within it. The image of the origami is usually very noisy. Since the computational cost to do this work is prohibitive even for problems of moderate sizes, we adopt a genetic algorithm in conjunction with hill climbing search technique to reduce the complexity. Experimental results show that good solutions can be found with lower cost using our method.

1 Introduction

Origami, which starts with just a sheet of paper but can be folded into various complicated shapes such as a beautiful flower, a dear animal, etc., has been loved by many people since ancient times. Researches conducted in recent years also proved that origami has great possibilities for education and rehabilitation effects [1]. In Japan, traditional and excellent origami works are conventionally collected into origami drill books. Such drill books have become a main way in which people can comfortably learn and enjoy origami art.

However, it is usually the case that people give up obeying the instruction of a drill book halfway because origami illustrations, the major constituent elements of origami drill books, are often too complicated to understand in the books

J. Lladós and Y.-B. Kwon (Eds.): GREC 2003, LNCS 3088, pp. 235–244, 2004.
© Springer-Verlag Berlin Heidelberg 2004

published in recent years. The difficulties in understanding origami drill books leads to the growing interests in 3D animated expression approaches [2]. For example, an origami playing simulator in 3D virtual space has been developed in 1996 [3]. A recognition system which aims to convert a sequence of illustrations printed on origami drill books into a 3D animation has also been reported in [4], [5], [6]. As on extension of the researches addressed in [4], [5], [6], this paper proposes a method that recognizes a target graph corresponding to an origami shape from an origami illustration image.

2 Approach

An origami illustration depicts both a shape of origami immediately before a folding operation and the folding operation that is going to be performed. The folding operation is specified graphically by the position(s) and the type(s) of crease(s) (see Fig. 1). If the *state* of origami corresponding to an illustration (namely, at one folding step) can be recognized through the illustration, it is possible to infer the folding operation applied to the origami in this state, according to the positions and types of the related creases.

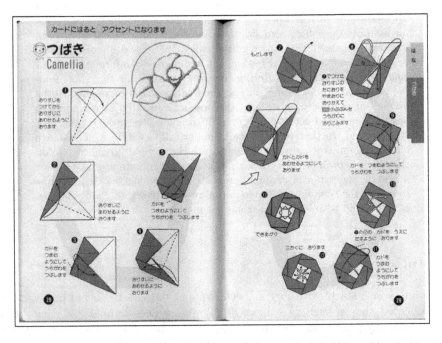

Fig. 1. An two-facing-page image from an origami drill book

However, given the same *shape* of origami and the same creases (namely, given the same illustration), there may exist several interpretations for the folding operation, so that the states of the origami associated with the different interpretations are distinct. To solve this problem, we construct an *internal model* that maintains 3D information about changes of origami states, step by step, during the interpretation for the whole folding process. Introducing this internal model enables us to simulate all possible folding operations against the model, and moreover to obtain the possible state changes of the origami caused by a specified folding operation. For associating the internal model at a folding step with a certain illustration, the state-changed internal model is projected on a 2D plane, usually from an orthogonal viewpoint with the origami face where a folding operated is defined, to form a 2D graph called ISG (Ideal Shape Graph). Obviously, the ISG generated under a correct interpretation should have the similar shape with the origami presented in the illustration that corresponds to the next folding step. The purpose of the method proposed in this paper is to match an ISG against a USG (Unrefined Shape Graph), which stands for the origami shape in illustrations, so as to find the correct interpretation for a folding operation. The USGs can be obtained from illustration images by image processing techniques.

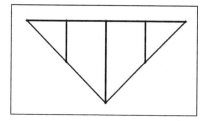 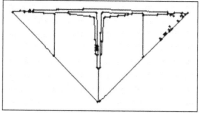

Fig. 2. An example of ISGs (left) and related USGs (right)

Figure 2 gives an example of a USG and its related ISG. The comparison of the USG with the ISG reveals that there are two characteristics regarding the two different kinds of graphs. One is that they are similar figures, and another is that a USG usually has much more vertices and edges than the related ISG due to the noise. Namely, ISGs are considered more reliable no-noise graphs that well express the shapes of origami.

In the light of these characteristics, the issue to match an ISG with a USG can be actually viewed as the optimization problem how to choose feature points from the USG that compose a one-to-one correspondence with feature points of the ISG, so that the graph shape generated by these feature points of the USG is best matched with the shape of the ISG. Provided the USG and ISG have M and N feature points, respectively, there exist $_MP_N$ different possible combinations of feature points for selection, which make the computing cost too expensive to find an exact solution. From this viewpoint, we abandon the idea of seeking exact solutions but instead adopt a genetic algorithm [7] with an evaluation function based on the similarity between USGs and ISGs. This algorithm is able to achieve a good approximate solution using much lower computing cost than exhausted searching. To make the algorithm converge fast, we finally use hill climbing searching technique to revise the matching results obtained from the genetic algorithm.

3 Extracting Feature Points and Neighboring Relations

To relate USGs with ISGs, it is necessary to look for the feature points of them. The feature points of USGs are straightforwardly the vertices of USGs, the terminal points of the edges detected from illustration images in preprocessing. On the other hand, the feature points of ISGs are slightly complex: include not only the vertices of visible faces of the internal model but the points of intersection formed by two faces as shown in Fig. 3.

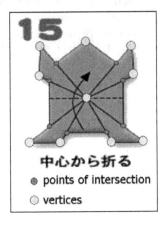

Fig. 3. Feature points of ISGs include both of vertices and points of intersection formed by face overlap

In addition to feature points, the neighboring relations among feature points are also needed to construct the evaluation function for the genetic algorithm. The neighboring relations are extracted based on ISGs, because ISGs are more trustworthy than USGs and do not suffer from noise.

4 Matching ISGs to USGs

4.1 Definitions

The Chromosome. The number of genes in a chromosome is supposed same with the number of feature points in the ISG. Information regarding every gene is defined to be the ID number of the feature point in the USG the feature point in the ISG that gene stands for is related to. So, a chromosome actually provides one possible correspondence of the ISG to the USG. For example, if a chromosome consisting of four genes has data of $5, 3, 2, 1$, it means that the feature points with IDs $1, 2, 3, 4$ of the ISG correspond to the feature points with IDs $5, 3, 2, 1$ in the USG, respectively.

The Evaluation Function. The evaluation function for a chromosome measures the similarity of a correspondence between the USG and the ISG.

According to the characteristics that an ISG and its related USG should be similar figures, the evaluation function is defined by total differences in angles and in length of edges of two graphs, i.e.,

$$F(I) = \frac{1}{\sum_{i \in I} E_{len}(i) \times \sum_{i \in I} E_{arg}(i)}, \tag{1}$$

where I and i indicate a chromosome and a constituent gene in it, respectively. The first term in the denominator measures the ratio of edges. That is,

$$E_{len}(i) = \sum_{j \neq js, j \in J} \left| \frac{I_j}{I_{js}} - \frac{U_j}{U_{js}} \right|, \tag{2}$$

where J stands for the set of feature points in the ISG which have neighboring relations with the feature point i, and js indicates such a specific feature point that the edge between itself and i is longest in all the edges originating from i. I_j and U_j express the length of edge $i - j$ in the ISG, and the length of the corresponding edge in the USG related by the information written in genes. I_{js} and U_{js} means the longest edge in those originating from i of the ISG and the corresponding edge in the USG, respectively.

The second term in the denominator in Eq. (1) measures error in angles, i.e.,

$$E_{arg}(i) = \sum_{j \neq js, j \in J} |IA_j - UA_j|, \tag{3}$$

where j and js have the same meaning with Eq. (2). Analogously, IA_j and UA_j express the angle generated by edge $i - j$ and edge $i - js$ in the ISG, and the angle generated by corresponding edges in the USG, respectively.

By definition, a better matching of the ISG to the USG will lead to smaller $\sum_{i \in I} E_{len}(i)$ and $\sum_{i \in I} E_{arg}(i)$, in other words, a bigger $F(I)$. The use of the reciprocal of the multiplication of $E_{len}(i)$ and $E_{arg}(i)$ in Eq. (1) enable us to take no account of the possible difference in scales between angles and length.

GA Operators. Because the value of the evaluation function we have defined rapidly increases as a solution gets closer to the optimal one, we adopt fitness scaling strategy to positively cross such hopeful chromosomes that have higher values of the evaluation function. The scaling is set to be the square of fitness of chromosomes. Fitness for a chromosome is calculated by Eq. (1), and that for a gene by the same function but sum operations are dropped, i.e.,

$$F(i) = \frac{1}{E_{len}(i) \times E_{arg}(i)}. \tag{4}$$

To keep solutions not diffusing, we furthermore shift excellent chromosomes directly to the next generation as their stands based on the idea of elite preservation.

When a gene has lower fitness than the average fitness of other genes in the same chromosome, this gene is selected as the target of crossover operator whose position will be later interchanged with another target. Introducing crossover operator can potentially enhance the fitness of parents chromosomes. Mutation operator is applied to those chromosomes a crossover operator has been just performed to. The bit data of all the genes are independently changed into ID numbers of other feature points in the USG with a certain probability. By this operation, we try to avoid over-narrowing the searching space.

The situation where one feature point of the USG appears at several gene locations in a chromosome might happen due to crossover operations. That means a single feature point of the USG corresponds to several feature points of the ISG. Since such chromosomes obviously can not lead to the true solution, we reject them and instead re-generate the same numbers of new chromosomes at random.

Our genetic algorithm is terminated when the number of generations has exceed a predeterminated number. The chromosome having highest fitness at that moment is chosen to be the approximate solution for the matching problem.

5   Optimization Using Hill Climbing Searching

5.1   The Idea

It is usually the case that there exist much more feature points in a USG than its related ISG as shown in Fig. 2(b). That leads to the problem that a huge number of GA operations may be needed to reach a chromosome whose genes all exactly correspond to right feature points of the USG. From this viewpoint, we repeat the genetic algorithm only a certain number of generations to obtain an approximate solution and then optimize the approximate solution using hill climbing searching technique to reduce the computing cost.

Hill climbing is a simple and fast heuristic searching method that extends a node into a node set from the current state first, then selects one node most close to the optimal state, and finally applies the same procedure repeatedly to the selected node. This method does not guarantee to reach a global optimal solution, but since we start it with an approximate solution, we do not take this problem seriously.

5.2   The Heuristic Function

Defining an appropriate heuristic function is important. Because this function measures how state x is close to the optimal state, it is possible to define it in the same way we define fitness of chromosomes, i.e.,

$$h(x) = \sum_{i \in I} E_{len}(i) \times \sum_{i \in I} E_{arg}(i). \tag{5}$$

5.3   Extending the Nodes

The nodes are extended by the following steps. (1) Calculate fitness for every gene of a chromosome based on Eq. (4). (2) Find the gene, i, with lowest fitness and also find its corresponding feature point, j, in the USG. (3) Replace the information written in the ith gene by the information regarding the feature points neighboring to the jth feature point in the USG. As to all the neighboring feature points, the heuristic function (Eq. (5)) is evaluated. The feature point with the lowest function value is the the node to be extended next. Steps (2) and (3) will be repeated for all the genes with lower fitness.

6 Experiments

This section describes the experimental results and evaluates the proposed matching method. The input to the genetic algorithm is such an image in which various constituent elements have been extracted and grouped into clusters (corresponding to folding steps), and also the order of these clusters has been recognized, as shown in Fig. 4. The genetic algorithm is performed under the following conditions: the number of chromosomes is 200, the mutation probability is 3%, and the number of generations is limited to 1000.

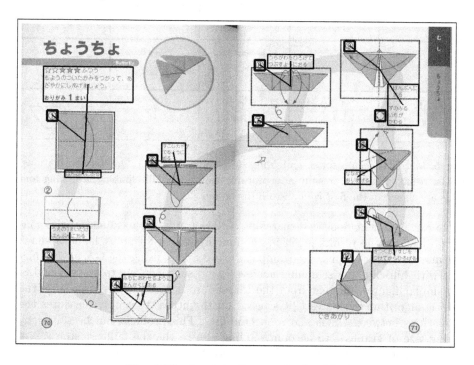

Fig. 4. The input to the genetic algorithm

Some results matching USGs obtained from illustrations to ISGs generated from an internal model using proposed method are given in Fig. 5. These results correspoind to the seven folding steps described in Fig. 4. Original illustrations, USGs, results from GA, results after optimization using hill climbing searching and ISGs are shown in the first column through the fifth column, respectively.

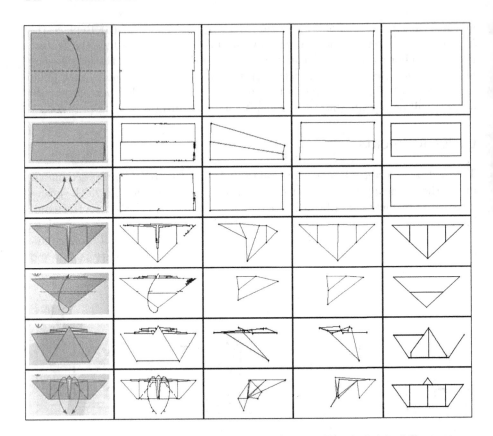

Fig. 5. Matching results for seven folding steps shown in Fig. 4. Original illustrations, USGs, results from GA, results after optimization using hill climbing searching and ISGs are shown in the first column to fifth column

From Fig. 5, it is obvious that matching simple graphs such as quadrangles converges fast, as the results given in the fourth column for steps 1 and 4 show. For more complex graphs, for example, steps 3 and 5, using the GA in conjunction with hill climbing searching achieves good solutions. As to steps 6 and 8, the similar figures different from the targets are detected. This is because the genetic algorithm evaluates USGs based on the fitness that only measures the similarities between USGs and a specific ISG. This problem can be solved by taking size of graphs into account. Giving rise to the the fault at step 7 is a mistake existing in the ISG: the ISG can not be correctly generated because of accumulated errors during the transformation of the internal model. We do not further discuss this problem here since it has been out of the scope of this paper.

The proposed method has been tested on a number of sequences of origami illustrations acquired from an ordinary origami drill book. Experimental results show that as shapes of origami become complex, the number of feature points of USGs and ISGs grows, and the searching space spreads. As a consequence, the chromosomes with higher fitness in the early stages of the evolution almost do not exist. It leads to slow speed of converging in the early evolution stages. While, when the number of chromosomes with higher fitness reaches to a certain level, the converging speed will increase rapidly. Therefore, developing some GA operations which are able to positively enhance the initial converging speed will be the subject.

References

1. T. Okamura, "My Origami World", http://www.oklab.com/origami/ori_wold. html 2000.
2. T. Agui, T. Takeda and M. Nakajima, "An Origami Playing Folds by Computer", *Computer Vision, Graphics and Image Processing*, Vol. 24, No. 6, pp. 244–258, 1983.
3. S. Miyazaki, T. Yasuda, S. Yokoi and J. Toriwaki, "An Origami Playing Simulator in the Virtual Space", *J. Visualization and Computer Animation*, Vol. 7, No. 6, pp. 25–42, 1996.
4. J. Kato, T. Watanabe, et al., "A Model-based Approach for Recognizing Folding Process of Origami", *Proc. of 14th Int'l. Conference on Pattern Recognition*, pp. 1808–1811, 1998.
5. J. Kato, T. Watanabe, H. Hase and T. Nakayama, "Understanding Illustrations of Origami Drill Books", *Trans. on Information Processing Society of Japan*, Vol. 41, No. 6, pp. 1857–1873, 2000.
6. H. Shimanuki, J. Kato and T. Watanabe, "Constituting Feasible Folding Operations Using Incomplete Crease Information", *Proc. of IAPR Workshop on Machine Vision Applications*, Nara, Japan, pp. 67–71, 2002.
7. D.E. Goldberg, *Genetic Algorithms in Search, Optimization, and Machine Learning*, Addison-Wesley, 1989.

A Recognition System for Folding Process of Origami Drill Books

Hiroshi Shimanuki, Jien Kato, and Toyohide Watanabe

Nagoya University, Furo-cho, Chikusa-ku, Nagoya, Aichi, 464-8603 Japan,
simanuki@watanabe.nuie.nagoya-u.ac.jp,
http://www.watanabe.nuie.nagoya-u.ac.jp/

Abstract. This paper describes a framework of a recognition system for folding process of origami drill books, with a view to converting a sequence of origami illustrations printed in an origami drill book into a 3D animation automatically, so that users can observe how an origami is folded from different viewpoints. The internal model, which maintains the changes of origami states during interpretation of the folding process, plays an important role in the recognition phase. The model also makes it possible for a CG simulator to reconstruct the recognized folding process. Several experimental results of this system have shown the validity of the proposed framework.

1 Introduction

Origami is the Japanese century-old art of paper folding. Now, it is loved by not only Japanese but also many people all over the world. Various origami works have been created, folded and inherited for hundreds of years. Furthermore, a lot of new works are still published every year as origami drill books by origami creators.

In origami works, a considerable number of them are generated by complicated ways of folding. This is the main reason why origami drill book readers often give up following the instructions of the drill books halfway. Namely, the origami illustrations, which explain the folding process in an origami drill book, are too difficult to understand. To deal with this problem, it is desirable to pick up an origami model, and to present how the model is folded and how the situation of the model changes in three-dimensional virtual space.

Miyazaki et al. [1] proposed a virtual simulation system of origami which realizes interactive folding operations in three-dimensional virtual space. This system focuses on user's manipulation of the three-dimensional origami model. However, the support for the user's origami operations is not considered.

In this paper, we propose a system that recognizes and reconstructs folding process of origami based on a sequence of illustrations printed in an origami drill book, with a view to converting a sequence of origami illustrations into a 3D animation automatically, so that people can observe how an origami is folded from different viewpoints.

J. Lladós and Y.-B. Kwon (Eds.): GREC 2003, LNCS 3088, pp. 244–255, 2004.
© Springer-Verlag Berlin Heidelberg 2004

2   Recognition System for Folding Process

Figure 1 gives the framework of the proposed system. The system is composed of three functional units: extraction of graphic elements, generation of folding operations, and recognition of folding operations. One internal model that records the changes of origami states during interpretation of a folding process is also an important element of the system.

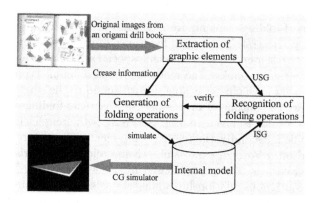

Fig. 1. The framework of recognizing and recreating folding process

Firstly, crease information is extracted from an origami illustration image using image processing techniques. Crease information here includes both the positions and types of the creases which specify the corresponding folding operations.

Secondly, the "feasible" folding operations are constituted based on the crease information. The crease information extracted from the illustrations by image processing techniques is superficial and incomplete. One reason is that there are usually some noises on the image, and the other reason is that the illustrations are two-dimensional. Only with this kind of information, generated folding operations include both feasible and infeasible ones. The "feasible" folding operations are obtained by maintaining consistency of crease patterns under some geometrical constrains.

Thirdly, the most likely folding operation is found out from the remaining feasible candidates by the unit of recognition of folding operations. All the possible ways of folding (candidates) are first simulated against a data structure, the internal model, which maintains the state transformation of a 3D origami work under folding operations step by step. The result of simulation, called ISG (Ideal Shape Graph), is then compared with the result of graphics recognition, called USG (Unrefined Shape Graph) which corresponds to the state of the origami in the next illustration. The ISG can be generated by projecting the internal model onto a 2D plane, from the same viewpoint as that of the next illustration. The folding operation corresponding to the ISG that most agrees with the USG related to the next illustration is finally chosen as the way of folding for the next step. The internal model is then updated in accordance with the recognized folding operation.

A sequence of "correct" folding operations described by the internal model (i.e. a folding process) can be generated and reconstructed by a CG simulator.

3   Recognition Processing

3.1   Extraction of Graphic Elements

As to extraction of folding elements from origami drill books, we have proposed a method [2] that successfully extracts five types of graphic elements (i.e. illustrations, explicative sentences, step numbers, special symbols and sketches) from a page image of origami books. The method groups different types of elements into a cluster so that each cluster is able to correspond to the single folding step.

Figure 2 shows the outline of processing that extracts folding elements. The example of the results is given in Fig. 3. Firstly, different elements are detected and classified. Secondly, the related component elements are grouped into "clusters" based on a Voronoi expression schema and some heuristics. Thirdly, a contiguous network is constructed based on a Delaunay diagram. The network expresses contiguous relationship among stepwise units (clusters). The path which passes all units every one time is unicursal. Then, an evaluation value is established based on the information acquired by number recognition. The path which satisfies both conditions of being unicursal and giving the greatest evaluation value is detected by best-first search method. Finally, crease information, which includes the positions and directions of folding operations, is also obtained by using the estimated order of the units (clusters) and the line detection technique.

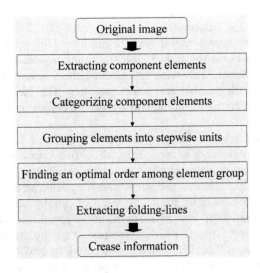

Fig. 2. The outline of processing that extracts folding elements

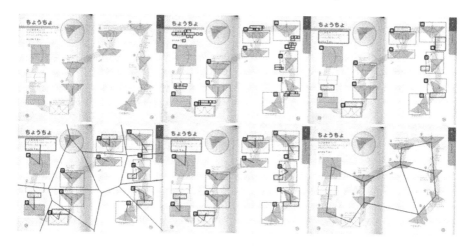

Fig. 3. An example of extracting folding elements

3.2 Calculation of Folding Operations

The crease information includes both of the position and direction of a folding operation. However, the information obtained from two-dimensional images such as origami drill books is superficial and incomplete. Moreover, given the incomplete crease information, many interpretations about the way of folding can be made. As the result, the creases cannot be determined uniquely. So, the feasible folding operations are obtained by maintaining consistency of crease patterns under some geometrical constrains [3].

We classify folding operations into basic operations and complex operations. Basic operations only consist of mountain and valley folding, and the resulting creases have uniform attributes (mountain or valley). On the other hand, complex operations mainly include tucking in, covering and expanding, and produce the creases with mixed attributes.

We mainly discuss on the assumption that the generation of creases is performed through a sheet of "extended" paper called *unfolded plan*. The complete creases made by each folding operation are specified by the given crease information. When an operation is applied on a face of origami, the moving portion of the face is usually folded up (rotate 180 degrees around the crease). That leads to a restriction called flatness of the origami model. This restriction requires that during a folding process all the faces of the origami model must be in parallel. Necessary and sufficient conditions for the creases connected with an inner point of the unfolded plan to keep an origami model flat, called local flatness conditions, are described in [4, 5, 6].

An example of the basic folding operation is shown in Fig. 4. The given crease l_0 is generated on the Face 1, and the complete crease l_1 is generated base on local flatness conditions at the local point p_0.

Figure 5 shows the present state of the origami model that consists of two triangle-faces. A new crease, also shown in the figure, is now generated on the

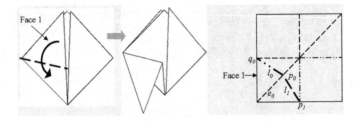

Fig. 4. An example of a basic folding operation

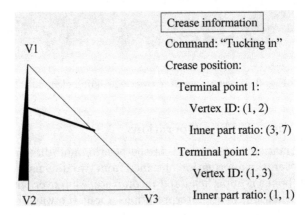

Fig. 5. Crease information

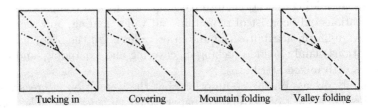

Fig. 6. The calculation result on unfolded plans

faces by a folding operation. The prospective creases on the "unfolded plans" are shown in Fig 6. And the resulting origami models in three-dimensional virtual space are also depicted in Fig. 7.

3.3   Updating an Internal Model

Constructing an Face List. The internal model is primarily composed of a face tree, in which nodes indicate faces and edges indicate connectivity relationships among the faces separated by one folding operation. In addition to connectivity relationships, another kind of important information is overlapping

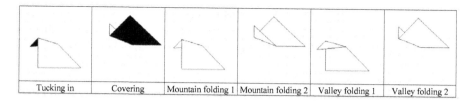

Tucking in	Covering	Mountain folding 1	Mountain folding 2	Valley folding 1	Valley folding 2

Fig. 7. The resulting origami models in 3-D virtual space

relationships, which describe the order of faces that overlap each other and furthermore locate at the same plane surface. This information is also maintained in the form of face trees.

When a folding operation is simulated against the internal model, the corresponding face tree has to be renewed suitably for the new situation of the model. That means not only some terminal nodes (leaves) will be broken up (grow), but also a data structure called face list that holds the overlapping relationships among faces (nodes) has to be updated. The latter updating is usually much more complicated than the former one. In this section, we describe the updating procedures for face lists with respect to basic folding operations.

"Mountain folding" and "valley folding" are the simplest and most frequently used operations in origami. Obviously, "mountain (valley) folding" is the reverse of "valley (mountain) folding" in the sense of moving faces in the opposite direction. Figure 8 illustrates how an origami model changes and how the face trees vary under a "valley folding". From the face tree given in Fig. 8, it can be easily observed that the initial situation of the face tree possesses only two faces F1 and F2, and that F2 is located behind F1. So, the face list corresponding to the upper level of the tree holds the order of overlapping as F1→ F2 (from left to right). After the "valley folding" is performed, the node of F1 split into F3

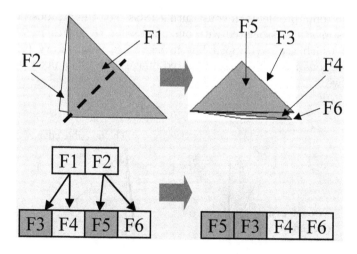

Fig. 8. Updating a face list in case of "valley folding"

and F4 because face F1 has been separated into two smaller faces. For the same reason, the node of F2 split into F5 and F6 simultaneously. Additionally, during this folding operation, two faces (F3 and F5) are moved and the others (F4 and F6) are stationary.

Now, we have four faces (F3, F4, F5 and F6) overlapping each other. The new face list corresponding to the lower level of the face tree has to be updated so that the list maintains the overlapping relationships among the present faces. We update the face list by the following steps. Firstly, a new sub-list is generated by picking out all moved (hatched) nodes and reversing the order of them. In the example of Fig. 8, this sub-list is F5→ F3. Secondly, the remaining nodes in the old face list are just added to the end of the sub-list made at the previous step. The updated face list for the example in Fig. 8 is F5→ F3→ F4→ F6 as shown at the right of the face tree.

It is not difficult to prove above-mentioned updating procedure to be true even for the case that "valley folding" is applied to several faces at the same time. On the other hand, the updating procedure for "mountain folding" can be simply obtained by modifying the above procedure a little. Namely, at the second step, we should not add the remaining nodes to the end of the sub-list, but should add the sub-list to the end of the remaining nodes, instead.

Constituting ISGs. The ISG assumes the role of two-dimensional representation of the present origami model as well as "interface" between graphic recognition and the logical data structure which is the internal model. In this section, the method of constituting the ISGs is described.

Each objects in the internal model, such as the face, the edge and the node, is assigned unique identifier. Information in the system is exchanged according to the identifiers. Therefore, it is necessary to understand correspondence between creases extracted by graphic recognition and objects' identifiers in the internal model.

There are some problems in constituting ISGs. For the composition of face, some objects must be associated with one pixel when the edges are overlapped, and objects which are overlapped but invisible are unnecessary (see Fig. 9). Therefore, we constitute ISGs as structured images. An ISG's pixel is the structure as follows.

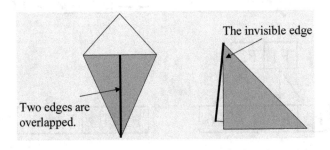

Fig. 9. Consitution of ISGs

```
typedef struct _Pixel
{
  unsigned char data;    // pixel data
  char *object_type;     // type of objects
  int *object_ids;       // the array of object identifications
} Pixel;
```

Figure 10 shows a structure of faces. The structure is grouped faces on the same plane. The way of updating the face lists is described in the preceding subsection. The constituting method of an ISG is as follows:

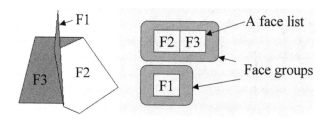

Fig. 10. A structure of faces

1. Calculate the centers of gravity of all the faces in every face group.
2. Convert coordinates of the centers of gravity, and sort in order of groups in the back (Z-sorting).
3. The following processing is repeated in the order of groups in the back.
   a. Convert coordinates of faces in the reverse order of the face list, and project them onto a screen.
   b. Object identifiers are then restored for every pixel.

This is the hidden surface removal method by two steps of Z-sorting. Generally, by the Z-sorting method, the judgment before and behind every face may not be able to be performed, but faces do not collide in origami.

However, using above-mentioned method, some object identifications are not matched with one pixel. It is necessary to detect edges which overlap and are visible. Therefore, we calculate three-dimensional physical relationship among edges, the pixel structure is added object identifications when edges are overlapped and visible.

3.4   Recognition of Folding Process

By using above-described methods, all the feasible folding operations are constituted. The most likely folding operation is then found out from the remaining feasible (possible) candidates by the unit of recognition of folding operations. All the possible ways of folding (candidates) are first simulated against the data structure, the internal model, which maintains the state transformation of a three-dimensional origami work under folding operations, step by step. The result of simulation, called ISG, is then compared with the result of graphics recognition called USG which corresponds to the state of the origami in the next illustration (see Fig. 11). The ISG can be generated by projecting the internal model onto a two-dimensional plane, from the same viewpoint as that of the next illustration. The folding operation corresponding to the ISG that most agrees with the USG related to the next illustration is finally chosen as the way of folding for the next step [7].

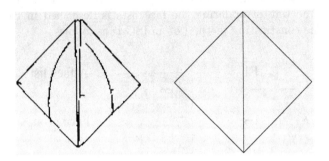

Fig. 11. An example of USG and ISG

4   Experimental Results

We have implemented a prototype system based on the proposed method. Figure 12 shows the user interface of the system. When a page image is input to the system, the system automatically extracts crease information. Then, by using the information, folding operations are calculated on the unfolded plan. The

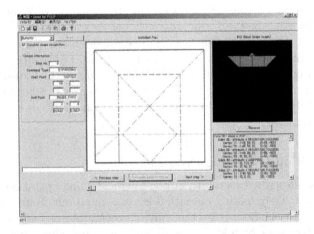

Fig. 12. The user interface of the prototype system

result is expressed on the unfolded plan of the middle of the interface. Moreover, the result of carrying out a folding operation on three-dimensional virtual space is displayed on upper right of the screen. This function allows users to see the origami model from all viewpoints.

We use an image of two facing pages of an origami book as input (see Fig. 13). Figure 14 shows the result of the stepwise calculation and the result of matching the ISG with the USG.

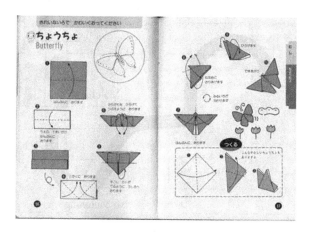

Fig. 13. The input image

The figure shows that our method gives a good performance at most steps. However, the image at step two could not be extracted because folding elements could not be detected or classified due to the noise on the image. The right ISG candidate is chosen manually, and processing is continued. At step seven, two ISG candidates are constituted, but neither can be matched with the USG. The reason is that the accuracy of matching is not sufficient. Therefore, we must still improve the precision of recognition.

5   Conclusion

This paper presented a system for recognizing and reconstructing folding process of origami drill books. The proposed updating algorithm for folding operations makes it possible to maintain consistency of data (internal models) which describe the transformation of origami models in 3D virtual space during a folding process. Furthermore, the proposed constituting method of ISGs makes it possible to associate information obtained from image processing with the logical data structure. The experimental results have demonstrated that our present work is able to recognize a sequence of folding processes from origami drill books whose layouts are motley.

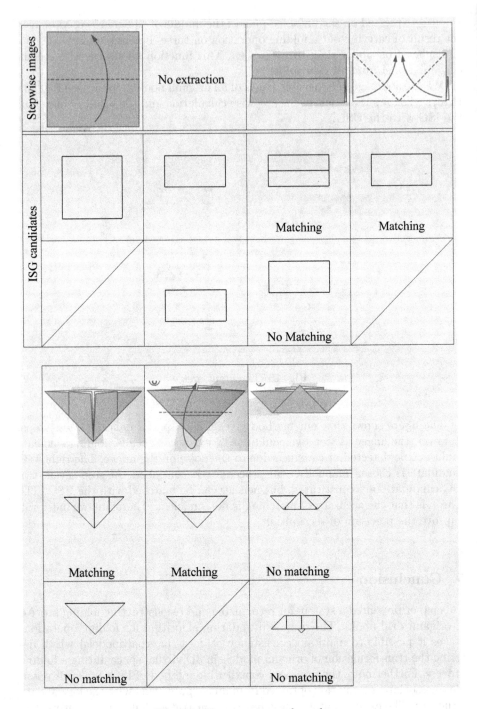

Fig. 14. The experimental result

As the future work, it is necessary to improve the recognition processing and to evaluate the results using more samples. Moreover, in order to make clearly understandable origami models in three-dimensional virtual space, animation representation which considers the feel of a paper material is required.

References

[1] S. Miyazaki, S., Yasuda, T., Yokoi, S., Toriwaki, J.: INTERACTIVE MANIPULA-TION OF ORIGAMI IN 3D VIRTUAL SPACE. J. IPS Japan **34** (1993) 1994–2001

[2] Suzuki, T.,Kato,J.,Watanabe, T.:Extraction of Contextual Information Existing among Composite Elements of Origami Books. In: Proc. of 4th IAPR International Workshop on Graphics Recognition. (2001) 195-207

[3] Shimanuki, H., Kato, J., Watanabe, T.: Constituting Feasible Folding Operations Using Incomplete Crease Information. In: Proc. of IAPR Workshop on Machine Vision Applications. (2002) 68–71

[4] Kawasaki, T.: On the Relation Between Mountain-creases and Valley-creases of a Flat Origami. In Huzita, H.,ed.: Proc. of the First International Conference on Origami in Education and Therapy (COET91), British Origami Society (1991) 229–237

[5] Auckly, D., Cleveland, J.: Totally Real Origami and Impossible Paper Folding. Am. Math. Monthly **102** (1995) 215–226

[6] Hull, T.: On the Mathematics of Flat Origamis. Congressus Numerantium **100** (1994) 215–224

[7] Kato, J., Watanabe, T., Hase, H., Nakayama, T.: Understanding Illustrations of Origami Drill Books. J. IPS Japan **41** (2000) 1857–1873

[8] sarah-marie belcastro, Hull, T.: Modelling the Folding of Paper into Three Dimensions Using Affine Transformations. Linear Algebra and its Applciations **348** (2002) 273–282

[9] Shimanuki, H., Kato and J., Watanabe, T.: Recognition of Folding Process from Origami Drill Books. In: Proc. of 7th International Conference on Document Analysis and Recognition. (2003) 550–554

Shape Description for Automatically Structuring Graphical Data

Laura Keyes and Adam Winstanley

Dept. of Computer Science, National University of Ireland, Maynooth, Co. Kildare, Ireland
lkeyes@cs.may.ie, adam.winstanley@may.ie

Abstract. This work explores automatic object recognition and semantic capture in vector graphics through shape description. The low-level graphical content of graphical documents, such as a map or architectural drawing, are often captured manually and the encoding of the semantic content seen as an extension of this. The large quantity of new and archived graphical data available on paper makes automatic structuring of such graphical data desirable. Contour shape description techniques, such as Fourier descriptors, moment invariants play an important role in systems for object recognition and representation. However, most work carried out in this area has concentrated on categories of object boundaries representing very specific shapes (for example, a particular type of aircraft). Two classifiers were implemented and proved accurate in their automatic recognition of objects from drawings in different domains. Classical classifier combination techniques were used to improve performance. Further work will employ more complex fusion techniques and it is envisaged they will be used in combination with recognition based on object context using various modelling methods. A demonstration system has been constructed using all these techniques.

1 Introduction

Increased use of graphical information systems (such as GIS, CAD and multimedia systems) has motivated research in developing and applying graphical object recognition. A vast amount of data archived by organisations in the world is in graphical form (for example, diagrams, maps, technical drawings, and architectural plans). For this to be searched, analysed and synthesised automatically, it must be parsed and converted from simple graphics (points, line, symbols, polygons) to semantically rich graphical information ("circuit breaker", "building", spark-plug", "extractor fan"). Much work has been done in computer vision on the identification and classification of objects within images. However, less progress has been made on automating feature extraction and semantic capture in vector graphics. This is partly because the low-level graphical content of graphical documents has often been captured manually (on digitising tables) and the encoding of the semantic content seen as an extension of this. The successful automation of raster-vector conversion plus the large quantity of new and archived graphical data available on paper makes the automation of feature extraction and recognition of graphical data desirable.

Data capture for graphical information systems consists of two parts: the digitisation of the geometry and the addition of attributes indicating the object type

J. Lladós and Y.-B. Kwon (Eds.): GREC 2003, LNCS 3088, pp. 256–264, 2004.

being depicted. Whereas the former can be automated using image processing and similar techniques, the latter is often a manual task. The manual structuring into composite objects and addition of labelling attributes is a labour-intensive, expensive and error prone process. One possible means of automatically structuring graphical data is through shape. Shape is an important part of the semantic content of an object within a graphical information system. Shape description methods used in image processing include Fourier Descriptors (FD) and Moment Invariants (MI).

Traditionally shape description methods are applied to the recognition of very specific shapes (for example, a particular make and model of aircraft). However, there are situations when, due to the nature of the data, we wish to classify previously unseen shapes into general classes representing categories of object. For example, in topographic object classification, a specific building shape may be unique. However, all building shapes have particular properties that distinguish them from objects in other classes. If descriptors can capture these properties, it would allow us to classify new examples. Other applications of general descriptors include the domain analysis of documents (for example as an electrical circuit diagram or a computer flow chart) and the segmentation of documents into different regions.

Previous work has applied this idea to topographic data from large-scale mapping [1]. As part of a project to speed up data capture and structuring of architectural and engineering drawings for a web-based multimedia Operations and Maintenance (O&M) management system, an initial attempt has been made to apply the same concept to this data domain. Standard shape description techniques are applied to object boundaries extracted from drawings represented as vector descriptions. The outputs obtained by the description methods provide a measurement of shape that characterises the object type. We then test the techniques' effectiveness at classifying shapes into general categories using standard data sets.

Different classifier schemes produce different classifications of the same data set. By analyzing these results against a standard data set for which ground-truth values are available, their effectiveness can be analysed and compared. It is usually seen that, although one technique yields the best performance, the set of features miss-classified by the different classifiers do not necessarily overlap. This suggests that different classifier techniques can offer complementary descriptions of the shapes to be classified, and a combination of classifiers would give optimal performance. A fusion methodology based on a Bayesian framework and using *max*, *min*, *sum* and *majority vote* rules [12], is applied to combine the results of the individual classifiers to derive an overall consensus decision. Results are presented here for the shape description task and matching module for identifying architectural features and symbols on drawings.

2 Automatically Structuring Graphical Data

Automating the structure of graphical data requires the recognition and representation of objects that are defined by a set of general shape properties. This involves the classification of a particular shape into a general class of similar object shapes. For example, the human visual system can recognise and identify a given chair from its shape properties, though the shape describing any particular chair may vary considerably. The shape properties of a given feature may vary while semantically they describe the same object. This semantic similarity must be considered when attempting to classify graphical data. In this work, boundary shape description is investigated and evaluated on the problem of automatically recognising and interpreting graphical data on technical drawings for the development of an operation and maintenance information system for plans within buildings and other facilities.

2.1 Operation and Maintenance Information System

An Operation and Maintenance Information System holds centrally all relevant information pertaining to the operation and maintenance of plant and equipment within buildings and other facilities. This information is presented through a multimedia web interface and consists of drawings, data sheets, operating instructions, parts listings, suppliers, installers, manufacturers and other details of all the service utilities. The information on each component is comprehensively cross-referenced using links between corresponding items in drawings, data sheets, photographs and so on. The system can be implemented for all sizes of installations but comes particularly suited for the infrastructure management of large industrial or service sites. Current use includes a sports complex and large private dwelling.

The Operation and Maintenance Information System allows a user to select an example object (simple or composite) and the software finds similar objects in the same or other drawings. The tool generates data structures that can be used to build multimedia linkages between objects, drawings and related information. The information is accessed through a standard web browser interface including navigation through hot-links and key-word search facilities.

CAD drawings showing the location of utilities and services also act as browser navigational maps. In operation, the system's main use concerns day-to-day operation and maintenance tasks, for example retrieving plant operating and servicing instructions or keeping maintenance records. Systems commissioned so far have been constructed manually through digitising and structuring of this information appropriately. For the system to be economic, it is desirable to automate as much as possible of this compilation process. Automation possibilities include:

- Recognition and labelling objects/components on drawings through
  - shapes of objects within drawings
  - text labels in proximity to objects
  - meanings of standard symbols
  - context of objects, for example a water pump on a water pipe
- Generating links through string matching
- Compilation of databases of information from scanned text/drawings

Once recognised and classified, these objects can be assigned unique identifiers in the system. This allows their inclusion in the search and navigation functions. In this paper we evaluate the classification of objects and components on drawings based on their isolated shape. Other work is in progress to incorporate techniques based on context into the classification process.

2.2 Shape Description for Object Recognition and Representation

The recognition and description of objects plays a central role in automatic shape analysis for computer vision and it is one of the most familiar and fundamental problems in pattern recognition. Common examples are the reading of alphabetic characters in text and the automatic identification of aircraft. The shape description techniques used include Fourier Descriptors (FD) Moment Invariants (MI) and Scalar Descriptors (SD) (area, elongation, number of corners etc.) []. Most applications using these for shape recognition deal with the classification of such definite shapes. However, this application (structuring components and symbols on technical drawings) is one of a number requiring the recognition and representation of object shapes that are defined by a set of general shape properties. Other examples include extracting buildings from topographic data and architectural drawings. In these cases, the semantic classes are reflected in the general properties of the objects shape as opposed to an exact template match. To identify graphical objects, each of the techniques needs to be extended to deal with general categories of shapes found in graphical documents, for example buildings.

The recognition of objects is largely based on the matching of numerical descriptions of shapes with a database of standard shapes. Fourier Descriptors, Moment Invariants and Scalar Descriptors are well understood when applied to images and can be normalised to describe shapes irrespective of position, scale and orientation [2]. They can also be easily applied to vector graphical shapes. Each technique is computed based on the shape boundary. The shapes can then be described using a small set of descriptor values (typically 7 to 10 real numbers). The results produced are used in the classification process. The recognition and classification is based on matching the descriptors of each shape to standard values representing typical shapes and choosing the closest match.

2.3 Classification

Shape description techniques generally characterise an object's shape as a set of real numbers. Classification of objects based on shape therefore consists of comparing these descriptors. In this work we are using supervised classification through Bayesian statistics [11,12].

Supervised classification involves two stages: a learning stage where criteria and methods are tried on the prototypes and recognition when the trained system is used to classify new data. Bayesian statistics uses the distribution of the values for each descriptor, for each class of object, in determining the probability that a particular object belongs to that class. Given a particular value for a descriptor, the likelihood of that value occurring in the distribution of values for a particular class can be determined. Applying Bayes theorem, the probability of the object belonging to that class is computed. Such a probability can be calculated for each class. The object then belongs to the class for which that descriptor gives the highest probability. The objective is to design classifiers that will classify an object in the most probable of the classes given.

2.4 Combining Classifiers

When setting out to design a shape recognition system the ultimate goal is to achieve the best possible classification performance. Attaining this goal involves the application of suitable classification schemes/techniques to the problem. Traditionally, choosing a classifier scheme as a final solution for the task at hand was based on an analysis of the results produced by each technique. However, although one technique would yield the best performance, the set of features miss-classified by the different classifiers would not necessarily overlap. This suggests that different classifier techniques can offer complementary descriptions of the shapes to be classified, which leads to the combining of the classifiers for improved performance.

A central problem for the fusion algorithm is how to integrate several classifiers to produce a single final classification. The fusion technique employed here follows a methodology based on *max*, *min*, *sum* and *majority vote* strategies [12] and utilises a decision combination topology with a Bayesian approach. All three shape description methods (Fourier descriptors, scalar descriptors and moment invariants) are used for the decision making by combining their individual results to derive a consensus decision. Using the set of real descriptor values produced by each shape description method, a *likelihood* and *probability* of an input feature belonging to a particular class is calculated. Each strategy obtains a decision by computing the a-posteriori probabilities for each class (for example, the sum rule will compute the sum of the probabilities), taking the resulting maximum value as the combined result.

These fusion algorithms can be used in two configurations. When used to evaluate the effectiveness of these shape recognition techniques using a fully structured training set, it outputs measures of performance of individual classifiers as well as combinations of classifiers using different combination algorithms. Alternatively, when a particular configuration is known to be effective for a particular recognition problem, it can be parameterised to implement this combination and label the shapes according to the derived classifications.

3   Case Study: Shape Recognition in Architectural Drawings

Shape description techniques previously developed and implemented were applied to architectural data. The performance of all techniques is statistically analysed for the automatic recognition and labelling of features on the drawings. Figure 1 describes the architecture of the overall shape recognition system employed.

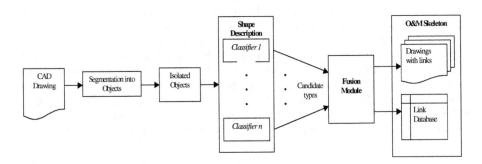

Fig. 1. Graphical Shape Recognition System configuration

3.1   Data Pre-processing

Before implementation of the shape techniques can be carried out there needs to be some pre-processing performed on the graphical data set. The architectural data available for construction of O&M systems is generally in a CAD vector format. Therefore, many of the problems of raster data and vectorisation do not apply. First, the technical plan is segmented into its component objects for extraction. The data extracted must form separate/minimal isolated closed polygonal shapes and are stored in vector format for further processing. An interpolation method is applied to this data to sample the shape boundary, using a finite number (N) of equidistant samples representing the x and y co-ordinates of the objects shape. These points are stored in the appropriate format (complex valued data in the case of the FD method and x-y co-ordinates for the MI and SD methods) for processing with each shape description technique.

The data is extracted and stored as individual polygon shapes in a format suitable for processing with the shape descriptor techniques, Fourier Descriptors, Moment Invariants and Scalar Descriptors. These shape description techniques are calculated from the object boundary. The output from each shape description method can be used in subsequent stages of the overall system, that is, the component matching and later online database retrieval. Fourier Descriptors and Moment Invariants produce a set of real valued numerical descriptors to describe each object. So, for each component shape in the set we have twenty-one descriptor values, (the sixteen scalars, seven moments and fourteen Fourier descriptors, (FD(2) to FD(16)). FD(0) and FD(1) are redundant due to normalisation (translation, scale rotation) performed for each method.

3.2 Experimental Results

To evaluate the effectiveness of this method, an experiment was carried out on a corpus of technical drawing objects from the GREC 2003 Symbol Recognition Contest: architectural, electrical and symbols (figure 2). The aim of this experiment is not to recognise each individual shape but to classify each set of graphical objects into their respective domain. The sample datasets include an ideal set of all symbols used for training plus several sets containing various types of distortion and degradation. For this application, binary degradation is not a problem, therefore only vectoral distortion including scale and rotation were considered (figure 3).

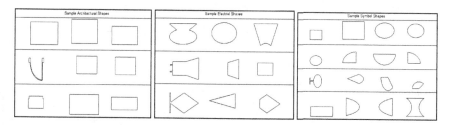

Fig. 2. Sample contour shapes from training sets

From each symbol image, closed contours were generated. Most symbols produce several contours. For each contour, Fourier and moment invariant descriptors were calculated. The ideal set was used to produce descriptor value distributions for each domain. The descriptors obtained from the testing data sets were used to classify the contours as belonging to one of the three classes through a maximum likelihood measure derived from the distributions. In this way, the data sets were used to test the effectiveness of each descriptor individually and combined using the implemented fusion algorithms.

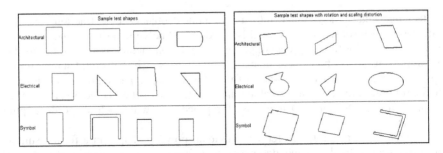

Fig. 3. Sample contour shapes from testing sets

To evaluate the performance of the graphical shape recognition system, standard precision and recall information retrieval metrics are employed. Precision, given here as a percentage, is a measure of selected shapes that the recognition system classified correctly (so-called true-positives as a fraction of all positives). Recall, also given as a percentage, is the measure of the proportion of the target class that the system detected. Tables 1, 2 and 3 show the results obtained for each shape description technique on a set of ideal tests and tests with scaling and rotation distortion, respectively. Each test set consists of Architectural, Electrical and Symbol data to be classified. Overall, the Fourier Descriptor method seemed to perform well when classifying Architectural data but poorly on Symbol data. Conversely, moment invariants performed well for classifying Symbol data but poorly for Architectural data. For Electrical, both techniques mis-classified the data as Symbols.

Table 1. Precision and recall of training set (59 objects, 212 contours)

Fourier Descriptors		Majority %	Max %	Min %	Median %	Sum %	Product %
Architectural	Precision	25.8	100	89.4	30.7	100	28
	Recall	96.0	76.0	84.0	92.0	92.0	92.0
Electrical	Precision	0	0	100	0	0	12.5
	Recall	0	0	7.1	0	0	3.57
Symbol	Precision	37.5	100	21.5	89.3	83.8	84.4
	Recall	15.7	35.8	26.1	18.7	23.1	20.9
Moment Invariants							
Architectural	Precision	0	100	2.5	100	100	11.1
	Recall	0	2	4	2	2	2
Electrical	Precision	0	0	100	0	0	1.3
	Recall	0	0	3.6	0	0	3.6
Symbol	Precision	42.3	100	94.5	99.3	63.8	98.4
	Recall	100	100	94.8	100	100	94.8

Using the ideal test data, results show that as descriptors for classifying Architectural data, Fourier descriptors prove best with 100% precision and 92% recall using max and sum rule combination strategies. Moment invariants proved best with 100% precision and 96% recall using the max rule and 98.1% precision and 99% recall using median rule. For the test set with scaling and rotation distortion, Fourier descriptors showed best results at 100% precision and 80.1% recall using the sum rule for Architectural data. On the other hand, moment invariants scored 100% and 99.8%

Table 2. Precision and recall for ideal test set (50 objects, 180 contours)

Fourier Descriptors		Majority %	Max %	Min %	Median %	Sum %	Product %
Architectural	Precision	29.8	100	89.7	33.1	100	32.2
	Recall	96.0	92.0	84.0	96.0	92.0	92.0
Electrical	Precision	0	0	100	0	0	22.2
	Recall	0	0	7.1	0	0	7.1
Symbol	Precision	38.9	100	20	84.2	80.8	66.7
	Recall	13.7	28.4	25.5	15.7	20.6	19.6
Moment Invariants							
Architectural	Precision	0	100	2.5	16.7	100	12.5
	Recall	0	2.0	4.0	2.0	2.0	2.0
Electrical	Precision	0	0	100	0	0	2.53
	Recall	0.0	0.0	3.6	0.0	0.0	7.1
Symbol	Precision	40.5	100	96	98.1	57.1	98
	Recall	100	96	94.1	99	98	94.1

Table 3. Precision and recall for deformed test set (scaling/rotation) (250 objects, 1147 contours)

Fourier Descriptors		Majority %	Max %	Min %	Median %	Sum %	Product %
Architectural	Precision	35.2	100	76.8	36	100	37
	Recall	81.2	78.6	76.6	81.2	80.1	78.1
Electrical	Precision	0	0	100	0	0	4
	Recall	0	0	4.2	0	0	2. 8
Symbol	Precision	30.9	100	20.7	53.8	83.2	45 .2
	Recall	24.4	27.9	23.9	24.5	25.8	18.6
Moment Invariants							
Architectural	Precision	26.1	100	5.7	14.6	100	18 .6
	Recall	1.5	2.3	8.1	1.5	1.5	4. 1
Electrical	Precision	0	0	100	0	0	0. 4
	Recall	0	0	1.4	0	0	1. 4
Symbol	Precision	37.6	100	91.1	99.8	54.2	98 .6
	Recall	97.7	96	90.9	97.9	96.7	93. 6

precision and 96% and 97.9% recall for the max and median rule, respectively. These results indicate the potential for using Fourier descriptors and moment invariants for the general classification of graphical domain data. Also the results show the potential of further combining each shape classifier to arrive at an improved consensus decision across all domains, as each provides complementary information, most notably on the Architectural and Symbol domains. Fusing the individual descriptors (14 FDs and 7 MIs) improves precision and recall of results for each test set.

4 Conclusions

Two types of contour/boundary shape description methods were investigated and their effectiveness evaluated on the problem of automatically recognising and interpreting graphical data on technical documents where generalized shape properties are required. A demonstration system has been developed to assess the potential of this approach to automatically structuring graphical data for the development of an online operation and maintenance information system.

Automating the structure of graphical data requires the recognition and representation of objects that are defined by a set of general shape properties. This involves the classification of a particular shape into a general class of similar object shapes; for example, the shape properties representing an office on a building plan may vary while still describing the same object. Such semantic properties must be considered when attempting to classify graphical data.

Each device was classified by the individual and fused descriptors with an accompanying measure of certainty and confidence. Both techniques, Fourier Descriptors and Moment Invariants proved reasonably successful in certain domains but not in all. Some classical Bayesian fusion techniques were implemented to try to optimise recognition by combining classifiers with limited success. It is planned to implement a more sophisticated fusion approach based on neural networks in the future.

Further work currently being carried out is evaluating this approach on more complex, variable and larger sets of graphical data found on building plans. Also envisaged, as a natural extension of this is work, is the combination of recognition through shape with recognition based on object context using various context-modelling methods. The results presented here from the initial system based on shape indicate the potential for this approach.

References

1. Winstanley, A.C.: Structuring Vector Maps using Computer Vision Techniques, Conf. of the Association of Geographic Information, Birmingham, pp. 8.11.1–8.11.2, (1998).
2. Winstanley, A.C. and Keyes, L.: Applying Computer Vision Techniques to Topographic Objects, Int. Archives of Photogrammetry and Remote Sensing, 33 (B3): 480–487, (2000).
3. Keyes L. and Winstanley A.C.: Using Moment Invariants for Classifying Shapes on Large-scale Maps, Computers Environment and Urban Systems, 25, 119–130, (2001).
4. Keyes L. and Winstanley A.C.: Data Fusion for Topographic Object Classification, IEEE/ISPRS Workshop on Remote Sensing and Data Fusion, 8-9, Rome, Nov 2001.
5. Gonzalez, R.C., Wintz, P.: Digital Image Processing, Addison-Wesley, 1977.
6. Granlund, G.H.:   Fourier Pre-processing for Hand Print Character Recognition, IEEE Transactions on Computers, C-21: 195–201, 1972.
7. Wood, S. L.: Fourier Analysis of Object Boundaries From Two Dimensional Digitised Images, ICASS, 1986.
8. Hu, M. K.: Visual Pattern Recognition by Moment Invariants, IEEE Transactions on Information Theory, IT-8: 179–187, 1962.
9. Dudani, S. A., Breeding, K.J., McGhee, R. B., Aircraft Identification by Moment Invariants, IEEE Transactions on Computers, C-26 (1): 39–45, 1977.
10. Chaur-Chin Chen: Improved Moment Invariants for Shape Recognition, Pattern Recognition, 26(5): 683–686, 1993.
11. Costa, L.F., Cesar, R.M., Shape Analysis and Classification: Theory and Practice, CRC Press, 2001.
12. Kittler, J., Hatef, M., Duin, R.P.W., Matas, J., On Combining Classifiers, IEEE Transactions on Pattern Analysis and Machine Intelligence, 20(3), 1998.

Graphic Recognition: The Concept Lattice Approach

Karell Bertet and Jean-Marc Ogier

L3I, University of La Rochelle, av M. Crépeau, 17042 La Rochelle Cédex 1, France
{kbertet, jmogier}@univ-lr.fr

1 Introduction

Object recognition is a very large problem that can be derived in different forms. In the domain of graphic recognition, many strategies are proposed, but many of them depend on the context in which they are applied [LVSM01]. This aspect implies the necessity to find a model for this context, and to use it for the implementation of dynamic and adaptative systems. In this paper, we focus on the object recognition problem where a knowledge base defined by a finite set of representative prototypes or class objects is given. Such a problem can then be formulated as follows:

Given a graphic object x,
which prototype of the knowledge base is closest to x?

Remark that, for such a problem, x isn't a prototype, but is close to a prototype, hence x is a noisy prototype or a noisy graphic object. This problem clearly depends on the knowledge base representation. In this paper, we propose and define a new approach issued from the formal concept analysis [GW99] where a concept lattice is used as knowledge representation, and where some relevant properties of this lattice can be extended to the object recognition problem. This approach can be precised as follows:

Knowledge Representation: How to define a relevant concept lattice from the knowledge base of representative prototypes?
Object Recognition: How to derive from this concept lattice efficient recognition algorithms?

One can generate a concept lattice from a knowledge base when each prototype of the base is characterised by a set of attributes. In this paper, we deal with prototypes given by some statistical descriptors, and from this descriptors we compute a set of attributes aimed at characterizing the prototypes. The concept lattice is a very useful tool for knowledge representation since it represents all the possible combinations of attributes (i.e. attributes shared by some prototypes of the knowledge base), and all the possible sequences of attributes from the more generalized one (i.e. shared by a lot of prototypes) to the more specialized one (i.e. shared by few prototypes).

J. Lladós and Y.-B. Kwon (Eds.): GREC 2003, LNCS 3088, pp. 265–278, 2004.
© Springer-Verlag Berlin Heidelberg 2004

This lattice based representation can be considered as a research area useful to guide some object recognition treatment by online providing a relevant sequence of attributes to be validated. Moreover, in the case of noisy graphic object, i.e. object where some attributes can't be validated, the concept lattice can be used to infer attributes for a recognition treatment. As a basic example, consider an attribute shared by all the prototypes. In this case, a validation of this attribute is clearly non-relevant for an object recognition.

In Section 2, the knowledge representation by a concept lattice is first formally defined (Section 2.1), before being applied to a knowledge base of prototypes given by statistical descriptors (Section 2.3). The two categories of techniques allowing to obtain a description of a prototypes base, and used when dealing classical graphic recognition approachs are described in Section 2.2.

Section 3 deals with the object recognition problem: some basic treatments useful for an object recognition are derived from relevant properties of a concept lattice in Section 3.1; such basic treatments are then combined and extended to the particular case of graphic recognition where graphic objects are given by statistical descriptors (Section 3.2).

2   Knowledge Representation by a Concept Lattice

Section 2.1 formally defines a concept lattice from a *formal context*, i.e. a binary relation between a set of *objects* and a set of characteristic *attributes*. In our case, objects corresponds to the representative prototypes, whereas attributes have to be derived from a prototype representation issued from image analysis. Section 2.2 enumerates all the possible ways to obtain a prototype description when dealing with classical graphic recognition approachs, and Section 2.3 illustrates our approach by generating a context (and so a concept lattice) from a set of prototypes given by statistical descriptors.

2.1   Concept Lattice: Mathematical Foundations

As previously mentionned, a concept lattice is defined from a *formal context* by the formal concept analysis [GW99]. A formal context $C = (G, M, R)$ consists of two sets G and M and a relation R between G and M. The elements of G are called the *objects*, and the element of M are called the *attributes* of the context. In order to express that an object g is in relation with an attribute m, we write gRm: "the object *has* the attribute m".

For a set $A \subseteq G$ of objects, we define A', the set of attributes common to the objects in A. Correspondingly, for a set $B \subseteq M$ of attributes, the set of objects which have all attributes in B is B':

$$A' = \{m \in M \mid gRm \text{ for all } g \in A\}$$
$$B' = \{g \in G \mid gRm \text{ for all } m \in B\}$$

A *formal concept* of the context (G, M, R) is a pair (A, B) with $A \subseteq G$ a set of objects, $B \subseteq M$ a set of attributes, and $A' = B$, that is equivalent to

$A = B'$. $\beta(C)$ denotes the set of all concepts for a context C. Let $\leq$ be an order relation (i.e reflexive, antisymmetric and transitive) defined on $\beta(C)$ as follows, with (A_1, B_1) and $(A_2, B_2) \in \beta(C)$ two concepts:

$$(A_1, B_1) \leq (A_2, B_2) \iff A_1 \subseteq A_2 \text{ (that is equivalent to } B_1 \supseteq B_2) \quad (1)$$

By $<$ we denote the irreflexive relation associated to $\leq$. The order $\leq$ on $\beta(C)$ is the transitive closure of the *cover relation* $\prec$ on $\beta(C)$ defined by $(A_1, B_1) \prec (A_2, B_2)$ if $(A_1, B_1) < (A_2, B_2)$ and there exists no concept (A_3, B_3) such that $(A_1, B_1) < (A_3, B_3) < (A_2, B_2)$. The set $\beta(C)$ equipped with this relation is a lattice denoted the *concept lattice* $(\beta(C), \leq)$ of the context $C = (G, M, R)$, also denoted the *Galois lattice* [BM70]. When equipped with the cover relation $\prec$, $(\beta(C) \prec)$ is the Hasse diagram of the concept lattice. Figure 1 represents a context C and its concept lattice represented by its Hasse diagram.

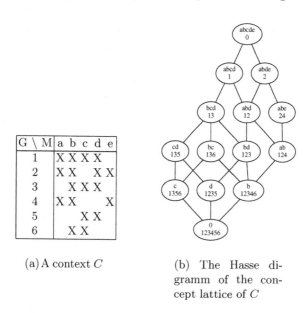

G \ M	a b c d e
1	X X X X
2	X X X X
3	X X X
4	X X X
5	X X
6	X X

(a) A context C

(b) The Hasse diagramm of the concept lattice of C

Fig. 1. A context and its concept lattice

There exists a lot of algorithms aimed at generating the concept lattice from a context. Among all of these algorithms, the most efficient is described in [NR99].

2.2   Image Prototypes Descriptors

With image analysis techniques, one can find several objects representations (vector, graph, ...), and the characteristic sets of attributes have to be derived from such representations. When dealing classical graphic recognition problems, one meets two principal categories of techniques allowing to describe objects, and that may be used in our case.

Statistical Description. The first category deals with statistical descriptions of objects, that are generally based on the computation of an invariant features vector, on the basis of mathematical concepts, like Fourier Mellin Transform, Fourier descriptors, Zernike moments, Radon Signature, and so on. For this category of technique, the first stage consists of a computation of the signature, that is then introduced in a classifier process (neural network, Bayesian classifier, ...) [TJT96, AJC+99].

Because of the difficulty to define the most relevant signatures, some authors propose to combine invariant features vectors by using some optimization process, like genetic algorithms or simulated annealing, in order to obtain the most adequate signature. However, even if these combinations allow to improve the good classification rate, these techniques often depend on contextual information and require to be adapted for each new situation. Furthermore, they often suffer of a lack of explanation of the chosen combination, since this operation is led by a numeric optimisation process.

Structural Representation. The second category of technique relies on structural representation of the objects. In this case, the objects are described by using graph representation, and the classification problem often relies on isomorphism research techniques [LVSM01].

Actually, these techniques suffer of a high computation complexity, and most of the techniques try to reduce to the search process complexity, by using heuristics or statistical based hypotheses (Region of Interest). Furthermore, these techniques also suffer of a lack of possibility to combine or select relevant features in the classification process.

In our case, both of these techniques may be used to represent the knowledge in the global process [LVSM01]. For the illustration of our approach, we choose a technique using statistical descriptors of the representative prototypes.

2.3   Defining a Context from Statistical Signatures

The statistical descriptor provides a descriptors vector or a signature for each prototype of the knowledge base. The problem is then to derive from this knowledge base a set of characteristic attributes, and to define a context, therefore a concept lattice can be computed.

More formaly, let $\{P_i\}_{i \leq n}$ be a set of n prototypes. A signature of a prototype P_i is a vector $(v_{ij})_{j \leq m}$ of m values. The knowledge base is the set $\{(v_{ij})_{i \leq n, j \leq m}\}$ of vectors for the n prototypes. Let $inv_j = (v_{1j}, v_{2j}, \dots, v_{nj})$ be the set of the jth values for all prototypes. The set of attributes is obtained by sampling these values in separate intervals $C_j = \{I_{j1}, \dots, I_{jp}\}$ with $p \leq n$, and the context (G, M, R) directly follows, with:

set of objects: $G = \bigcup\limits_{i \leq n} P_i$

set of attibutes: $M = \bigcup\limits_{j \leq m} C_j$

relation between G and M: $\forall P_i, \ \forall I_{jk} \in C_j \ (P_i R I_{jk} \iff v_{ij} \in I_{jk})$

To be *valid*, a context must associate a characteristic set of attributes to each prototype, i.e. it has to verify the vollowing property:

$$\forall P_i, P_{i'}, \ \{I_{jk} \ | P_i \ R \ I_{jk}\} \neq \{I_{jk} \ | P_{i'} \ R \ I_{jk}\} \tag{2}$$

The smallest set of attributes is obtained by sampling the values of inv_j, $j \leq m$, in one interval $C_j = \{I_{j1}\}$, and the obtained context is not valid because it doesn't verify (2). By sampling the n values of inv_j in n intervals (one interval by value), we obtain a greatest valid context of $n * m$ attributes. Some intermediate samplings can be obtained by a basic cut of interval as follows: consider a sampling $\cup_{j \leq m} C_j$ of all the values; consider the interval $I_{jk} = [a, b] \in C_j$ containing two consecutives values $v_{ij} < v_{i'j}$ such that $|v_{ij} - v_{i'j}|$ is maximal; a new sampling is then obtained by replacing I_{jk} with the two intervals $[a, v_{ij}]$ and $[v_{i'j}, b]$. Function **context** in Algorithm 1 first computes the smallest sampling $C_j = \{I_{j1}\}$, with $j \leq m$, and iterates the cut described below until a valid sampling is obtained. Note that it is possible to iterate again some cuts nb times by adding a parameter nb to Function **context**. We then obtain some more precise but greater context.

Example 1. To illustrate Function **context** in Algorithme 1, consider as a basic example the following statistical descriptors of $n = 4$ prototypes obtained by the Fourier Mellin Transform, where a line represents the index of a prototype (from 1 to 4), and the $m = 5$ values of its signature:

```
1  0.016201    0.000258   -0.000000   -0.004425    0.000000
2  0.229363   -0.192015   -0.029122    0.115654    0.020098
3  0.279948   -0.117589   -0.013490   -0.023691    0.001997
4  0.311336    0.027862   -0.003052   -0.107714   -0.006230
```

From this base of signature, Function **context** in Algorithm 1 computes the following context where each interval in C_j, $j \leq 4$, is represented by its minimal and maximal values. Figure 2 gives the associated concept lattice where each concept (A, B) is represented by the set A of candidates prototypes above the set B of validated attributes.

	I_{01}	I_{11}	I_{12}	I_{21}	I_{31}	I_{32}	I_{33}	I_{41}
min	0.016201	0.000258	-0.117589	-0.029122	-0.107714	-0.023691	0.115654	-0.006230
max	0.311336	0.027862	-0.192015	-0.000000	-0.107714	-0.023691	0.115654	-0.006230
prot. 1	×	×		×		×		×
prot. 2	×		×	×			×	×
prot. 3	×		×	×		×		×
prot. 4	×	×		×	×			×

3 Object Recognition

In this section, at first we presente some basic treatments that have to be iterated and combined to obtain an object recognition treatment (Section 3.1). Such basic treatments aim at exploring the concept lattice as a research area: a *validation*

Name: `context`

Input: $\{P_i\}_{i \leq n}$ a set of n prototypes;

$\{(v_{ij})_{i \leq n,\, j \leq m}\}$ a set of n vectors containing m values;

Output: a context (G, M, R)

begin

/* compute the sampling */

foreach $j \leq m$ **do** let $(v'_{ij})_{i \leq n}$ the sorted vector $(v_{ij})_{i \leq n}$;

foreach $j \leq m$ **do** $C_j = \{[v'_{1j}, v'_{nj}]\}$;

while *the sampling is not valid (2)* **do**

let $I_{jk} = [a, b]$ containing the values $v'_{ij} < v'_{(i+1)j}$ such that

$|v'_{(i+1)j} - v'_{ij}|$ is maximal;

$C_j = C_j \setminus [a, b] \cup [a, v'_{ij}] \cup [v'_{(i+1)j}, b]$;

/* compute the context */

$G = \emptyset$; **foreach** $i \leq n$ **do** $G = G \cup P_i$;

$M = \emptyset$; **foreach** $j \leq m$ **do** $M = M \cup C_j$;

foreach $i \leq n, j \leq m, I_{jk} \in C_j$ **do**

if $v_{ij} \in I_{jk}$ then $P_i R I_{jk}$

return $[(G, M, R)]$

end

Algorithm 1. Computes a context from a knowledge base of statistical descriptors of prototypes

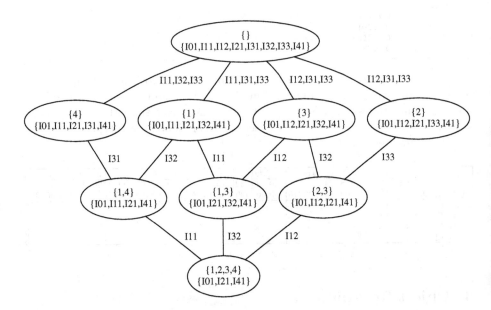

Fig. 2. Concept lattice generated

treatment increases the set of validated attributes whereas a *reduction* treatment decreases the set of validated attributes. Each treatment depends on a selection function to select some attributes to be (un)validated. We propose in Section 3.2 a general graphic recognition algorithm for a graphic object given by a statistical descriptors, this algorithm relies on a combination of basic treatments together with specific selected functions.

3.1   The General Case

Let us recall the graphic recognition problem:

Given a graphic object x,
which prototype of the knowledge base is closest to x?

When a knowledge base of prototypes is given by a context (G, M, R), where each prototype g in G is characterised in terms of owning attributes (i.e. attributes in M in relation with g), the concept lattice represents an area research well-suited to guide an object recognition treatment: it consists of a validation or unvalidation sequence of some attributes guiding by an exploration of the lattice.

Let (A, B) be a concept, then prototypes in A share a common set of attributes in B, maximal under inclusion. In terms of object recognition, a concept (A, B) represents a step of the recognition where B contains some validated attributes from x, and A contains the candidates prototypes to be associated to x. The smallest concept according to the relation $\leq$ can be the concept $(G, \emptyset)$ meaning that still no attribute is validated, and that all the prototypes in G are candidates. In the general case, the smallest concept is a concept (G, C) with $C \subseteq M$ possibly empty, and where attributes in C are shared by all the prototypes. In Figure 2, we have a non empty set C of initial validated attributes since $C = \{I_{01}, I_{21}, I_{41}\}$. All the concepts are reachables from (G, C) according to $\leq$, in particular the concepts $(A = \{a\}, B)$ meaning that only one prototype a is candidate to correspond to x. For each sequence of concepts from (G, C) to $(A = \{a\}, B)$, the set of validated attributes increases while the set of candidates prototypes decreases. The object recognition problem can then be decomposed as a sequence of validation/unvalidation attributes, each step being represented by a concept (A, B) where a set of attributes to be examined can be computed in order to define a new concept (A_1, B_1) for the next step. The lattice can be explored from (G, C), either according to the binary relation $\leq$, or to the cover relation $\prec$.

Global Validation.   When dealing with the relation $\leq$, the set P_{global} of attributes to be examined at each step (A, B) is obtained from the concepts (A_1, B_1) such that $(A_1, B_1) \geq (A, B)$ by (3).

$$P_{global} = \bigcup \{B_1 \backslash B \mid (A, B) \leq (A_1, B_1) \text{ and } |A_1| = 1\} \qquad (3)$$

The condition $|A_1| = 1$ has to be tested to avoid dealing with the maximal concept $(M, \emptyset)$ what means "no prototype corresponds to the total set M of validated attributes". From a subset $V \subseteq P_{global}$ of validated attributes, the smallest concept (A_1, B_1) of the concept lattice containing $B \cup V$ is computed. Then $B_1 = B \cup V \cup I$, where I are inferred attributes. (A_1, B_1) corresponds to a new step of the sequence recognition with $B_1 \subseteq B$ the increased validated attributes, and $A_1 \supseteq A$ the decreased candidates prototypes.

This basic recognition treatment according to relation $\leq$ is described by Function `global_validation` in Algorithm 2. As input, it requires a selection function that aims at validating some attributes between the attributes in P_{global}.

Name: `global_validation`
Input: a concept (A, B);
       the concept lattice given by its contexts $\beta(C)$ and the relation $\leq$;
       `global_select_valid`, a function aimed at validating some attributes between a given set of attributes;
Output: a concept $(A_1, B_1) \geq (A, B)$
begin
    $P = \emptyset$;
    foreach $(A_1, B_1) \geq (A, B)$ *such that* $|A_1| = 1$ **do** $P = P \cup (B_1 \backslash B)$;
    $V =$ `global_select_valid`(P);
    foreach $(A_1, B_1) \geq (A, B)$ **do**
        if $V \subseteq B_1$ *and* A_1 *is minimal* **then**
            print($B_1 \backslash B$ "validated attributes");
            print($B_1 \backslash B \backslash V$ "inferred attributes");
            return $[(A_1, B_1)]$

end

Algorithm 2. Validates some attributes by a global exploration

Local Validation. When dealing with the cover relation $\prec$, each concept (A_1, B_1) such that $(A_1, B_1) \succ (A, B)$ gives rise to the set $B_1 \backslash B$ of attributes to be examined. So all such concepts imply to examine a family P_{local} of attributes (i.e. a set of subsets of attributes) as in (4).

$$P_{local} = \bigcup \{\{B_1 \backslash B\} \mid (A, B) \prec (A_1, B_1)\} \qquad (4)$$

From definition of a concept lattice, it's easy to check that these subsets don't intersect, and the validation of a subset V of cardinality at least 1 in the family P_{local} is sufficient to deduce the entire subset of P_{local} it belongs to, and then to compute the concept (A_1, B_1) for the next recognition step. Then $B_1 = B \cup \{v\} \cup I$, where I are inferred attributes. We also have increased the validated attributes since $B \subseteq B_1$, and decreased the candidates prototypes since $A \supseteq A_1$.

This basic recognition treatment according to relation $\prec$ is described by Function `local_validation` in Algorithm 3. As input it requires a selection function that aims at validating one attribute between the family P_{local}.

Name: `local_validation`
Input: a concept (A, B);
  the concept lattice given by its contexts $\beta(C)$, and the relation $\prec$;
  `local_select_valid`, a function aimed at validating one attribute between a family on M;
Output: a concept $(A_1, B_1) \succ (A, B)$
begin

$\quad P = \emptyset;$
$\quad$ **foreach** $(A_1, B_1) \succ (A, B)$ **do** $P = P \cup \{B_1 \backslash B\};$
$\quad V =$ `local_select_valid`(P);
$\quad$ **foreach** $(A_1, B_1) \succ (A, B)$ **do**
$\quad\quad$ **if** $V \subseteq B_1$ **then**
$\quad\quad\quad$ print($B_1 \backslash B$ "validated attributes");
$\quad\quad\quad$ print($B_1 \backslash B \backslash V$ "inferred attributes");
$\quad\quad\quad$ **return** $[(A_1, B_1)]$

end

Algorithm 3. Validates some attributes by a local exploration

Let us remark that some attributes can be validated in a bad way when dealing with a deteriorated graphic object x. In particular, with Function `global_validation`, the concept $(\emptyset, M)$ can be reached when some deteriorated attributes are validated. $(\emptyset, M)$ means that the validated attributes are the entire set M of attributes, and the set of candidate prototypes sharing these attributes, and therefore attributes to examine, is the empty set. Function `global_reduction` in Algorithm 4 and Function `local_reduction` in Algorithm 5 are provided to invalidate attributes, the first is conversely similar to Function `global_validation` while the second is conversly similar to Func-

Name: `global_reduction`
Input: a concept (A, B);
  the concept lattice given by its contexts $\beta(C)$, and the relation $\leq$;
  `global_select_reduc`, a function aimed at unvalidating some attributes between a given subset of attributes;
Output: a concept $(A_1, B_1) \leq (A, B)$
begin

$\quad V =$ `global_select_reduc`(B);
$\quad$ **foreach** $(A_1, B_1) \leq (A, B)$ **do**
$\quad\quad$ **if** $V \cap B_1 = \emptyset$ *and* A_1 *is maximal* **then**
$\quad\quad\quad$ print($B \backslash B_1$ "unvalidated attributes");
$\quad\quad\quad$ print($B \backslash B_1 \backslash V$ "unvalidated inferred attributes");
$\quad\quad\quad$ **return** $[(A_1, B_1)]$

end

Algorithm 4. Unvalidates some attributes by a global exploration

Name: `local_reduction`
Input: a concept (A, B);
        the concept lattice given by its contexts $\beta(C)$, and the relation $\prec$;
        `local_select_reduc`, a function aimed at validating some attributes   between a given family on M;
Output: a concept $(A_1, B_1) \prec (A, B)$
begin

    $P = \emptyset$;
    foreach $(A_1, B_1) \prec (A, B)$ **do** $P = P \cup \{B \backslash B_1\}$;
    $V =$`local_select_reduc`(P);
    foreach $(A_1, B_1) \prec (A, B)$ **do**
        if $V \not\subseteq B_1$ **then**
            print($B \backslash B_1$ "unvalidated attributes");
            print($B \backslash B_1 \backslash V$ "unvalidated inferred attributes");
            return $[(A_1, B_1)]$

end

Algorithm 5. Unvalidates some attributes by a local exploration

tion `local_validation`. Note that Function `global_reduction` has to invalidate some attributes between the attributes in B for a step (A, B), whereas Function `local_reduction` deals with a smaller set of attributes organised in a family.

A recognition treatment of a given graphic object x can be obtained by an iteration of Function `local_validation`, or by an iteration of Function `local_validation`, or by a combination of these two functions, with $(\emptyset, M)$ as first input, and until a concept $(A = \{a\}, B)$ has been reached, and each iterative step is corresponding to a concept. Function `global_reduction` and Function `local_reduction` can also be on-line used to invalidate attributes, in particular in the case where the concet $(\emptyset, M)$ is reached.

The choice of a validation function only depends on the attributes issued from the initial context. When a deteriorated attribute can't be validated from a big set of attributes, its validation may be performed by using some specific image analysis function from the smallest set of attributes well-organised in a family. So a local treatment is more appropriate. However a local validation deals with attributes from the more general one (i.e. shared by several prototypes) to the more specific one (i.e. shared by few prototypes), and would be unsuccessful when global attributes are deteriorated.

When attributes are obtained by image analysis function in a global way, the global validation is more appropriate : the number of iteration depends on the initial graphic object x, and so on its deterioration rate. In this case, it is possible to deal with some approximation treatment on attributes at each iteration.

3.2   Object Recognition for Statistical Analysis

In the case where prototypes are given by statistical descriptors, the object recognition problem becomes:

Given a signature $(x_1, \ldots, x_m)$ of a graphic object x,
which prototype is closest to x?

Since statistic signatures are directly computed from a graphic object, a global recognition treatment is more appropriate in this case. It consists of a sequence of Function `global_validation`, with the smallest concept (G, C) as first input, and until a concept (A, B) such that $A = \{a\}$ or $A = \emptyset$ is reached. When the concept $(\emptyset, M)$ is reached, an iteration of Function `local_reduction` unvalidates some attributes to reach a concept $(A = \{a\}, B)$. The prototype a is then the result of the recognition treatment. Function `recognition` in Algorithm 6 precises such recognition treatment, and uses the two following selected functions:

- the selected function `select_valid` aims at validating (and so infering) some attributes at each iteration of Function `global_validation`,
- the selected function `select_reduc` aims at invalidating some attributes when an iteration of Function `local_invalidation` is needed.

Name: `recognition`
Input: a concept lattice given by its contexts $\beta(C)$, and the relation $\prec$;
an object x given by its signature $(x_1, \ldots, x_n)$;
Output: a prototype a, result of the recognition process of x
begin

/* iteration of global validation treatments */
let (G, C) be the smallest concept of the concept lattice;
$A = G$ and $B = C$;
$s = 1$;
while $|A| > 1$ **do**
$\quad (A, B) =$ `global_validation`$((A, B), (\beta(C), \prec),$`select_valid`$(x, s))$;
$\quad s = s - 0.1$;
/* one local reduction treatment, if needed */
if $|A| = 0$ **then**
$\quad (A, B) =$ `local_reduction`$((A, B), (\beta(C), \prec),$`select_reduc`$(x, s))$;
/* now $|A| = 1$ */
let $a \in A$;
return $[a]$

end

Algorithm 6. Graphic recognition

Before precising these two functions, let's consider the following set I_x of intervals in (5):

$$I_x = \{I_{jk} \mid x_j \in I_{jk} , I_{jk} \in C_j , j \leq m\} \tag{5}$$

This set I_x can be used in the first validation iteration to validate the intervals in I_x, and so infer some other intervals. Remark that intervals in C_j are disjoint for each $j \leq m$, so I_x contains at most one interval in C_j. Remark also that the size of I_x decreases when the deterioration rate of x increases.

By extending an interval in M to a fuzzy interval depending on ε (see Figure 3), the membership degree $\alpha \in [0.1]$ of x to an interval $I_{jk} = [a, b] \in C_j$ is defined as:

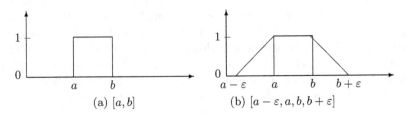

(a) $[a, b]$ (b) $[a - \varepsilon, a, b, b + \varepsilon]$

Fig. 3. An interval $[a, b]$, and the associated fuzzy interval according to ε

$$
\begin{aligned}
\alpha^{\varepsilon}_{I_{jk}}(x) &= \quad 1 \qquad \text{if } a \leq x_j \leq b \\
&= \quad 0 \qquad \text{if } x_j \leq a - \varepsilon \text{ or } x_j \geq b + \varepsilon \\
&= \tfrac{v_j - a + \varepsilon}{\varepsilon} \quad \text{if } a - \varepsilon \leq x_j \leq a \\
&= \tfrac{b + \varepsilon - v_j}{\varepsilon} \quad \text{if } b \leq x_j \leq b + \varepsilon
\end{aligned}
$$

The set I_x is derived to I_x^s, where $s \leq 1$ is the bound of membership degree intervals accepted. Remark that $I_x = I_x^1 \supseteq I_x^{0.9} \supseteq I_x^{0.8} \ldots \supseteq I_x^0 = M$.

$$I_x^s = \{ I_{jk} \mid \alpha^{\varepsilon}_{I_{jk}}(x) \leq s , I_{jk} \in C_j , j \leq m \} \qquad (6)$$

Let us now precise the two selected functions used by Function `recognition` in Algorithm 6. Each iteration i of Function `global_validation` calls the selected function `select_valid` in Algorithm 7 with the extra input $s = 1 - 0.i$ in order to computes $I_x^{1-0.i-0.1} \setminus I_x^{1-0.i}$ and to validate and infer some attributes. If the last iteration l outputs the concept $(\emptyset, M)$, a local reduction is performed by using the selected function `select_reduc` in Algorithm 8 with the extra input $s = 1 - 0.l$. Therefore the recognition treatment ends with a concept $(A = \{a\}, B)$ representing the prototype a as output.

Name: `select_valid`
Input: a set P_{global} of attributes;
         an object x given by its signature $(x_1, \ldots, x_n)$;
         a bound $s \leq 1$;
Output: a subset of P_{global}
begin
     compute $I_x^{s-0.1}$ and I_x^s;
     $I = I_x^{s-0.1} \setminus I_x^s$;
     return $[I \cap P_{global}]$
end

Algorithm 7. Selects attributes in P_{global} for a global validation

Name: `select_reduc`
Input: a family P_{local} on the set of attributes;
an object x given by its signature $(x_1, \ldots, x_n)$;
a bound $s \leq 1$;
Output: a subset of $P \in P_{local}$
begin

> compute $I_x^{s-0.1}$ and I_x^s;
> $I = I_x^{s-0.1} \backslash I_x^s$;
> **foreach** $V \in P_{local}$ **do** $nb[V] = |V \cap I|$;
> let V such that $nb[V]$ is maximal;
> **return** $[V \cap I]$

end

Algorithm 8. Selects attributes in P_{local} for a local reduction

Example 2. To illustrate Function 6 in Algorithm 6, consider as a basic example the concept lattice in Figure 2, and an object x given by its signature:

0.491243	0.219234	0.061987	0.115661	0.022276

The minimal concept $(\{1,2,3,4\}, \{I_{01}, I_{22}, I_{41}\})$ is the first step of the recognition treatment, and means that "all the prototypes are candidates, whereas the values 0, 2 and 4 of the are respectivly inferred belonging to intervals I_{01}, I_{22} and I_{41}".

We have $I_x = \emptyset$ and $I_x^{0.9} = \{I_{33}\}$. Since the first global validation step deals with I_x to select attributes, the associated concept is still the same. The second global validation step deals with $I_x^{0.9}$. So I_{33} is validated, and I_{11} is inferred since the smallest concept containing I_{33} is the concept $(\{2\}, \{I_{01}, I_{11}, I_{22}, I_{33}, I_{41}\})$. This means that the first value of the descriptor of x is inferred belonging to interval I_{11}. But this also means that the recognition treatment ends with the prototype 2 as result.

4 Conclusion and Perspectives

In this paper, we propose an original approach allowing to represent knowledge domain when dealing with a graphic recognition problem. The chosen formalism relies on Concept lattice (Galois lattice), that is a particularly interesting tool when trying to classify objects, by integrating contextual information. Based on an exhaustive extraction of attributes, this approach allows to select the relevant features, dynamically, as a function of the context. Furthermore, this kind of approach allows to determine a posteriorly the set of inferred attributes in the recogniton process, i.e. the useful descriptors. We formally precise in this paper the different relevant points of this approach, and its experimentation with some statistical information reprenting the prototype base.

A first perspective concerning this work consists of applying this approach for some structural representation, and in extending the basic treatments for the implementation of dynamic analysis scenario, as a function of contextual information.

Another perspective would be an experimentation study, by precising the rate of validated attributes, i.e. the attributes selected in the recognition process; the rate of inferred attributes, i.e. attributes that are not directly validated; and the global recognition rate, and so the reject rate.

Another important study of this approach concerns the algorithmical aspects: the recognition algorithms need a concept lattice as input. Since such a lattice can be very large (exponential if the worst case) and since only some parts of this lattice are necessary for the recognition treatments, it is possible to perform the same treatments without computing the whole lattice by an on-line generation of some parts of the lattice using specific representation of a lattice. Among all the studied representation of a lattice [Bir67], the implicational systems [BN04] must be very efficient to an on-line generation.

Acknowledgment

The authors wish to thank Uttama Surapong for its useful corrections on this paper.

References

[AJC+99]   S. Adam and J.M. Ogier, C. Cariou, R. Mullot, J. Gardes, and Y. Lecourtier, Combination of invariant pattern recognition primitives onn technical documents. In *Proceedings of GREC'99*, Pages 203–210, Jaipur, India 1999.

[Bir67]   G. Birkhoff, *Lattice theory*, volume 25. American Mathematical Society, 3rd edition, 1967.

[BM70]   M. Barbut and B. Monjardet. *Ordre et classification, Algèbre et combinatoire*, Hachette, Paris, 1970. 2 tomes.

[BN04]   K. Bertet and M. Nebut, Efficient algorithms on the Moore family associated to an implicationnal system. *DMTCS*, 2002, to appear.

[GW99]   B. Ganter and R. Wille, *Formal concept analysis, Mathematical foundations*, Springer Verlag, Berlin, 1999.

[LVSM01]   J. Lladós and E. Valveny and G. Sánchez and E. Martí. Symbol Recognition: Current advances and perspectives, In *Proceedings of GREC'01*, Kingston, Canada 2001.

[NR99]   L. Nourine and O. Raynaud, A fast algorithm for building lattices. In *Third International Conference on Orders, Algorithms and Applications*, Montpellier, France, August 1999.

[TJT96]   O.D. Trier and A. K. Jain, and T. Taxt. Features extraction methods for character recognition – a survey. *Pattern Recognition*, 29:641–662, 1996.

A Topological Measure for Image Object Recognition

Patrick Franco, Jean-Marc Ogier, Pierre Loonis, and Rémy Mullot

Laboratoire Informatique, Image, Interaction (L3I) - UPRES EA 2118
Université de La Rochelle - Pôle Sciences et Technologies
17042 La Rochelle Cedex 1 France
{patrick.franco, jean-marc.ogier,...}@univ-lr.fr

Abstract. All the effective object recognition systems are based on a powerful shape descriptor. We propose a new method for extracting the topological feature of an object. By connecting all the pixels constituting the object under the constraint to define the shortest path (minimum spanning tree) we capture the shape topology. The tree length is in the first approximation the key of our object recognition system. This measure (with some adjustments) make it possible to detect the object target in several geometrical configurations (translation/rotation) and it seems to have many desirable properties such as discrimination power and robustness to noise, that is the conclusion of the preliminary tests on characters and symbols.

1 Introduction

The template matching problem can be described as : suppose that we have a prototype of an object and we want to detect its instance in a given image. A direct solution is to place the prototype (template) in the image and detect its presence by comparing intensity values of the prototype with the corresponding values in the image. Classically that is the schema of cross-correlations approaches. Because the heart of the problem is to efficiently characterize the objects, different models can be used and they define many classes of solution, we are in the general framework of pattern recognition. Usually a partition is made between descriptors based on local or global features of an object.

In the first case, contours are commonly used in order to obtain invariant descriptions of patterns through Fourier descriptors [14, 11]. Circular primitives, which are, by definition, well adapted to rotation invariant recognition, have been used in [7]. These are based on the analysis of the shape through a set of circles.

Many features can be used to describe the global aspect of a shape. Since the works of Hu in 1961, invariant moments [5, 16] which are based on combinations of regular moments, have been very frequently used. One can thus cite Zernike moments [21, 6]. We can cite morphological approaches [12] in which objects are decomposed by geometrical primitives and relations among then. These links are synthesized by graphs and the object recognition task is transformed into a graph matching problem (graph/sub-graph isomorphism).

J. Lladós and Y.-B. Kwon (Eds.): GREC 2003, LNCS 3088, pp. 279–290, 2004.

In this article we propose anew model based on the capture of the topologic-alproperties of ashape. This approach was inspired by the works of O. Michel, A. Hero, B. Ma [3, 1]. Any object is described in the image system coordinates by a multi-dimensional points set with a specific topology. By computing a Minimum Spanning Tree (MST) on this points set we define a measure of the object's topology because for a given points distribution the MST length is single. We show that the MST length can define a metric capable to discriminate a prototype object from an unknown one. A mixture of both objects is realized before computing the variation of the lengths from the prototype length. This stage makes possible to detect translations and rotations of the prototype in the image.

The principle is detailed in Section 2.2 and illustrated through an example. The technique is tested in Section 3.1 on binary images in the multi-oriented character recognition problem. Then it's applied (Section 3.2) to the classification of complex and noisy symbols. The results are analyzed and the discrimination power in front of noise is studied.

2   Object Recognition by Minimum Spanning Tree

2.1   Minimum Spanning Tree: Definition

An image object $O(x, y)$ can be represented in the image system coordinates by a points set evolving in $\mathbb{R}^d$ ($d = 2$ for a binary image, $d = 3$ for a gray scale). A MST, called G, build on this points set $O = \{p_1, p_2, .., p_i, .., p_N\}$ is a:

- *completely connected tree*: all the points $p_i \in O$ are connected.
- *not directed tree*: there is no read sense of the edges $e_{i,j}$ connecting the points p_i to p_j.
- *tree without cycle*: the tree does not describe a loop, so two points are connected by a single path.
- *weighted tree*: the lengths of the $e_{i,j}$ edges are weighted.

G is represented by a list of nodes (the points p_i) and connections (the edges $e_{i,j}$) between these nodes. The total γ order length of the tree is the sum of the edges length (Euclidian norm) weighted by $\gamma \in]0, d[$:

$$L_\gamma = \sum_{e_{i,j} \in G} \| e_{i,j} \|^\gamma \tag{1}$$

Among all the completely connected acyclic trees that it is possible to build, the MST is the tree with the minimal length:

$$G^\star = \underset{G}{Argmin}\ L_\gamma \tag{2}$$

The fundamental algorithms are due to Kruskal and Prim [10], for an history of the problem we can see [2].

Note: sometimes two or more edges may have the same length, so different trees may result, but they will all have the same total length (which will always be the minimum). In this work, the MST and its length are computed thanks to the algorithm proposed in [4].

2.2   Matching by Minimum Spanning Trees

In this section, we show through an example how two objects can be discriminated by considering the topology of theirs points distributions, the MST length of which is a signature. We assume that the preliminary noise cleaning and segmentation tasks have been yet performed on the image. Let O_1 be the prototype and O_2 be a given object.

Algorithm

To address the template matching problem two MSTs are performed. A MST is computed off line on the prototype O_1, let L_1 be the tree length. An other one is defined on the mixture of the prototype and the input object, let L_{12} be the tree length. By comparing the MST lengths L_1 and L_{12} we can define an error measure between the two objects. When the prototype completely match to the unknown object, the topology defined by theirs union points sets is identical to the prototype one. In this case, the two MSTs have the same length and the error measure is minimum. This reasoning is illustrated by the Figures 1 to 9.

In the real world problem the objects can be multi-oriented. So we can iteratively apply translations and rotations on the input object to really estimate the similarity between the objects. Finally the distance is given by the geometrical transformation who minimize the criterion error. This rule is synthesized by the following algorithm.

Data   : $O_1 = \{p_1, .., p_i, .., p_N\}$, $O_2 = \{q_1, .., q_j, .., q_N\}$, γ
begin

  Build a MST on the prototype set O_1, let L_1 its γ order length.
  for *Several matrix transformation T* **do**
    1. Define the transformed object :
    $$O_2^T = T * O_2 = \{q_1^T, ..., q_N^T\}$$

    2. Define the union ("mixture") between the prototype and the transformed object :
    $$O_{12} = O_1 \cup O_2^T = \{p_1, ..., p_N, q_1^T, ..., q_N^T\}$$

    3. Build a MST on O_{12}, let L_{12} its length.
    4. Compare O_2 with O_1 by :
    $$E^T = |L_{12} - L_1|$$

  end
  Finally, the γ distance between the prototype and the unknown object is :
  $$E^\star = \min\{E^T\} \quad \text{with} \quad T^\star = \underset{T}{Argmin}\ \{E^T\}$$

end

Algorithm 1: Template matching by MST

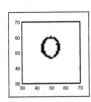

Fig. 1. A prototype of the character 'O'

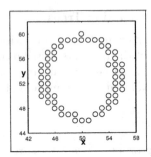

Fig. 2. The prototype in the image system coordinates

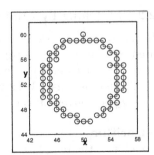

Fig. 3. The MST built on the prototype

Fig. 4. An unknown object ('O' translated and rotated)

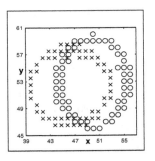

Fig. 5. The mixture for a non optimal geometrical transformation: the two objects don't match

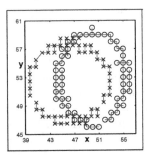

Fig. 6. The MST built on the mixture

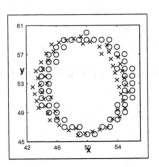

Fig. 7. The mixture for an "optimal" transformation: the two objects match

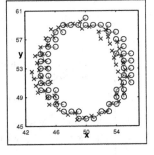

Fig. 8. The MST built on the mixture

Discussion on the Use of the Mixture

Statistical point of view
The MST length is linked to an entropy measure called Rényi's entropy [17]. The recent work of A. Hero and O. Michel [3] shows that a family of

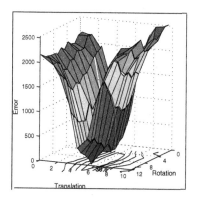

Fig. 9. Evolution of the error E^T according to some geometrical transformations T

tree[1] (of which the MST) which satisfies the Redmond's quasi-additivity property [15], built on one d dimensional points distribution are robust estimators of the Rényi's entropy of this distribution. These works are a multi-dimensional generalization of the results initially obtained in $2d$ by R. Ravi et al. [18]. This property find a natural application in the image registration problem. B. Ma et al. [1] developed a solution based on the following analysis. When two images are perfectly matched, theirs points distributions are overlapped and the joint probability function is maximum, consequently the Rényi's entropy of the mixture distribution is minimum.

Pattern recognition point of view
The idea consists in using the MST length to characterize the topology of a points set. Nevertheless, the comparison of two pattern is not based on the individual tree lengths defined on each set because the mathematical relationship between a points set and the tree length is not bijective, so two different objects may present the same tree length[2]. To take into account this situation an MST is defined on the mixture of the sets to be matched.

3   Application to Characters and Symbols Recognition

The technique is tested on the multi-oriented characters and symbols recognition problem. Here we present some preliminary results obtained on few samples. That is a first step to see how the algorithm works and to observe the discrimination power of the technique.

---

[1] The Steiner tree, the minimal spanning tree, and the trees related to Traveling Salesman Problem.
[2] This appears because the MST is the relative neighborhood graph.

3.1   Characters Recognition

We considered isolated characters on small ($1cm$ x $1cm$), binary and low resolution images (< 240 dpi). The font is 32 Times New Roman. To check the property of invariance recognition in front of translations and rotations we have considered special cases. First, the distance between the prototype 'O' and multi-oriented samples $0, 30, 60, 90°$ have been estimated. Moreover we have pointed out the distance between 'O' and a priori topologically nearest neighbor as 'Q' and '0' (cf Figure 14).

The level of discrimination measured by a criterion D is defined as:

$$D = \frac{min(d_1, .., d_k, .., d_n) - max(d_1, .., d_i, .., d_n)}{max(d_1, .., d_i, .., d_n)}$$

where:

d_k, the distance between the prototype and the false neighbors number k;

d_i, the distance between the prototype and the multi-oriented sample number i.

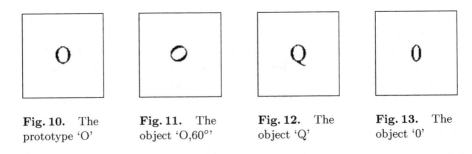

Fig. 10. The prototype 'O'

Fig. 11. The object 'O,60°'

Fig. 12. The object 'Q'

Fig. 13. The object '0'

We remark that the error concerning the samples $30, 60, 90°$ is not null. Quantifications errors exist ('O' and 'O,30°' don't have the same black pixels number). We also note that the maximal error between 'O' and the multi-oriented samples is lower than the minimal error between 'O' and the considered false neighbors ($37.189 < 66.585$). That emphasizes the discrimination level of the technique ($D = 66.585 - 37.189 = 79.04\%$). We observe a similar discrimination in others cases (cf Figure 15).

In order to estimate the real performance of the MST solution we have studied its noise resistance. Many objects have been deeply degraded by salt noise (black pixels random removed, cf Figure 16). The Figure 17 shows the evolution of the distances between the original prototype and degraded objects in front of increasing noise level ($0, 10, 20, 30\%$). The mean distances are computed after ten random samples of corrupted objects per noise level, the standard deviations (root mean square error) are represented by errors bars. These results are completed by the evolution of the discrimination level (cf Table 18).

In the range noise $[0; 30\%]$ the character 'O' in multi-oriented configurations and the false neighbors 'Q' and '0' still be well discriminated (cf Figure 17). For example, with a 30% noise level the discrimination factor remains significant $D = 21.93\%$ (cf Figure 18).

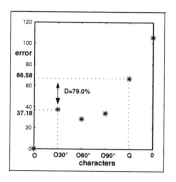

Fig. 14. $\gamma = 1$ order distance between the character 'O' and multi-oriented and false neighbor samples

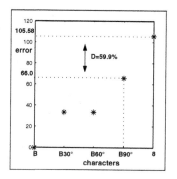

Fig. 15. $\gamma = 1$ order distance between 'B' and multi-oriented and false neighbor samples

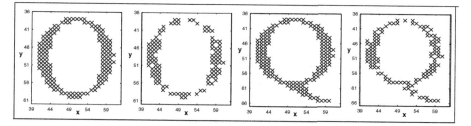

Fig. 16. Some originals and corrupted objects (30% salt noise)

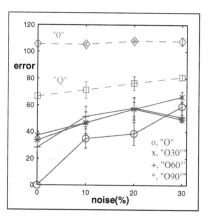

Fig. 17. Behaviour of the metric in presence of noise: $\gamma = 1$ distances evolution

	noise level (%)			
	0	10	20	30
$D(\%)$	79.04	38.70	32.11	21.93

Fig. 18. Evolution of the discrimination factor in presence of noise

Globally the MST metric means within the frame of the assumptions formulated in this experience (noise model, level etc) robust to noise effects. We explain this relative resistance in the following way. The MST defines the dominant skeleton of the character by mapping the shortest path of nearest neighbor points set. The action of the uniform salt noise is diffused on the pattern (cf Figure 16), so the global topology of the character is not yet damaged and consequently this dominant skeleton is preserved. These results are confirmed in other cases (cf Figures 19,20).

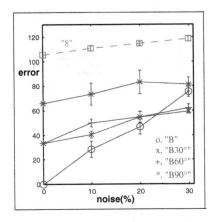

	noise level (%)			
	0	10	20	30
$D(\%)$	59.97	51.05	37.93	41.85

Fig. 20. Evolution of the discrimination factor in presence of noise

Fig. 19. Behaviour of the metric in presence of noise: $\gamma = 1$ distances evolution

3.2   Symbols Recognition

The technique can be easily applied to symbols recognition. Here two kinds of symbols have been considered. Architectural prototypes (cf Figure 21) are similar to the one referenced in [22] and we can find the electrical ones (cf Figure 23) in [23]. The objects to be classified (cf Figures 22,24) have been generated in the following way. First, all prototypes (sometimes rotated) have been grouped together in one image. The ideal image has been in the second stage artificially degraded by 30% of salt and pepper noise. Then classical noise cleaning and segmentation tasks have been computed on this deteriorated image.

Fig. 21. Some prototypes of architectural symbols

The MST metric is used as classification criterion. The Tables 1 resp. 2 show the $\gamma = 1$ distances between objects and architectural resp. electrical symbols. A classification is performed by comparing all input objects with symbol prototypes. The symbol's identity is assigned as the identity of the prototype which minimize the γ distance.

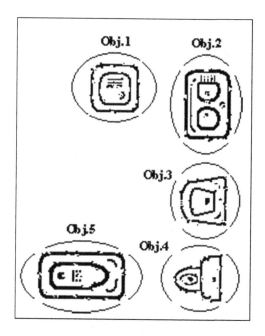

Fig. 22. Objects to be classified

Table 1. Recognition of architectural symbols based on MST metric ($\gamma = 1$)

	Objects				
	obj.1	obj.2	obj.3	obj.4	obj.5
shower	**137.475**	687.274	397.574	442.207	874.910
sink	725.459	**217.119**	784.588	822.871	671.442
washbasin	360.129	774.210	**141.932**	355.456	910.983
wc	457.307	787.731	354.197	**134.664**	917.213
bath	928.695	685.617	931.168	975.321	**342.554**
Reality	shower	sink	washbasin	wc	bath

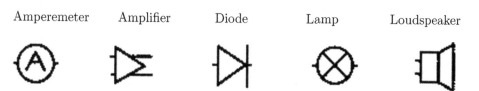

Fig. 23. Some prototypes of electrical symbols

In the two school cases all the objects have been rightly recognized. For example, in the experiment dealing with architectural symbols (cf Table 1) the first object was correctly classified as the *shower*. The $\gamma = 1$ order distance between this object and the shower's prototype was estimated at 137.475. The second ranked symbol is the *washbasin* with 360.129. That's not a surprise because

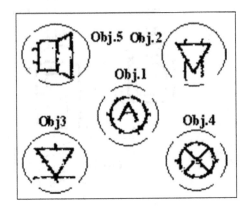

Fig. 24. Objects to be classified

Table 2. Recognition of electrical symbols based on MST metric ($\gamma = 1$)

	Objects				
	obj.1	obj.2	obj.3	obj.4	obj.5
amperemeter	**110.120**	266.928	273.014	155.686	246.656
amplifier	248.392	**106.658**	204.757	268.846	273.313
diode	260.899	147.514	**143.139**	269.313	246.485
lamp	205.343	276.928	282.901	**111.100**	277.899
loudspeaker	252.928	300.514	293.139	275.686	**38.514**
Reality	amperemeter	amplifier	diode	lamp	loudspeaker

among all of the treated symbols the *washbasin* is geometrically the nearest of the *shower* (cf Figure 21). The same observation can be made with the identification of electrical symbols in the Table 2. The *amplifier* was correctly recognized (second column) but it is rather close to the *diode* (106.658 vs. 147.514). The discrimination level is evaluated at $D = \frac{147.514 - 106.658}{106.658} = 38.3\%$. It is a significant result when we see the geometrical similarity which exists between the two symbols (cf Figure 23). Objectively this kind of property must be confirmed by the study of more cases.

4   Complexity

The time processing is a critical point because the MST is performed with a polynomial cost estimated at $N^2 \log N$ (with N the number of shape pixels, see [4]). Several solutions exist to reduce this cost.

Firstly by using a faster algorithm, D. Karger and P. Klein present a randomized linear-time algorithm to find a MST from a connected and weighted graph [8].

This solution can be completed by the optimization of the construction of the trees specially on the mixture. For example the MST on the mixture (prototype - input object) can be built from the tree already computed on the prototype. In this case the MST built on the prototype must be initially stored in memory. This incremental approach is possible because a sub-tree of a MST is itself a MST. So the implementation schema proposed by M. Soss in [20] can be considered.

Another class of solution based on data reduction can be used. Morphological mathematics [19] guided by erosion operations can reduce the number of pixels describing a shape. Erosion is a way to remove pixels from the boundaries of features in order to smooth them and to remove isolated pixel noise from the image. Skeletonization is a specialized erosion that preserves an important characteristic of feature shapes. The skeleton is the set of mid-lines that preserves much of the topological shape information of the features. It is produced by an iterative erosion that removes all pixels that are not part of the skeleton. Moreover, works [13, 9] dealing with reduction of skeleton redundancy provide methods to extract the minimal skeleton of an image.

5 Conclusion

Behind any image object recognition system there is a powerful shape descriptor. In this article a new topological measure is proposed and its properties are checked through the problem of characters and symbols recognition. Invariance in front of shift and multi-oriented object extended by the noise resistance were studied in the context of small and low resolution binary images. In addition the discriminating power was evaluated. In the framework of experiments led the MST technique seems competitive specially for complex patterns composed by disjoint regions. It can be seen like region based technique because all the shape pixels are connected by the trees as the opposite of methods only based on contour.

Many points remain under study. For instance, the result dependence at the angular step size specially for symbols randomly oriented. The norm used for object description is provided by γ and the question of its best adaptation is open. The time consuming remains the main drawback nevertheless many ways exist to reduce this cost (cf Section 4). This survey offers new prospects. The integration of a similar technique at the segmentation level is a future challenge.

Acknowledgments

The authors would like to thanks Pr. Alfred Hero (University of Michigan, E.E.C.S. Department) and Pr. Olivier Michel (University of Nice Sophia-Antipolis, Astrophysical Laboratory) for their advices and the use of their original software.

References

1. B. Ma A. Hero J. Gorman and O. Michel. Image registration with minimal spanning tree algorithm. In *IEEE International Conference on Image Processing*, Vancouver October 2000.

2. R. Graham and P. Hell. On the history of minimum spanning tree problem. *IEEE Annals of the History of Computing*, 7(1):43–57, 1985.
3. A. Hero and O. Michel. Robust entropy estimation strategies based on edge weighted random graphs. In *SPIE, International Symposium on Optical Science, Engineering and Instrumentation*, San Diego July 1998.
4. A. Hero and O. Michel. Asymptotic theory of greedy approximations to minimal k-point random graphs. *IEEE Transactions on Information Theory*, IT 45:1921–1939, 1999.
5. M. Hu. Visual pattern recognition by moment invariants. *IEEE Transactions on Information Theory*, IT 8:179–187, 1962.
6. A. Khotanzad and Y. Hong. Rotation invariant image recognition using features selected via a systematic method. *Pattern Recognition*, (23):1089–1101, 1990.
7. N. Kita. Object locating based on concentric circular description. In *Proceedings of 11th IEEE International Conference of Pattern Recognition*, pages 637–641, The Hague 1992.
8. D. Karger P. Klein and R. Tarjan. A randomized linear-time algorithm to find minimum spanning trees. *Journal of the Association for Computing Machinery (ACM)*, 42(2):321–328, 1995.
9. R. Kresch and D. Malah. Morphological reduction of skeleton redundancy. *Signal Processing*, 38:143–151, 1994.
10. T. Cormen C. Leiserson and R. Rivest. *Introduction to algorithms*. The MIT Press, 1994.
11. C. Lin. New forms of shape invariants from elliptic fourier descriptors. *Pattern Recognition*, (20):535–545, 1987.
12. Luong Chi Mai. *Introduction to computer vision and image processing*. United Nations Educational, Scientific and Cultural Organisation (UNESCO), 2000.
13. P. Maragos and R. Shafer. Morphological skeleton representations and coding of binary images. *IEEE Transactions on Accoustics, Speach and Signal Processing*, 34(5):1228–1244, 1986.
14. S. Pei and C. Lin. Normalisation of rotationally symmetric shapes for pattern recognition. *Pattern Recognition*, (25):913–920, 1992.
15. C. Redmond and J.E. Yukich. Limit theorems and rates of convergence for euclidean functionals. *Annals of Applied Probability*, 4(4):1057–1073, 1994.
16. T. Reiss. Recognizing planar objects using invariants image features. In *Lecture Notes in Computer Science*, Springer-Verlag, Berlin 1993.
17. A. Rény. On measures of entropy and information. In *Symposium on Mathematics Statistics and Probabilities*, pages 547–561, Berkeley 1961.
18. R. Ravi M. Marathe D. Rosenkrantz and S. Ravi. Spanning trees short or small. *SIAM, Journal on Discrete Mathematics*, 9:178–200, 1996.
19. J. Serra. *Image analysis and mathematical morphology Volume 2: Theoretical Advances*. Academic Press, London, 1988.
20. M. Soss. *On the size of the sphere on influence graph*. PhD thesis, Mc Gill University Scholl of Computer Science Montreal, 1998.
21. M. Teague. Image analysis via the general theory of moments. *Journal of the Optical Society of America*, 70:920–930, 1980.
22. S. Tabbone L. Wendling and K. Tombre. Indexing of technical line drawings based on f-signatures. In *6th International Conference on Document Analysis and Recognition (ICDAR)*, pages 1220–1224, Seattle, Washington, USA Sept 2001.
23. Ming Ye. Symbol recognition package (2000). In *http://www.ee.washington.edu/research/...*, by the Intelligent Systems Lab. Depart. of Elect. Engin. University of Washington.

On-line Graphics Recognition: State-of-the-Art

Wenyin Liu

Department of Computer Science
City University of Hong Kong, Hong Kong SAR, PR China
csliuwy@cityu.edu.hk

Abstract. A brief survey on on-line graphics recognition is presented. We first present some common scenarios and applications of on-line graphics recognition and then identify major problems and sub-problems at three levels: primitive shape recognition, composite graphic object recognition, and document recognition and understanding. Representative approaches to these problems are also presented. We also list several open problems at the end.

1 Introduction

Graphics is a visuospatial means for expressing and communicating ideas, thoughts, and knowledge, or in general, information. Although graphics is usually considered as an auxiliary and supplementary means to text in expression and presentation, it cannot be replaced by pure text in some situations, e.g., engineering design and art design. This is because graphical expression is more vivid and concrete, by showing both elements and their spatial relations directly and comprehensively at the same time, than text, which is linear, and in those situations, indirect, abstract, and ambiguous. Hence, a Chinese proverb says, "one picture is worth a thousand words."

In the information era, graphical information is exchanged between human and machines and among machines, and is processed by machines. However, how to effectively and efficiently input graphics into machines is a non-trivial problem. Currently, most graphics input/editing systems, including Microsoft Office, Visio, and many CAD systems, ask users to input graphic objects using mouse/keyboard to select explicit shapes from lots of toolbar buttons or menu items. For instance, in Microsoft Office, certain predefined simple shapes or composite objects are listed in the AutoShapes menu. This kind of user interface (explicit indication of shapes) is clumsy for graphics input. Users frequently find that it is inconvenient to draw their intended shapes via many mouse clicks. Moreover, if there are many predefined objects/shapes, it is hard to remember where to find an intended one. For instance, in Microsoft Visio, there are nearly 10,000 composite shapes, which are also known as master objects, listed in many stencils for users to select. Such complex user interfaces often make users feel frustrated.

Admittedly, the most natural and convenient way to input graphics is to draw sketches on a tablet using a digital pen, just like drawing freehand graphics on a real sheet of paper using a pencil. However, the sketchy graphic objects and freehand drawings drawn in this way are usually not clear (or not neat/beautiful) in appearance,

J. Lladós and Y.-B. Kwon (Eds.): GREC 2003, LNCS 3088, pp. 291–304, 2004.

not compact in representation and storage, and not easy for machines to understand and process. The effect of expression and communication of freehand graphics can be better if we can recognize and convert them to neat and regular forms. Moreover, it is even better if we can do recognition and conversion while the user is sketching since the recognized/converted parts can provide immediate and useful feedback to the user so that he can realize errors or inappropriateness earlier and therefore draw the graphics more perfectly. This immediate recognition and conversion process is referred to as on-line graphics recognition (Liu et al. 2001), which can be specified in detail as the following three sequential sub-processes (levels).

1. Primitive shape recognition: while the user is drawing or immediately after he has drawn a freehand stroke, determine the type and parameters of its primitive shape (which can be line, triangle, rectangle, ellipse, etc.) and if necessary, replace on the screen the freehand one with its regular form (determined by its parameters).

2. Composite graphic object recognition: after recognizing and converting the current stroke, if possible, combine together the current stroke (recognized primitive shape) with the ones previously drawn by the user based on their spatial relationship, determine or predict the type and parameters of the composite graphic object that the user is intending to input, and then replace on the screen the freehand one with its regular form.

3. Document recognition and understanding: after recognizing and converting the graphical elements (primitive shapes and composite graphic objects), if possible, understand the connections and relationship among the elements, and semantics in the current (part or whole) drawing as one document, beautify and re-display it with a neat layout.

In this paper, we will present a brief survey of on-line graphics recognition. Specifically, we will first present some common scenarios and applications of on-line graphics recognition in Section 2. Then, we present in Section 3 the basic problems and sub-problems involved in the above three sub-processes of on-line graphics recognition and current approaches. Finally, we present a short summary and some open problems in Section 4.

2 Applications

Let us first examine several common scenarios of applications of on-line graphics recognition. As we can see from these scenarios, the most common, basic, and important application of on-line graphics recognition is the user interface for inputting graphics into machines. On-line graphics recognition is the enabling technique for this kind of user interface.

1. While a user is drawing a stroke, it is continuously morphed to the predicted primitive shape (Arvo and Novins 2000). We refer to this type of recognition as simultaneous recognition since recognition is simultaneously and continuously done while the user is inputting. This application is mainly for simple shape graphics input. Other systems for simple shape recognition may not do continuous recognition and morphing. Instead, they do primitive shape recognition after the user finishes a stroke. We refer to this type of recognition as immediate recognition since recognition is

only done right after the stroke is completely drawn. These systems include Smart-Sketechpad (Liu et al. 2001) and CALI (Fonseca et al. 2002). Moreover, Fonseca et al. (2002) also refer to this kind of interface for graphics input as calligraphic interfaces.

2. After a user draws a freehand stroke, it is recognized (and regularized) as a primitive shape. At the same time, as one component, it is combined with previously inputted components together (based on their spatial relationship) to form a query for searching for similar objects in the model database. The purpose of this kind of approach is to guess what composite graphic object the user is intending to input. The matched candidates ranked according to their similarity to the query are displayed and suggested for the user to select. The object selected by the user then replaces these components on the screen. In this way, the user does not need to finish the entire object and can therefore save some of his time. The application is particularly useful for graphics input on small screen devices. This is also a type of simultaneous recognition. Actually, it is also possible to recognize a composite object after all of its components are completely drawn, as in immediate recognition.

3. After a user draws a sketch of a design of a graphic user interface (GUI) with freehand shapes of menus, buttons, palettes, and panels in the sketchy layout, it is automatically transformed into a neat design (i.e., beautified layout with regularized, aligned and grouped objects) of the GUI. Landay and Myers (2001) present such a system called SILK (which stands for Sketching Interfaces Like Krazy), which is an informal sketching tool that combines many of the benefits of paper-based sketching with the merits of current electronic tools. JavaSketchIt is another system for this purpose, which is developed by Caetano et al. (2002) and can generate a Java interface from hand-drawn geometric shapes. This application is particularly important in the early stages of GUI design, when designers need the freedom to sketch rough design ideas quickly, the ability to test designs by interacting with them, and the flexibility to fill in the design details as they make choices. Actually, this well-known application is desirable for general creative design and requires sketch recognition and understanding as supporting techniques. For instances, Zeleznik et al. (1996) invent an interface to input 3D sketchy shapes by recognizing the predefined patterns of some 2D shapes that represent certain sketchy solid shapes, and Matsuda et al. (1997) present a Freehand sketch system for 3D geometric modelling. Lipson and Shpitalni (2002) present a system for reconstructing a 3D object from a single 2D freehand line drawing. Igarashi, Matsuoka, and Tanaka (1999) present a gesture–based sketching interface (TEDDY) to quickly and easily design 3D free–form models out of 2D sketchy strokes. In their system the designer first interactively draws 2D free–form strokes depicting a 2D silhouette. A 3D polygonal object is automatically constructed by inflating the region surrounding the silhouette, making wide areas fat and narrow ones thin. Hsu and Lee (1994) present an animation system for producing 2.5D animations using skeletal strokes as the basic primitive. In their paper, skeletal strokes can be regarded as a realization of the brush and stroke metaphor using arbitrary pictures and its deformations as ink. Since any arbitrary picture can be defined to be a skeletal stroke, a huge variation in styles is possible. However, the animator still has to cope with a lot of additional work (e.g., providing input images and deforming images) in comparison with traditional animation. More recently, Vansichem

et al. (2001) propose an approach to drawing and manipulating stylized curves without the need to explicitly manipulate (i.e., point, click and drag) control points of underlying splines. Their approach generates curves on-the-fly by processing (pressure sensitive) stylus data in real-time. This simplifies the interaction drastically because the animator can exploit direct manipulation tools on the curves themselves. Using a similar technique, Di Fiore and Van Reeth (2002) present a sketching tool that assists the animator throughout multiple stages of the animation process. This tool helps retaining the natural way of drawing and editing, and offers additional functionality such as rapidly creating approximate 3D models and deforming animation objects. Other well-known application domains of sketch recognition and understanding include flowcharts (Gross 1994), architectural drawings (Gross 1996; Do 2002; Leclercq 1999), mathematic expressions (Tapia and Rojas 2003), music notations (Forsberg, Dieterich & Zeleznik 1998), and UML diagrams (Lank et al. 2001; Hammond and Davis 2002; Blostein et al. 2002).

4. When the user wants to delete some elements, he can simply draw a symbol like "X" or some other doodle lines (like using an eraser on paper) on those elements. This application is known as gesture recognition for editing. Actually, many sketching systems, such as SILK (Landay and Myers 2001) and CALI (Fonseca et al. 2002), have embedded such functions and gestures for those common commands, including "delete", "move", "copy", etc. Bimber (1999) describes a system that can recognize dynamic gestures (required information is dynamically extracted using a particular grammar) to support the sketching interface for 3D input. A well-known application of graphical gesture recognition is a pen-based interface for interactive editing (Saud et al. 2002) on both text and graphics.

3 Problems and Approaches

The fundamental and common problems in the above applications can be classified and specified as follows.

1. Primitive shape recognition: given one or several freehand strokes, determine the type and parameters (e.g., size, angle, etc.) of its primitive shape that the user is intending to draw. The primitive shapes include lines, free curves, common convex polygons (e.g., triangles and rectangles), and ellipses. Some pre-defined shapes, such as those used for gesture commands, can also be included.

2. Composite graphic object recognition: given several primitive shapes that the user draws (hopefully) consecutively and adjacently, determine the type and parameters of the composite graphic object that the user is intending to input. The composite graphic objects are usually predefined in a model database, e.g., those graphic symbols commonly used in engineering drawings.

3. Document recognition and understanding: given a set of primitive shapes and composite objects as elements of current (part or whole) drawing, determine the syntaxes (connections and relationship among the elements) and semantics of the drawing as one document in general/ specific application domains, e.g., GUI design and 3D object description.

Next we investigate the above problems in detail and present related approaches to them in the following sub-sections.

3.1 Primitive Shape Recognition

This problem can be divided into the following four sub-problems (Jin et al. 2002).

(1) Stroke Curve Pre-processing

Input: a freehand stroke; Output: a refined polyline.

Requirement: the refined polyline should be similar to the freehand stroke but in a more compact and perfect representation.

(2) Shape Classification

Input: the refined polyline.

Output: a basic shape type id: e.g., line, triangle, quadrangle, pentagon, hexagon, ellipse, or free curve, etc.

Requirement: the output shape type id is consistent with the user's intention.

(3) Shape Fitting

Input: the type id and the stroke (the original and refined polyline).

Output: the fitted shape (characterized by parameters).

Requirement: the fitted shape, which is of the same basic shape type, has the lowest average distance to the input stroke.

(4) Shape Regularization

Input: the fitted shape and the original stroke.

Output: the regularized shape (characterized by parameters).

Requirement: the regularized shape is similar to the original freehand stroke but also appears in its most beautiful form, e.g., conforming as much as possible to connectedness, perpendicularity, congruence, and symmetry, intended by the user. This sub-problem (or process) is also referred to as beautification (Igarashi et al. 1997).

3.1.1 Stroke Curve Pre-processing

Due to non-proficiency or un-professionalism, the freehand stroke for an intended shape input is usually very cursive/unshaped and free-formed. For example, without using a ruler, a straight line drawn by a drafter is not so straight if measured strictly no matter how much attention the drafter is paying to the drawing operation. More often, the sketchy line is not properly closed. Hence, the freehand line is not suitable for feature extraction and shape classification directly. Pre-processing is needed to reduce all kinds of noises. Liu et al. (2002) have used four sub-processes in the pre-processing stage: polygonal approximation, agglomerate points filtering, end point refinement, and convex hull calculation.

Many intermediate points on the sketchy line are redundant because they lie (approximately) on the straight-line segment formed by connecting their neighbors. These points are referred to as non-critical points and can be removed from the chain so that the sketchy line can be approximately represented by a polyline (an open polygon) with much fewer critical vertices. The procedure of removing non-critical points is referred to as polygonalization or polygonal approximation. There are many algorithms for this purpose, such as the one developed by Sklansky and Gonzalez (1980). Some of these intermediate points, although undesirable but still cannot be eliminated using the polygonalization procedure since they are far away from the desired/intended line segments. Chen and Xie (1996) refer to these undesirable points as sick points and filter out them using a fuzzy rule according to the features around the point (including drawing speed and change of angle).

Due to the shaky operations caused when the pen-tip touches the tablet and when it is lifted up, there are often some hooklet-like segments at the ends of the sketchy lines. There might also be some circlets at the turning corners of the sketchy line. These noises usually remain after polygonal approximation. The agglomerate points filtering process can be introduced to reduce these noises. The main idea lies in the difference of point density. A segment of hooklet or circlet usually has much higher point density than the average value of the whole polyline. The task of agglomerate points filtering is to find such segments and use fewer points to represent them.

Because it is difficult for the user to draw a perfectly closed shape, the sketchy line is usually not closed or forms a cross near its endpoints. In other words, it has improper endpoints. These improper endpoints are great barriers for both correct shape recognition and well regularization. The solutions to these situations are intuitively simple. For a freehand stroke that has cross endpoints, its extra points can be erased to make it properly closed. For a sketchy line that is not closed, its endpoints can be extended along its end directions to make it closed. After that it can undergo other processing as if it were previously closed.

The input stroke is often very cursive, and might also be concave. These noises have strong impact on the later feature extraction stage, especially for convex shape classification. Sometimes, its convex hull can be used to represent its original line and therefore those noises are removed. A classical algorithm developed by Graham (1972) can be used obtain the convex hull of the vertices set of the input stroke.

Some methods (e.g., Chen and Xie 1996 and Calhoun et al. 2002) also segment an entire stroke into multiple primitive strokes such that each can be recognized as a primitive shape (e.g., line segments or arcs). Chen and Xie (1996) use a fuzzy rule to determine the turning points according to the features around the points (including drawing speed/acceleration and change of angle) on the original stroke. The stroke can then be segmented at these turning points.

3.1.2 Shape Classification

After pre-processing, the refined stroke can be used for feature extraction and shape classification. There are already many works done for the shape classification problem. We mainly classify them into four groups. They are decision-tree based approaches, filter-based approaches, energy minimization approaches, and statistical approaches. Next, we present brief reviews of these approaches.

(1) Decision-Tree Based Approaches

Chen and Xie (1996) use a decision tree based on several fuzzy classifiers to determine whether a stroke/segment is a straight line, circle/arc, ellipse/elliptical arc, or free curve. In their method, each fuzzy classifier generates a possibility of "the segment being a specific shape" by calculating the average of the possibilities of all the points (on the segment) being on the inferred geometric line/curve, which is calculated based on the hypothesized shape model and some sampling points. The possibility of a point being on the inferred line/curve is calculated based on its distance from the line/curve and the drawing speed at the point. The performance of this method is not known since it is not fully tested and reported.

(2) Filter-Based Approaches

Apte et al. (1993) have proposed another way to classify shapes based on filters. However, these filters are sensitive to orientation of the geometric objects. All the shapes, except for circles and lines, should be drawn in parallel with the X-axis and Y-axis. This precondition is somewhat too strict. Fonseca and Jorge (2000) have extended Apte et al.'s work by adding some new filters. First they calculate some global attributes of the given shape, such as convex hull, largest-area inscribing triangle, largest-area inscribed quadrilateral (Boyce et al. 1985), and enclosing rectangle (Freeman and Shapira 1975). Then, they form a group of filters based on these attributes to do shape classification, and fuzzy logic is also employed in their algorithm. Compared with Apte et al.'s work, their recognition approach is orientation independent. Instead of outputting a definite shape type, their approach introduced some uncertainty and can output several types in a ranked list. This is reasonable for ambiguous situations in on-line shape classification. However, the filters they used can hardly distinguish very ambiguous shapes such as pentagon and hexagon, and this ad hoc approach is not easily extensible.

(3) Energy Minimization Approaches

The shape classification approach reported by Arvo and Novins (2000) continuously morphs the sketchy curve to the guessed shape while the user is drawing the curve. Their approach only handles two simplest classes of shapes (circles and rectangles) drawn in single strokes. Liu et al. (2001) propose another Hypothesis-and-Test approach for shape classification. It is also a model-based approach. They first hypothesize the input shape as a triangle, a rectangle, or an ellipse. Then, they calculate the difference between each hypothesized shape and the normalized original sketchy stroke. In order to evaluate all possibilities, each model should be scaled and rotated many times for such comparisons. The energy is the average distance of each vertex of the normalized stroke to the hypothesized shape. The model with the smallest energy is selected as the shape classification result. Unfortunately, the model with the smallest energy is only the most similar one to the user sketch, but may not be the one that the user has in his/her mind. Jin et al. (2002) develop a locally optimal method, which is based on the Attraction Force model, to combine the adjacent vertexes progressively until the maximal attraction force is under a threshold. The main idea is that a vertex is simultaneously attracted by its two neighbours. The attraction force between two vertexes depends on their distance and inner angles. The vertex is merged to the neighbour with the bigger force (if it is larger than a threshold). After no vertex can be merged, the type of the shape can be determined by the number of remaining vertexes.

(4) Statistical Approaches

In SILK, Landay and Myers (2001) recognize gestures through the algorithm of Rubine (1991), which uses statistical pattern recognition techniques to train classifiers. The resulting classifier is based on the features (including angles and point-to-point distances) extracted from several examples. SILK uses 15 to 20 examples for each primitive component. SILK can also learn gestures that particular designers use to form the primitive components. In the work reported by Liu et al. (2001, 2002), two statistical machine-leaning based approaches, which are based on neural networks (NN) and support vector machines (SVM), are employed in shape recognition. The feature used is the turning function (Arkin et al. 1991). However, the computational cost is very high and the number of primitive shapes is limited. Peng et al. (2003) have presented an SVM-based recognition method for 14 classes of pre-defined strokes (primitive shapes). The feature used is also the turning function. Their method is user-adaptive since it is designed for incremental learning.

3.1.3 Shape Fitting and Regularization

After the shape type is known, fitting is employed to adjust the shape parameters (e.g., three vertices for a triangle) such that the recognized shape can best fit its original closed curve. The method of fitting depends on the type of shape. Least-square is a frequently used method for line fitting, e.g., used by Chen and Xie (1996). They also use fuzzy logic for circular fitting and elliptical fitting. The parameters of the fitted circle or ellipse are weighted sum of the ones inferred from various sets of sampling points. The classified free curves are represented by the fitted B-splines. Jin et al. (2002) employ two basic types of fitting processes: ellipse fitting and polygonal fitting. For ellipse fitting, they first determine its axes orientations by finding the eigenvectors of the covariance matrix of the sampling points along the original curve at equi-length steps. The stroke's enclosing rectangle whose edges are parallel to the axes is used to determine the centre and axes lengths of the ellipse. For N-edge polygonal fitting, they first find its inscribed N-edge polygon that has the maximal area. As a result, they cut the original stroke into N pieces by the vertices of this inscribed polygon. By finding the linear regression result of each piece, the edges of the optimized N-edge polygon can be obtained.

Unlike the shape classification problem, very few related work has been done for the shape fitting and regularization/rectification/beautification problems. Usually these problems are regarded as parts of shape classification problem. Probably the earliest and the most valuable paper dedicated to the problem of beautification is the one presented by Pavlidis and van Wyk (1985). Igarashi et al. (1997) have developed an interactive beautification system, which can transform an original sketch into a diagram that looks like being carefully drafted. Liu et al. (2002) and Jin et al. (2002) have done shape regularization systematically. In particular, they have done inter-shape regularization (e.g., alignment among a group of adjacent shapes) in addition to inner-shape regularization (within single shapes).

3.2 Composite Graphic Object Recognition

Currently, there are mainly two categories of approaches to this problem: classifier-based approaches and similarity-based approaches.

The main idea of classifier-based approach is to build a binary decision tree where each leaf represents a symbol and each edge represents a rule to classify the shapes into branches. The sketchy object is recognized according to these rules descending from the top of the tree. However, this approach suffers from the problem that it is not extensible. For different graphic objects, specific rules must be added. Hence, it is impractical to build a general system that works for any domain without change of the software using this approach. Hence, this approach only appears in 1960s for a very short time and then was abandoned to a large extent by researchers. This approach has been rejuvenated recently with the incorporation of fuzzy rules and visual language grammars that use statistical information on the frequency of occurrence of particular features. Peng et al. (2003) also use a decision-tree based method for composite object recognition. Particularly, they adopt an incremental decision tree induction method (Utgoff 1996) to construct dynamic user models. They build and store a specific tree for each specific user. The root of the decision tree records the user id and each leaf node records the class label of the input object. They organize the branch nodes according to the input sequence of the strokes and use three attributes to identify/match an input stroke: the class of the stroke, the direction of it and the relationship between the current stroke and its previous stroke. By doing so, they can provide user-adaptation when recognizing composite graphic objects.

In similarity-based approaches, similarities between two graphic objects are defined and calculated. Usually, the graphic object is firstly divided into primitives, which can be segments of strokes or simple closed shapes. Then, a graph is built by utilizing these primitives as nodes and their relations as edges. These graphs are called Attributed Relation Graph (ARG) (Li et al. 2000), Region Adjacent Graph (RAG) (Lladós 2001), or others according to different authors. In general, these graphs may be matched by comparing nodes and edges according to their contribution to a relational distance metric (Shapiro 1993). (Similarity metrics definition is a fundamental issue for all pattern recognition problems, including on-line graphics recognition, but is beyond the scope of this paper.) Finally, the most similar graphic object is selected from the database as the recognition result. One advantage of this approach is that it is easily extensible. Another advantage is that they do not require a large amount of training data. New graphic objects can be added into the database freely without any modification of the software. However, these approaches usually include a subgraph-matching problem, which requires a high computational cost and has been proven to be NP-complete (Mehlhorn 1984). Another disadvantage of these approaches is that they are sensitive to the noise and not robust. Calhoun et al. (2002) first segment a composite object into multiple primitive strokes (line segments or arcs) and then represent their relations in a semantic network. The definition of each type of object is learned by examining a few (3 or 4) examples of the type and identifying which properties and relationships occur frequently. Pen speed and stroke curvature are used as features to segment a stroke into its constituent primitives. During recognition, an input object is identified by determining which definition matches it with the least error. The SmartSketchpad (Liu et al. 2002) also uses a similarity-based approach to composite object recognition. In particular, the user-intended object can be predicted even before it is completely drawn due to the use of a partial structural similarity calculation strategy. This process is a continuous recognition process while the user is drawing. In contrast, Calhoun et al. (2002) ask the user to tell the system that the object is completely drawn such that the system can start recognition.

3.3 Document Recognition and Understanding

Gross (1994) develops a prototype system called Sketch-A-Sketch, which can recognize primitive shapes (glyphs), and detect and maintain their spatial relationship represented as constraints. After the glyph recognizer recognizes the primitive shapes, the spatial relations among them are analyzed. The relations are binary and are represented as predicates. The relations are defined in terms of the bounding box, size, and starting and ending points of the primitive elements. Since many true but uninteresting relations can be reported, several methods are used to screen them. First, spatial relations are organized in a hierarchy or specificity, and only the most specific relations are desired. E.g., "concentric" is more specific than "contains". Second, spatial relations are also organized by the type of element they can apply to. For instances, "connects" only applies to lines and "contains" only applies to closed shapes. Finally, a list of commutative (e.g., "overlap") and transitive properties of relations is consulted to avoid redundant relations. As a by-product of the whole document recognition and understanding, the system can also learn objects of high-level configurations from examples, represent their definitions using the elements and constraints, and then recognize them later. The system can also maintain the essential relations in these configurations as the user edits the diagram.

Pinto-Albuquerque et al. (2000) present an approach to graphic document design based on sketch recognition. In particular, they develop a visual language for describing the graphical elements and their spatial relationship in the document. The lexical elements in this language are a set of predefined primitive shapes and the syntax used is a fuzzy relational adjacency grammar. The freehand strokes are first recognized and converted to primitive shapes (with their types and attributes) by a stroke recognizer. The recognized primitive shapes are then input to the visual syntax analyzer, which matches them against the productions in the fuzzy relational adjacency grammar. Semantic analysis and feedback are also side-effects of the syntax analyzer. An understood layout of document is finally obtained. Currently, their prototype system, DocSketch, can identify simple sketched shapes. It recognizes the visual characteristics of the shapes and the relations among them by choosing the most likely classification. The most likely document design composition can then be inferred from them. A promising extension of this system includes beautification automation of the document layout while still keeping correct spatial relationship.

Other well-known prototype systems that can achieve some understanding from on-line sketches include ASSIST (Alvarado and Davis 2001) and ESQUISE (Leclercq 1999, 2003; Leclercq and Juchmes 2002). ASSIST (which stands for A Shrewd Sketch Interpretation and Simulation Tool) can understand mechanical engineering sketches and then interpret their mechanisms using simulation. ESQUISE can capture and understand architectural sketches and then evaluate the energy needs of the project.

Sketch-based 3D construction or understanding uses similar techniques at the 2D level of recognition and understanding. However, more techniques specific to the 3D level are required and are therefore beyond the scope of this paper.

4 Summary and Concluding Remarks

We have presented a brief survey of the state of the art of on-line graphics recognition techniques. We first examined various applications and then identified the problems at three levels. Representative works and related approaches to these problems have also been presented.

As an enabling technology of pen-based user interfaces for graphics input, on-line graphics recognition has not attracted full attention yet, compared with on-line handwriting character recognition. One of the reasons is probably due to lack of suitable applications, killer applications, or urgent applications. However, as Tablet PCs and other mobile devices equipped with pens become more and more popular, these applications will be demanded soon. Although many related works have already been done, we think more works should be done, especially in the following aspects.

1. Editing gestures recognition and editing-related applications. Although a gesture may consist of one stroke, which is usually considered at the primitive or simple graphics level, the shapes of most gestures may be more complicated than those simple shapes, e.g., triangles, circles/ellipses, etc. The number of complex gestures for editing can also be up to several hundreds. The environment can make the problem even more complex. Sometimes, we do not know whether it is an editing gesture or just a character or a graphic object in the context. Hence, recognition/classification of them is usually not so easy. Both classification methods and basic features should be investigated. Context-aware recognition is especially necessary.

2. Composite object recognition, mainly for graphics input (e.g., diagramming) applications. For composite object recognition, while on the one hand, we continue to pursue higher accuracy of recognition/classification at the primitive graphics level, on the other hand, we should also take into consideration of error-tolerance when matching the components of composite objects. The reason is that it seems that we will never achieve a recognition accuracy of 100% at any recognition level and the user's intention is sometimes ambiguous as well. Peng et al. (2003) have tried application of fuzzy matching and obtained better result than exact matching. Meanwhile, their effort on user-adaptation is also a correct direction since the problem of learning capability which can handle sketches from new domains and new users (in terms of styles and preferences of sketching) is seldom addressed. Efficient matching algorithms for composite objects is also an important problem. The algorithm complexity of matching composite objects should be lowered down since we may have more than 10,000 objects (as in Microsoft Visio) to match for each input. Reinforcement between recognitions at the two levels could also be investigated to achieve higher recognition accuracy at both levels.

3. Semantic level understanding for creative design. Applications for creative and conceptual design are among the most useful applications of sketching or on-line graphics recognition. Although some works at this level have been reported, e.g., by Leclercq (1999, 2003) and Alvarado and Davis (2001) in certain limited domains, currently, sketching understanding is still a challenging problem requiring domain knowledge and integration of multidisciplinary technologies, e.g., both graphics recognition and imaginal thinking research. More research works should be done such that reasoning and prediction of the user's intentions can be made from the sketches he/she draws in order to support and facilitate his/her conceptual design, e.g., in creative design tasks.

We hope this paper can provide some insights in this area. However, due to the limitation of both the author's knowledge in this area and the number of pages, there are definitely many other works that are important but not mentioned in this paper. We welcome criticism, comments and suggestions from readers and reviewers and hope we can extend this paper with more comprehensive works in the future.

Acknowledgement

The work described in this paper is fully supported by a grant from the Research Grants Council of the Hong Kong SAR, China [Project No. CityU 1073/02E]. The author would like to thank Dr. Eugene Bodansky and other anonymous referees for their constructive comments and recommendation of additional references.

References

1. Alvarado, C. and Davis, R: Resolving Ambiguities to Create a Natural Computer-Based Sketching Environment. In: Proc. IJCAI (2001) 1365–1371
2. Apte, A., Vo, V. and Kimura, T.D.: Recognizing Multistroke Geometric Shapes: An Experimental Evaluation. In: Proc. ACM Symposium on UIST (1993) 121–128
3. Arkin, E.M., et al.: An Efficiently Computable Metric for Comparing Polygonal Shapes. IEEE Trans. on PAMI 13(3) (1991) 209–216
4. Arvo, J. and Novins, K.: Fluid Sketches: Continuous Recognition and Morphing of Simple Hand-Drawn Shapes. In: Proc. ACM Symposium on UIST, San Diego, California (2000)
5. Bimber, O.: Rudiments for a 3D Freehand Sketch Based Human–Computer Interface for Immersive Virtual Environments. In: Proc. ACM VRST'99 (1999) 182–183
6. Blostein, D., Rose, A., and Zanibbi, R.: User Interfaces for On-Line Diagram Recognition. Lecture Notes in Computer Science 2390 (2002) 92–103 (GREC2001)
7. Boyce, J.E., Dobkin, D.P., Drysdale, R.L., and Guibas, L.J.: Finding Extremal Polygons. SIAM Journal on Computing 14(1) (1985) 134–147
8. Caetano, A., Goulart, N., Fonseca M.J., and Jorge J.A.: JavaSketchIt: Issues in Sketching the Look of User Interfaces. In: Proc. AAAI Sym. Series--Sketch Understanding (2002)
9. Calhoun, C., Stahovich, T.F., Kurtoglu, T., Kara, L.M.: Recognizing Multi-Stroke Symbols. In: Proc. AAAI Spring Symposium Series--Sketch Understanding (2002)

10. Chen, C.L.P. and Xie, S.: Freehand drawing system using a fussy logic concept. Computer-Aided Design, 28(2) (1996) 77–89
11. Di Fiore, F. and Van Reeth, F.: A Multi–Level Sketching Tool for "Pencil–and–Paper" Animation. In: Proc. AAAI Spring Symposium Series--Sketch Understanding (2002)
12. Do, E.Y.-L.: Functional and Formal Reasoning in Architectural Sketches. In: Proc. AAAI Spring Symposium Series--Sketch Understanding (2002)
13. Fonseca, M.J. and Jorge, J.A.: Using Fuzzy Logic to Recognize Geometric Shapes Interactively. In: Proc. 9th IEEE Conf. on Fuzzy Systems, Vol. 1 (2000) 291–296
14. Fonseca, M.J., Pimentel, C., and Jorge, J.A.: CALI: An On-line Scribble Recognizer for Calligraphic Interfaces. In: Proc. AAAI Spring Sym. Series--Sketch Understanding (2002)
15. Forsberg, A., Dieterich, M., and Zeleznik, R.: The Music Notepad. In: Proc. ACM Symposium on UIST, San Francisco, CA (1998)
16. Freeman, H. and Shapira, R.: Determining the Minimum-area Enclosing Rectangle for an Arbitrary Closed Curve. Communication of the ACM 18(7) (1975) 409–413
17. Graham, R.L.: An Efficient Algorithm for Determining the Convex hull of A Finite Planar Set. Information Processing Letters 1(4) (1972) 132–133
18. Gross, M. D.: Stretch-A-Sketch: a Dynamic Diagrammer. In: Proc. IEEE Sym. on Visual Languages (1994) 232–238
19. Gross, M. D.: The Electronic Cocktail Napkin – Computer Support for Working with Diagrams. Design Studies 17(1) (1996) 53–70
20. Gross, M.D. and Do, E.Y.L.: Ambiguous Intentions: A Paper-like Interface for Creative Design. In: Proc. ACM Symposium on UIST, Seattle, WA (1996) 183–192
21. Hammond, T. and Davis, R.: Tahuti: A Geometrical Sketch Recognition System for UML Class Diagrams. In: Proc. AAAI Spring Symposium Series--Sketch Understanding (2002)
22. Hsu, S.C. and Lee, I.H.H.: Drawing and Animation using Skeletal Strokes. In: Proc. of SIGGRAPH94 (1994) 109–122
23. Igarashi, T., Matsuoka, S., and Tanaka, H.: Teddy: A Sketching Interface for 3D Freeform Design. In: Proc. of SIGGRAPH (1999) 409–416
24. Igarashi, T., Matsuoka, S., Kawachiya, S., and Tanaka, H.: Interactive Beautification: A Technique for Rapid Geometric Design. In: Proc. ACM Sym. on UIST (1997) 105–114
25. Jin, X., Liu, W., Sun, J., and Sun, Z.: On-line Graphics Recognition. In: Proc. of Pacific Graphics (2002) 256–264
26. Landay, J.M. and Myers, B.A.: Sketching Interfaces: Toward More Human Interface Design. IEEE Computer 34(3) (2001) 56–64
27. Lank, E., Thorley, J., Chen, S., Blostein, D.: On-line Recognition of UML Diagrams. In: Proc. 6th ICDAR (2001) 356–360
28. Leclercq, P. and Juchmes, R.: The Absent Interface in Design Engineering. In: Artificial Intelligence for Engineering Design, Analysis and Manufacturing 14(3) (2002) 219–217
29. Leclercq, P.: Absent Sketching Interface for Architectural Engineering. In: Proc. GREC (2003) 415–423
30. Leclercq, P.: Interpretative Tool for Architectural Sketches. In: Visual and Spatial Reasoning in Design (Gero, J., and Tversky, B., Eds.) (1999) 69–80
31. Li, C., Yang, B., and Xie, W.: On-line Hand-Sketched Graphics Recognition Based on Attributed Relation Graph Matching. In: Proc. 3rd World Congress on Intelligent Control and Automation, Hefei, China (2000) 2549–2553
32. Lipson, H. and Shpitalni, M.: Correlation-Based Reconstruction of a 3D Object from a Single Freehand Sketch. In: Proc. AAAI Spring Sym. Series--Sketch Understanding (2002)

33. Liu, W., Jin X., Sun, Z.: Sketch-Based User Interface for Inputting Graphic Objects on Small Screen Devices. Lecture Notes in Computer Science 2390 (2002) 67–80

34. Liu, W., Qian, W., Xiao, R., and Jin, X.: Smart Sketchpad—An On-line Graphics Recognition System. In: Proc. 6th ICDAR (2001) 1050–1054

35. Lladós, J., Martí, E., and José, J.: Symbol Recognition by Error-Tolerant Subgraph Matching between Region Adjacency Graphs. IEEE Trans. on PAMI 23(10) (2001) 1137–1143

36. Matsuda, K., et al.: Freehand Sketch System for 3D Geometric Modelling. In: Proc. International Conference on Shape Modeling and Applications (1997) 55–62

37. Mehlhorn, K.: Graph Algorithm and NP-Completeness. Springer-Verlag (1984)

38. Pavlidis, T. and van Wyk, C.J.: An Automatic Beautifier for Drawings and Illustrations. In: Proc. SIGGRAPH (1985) 225–234

39. Peng, B., Sun., Z., Liu, W., and Cong, L.: Dynamic User Modeling for Sketchy Shape Recognition. In: Proc. GREC (2003) 355–365 (A revised version also appears in this volume.)

40. Pinto-Albuquerque, M., Fonseca, M.J., and Jorge, J.A.: Visual Languages for Sketching Documents. In: Proc. of IEEE Int. Sym. on Visual Languages (2000) 225–232

41. Rubine, D.H.: The Automatic Recognition of Gestures. Ph.D. Dissertation, Carnegie Mellon University, Computer Science, Pittsburgh, USA (1991)

42. Saund, E., et al.: Perceptual Organization as a Foundation for Intelligent Sketch Editing. In: Proc. AAAI Spring Symposium Series--Sketch Understanding (2002)

43. Shapiro, L.: Relational Matching: In: Handbook of Pattern Recognition and Image Processing: Computer Vision (Young, T.Y., ed.) (1993) 475–496

44. Sklansky, J. and Gonzalez, V.: Fast Polygonal Approximation of Digitized Curves. Pattern Recognition 12 (1980) 327–331

45. Tapia, E. and Rojas, R.: Recognition of On-Line Handwritten Mathematical Expressions using a Minimum Spanning Tree Construction and Symbol Dominance. In: Proc. GREC (2003)

46. Utgoff, P.E.: Decision Tree Induction Based on Efficient Tree Restructuring. Technical Report 95-18, University of Massachusetts, Dept of CS, Amherst, MA (1996)

47. Vansichem, G., Wauters, E., and Van Reeth, F.: Real–time Modeled Drawing and Manipulation of Stylized Cartoon Characters. In: Proc. IASTED International Conference on Computer Graphics and Imaging (2001) 44–49

48. Zeleznik, R.C., Herndon, K.P., and Hughes, J.F.: SKETCH: An Interface for Sketching 3D Scenes. In: Proc. SIGGRAPH, New Orleans (1996) 163–170

User Adaptation for Online Sketchy Shape Recognition

Zhengxing Sun[1], Wenyin Liu[2], Binbin Peng[1], Bin Zhang[1], and Jianyong Sun[1]

[1] State Key Lab for Novel Software Technology, Nanjing University, 210093, PR China
szx@nju.edu.cn
[2] Dept. of Computer Science, City University of Hong Kong, Hong Kong SAR, PR China
csliuwy@cityu.edu.hk

Abstract. This paper presents a method of online sketchy shape recognition that can adapt to different user sketching styles. The adaptation principle is based on incremental active learning and dynamic user modeling. Incremental active learning is used for sketchy stroke classification such that important data can actively be selected to train the classifiers. Dynamic user modeling is used to model the user's sketching style in an incremental decision tree, which is then used to recognize the composite shapes dynamically by means of fuzzy matching. Experiments prove the proposed method both effective and efficient for user adaptation in online sketchy shape recognition.

1 Introduction

Even in this high-tech computer era, the most elementary form of written communication, sketching via pen and paper, is central to many of today's technological advances and will likely continue to be so. Unlike text-based or WIMP (Windows, Icons, Menus and Pointing) input, sketch-drawing tends to be highly informal, inconsistent and ambiguous in both intra-person and inter-person settings. The challenge for a sketch-based system to be of practical utility is that it must robustly cope with the variations and ambiguities inherent in sketchy drawings so as to interpret the visual scene the way the user intended. Though researchers have been making experimental progress in handling such forms of input, most shape recognition methods are too restrictive and few focuses on user diversity, while it is ubiquitous in sketching process. In fact, benefiting from advances in sketching recognition system could not be expected before the problem of user adaptation is well solved.

Many applications of pattern recognition, such as handwriting recognition [1] and speech recognition [2], have dealt with user adaptation. Although some training based learning methods, such as Neural Network (NN), Support Vector Machine (SVM) and Hidden Markov Model (HMM), have been adopted for writer adaptation of online handwriting recognition [1], they are not suitable for the recognition of composite shapes, which contain much more strokes, due to the two following reasons: the classes of composite shapes are too many to be enumerated, and it is even difficult for the system to know whether the composite shapes are drawn completely.

Usually, human cognition is performed incrementally and iteratively. Likewise, we propose that computers should incrementally, continuously, and automatically

J. Lladós and Y.-B. Kwon (Eds.): GREC 2003, LNCS 3088, pp. 305–316, 2004.

adapt to a particular user's sketching style. We identify two main questions that confront user adaptation of sketchy shape recognition. The first concerns stroke classification of sketchy objects without requiring the user to select and label new training samples manually during training (and re-training) of the classifier. Accordingly, we employ an SVM-based incremental active learning method to classify the user's sketching strokes, which can actively analyze the user's incremental data and only submit important data from the original large dataset to users for evaluation. This method largely reduces the workload of manual labeling and requires no re-training of the classifier without loss of classification precision. The second issue relates to the task of grouping the user's strokes into a composite object the user intends without requiring the user to indicate when one sketchy shape ends and the next one begins. For this purpose, we introduce a dynamic user modeling scheme to model the sequence of the user's sketching style for composite objects in an incremental decision tree. The model is then used to predict the 'possible objects' by means of fuzzy matching based on the visiting frequency of each object in the user model.

In Section 2, we briefly review some related works. Our framework of user adaptation for on-line sketchy shape recognition is described in Section 3. Some experimental results and evaluation are presented in Section 4. Some concluding remarks are given in Section 5.

2 Related Works

A large number of experiments on sketchy graphics recognition, for examples [5][6], have been achieved and the related works can be grouped into two categories: rule-based and statistical approaches. Nevertheless, even the latest experimental systems are typically limited to basic shapes such as rectangles, triangles and circles. Recent developments incorporate HMM and hybrid NN/HMM into sketchy stroke recognition, such as those used in speech recognition [2]. However, very few researches have addressed the problem of user adaptation of online sketchy shape recognition.

For shape classification, a lot of works have been done. Typically, a way to classify shapes based on filters has been proposed in reference [7]. However, these filters are sensitive to orientation of geometric objects. Another method of shape classification reported in reference [8] morphs continuously the sketchy curve to the guessed shape while the user is drawing the curve; however, it only handles the simplest classes of shapes drawn in single strokes.

3 The Proposed Approach

In our researches, the minimum input unit of a composite shape in the drawing process is a stroke, which is defined as the trajectory of the pen movement on a tablet between the time when the pen-tip begins to touch the tablet and the time when the pen-tip is lifted up from the tablet. To facilitate the processing of computers, we suppose that all composite shapes are composed of some continuous strokes and users always input similar stroke information when they draw the same shape. Accordingly, a framework of online adaptive recognition method is developed in our online sketchy shape recognition system [3][4] as shown in Fig. 1.

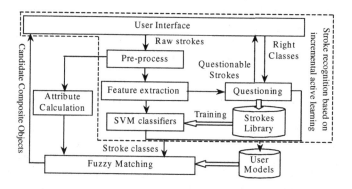

Fig. 1. Framework of user adaptation for on-line sketchy shape recognition

Firstly, raw stroke pre-processing and feature extraction are included. The raw stroke pre-processing is used to eliminate the noise caused by input conditions or input styles. It mainly undergoes the following processes [3][4]: redundant points reducing, polygonal approximation, agglomerate points filtering and end points refinement. Based on pre-processing, feature extraction is then applied to obtain the feature vector, which is an improvement of the turning function [9]. Details can be seen in reference [10].

Two steps of user adaptation are then applied. Firstly, an SVM-based incremental active learning method, mainly including SVM classifier and questioning of classification, is performed to adapt users' parameters of strokes. It can actively analyze users' incremental data and make full use of the historical data to reduce the workload of manual labeling and the training time of the classifier without loss of classification precision. Secondly, a dynamic user modeling method is adopted to build user models for each specific user in an incremental decision tree and recognize dynamically the "possible shapes" by means of fuzzy matching. We will present the two steps in detail in the following subsections.

Additionally, the sketchy shapes drawn by the user must undergo rectification so that the shape becomes regular and looks very similar to the one in his/her mind. Our approach is to rectify the fitted shapes to the regular form until its overall distortion is under the tolerable range. This process is currently rule based [3][4].

3.1 SVM-based Incremental Active Learning for Stroke Classification

Support Vector Machines (SVMs) have been proved efficient and suitable for learning with large and high dimension data sets. Furthermore, investigations [11][12] have shown that the incrementally trained SVMs are better than their non-incrementally trained equivalents. This rests mainly with the fact that the generalization property of an SVM does not depend on all the training data but only a subset which is referred to as Support Vectors (SVs). In other words, the number of

SVs typically is very small compared with the number of all training samples. In fact, that the SVs are those that lie the closest to the hyper-plane [12]. Nevertheless, there is a problem how to distinguish them from the rest in the sample sets before training. A solution is to minimize the collected data sets (S_{cl}) by making use of the historic result of training, so that the samples are close enough to the hyper-plane as SV sets (S_{sv}). That is, $Min(S_{cl}| S_{sv} \subset S_{cl})$. Additionally, the training process of SVMs itself may be very time consuming, especially when dealing with noisy data, and the samples used in incrementally training of SVM-classifier must be labeled artificially. This is tedious and burdensome, is even an interruption of the user's thinking process.

Therefore, we propose an SVM-based incremental active learning algorithm, which inserts a questioning process in the training process of SVM incremental learning. The training would only preserve the SVs at each incremental step and then add them instead of all historic data to the training sets collected in the questioning step. In other words, SVM classifier analyzes users' incremental unlabeled samples and picks out the most important instances for the user to endorse as training samples. This is so called active learning. Denoting the training process of SVM as *Train(SV)*, the question process as *Query(data)*, the initial training samples as *IS*, the incremental training samples as *INS*, the temporary training samples as *NS* and working data as *WS*, the process of SVM incremental active learning can be briefly described as:

1. *Γ=Train(IS)*, *WS=IS$_{sv}$*. The random training samples are collected and their correct classes are specified until they are sufficient for training the classifier initially. A subclassifier for every two classes is built if it does not exist, and is then trained or retrained with the historical SVs and newly added training samples to learn users' preferences of sketching strokes.
2. *Γ=Train(WS)*, *WS=WS$_{sv}$*. The features of the sketchy strokes are extracted in terms of the modified turning function [4], and are classified with every subclassifier. The outputs are the classes with the most votes from every subclassifier. The questionable samples are selected if they are close to the hyper-plane.
3. *NS=Query(INS)*, *WS=WS∪NS*. The questionable samples are questioned actively and then evaluated interactively by the user. The evaluation of the user is stored and gathered as the incremental training samples.
4. Repeat (2) and (3) until the results of SVM classifiers are satisfactory or enough training samples are obtained.

One important issue in our method, distinguished mainly from traditional SVM-classifiers, is to find whether the samples are in question and to be evaluated by the user. In our questioning process, the interrogative samples are determined by estimating their distance from the hyper-plane. Given a training set of l samples $F = \{(x_1, y_1), \cdots, (x_l, y_l)\}$, $y_i \in \{+1, -1\}$, the original data space can be mapped to a higher dimensional feature space f via a Mercer Kernel operator [13] $K(x,y) = \Phi(x) \cdot \Phi(y)$, where $\Phi: F \rightarrow f$, so as to make these samples linearly separable in the higher dimension feature space. We build the hyper-plane that separates the training data by maximization of the margin in the higher dimension feature space f and the hyper-plane can then be expressed as:

$$\sum_{x_i \in SV} \alpha_i y_i K(x, x_i) + b = 0 \, , \, 0 < \alpha_i \leq C \tag{1}$$

That is, $w_0 \Phi(x) + b = 0$, where, $w_0 = \sum_{x_i \in SV} y_i \alpha_i \Phi(x_i)$, coefficients α_i can be obtained from solving the following optimization problem:

$$\text{Minimize} : w(\alpha) = \sum_{i=1}^{l} \alpha_i - \frac{1}{2} \sum_{i,j=1}^{l} \alpha_i \alpha_j y_i y_j \Phi(x_i) \cdot \Phi(x_j), \tag{2}$$

subject to constraints: $\sum_{i=1}^{l} \alpha_i y_i = 0 \, , \, \alpha_i \geq 0 \, , \, i = 1, 2, ..., l$. $\tag{3}$

The distance between the sample x and the hyper-plane can be defined as:

$$d(x, w) = \frac{|w_0 \Phi(x) + b|}{\|w_0\|} \tag{4}$$

Since $\|w_0\| = 1$, $d(x, w) = |w_0 \cdot \Phi(x) + b| = |\sum_{x_i \in SV} \alpha_i y_i K(x, x_i) + b|$ $\tag{5}$

During questioning, there are three critical problems. The first is how to select the threshold value of the distance between the training samples and the hyper-plane. If we set the constant threshold value, a conflict between the precision and the speed occurs. Therefore, we use dynamic threshold values. At the beginning, when the precision of the classifier is low and a relatively large portion of the small dataset does not lead to a long retraining time, the threshold values can be set much larger. It then descends with the increase of the precision of the classifiers, and higher precision can be obtained in shorter training time. The second problem is how to deal with the samples classified incorrectly by the classifiers. In fact, the incremental active learning can automatically select the important samples that are close to the hyper-plane but are classified incorrectly. The third problem relates to multi-class classification. We only discuss the binary-classification problem previously. The multi-class classifiers (m classes and n samples in the training sets) are usually built with many binary sub-classifiers in two major structures, one-against-all and one-against-one. One-against-all structure needs m sub-classifiers (with n samples for each classifier), while one-against-one needs $m(m-1)/2$ sub-classifiers. In fact, the one-against-one is based on the max-win scheme [13], where each sub-classifier casts one vote for its preferred class, and the results are the classes voted with the most votes. It is generally believed that one-against-one structure has actually many advantages in training compared with traditional one-against-all structure.

3.2 Dynamic User Modeling for Sketchy Composite Shape Recognition

Following stroke classification, dynamic user modeling is used to capture users' styles of sketching composite shapes. The user model is actually an incremental decision tree [14]. Fuzzy matching is introduced to predict/recognize the 'possible shapes' dynamically.

3.2.1 Definition of User Model

In our work, the term 'user model' mainly means how a user draws a particular composite shape. In other words, a user model reflects the user's drawing/sketching style, e.g., the sequence of the strokes, etc. To construct user models, the following definitions are given.

Definition 1. The stroke is defined as $s=(type, dir)$, where '$type$' is the class of the strokes obtained by the incremental active learning or by users' feedback, and 'dir' is the direction of the stroke, which is set as one of the eight equiangular directions dividing a circle, denoted as I, II, ..., VIII, respectively.

Definition 2. The relationship between two continuous strokes can be expressed as $r=(rel)$, where 'rel' is defined as the direction (defined above) from the center of gravity of the previous stroke (v_m) to that of the current (v_{m+1}). In addition, in a user model, each node also includes an attribute 'possible shapes', which records the possible composite shapes that can be found along this branch (sub-tree) and their corresponding possibilities (frequencies). Using this attribute, the resulting shape can be predicted more efficiently and dynamic pruning can be conveniently performed to cut off those noisy or exceptional nodes.

Definition 3. The list of the possible shapes is expressed as $Glist=<w_1, w_2, ..., w_n>$, where $w_i=(GClass, weight)$, '$Gclass$' is one of objects that can be searched from the current node, and '$weight$' is the visiting frequency of the candidate object. These two values are obtained by learning from the user's historic dataset.

Definition 4. A single user model can be denoted as $T=(V, E)$, it is actually a tree structure, where $V=(v_1, v_2, ..., v_l)$, $v_i=(s_i, r_i, GList_i)$, and $E=(e_1, e_2, ..., e_k)$. $e=<v_m, v_{m+1}>$, expressing the sequence of the two strokes v_m and v_{m+1}, is one edge of the decision tree.

Definition 5. Multi-user models are composed of many single user models and can be denoted as $U=(T_1, T_2, ..., T_n)$.

In summary, our user model of composite shapes is a decision tree for each specific user. The root of the tree records the user's id and each leaf node records the class label of the input object. The branch nodes record the information of each input stroke, which is one part of the composite object represented by the leaf node.

3.2.2 Building User Models

In term of user model defined previously, we can build and store a specific tree for each specific user according to the stroke sequence and three attributes of each stroke: the type, the direction, and the relationship with its previous stroke. The type of the stroke, which is the key identifier of the stroke, is determined by the SVM-classifiers or collected by feedback from the user as described in Section 3.1. The other two attributes can be calculated by a rule-based method. These three attributes are put together to identify one stroke and used to avoid over-branching of the decision tree.

Along with the training process, the decision tree will grow and adjust to the user's style of stroke sequence and construction of the composite shapes. When a composite shape is being sketched in a sequence of strokes, they are tried to match with the strokes along the branch. If the matching is successful, the possible composite shape can be predicted or recognized, and, at the same time, the weights of related nodes in the user models are adjusted. Otherwise, a new branch of the tree is created starting from the unmatched node. If a composite shape does not exist in the pre-defined object database, the strokes are collected and the new object is added to the database after shape regularization.

Suppose m classes of strokes have been collected and there are mostly n strokes in the composites, the maximal complexity to build one branch should be $O(m \cdot n)$.

3.2.3 Fuzzy Matching

When being sketched in a sequence of strokes, a composite shape is tried to match every stroke along all branches of the decision tree. However, there exists a contradiction between the accuracy of calculating the attributes of strokes when building the decision tree and the illegibility of these strokes when drawing and predicting it. This may cause very lower precision of recognition, especially with a small training dataset. Therefore, a fuzzy matching method is introduced to search the 'possible shapes' that the user intents to draw.

Two fuzzy attributes, the direction and the type of stroke, are considered firstly. The main fuzzy attribute is the direction (including the direction of a stroke and that of the relationship between two continuous strokes). For example, the direction of a stroke with $\pi/9$ from the x-axis clockwise should be recognized as "II", but in fact, the user wants to input the stroke with the direction "I". Therefore, we introduce a subjective function of fuzzy matching to recognize the direction of stroke, which is defined as follows:

$$
f(x) = \begin{cases} \dfrac{1}{2} + \dfrac{1}{2}\sin(4x - \dfrac{2i-3}{2}\pi) & x \in (\dfrac{(i-2)\pi}{4}, \dfrac{i\pi}{4}) \\ 0 & x \le \dfrac{(i-2)\pi}{4} \quad x \ge \dfrac{i\pi}{4} \end{cases} \tag{6}
$$

Where, $i=1,2,...,8$ expressing 8 directions: I, II, ..., VIII. One stroke may have two possible directions if it is not inputted accurately in the defined eight directions.

The type/class of a stroke, which is recognized by the SVM-based incremental active learning method, may be wrong since the precision of stroke recognition is not always 100%. We use a subjective array of fuzzy stroke classes to solve this problem [10]. This subjective array is based on our statistic analysis of experiments in the stroke recognition, defined as follows:

$$
R =
$$

i\j	1	2	3	4	5	6	7	8	9	10	11	12	13	14
1	0.7	0.2		0.05	0.05									
2	0.1	0.9												
3	0.05	0.05	0.8							0.1				
4	0.1	0.1		0.6		0.05			0.05	0.05			0.05	
5		0.1		0.05	0.85									
6		0.1			0.05	0.85								
7							0.95	0.05						
8								1						
9									1					
10	0.05	0.05	0.05							0.85				
11	0.05			0.05		0.05	0.05		0.05		0.55	0.2		
12						0.05						0.85		0.1
13													1	
14												0.1		0.9

$$ \tag{7} $$

where, R_i is the row representing the classes determined by SVM classifiers, R_j is the column representing the correct classes, and R_{ij} is the possibility of the correct class 'j' being determined as class 'i' by SVM classifiers.

Let g' be the weight (visit frequency) of the current node and GList be the list of the candidate objects (possible shapes) of the current node, the weight of each candidate object in this node is g'·Glist. All candidate objects (possible shapes) from all visited nodes are ranked by their maximum weights (some objects may have different weights along different branches). When the next stroke is input, the fuzzy directions of this stroke can be calculated as s_1 and s_2, the fuzzy relations to the previous stroke are r_1 and r_2, and the possibility of being a particular stroke type is R_{ij}. Consequently, the weight/possibility of the next searching node is:

$$ g = g' s_m r_n R_{ij} , \tag{8}$$

where, m, $n=1$ or 2, and i, $j=1$, ..., 14. Table 1 illustrates the how to adjust the weights/possibilities of the candidate objects when a composite shape is being sketched.

Table 1. Adjust the possible shapes when inputting a composite shape

No.	Input stroke and the current look of the object	Rank of the desired object	Candidates sorted by the descending weight
1	○	25	◎ ♀ ⊕ ♀ ⊘ ◎ ○ et al.
2	♀	4	♀ ○ ⊕ ♀
3	♀	2	♀ ♀
4	♀	1	♀

Suppose that m classes of strokes are collected and there are n strokes in the most complex object and k visited nodes, the complexity of fuzzy matching should be $O(k·m·n)$. Therefore, this method should be efficient enough for real-time recognition because k is usually between 3 and 20.

4 Experiments and Evaluation

For experiments, one important problem must be considered: how the system knows whether the recognition result is correct, and if not, what the correct result should be. Alternatively, all learning can be carried out unnoticeably during the normal use and the user is assumed to agree all the recognition results. In fact, the user does not necessarily notice all the mistakes immediately if there is any or the user does not care to correct them. This problem can be avoided if the user is taught to draw shapes with a standardized sample sets. Accordingly, the experiments presented in this paper have been limited to 150 common composite objects, as shown in Fig. 2. All object samples are labeled with their correct types and they form the ground-truth database. Each standard object can be drawn in several styles, for example, as illustrated in Fig. 3. We have collected 537 styles for all the 150 objects, and 10 drawing samples for each style of an object. Totally, we collect 5370 drawing sample in the ground-truth database for the experiments.

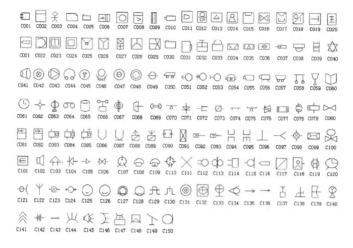

Fig. 2. Experiment sets of composite objects

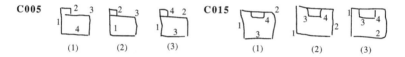

Fig. 3. Illustration of drawing style variations of composite objects

4.1   Experimental Results of Stroke Recognition

For the experiment of sketchy stroke recognition with SVM-based incremental active learning, we have collected 53302 strokes of the 14 classes as shown in Fig. 4, which are most commonly used in sketching. Every sample is represented as the modified turning function [4] with 20-dimensional features. 21932 samples are randomly selected as the testing data, and the rest are randomly grouped into 25 sets of incremental training. The first 5 sets have 300, 300, 370, 500 and 900 samples, respectively, and each of the later 20 set has 1500 samples. It is reasonable for an incremental learning because SVM has the ability to obtain a good performance under a small training set and maintains a relatively stable precision.

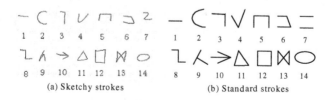

Fig. 4. The class of strokes used often in the composite objects

In our experiments, the training process using RBF kernel [15] is the same as SVMTorch [16]. All experiments are done on an Intel P4 PC with 1.4GHz CPU and 768 MB memory running Microsoft Windows. We compare our method with the repetitive learning, which add new dataset to all historic dataset, and SVM incremental learning algorithms reported in reference [11] and [12], respectively. The result of comparison is shown in Fig. 5. The results show that, while the classification precisions of these methods are nearly the same, as shown in Fig. 5(a), the training time and the numbers of incrementally added training samples of our method is the least, as shown in Fig. 5(b) and (c).

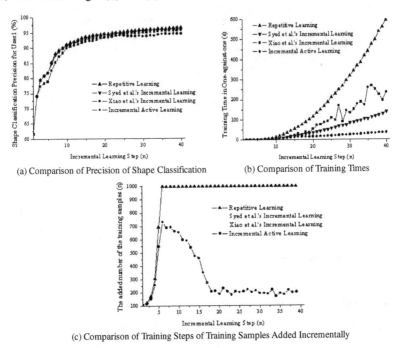

(a) Comparison of Precision of Shape Classification   (b) Comparison of Training Times

(c) Comparison of Training Steps of Training Samples Added Incrementally

Fig. 5. Recognition precision comparison

4.2 Experimental Results of Composite Shape Recognition

For our composite shape/object recognition experiment using dynamic user modeling, we first use one, three, five, or seven styles for every object as the training data (Denoted as T_1, T_3, T_5 or T_7), respectively, to train the model, and then use three styles as the test data (1611 samples in total). The precisions of object recognition using exact matching and fuzzy matching are illustrated in Table 2 and Table 3, respectively. A sketchy object is considered recognized correctly if appears in top i of the candidate list (i=1, 3, 5, 7).

Table 2. The object recognition precision with exact matching

Training Dataset	Top n in the candidate objects list			
	Top 1	Top 3	Top 5	Top 7
T_1 (in total, 537 samples)	47.61%	55.49%	58.29%	60.34%
T_3 (in total, 1611 samples)	76.16%	81.87%	85.16%	86.10%
T_5 (in total, 2685 samples)	85.35%	89.26%	91.19%	91.50%
T_7 (in total, 3759 samples)	89.14%	92.43%	93.92%	94.29%

Table 3. The object recognition precision with fuzzy matching

Training Dataset	Top n in the candidate objects list			
	Top 1	Top 3	Top 5	Top 7
T_1 (in total, 537 samples)	77.72%	88.08%	91.37%	92.68%
T_3 (in total, 1611 samples)	81.81%	92.99%	95.47%	96.96%
T_5 (in total, 2685 samples)	83.43%	93.67%	96.46%	97.77%
T_7 (in total, 3759 samples)	85.23%	94.60%	96.96%	98.63%

The results of experiments show that our user modeling method is effectual after training: the precision increases along with the increment of training number, and fuzzy matching is even more powerful than exact matching, especially when the training data set is very small.

5   Conclusions

In this paper, we have exploited an original principle of adaptation to various users' sketching styles in sketchy shape recognition. The adaptation principle is based on the combination of stroke classification performed by an incremental active learning method and composite shape recognition by means of dynamic user modeling. Firstly, we propose an SVM-based incremental active learning algorithm for stroke classification. This method reduces the workload of artificial labeling and the classifier's training time by analyzing the users' incremental data actively and discarding those unimportant samples that without loss of classification precision. It is efficiency for both users and training classifiers. Secondly, we introduce a dynamic user modeling method to build user models for each specific user in an incremental decision tree and recognize dynamically the 'candidate shapes' by means of fuzzy matching. Each time the user input a composite shape, the nodes along the corresponding branch in the tree are visited and matched again with the strokes of the object in that sequence. This enhances the weights of those frequently visited nodes and objects. Hence, the more the user models are used, the higher the accuracy of shape prediction/recognition. Experiments prove the proposed method both effective and efficient.

Acknowledgement

The work described in this paper is supported by the grant from the National Natural Science Foundation of China [Project No. 69903006 and 60373065] and the Research Grants Council of the Hong Kong Special Administrative Region, China [Project No. CityU 1073/02E]

References

1. Rejean P and Sargur N, On-line and Off-line Handwriting Recognition: A Comprehensive Survey, IEEE Trans. on PAMI, 2000, 22(1): 63–84.

2. Rottland J, Neukirchen C, and Rigoll G, Speaker Adaptation for Hybrid MMI/Connectionist Speech Recognition Systems. In Proc. ICASSP, 1998.
3. Liu W Y, Jin X Y and Sun Z X, Sketch-Based User Interface for Inputting Graphic Objects on Small Screen Devices, Lecture Notes in Computer Science, 2002 (2390): 67–80.
4. Sun Z X et al., Sketch-based Graphic Input Tool for Conceptual Design, J. of Computer-Aided Design & Computer Graphics (In Chinese), 2003,15(9): 205–206.
5. Gross M D, The Electronic Cocktail Napkin: a Computational Environment for Working with Design Diagrams. Design Studies, 1996, 17: 53–69.
6. Newman M W, James L, Hong J I, and Landay J A, DENIM: An Informal Web Site Design Tool Inspired by Observations of Practice, Human-Computer Interaction, 2003, 18: 259–324.
7. Apte A, Vo V and Kimura T D Ajay A, Van V, and Takayuki D K, Recognizing Multistroke Geometric Shapes: an Experimental Evaluation. ACM Symposium on User Interface Software and Technology, 1993: 121–128.
8. Arvo J, Novins K, Fluid Sketches: Continuous Recognition and Morphing of Simple Hand-Drawn Shapes, ACM Symposium on User Interface Software and Technology, San Diego, California, November, 2000.
9. Arkin E M, et al., An Efficient Computable Metric for Comparing Polygonal Shapes, IEEE Trans. on PAMI, 1999, 13(3): 209–216.
10. Sun Z X, et al., Study on User Adaptation for Online Sketchy Graphic Recognition, J. of Computer-Aided Design & Computer Graphics (In Chinese), 2004, 16.
11. Syed N, Liu H, and Sung K, Incremental Learning with Support Vector Machines, IJCAI-99, Stockholm, Sweden, 1999: 272–276.
12. Xiao R, et al., An Incremental SVM Learning Algorithm α-ISVM, Journal of Software (In Chinese), 2001, 12(12): 1818–1824.
13. Weston J and Watkins C, Multi-class Support Vector Machines, Technical Report CSD-TR-98-04, Department of Computer Science, University of London, 1998.
14. Utgoff P E, Decision Tree Induction Based on Efficient Tree Restructuring, Technical Report 95-18, Univ. of Massachusetts, Dept. of Computer Science, Amherst, MA, 1996.
15. Ratsaby J, Incremental Learning with Sample Queries, IEEE Trans. on PAMI, 1998, 20: 883–888.
16. Collobert R and Bengio S, SVMtorch: Support Vector Machines for Large-Scale Regression Problems, Journal of Machine Learning Research, 2001: 143–160.

Retrieving On-line Chinese Scripts with an Invariant Structural Descriptor

Su Yang

Dept. of Computer Science and Engineering, Fudan University, Shanghai 200433, China
suyang@fudan.edu.cn

Abstract. Driven by new applications running on Tablet PC, a new pattern descriptor was proposed for retrieval of on-line Chinese scripts. The descriptor is based on Attributed Relational Graph (ARG). Fuzzy description is employed to enhance the adaptability of this model. To simplify the matching, the graph model is transformed to statistical features. Another improvement is that the descriptor is rotation-invariant. The experimental results show that this descriptor is effective for rotation-invariant retrieval of characters in regular style.

1 Introduction

As Tablet PC comes into the markets, handwriting recognition has to face new problems driven by newly arising applications, such as note taking. It is a basic requirement for such a system that retrieval of specific information contained in a user's notes should be enabled. Retrieval of on-line scripts is different from recognition of on-line handwritings in the following aspect. The goal of handwriting recognition is to find the template that best matches the input so that the text code corresponding to this template can be selected as the interpreter of the input. As for the retrieval, the task is to find a piece of formerly saved ink that best matches the query. On one hand, the difficulty of retrieval is lower than that of recognition in the following aspects. First, a recognizer should be able to tolerate different writing styles but retrieval is performed only on an identical user's handwritings. Second, the matching for recognition purpose should be performed on the entire character set to find the best matching character but that for retrieval purpose only needs to be conducted on one's formerly saved scripts, which usually consist of a subset of the entire character set. On the other hand, retrieval is harder than recognition because some new requirements were put forward by newly arising applications. For example, rotation invariance is not crucial for on-line handwriting recognition because directions of input characters vary a little. But for retrieval of on-line scripts, rotation invariance cannot be neglected, because characters may be in different directions. For example, Fig. 1 is a handprint graph to show voltage versus time, in which the characters to label X-Y coordinates are in horizontal and vertical direction respectively. Another example illustrated in Fig. 2 is a handprint map of a site in Nanjing, where the characters to note two roads are in horizontal and diagonal direction respectively. For cases like those, techniques for rotation-invariant retrieval

J. Lladós and Y.-B. Kwon (Eds.): GREC 2003, LNCS 3088, pp. 317–328, 2004.
© Springer-Verlag Berlin Heidelberg 2004

of on-line scripts are in demand. In this sense, the difficulty for on-line retrieval is higher than that for on-line recognition.

Chinese characters may be the most complicated characters in terms of handwriting recognition. A large number of users need Chinese character recognition applications. So, this study was concentrated on rotation-invariant retrieval of on-line handwritten Chinese characters. Although the query can either be a character or a string, we will focus on one character's query. Also, we assume that the saved scripts have already been segmented into characters, which is the practice for many applications. What we are dealing with in this study is the most fundamental case.

Although a great progress has been made in Chinese character recognition, rotation-invariant recognition of Chinese characters is a challenge yet. There are two solutions. One is to build multiple templates for each character by taking into account several representative directions in which a character may be written [1]. As the rotation-invariant performance of this method is subject to the number of the templates built for each character, rotation invariance is achieved by increasing computational complexity. The other way is to utilize rotation-invariant descriptors. To date, only one approach based on ring projection has been developed [9][8][5][2]. However, this descriptor is not applicable to handwritten Chinese characters, because it is hard to find a stable center for handwritten characters when computing the ring projection. Both of the previously mentioned methods are for off-line recognition. So far, no rotation-invariant recognizer has been developed for on-line handwritten characters due to the lack of applicable cases. However, the situation changed with the coming of Tablet PC, for which rotation-invariant retrieval of on-line scripts is useful. In this study, we proposed a new pattern descriptor for rotation-invariant retrieval of on-line handwritten Chinese characters. Not like numerical measurement based ring projection, our method focuses on structural characteristics of Chinese characters. This descriptor is based on attributed relational graph [4][3][7]. Fuzzy description [10] is also utilized to enhance the adaptabilities of this model. To simplify the matching, the graph model is transformed to statistical features. Rotation invariance is achieved by using relative coordinates instead of fixed coordinates. The experimental results show that this descriptor is effective for retrieval of characters in regular style and can promise rotation invariance.

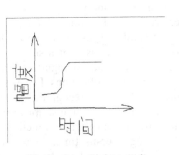

Fig. 1. A handprint graph

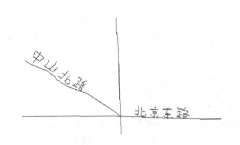

Fig. 2. A handprint map

2 Graph Based Representation of Chinese Characters

Chinese characters are fundamentally composed of line segments. Different types of line segments to construct a Chinese character can be regarded as primitives. For a given Chinese character, each line segment is constrained to the other line segments in accordance with certain rules. Such characteristics can be described using a graph model. An attributed relational graph consists of

$$\omega = (N, B, V_N, V_B, \mu, \varepsilon) \tag{1}$$

where N can be understood as the line segments to compose a character, B the relations between each pair of line segments in N, V_N a label set to denote all types of line segments, V_B a label set to denote all types of relations, μ a map set by which each line segment in N is associated with a label in V_N, and ε a map set by which each relation in B is associated with a label in V_B. In practice, the type of a line segment or a relation is sometime too ambiguous to be identified, so we describe the type of a line segment or a relation by assigning a membership degree for every possible case in terms of fuzzy set theory. This leads to the descriptor described below.

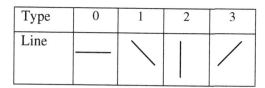

Type	0	1	2	3
Line	—	\	|	/

Fig. 3. Primitive line segments

2.1 Fuzzy Descriptor for Representing Types of Line Segments

A Chinese character can be segmented into line segments by using a dominant point detector such as the method proposed in [6]. As shown in Fig. 3, there are 4 types of line segments in Chinese characters in total, which are denoted as 0, 1, 2, and 3 respectively. A line segment's type is determined by its angle

$$\theta = arctg[(y_e - y_b)/(x_e - x_b)] \tag{2}$$

where (x_b, y_b) and (x_e, y_e) are the start and end point of the line segment respectively. Referring to Fig. 3, the typical angle values in correspondence with type 0,1,2,3 are $\theta_0 = 0°\pm k180°$, $\theta_1 = -45°\pm k180°$, $\theta_2 = -90°\pm k180°$, $\theta_3 = -135°\pm k180°$ respectively, where k is a positive integer. If the angle of a line segment is close to a typical angle value, its type is apparent. In case that the angle of a line segment is not close to any typical angle value, such as $-67.5°$, it would be hard to determine its type. In order to enable our system to tolerate such uncertainties, we use a vector

$$[\mu_0(\theta), \mu_1(\theta), \mu_2(\theta), \mu_3(\theta)] \tag{3}$$

to describe the possibility that a line segment belongs to every type. In terms of fuzzy set theory, type of a line segment can be regarded as linguistic variable, {0,1,2,3} are linguistic terms, each of which corresponds with a fuzzy set, and $\mu_i(\theta)$ is the membership function associated with linguistic term i, where $i=0,1,2,3$. The membership function of linguistic term i is defined as

$$
\mu_i(\theta) = \begin{cases}
1 & \theta \in [\theta_i - 10°, \theta_i + 10°] \\
0.5 + 0.5 \times \dfrac{\theta - (\theta_i - 22.5°)}{12.5°} & \theta \in [\theta_i - 35°, \theta_i - 10°] \\
0.5 + 0.5 \times \dfrac{(\theta_i + 22.5°) - \theta}{12.5°} & \theta \in [\theta_i + 10°, \theta_i + 35°] \\
0 & \theta \notin [\theta_i - 35°, \theta_i + 35°]
\end{cases}
\tag{4}
$$

where $i \in \{0,1,2,3\}$.

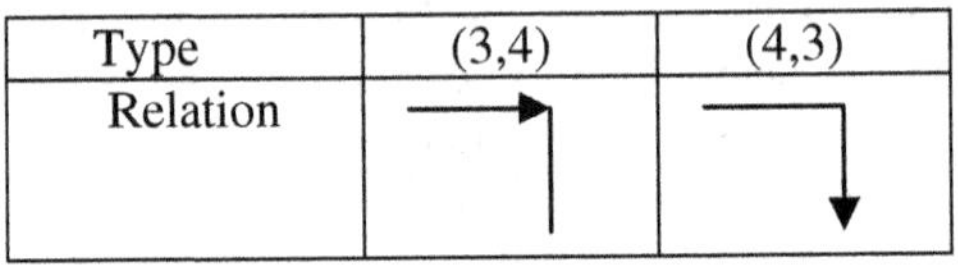

Type	(3,4)	(4,3)
Relation		

Fig. 4(a). 2 types of relations

Line segment A:
Line segment B:

Type	(0,0)	(0,1)	(0,2)	(1,0)	(1,1)	(1,2)
Relation						
Type	(2,1)	(2,0)	(2,2)			
Relation						

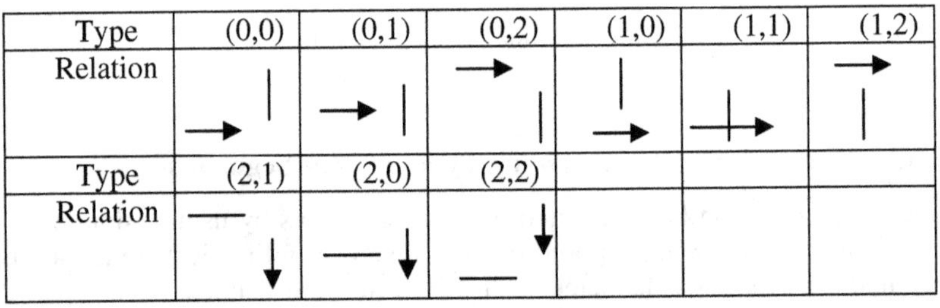

Fig. 4(b). The other 9 types of relations

Line segment A:
Line segment B:

2.2 Fuzzy Descriptor for Representing Types of Relations Between Line Segments

As illustrated in Fig. 4(a) and (b), there are 11 types of relations between two line segments in total. Figure 4(a) shows the 2 cases that the head of a line segment is meanwhile the tail of another line segment. Figure 4(b) shows the 9 cases that a line segment is positioned at the bottom-left, left, top-left, bottom, centre (crossover), top, bottom-right, right, and top-right of the other line segment.

The degree of how the 9 types of relations shown in Fig. 4(b) are fulfilled by two line segments is computed as follows. By projecting two line segments of interest onto X co-ordinate, we can obtain their projections, $[x_{a1}, x_{a2}]$ and $[x_{b1}, x_{b2}]$. Without losing generality, here, we assume that $x_{a1} \le x_{a2}$ and $x_{b1} \le x_{b2}$. As illustrated in Fig. 5, there are 3 types of relations between two projections on a co-ordinate, which are denoted as 0, 1, and 2 respectively. The three types correspond with such cases that a projection is at the left, centre, and right of the other projection on X co-ordinate. If two projections do not overlap with each other, the type of their relation is apparent. In the case of overlapping, the situation becomes complex. To enhance the capability of our system in dealing with the uncertainties caused by overlapping, we use a vector

$$[\mu_0(x_{a1}, x_{a2}, x_{b1}, x_{b2}), \mu_1(x_{a1}, x_{a2}, x_{b1}, x_{b2}), \mu_2(x_{a1}, x_{a2}, x_{b1}, x_{b2})] \tag{5}$$

to describe the possibility that a relation belongs to every type. In terms of fuzzy set theory, type of relation can be regarded as linguistic variable, {0,1,2} are linguistic terms, and $\mu_i(x_{a1}, x_{a2}, x_{b1}, x_{b2})$ is the membership function associated with linguistic term i, where $i=0,1,2$. Regarding the 3 linguistic terms, the membership functions are defined as

$$\mu_0(x_{a1}, x_{a2}, x_{b1}, x_{b2}) = \begin{cases} 1 & x_{a2} \le x_{b1} \\ 1-(x_{a2}-x_{b1})/r_{\min} & r_{\min} > 0 \wedge 0 < (x_{a2}-x_{b1})/r_{\min} < 1 \\ (m_b - m_a)/r_{\max} & r_{\min} = 0 \wedge r_{\max} > 0 \wedge m_a < m_b \\ 0 & else \end{cases} \tag{6}$$

$$\mu_1(x_{a1}, x_{a2}, x_{b1}, x_{b2}) = \begin{cases} 1 & m_a = m_b \\ (x_{a2}-x_{b1})/r_{\min} & r_{\min} > 0 \wedge 0 < (x_{a2}-x_{b1})/r_{\min} < 1 \\ (x_{b2}-x_{a1})/r_{\min} & r_{\min} > 0 \wedge 0 < (x_{b2}-x_{a1})/r_{\min} < 1 \\ 1-|m_a - m_b|/r_{\max} & r_{\min} = 0 \wedge r_{\max} > 0 \\ 0 & else \end{cases} \tag{7}$$

$$\mu_2(x_{a1}, x_{a2}, x_{b1}, x_{b2}) = \begin{cases} 1 & x_{b2} \le x_{a1} \\ 1-(x_{b2}-x_{a1})/r_{\min} & r_{\min} > 0 \wedge 0 < (x_{b2}-x_{a1})/r_{\min} < 1 \\ (m_a - m_b)/r_{\max} & r_{\min} = 0 \wedge r_{\max} > 0 \wedge m_a > m_b \\ 0 & else \end{cases} \tag{8}$$

where $r_{\min}=\min\{x_{a2}-x_{a1}, x_{b2}-x_{b1}\}$, $r_{\max}=\max\{(x_{a2}-x_{a1})/2, (x_{b2}-x_{b1})/2\}$, $m_a=(x_{a2}+x_{a1})/2$, and $m_b=(x_{b2}+x_{b1})/2$.

The relation between two projections on Y co-ordinate can be computed in the same manner. Here, $\mu_0(y_{a1}, y_{a2}, y_{b1}, y_{b2})$, $\mu_1(y_{a1}, y_{a2}, y_{b1}, y_{b2})$, and $\mu_2(y_{a1}, y_{a2}, y_{b1}, y_{b2})$ represent the possibility that a projection is at the bottom, center, and top of the other projection respectively.

Then, the relation between two line segments A and B in (X,Y) plane can be obtained by synthesizing the relations between their projections on both X and Y coordinate. Here, we let

$$\mu_{(i,j)}(A,B) = \mu_i(x_{a1}, x_{a2}, x_{b1}, x_{b2}) \times \mu_j(y_{a1}, y_{a2}, y_{b1}, y_{b2}) \tag{9}$$

It is the possibility that the relation between line segment A and B belongs to type (i,j) defined in Fig. 4(b), where $i,j=0,1,2$. For example, $\mu_0(x_{a1}, x_{a2}, x_{b1}, x_{b2})$ is the possibility that line segment A is at the left of line segment B when projected onto X co-ordinate, $\mu_0(y_{a1}, y_{a2}, y_{b1}, y_{b2})$ is the possibility that A is at the bottom of B when projected onto Y co-ordinate, and $\mu_{(0,0)}(A,B) = \mu_0(x_{a1}, x_{a2}, x_{b1}, x_{b2}) \times \mu_0(y_{a1}, y_{a2}, y_{b1}, y_{b2})$ is the possibility that A is at the bottom-left of B.

For the 2 cases shown in Fig. 4(a), we hold

$$\mu_{(3,4)}(A,B) = \begin{cases} 1 & x_{at} = x_{bh} \wedge y_{at} = y_{bh} \\ 0 & else \end{cases} \tag{10}$$

$$\mu_{(4,3)}(A,B) = \begin{cases} 1 & x_{bt} = x_{ah} \wedge y_{bt} = y_{ah} \\ 0 & else \end{cases} \tag{11}$$

where (x_{ah}, y_{ah}), (x_{at}, y_{at}), (x_{bh}, y_{bh}), and (x_{bt}, y_{bt}) are the start and end point of line segment A and B respectively.

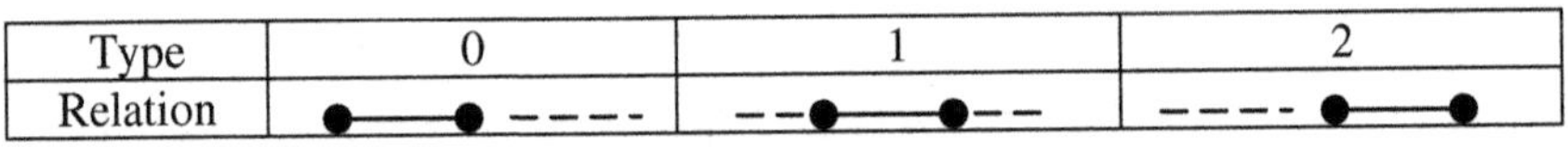

Type	0	1	2
Relation	●——● — — — —	— —●——●— —	— — — —●——●

Fig. 5. The 3 types of relations in one-dimensional space

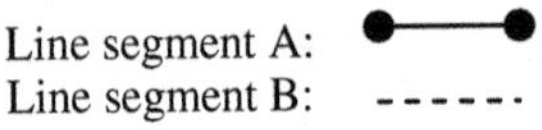

Line segment A: ●——●
Line segment B: — — — — —

2.3 Transformation of Graph Model to Statistical Features

Following the computation of types of primitives and relations as described above, we can obtain a graph representation for every Chinese character. The goal of retrieval is to find the best matching candidate with regard to a query. Hereby, the problem of retrieval becomes measuring the distance between two graphs, namely graph matching. It is known that graph matching is a difficult problem. Actually, we do not perform graph matching in the general sense. Instead, we solve the matching problem by transforming the graph model to a format that can enable an easy computation of the distance between two graphs. The goal of matching is to find correspondence in terms of node between two graphs. The distance between two graphs is actually the sum of the distance between every pair of matched nodes. So, the key problem is the computation of the distance between two nodes. This is realized as follows. We focus on every node in a graph separately and figure out how the other nodes distribute around it in the sense of statistics. This leads to a statistical feature associated with every node. This feature enables an easy computation of the distance between two nodes. Following is the detailed implementation.

Supposing a Chinese character is composed of L line segments denoted as $\{N_q|q=1,2,...,L\}$, the statistical feature associated with line segment $N_p \in \{N_q|q=1,2,..., L\}$ is defined as

$$F_{k,(i,j)}(N_p) = \sum_{q=1}^{L} \mu_{(i,j)}(N_p,N_q) \times \mu_k(N_q) \tag{12}$$

where $\mu_{(i,j)}(N_p,N_q)$ (see Eq. (9)~(11) for definition) is the possibility that the relation between line segment N_p and N_q belongs to type (i,j), and $\mu_k(N_q)$ (see Eq. (4) for definition) is the possibility that line segment N_q belongs to type k. $F_{k,(i,j)}(N_p)$ is a statistical summary of such line segments that their relation with N_p belongs to type (i,j) and their primitive type is k. Then, a feature matrix

$$F(N_p)=\{F_{k,(i,j)}(N_p)|\ k \in \{0,1,2,3\};(i,j) \in D\} \tag{13}$$

can be formed for line segment N_p, where $D=\{(0,0),\ (0,1),\ (0,2),\ (1,0),\ (1,1),\ (1,2),\ (2,0),\ (2,1),\ (2,2),\ (3,4),\ (4,3)\}$ represent all the relation types as defined in Fig. 4 and $k=\{0,1,2,3\}$ all the primitive types as defined in Fig. 3. Since the feature matrix has a fixed dimension, which is 4×11, computation of the distance between two nodes becomes very easy.

Figure 6(a) provides an example to show how the feature is computed. Let us focus on line segment N_1. $F_{0,(1,2)}(N_1)$ represents the number of such line segments that their relation with N_1 is $(1,2)$ and their primitive type is 0. It can be seen that only N_3 meets the above requirement: its relation with N_1 is $(1,2)$ (see Fig. 4(b) for definition) and its primitive type is 0 (see Fig. 3 for definition). So, $F_{0,(1,2)}(N_1)=1$. In case that the primitive type of a line segment or the relation between two line segments is not deterministic, the fuzzy computation defined in Eq. (4) and Eq. (9)~(11) should be employed.

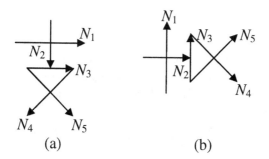

Fig. 6(a). A Chinese character   **6(b).** The rotation version

2.4 Rotation Invariance of the Descriptor

To achieve rotation invariance, we modified the above descriptor by letting line segment N_p act as X co-ordinate when computing its feature matrix $F(N_p)$. The detailed implementation is as follows. Firstly, the endpoints of all the line segments $\{N_q|q=1,2,...L\}$ are transformed from the original co-ordinates (x,y) to a new co-ordinates (x_{New},y_{New}) via the well known equation

$$x_{New} = x\cos\theta + y\sin\theta \qquad (14)$$
$$y_{Nwe} = -x\sin\theta + y\cos\theta$$

where θ is the angle of N_p in the old co-ordinates so as to let N_p act as the X axis in the new co-ordinates. Then, we compute the feature matrix $F(N_p)$ following Eq. (2), (4), and (6)~(13).

Why the above computations can guarantee rotation invariance is explained as follows. A Chinese character being composed of 5 line segments and a rotated version of it are shown in Fig. 6(a) and (b) respectively, where arrows indicate the end points of these line segments, and the line segments are labelled with the denotations N_1, N_2, N_3, N_4, and N_5 respectively. Without losing generality, we will show how rotation invariance can be guaranteed in computing the feature matrix $F(N_4)$. As described previously, we must take line segment N_4 as X co-ordinate when computing $F(N_4)$. It is obvious that the angle between line segment N_4 and every other line segment remains unchanged in the case of rotation as shown in Fig. 6. This means that the type of every line segment computed via Eq. (4) will not be affected by the rotation. Also, it is straightforward that the projection from every other line segment onto N_4 does not change with the rotation. So, the type of the one-dimensional relation between every other line segment and N_4 computed via Eq. (6)~(8) is not subject to the rotation. This means that the two-dimensional relation between N_4 and every other line segment is also invariant to the rotation because the two-dimensional relation is just the synthesis of the one-dimensional relation in both X and Y co-ordinate according to Eq. (9). It follows that the feature matrix $F(N_4)$ is rotation-invariant because $F(N_4)$ is merely the synthesis of the line segment type and the relation type of the other line segments in reference to N_4 according to Eq. (12) and (13). $F(N_1)$, $F(N_2)$, $F(N_3)$, and $F(N_5)$ are computed in the same manner so that they are also rotation-invariant.

3 Matching

Suppose that a Chinese character is composed of line segments $\omega=\{N_p|p=1, 2,...,L\}$ and another Chinese character consists of line segments $\omega'=\{N'_q|q=1,2,...,L'\}$. The distance between the two line segments N_p and N'_q is defined as

$$d(N_p, N'_q) = \sum_{k=0}^{3} \sum_{(i,j)\in D} | F_{k,(i,j)}(N_p) - F_{k,(i,j)}(N'_q)| \qquad (15)$$

where $F_{k,(i,j)}(N_p)$ and $F_{k,(i,j)}(N'_q)$, defined in Eq. (12), is the statistical feature associated with either line segment.

Matching two characters is to find the correspondence between their line segments. This can be achieved in the sense of nearest neighbor. Following is the computation:

```
for l=1 to min(L,L')
```

$$d_l=d(N_s,N'_t)=\min\{d(N_p,N'_q)\mid N_p\in\omega;\ N'_q\in\omega'\}$$

(N_s,N'_t) is selected as a matched pair

remove N_s from ω and remove N'_t from ω'

```
end
```

Following the above computation, there must exist $K=\min\{L,L'\}$ matched pairs and $|L-L'|$ unmatched line segments. Taking into account contributions of both matched pairs and unmatched individuals simultaneously, the distance between two characters is defined as

$$D=(1+\frac{|L-L'|}{L+L'})\sum_{l=1}^{K}d_l \tag{16}$$

where $\sum d_l$ is the cost of K matched pairs, and $1+|L-L'|/(L+L')$ accounts for the penalty for $|L-L'|$ unmatched line segments.

The objective of retrieval is to find the nearest neighbor against an input character in a given character set. Based on Eq. (16), the distance between every candidate character and the input character can be computed. Then, the character with the minimum distance to the input character is selected as the retrieved result.

4 Experiment and Discussion

Based on the proposed method, we developed a program using C for retrieval of on-line handwritten Chinese characters. The retrieval experiment was conducted as follows. First, a user is asked to write every character in a given set to produce a handwriting database for every character. Second, this user is asked to rewrite every character in the same set to retrieve the best matching character in the formerly produced database. A query character could be written in arbitrary orientation but samples in three directions as shown in Fig. 7 must be produced for every query character to evaluate the performance in terms of rotation invariance. Note that there is a restriction for both database and query production; that is, every character must be written in a regular style as shown in Fig. 7. In case that an input character does not comply with this requirement, we will ask the user reproduce the same character until a regular sample is available. Two sets of characters are used for performance evaluation. The first set contains 400 Chinese characters shown in Fig. 8. The second set contains 100 Chinese characters shown in Fig. 9. Because the stroke number of the characters in the first set is every close, which is from 9 to 11, the distinctions among these characters lie in the relations between the line components of which every character consists. Therefore, the first set is used for evaluating the discrimination power of the proposed descriptor. The second set is composed of the 100 leading characters in the standard codebook. The tests were carried out as follows. Three

Fig. 7. Handwritings of a user

Fig. 8. The first set

Fig. 9. The second set

users were asked to produce handwritten characters for set 1 and set 2 respectively. User 1 produced the characters in set 1. User 2 and user 3 produced the characters in set 2 respectively. Then, every user was required to retrieve his individual scripts in the database produced by him. The retrieval accuracy was 99.25% for user 1, and 100% for both user 2 and 3. However, we noticed that only slight deformation could be tolerated in the retrieval experiment. If a handwritten character was not in a regular style, the retrieved result is incorrect in most cases. So, a few characters had to be produced several times to get a correct retrieval in the tests. Also, we noticed the following fact in the tests. If a query without any rotation can lead to a correct retrieval, a correct retrieval is also available in any rotation case for the same character. This means that the proposed descriptor is rotation-invariant. Retrieval of each character can be completed within a tolerable time, about several seconds, on a P166 PC.

The above experiment shows the following evidence. (1) The discrimination power of the proposed descriptor is adequate for enabling classification of at least 400 Chinese characters. This means that the 4 types primitives and 11 types of relations described previously are sufficient for uniquely describing these characters. (2) The proposed descriptor is rotation-invariant due to the experimental results. A theoretical proof is also available, and one can ask for it via Email. (3) Only slight deformation is tolerable for the proposed descriptor. This limit is due to both the inevitable inaccuracy in decomposing a stroke into line segments and the nature of the graph based representation of a character. When a character contains arc components, the decomposition of this character into line segments will become unstable. As a result, types of primitives and relations in the graphical modeling of this character vary greatly from one sample to another. This often takes place in cursive handwriting. That accounts for why the proposed scheme is mainly effective for processing regular handwriting.

5   Summary

The contributions of this paper are as follows. (1) In terms of on-line handwriting recognition, this paper faces new problems arising from Tablet PC. (2) A new descriptor was proposed for rotation-invariant retrieval of on-line Chinese scripts. Its discrimination power and rotation invariance have been showed via experiment. Our future endeavor will be focused on seeking methods to improve robustness.

Acknowledgement

This work is partially supported by Natural Science Foundation of China under grant No. 60305002.

References

1. Chiu, H. P., Tseng, D. C.: A novel stroke-based feature extraction for handwritten Chinese character recognition. Pattern Recognition 32 (1999) 1947–1959
2. Chiu, H. P., Tseng, D. C.: Invariant handwritten Chinese character recognition using fuzzy min-max neural networks. Pattern Recognition Letters 18 (1997) 205–225

3. Liu, J. Z., Ma, K., Cham, W. K., Chang, M. M. Y.: Two-layer assignment method for online Chinese character recognition. IEE Proceedings-Vision Image and Signal Processing 147 (2000) 47–54
4. Tsai, W. H., Fu, K. S.: Error-correcting isomorphisms of attributed relational graphs for pattern analysis. IEEE Transactions on Systems Man and Cybernetics 9 (1979) 757–768
5. Tseng, D. C., Chiu, H. P., Cheng J. C.: Invariant handwritten Chinese character recognition using fuzzy ring data. Image and Vision Computing 14 (1996) 647–657
6. Yang, S., Dai, G. Z.: Detecting dominant points on on-line scripts with a simple approach. 8th International workshop on Frontiers in Handwriting Recognition, Ontario, Canada, (2002) 351–356
7. Yang, S., Zhu, Z. X., Li, Z. S.: Research and development of on-line handwritten Chinese character recognition system. Chinese Journal of Pattern Recognition and Artificial Intelligence 12 (1999) 121–124
8. Yang, T. N., Wang, S. D.: A rotation invariant printed Chinese character recognition system. Pattern Recognition Letters 22 (2001) 85–95
9. Yuen, P. C., Feng, G. C., Tang, Y. Y.: Printed Chinese character similarity measurement using ring projection and distance transform. Int. J. Pattern Recognition and Artificial Intelligence, 12 (1998) 209–221
10. Zadeh, L. A.: A fuzzy-algorithmic approach to the definition of complex or imprecise concepts. Int. J. Man-Machine Studies 8 (1976) 249–291

Recognition of On-line Handwritten Mathematical Expressions Using a Minimum Spanning Tree Construction and Symbol Dominance

Ernesto Tapia and Raúl Rojas

Freie Universität Berlin, Institut für Informatik
Takustr. 9, D-14195 Berlin, Germany
{tapia, rojas}@inf.fu-berlin.de

Abstract. We present a structural analysis method for the recognition of on-line handwritten mathematical expressions based on a minimum spanning tree construction and symbol dominance. The method handles some layout irregularities frequently found in on-line handwritten formula recognition systems, like symbol overlapping and association of arguments of sum-like operators. It also handles arguments of operators with non-standard layouts, as well as tabular arrangements, like matrices.

1 Introduction

Recognizing mathematical formulae is an important pattern recognition problem, because mathematical expressions constitute an essential part of the notation in most scientific disciplines. In *off-line* recognition, handwritten or printed formulas are given in the form of images or bit-maps, a *static representation* of the data. In *on-line* recognition, computers with pen devices (graphic tablets, contact sensitive whiteboards, Tablet PCs) store the data as *digital ink*, a *dynamic representation* which is in essence a sequence of points with temporal information.

We follow a two-step approach to recognize on-line handwritten mathematical expressions [5, 1, 2]. The first step is to divide static or dynamic data into groups of strokes, which are interpreted as single objects. A list of objects and their *attributes* (location, size, etc.) is returned. The only missing attribute for an object is its identity, which is determined using a classifier. The second step is to apply some *structural analysis* technique to obtain a hierarchical structure of the expression which describes the mathematical relationships among the symbols.

One important problem in structural analysis is the irregular writing of users, which derives in layout problems affecting the recognition of the expression. This difficulties can be overcome if the writer works with an editor which allows immediate feedback and has undo-redo and visualization capabilities [7]. A very different situation occurs when the recognition of mathematical expressions is

J. Lladós and Y.-B.Kwon(Eds.): GREC 2003, LNCS 3088, pp. 329–340, 2004.
© Springer-Verlag Berlin Heidelberg 2004

used as an auxiliary tool embedded in another system [4, 8]. This limits the interaction between the user and the recognition engine: structural analysis has to be so flexible as possible. Zanibbi et al. [9] propose a system which handles horizontal layout irregularities using a data structure which exploits the left-to-right reading of mathematical expressions. Matsakis [6] developed a method for stroke grouping called minimum spanning tree constraint, which bases the structural analysis on the proximity of symbols. Combining both approaches, we developed a method, which handles symbol overlapping and argument association for operators, besides horizontal layout irregularities.

This manuscript describes the structural analysis method we developed and is organized as follows. Section 2 introduces the concepts we need for the rest of the text. In Sect. 3 we describe the construction of the minimum spanning tree based on symbol dominance. Section 4 concludes with some comments about this work.

2   Structural Analysis of Mathematical Expressions

As mentioned in the previous section, the raw data considered in on-line recognition are points with time information. A stroke is a sequence of points generated between pen-down and pen-up events. A symbol is a sequence of strokes constructed by applying some grouping heuristic or segmentation algorithm.

To simplify structural analysis of the expression, we consider as the *basic attributes* of a symbol s its label and its bounding box. The label is obtained by means of a classifier and the bounding box is defined by the minimum x and y coordinates (x_s, y_s) of all points in the symbol, its height H_s, and weight W_s.

Once raw symbols are endowed with attributes, we collect them in *ordered attributed lists*. The order of a symbol in a list is determined by its leftmost x coordinate, i.e. if the list L is formed by the symbols $(s_1, \ldots, s_k)$, it means that $x_{s_i} \leq x_{s_j}$ for $i < j$. The attributes of a list L are its label and its bounding box attributes (x_L, y_L), H_L and W_L. The label of a symbol list is obtained during the structural analysis process by the spatial and geometrical relations between symbols, as described in Sect. 2.1.

2.1   Symbol Regions and Symbol Attributes

Relations and operator dominance in mathematical notation are defined explicitly or implicitly by the position and relative size of symbols in an expression. The spatial regions *top-left*, *above*, *superscript*, *right*, *subscript*, *below*, *below-left* and *subexpression* are used to determine such relations. For example, the operands (numerator and denominator) of the horizontal bar (fraction operator) are expected to lie in the regions above and below of the horizontal bar. See Fig. 1.

By comparing symbol attributes, we can test whether or not a symbol belongs to a determined spatial region. The *superscript threshold* and the *subscript threshold* are numeric attributes used to delimit the regions around symbols. The *centroid* is a point attribute used to determinate the symbol's location.

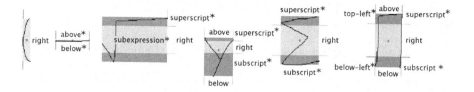

Fig. 1. Regions, thresholds and centroids of different symbol types. From left to right: non-scripted, horizontal bar, square root, scripted, sum-like and the product operator. The regions marked with an asterisk determine the range of different symbol types

To determine this symbol's attributes, we classify it as *ascendent, descendent* or *central*, as shown in Table 1. The reason for doing so becomes clear if we observe the layout differences in the subindex relation of the central symbol x_* and the descendent symbol y_*. The attributes for a symbol s are shown in Table 2. After obtaining symbol attributes we can determine which region symbols lie in. For example, given the symbols s and a we can define a boolean function to determine if a lies in the above region of s, as follows:

Table 1. The symbols used in our system

	scripted	superscripted	non-scripted	sum-like
ascendent	$b\ d\ \partial\ \Delta$	0 1 2 3 4 5 6 7 8 9		
descendent	y			
central	$a\ c\ x\ z\ )$	$e\ \pi\ \sqrt{\ }$	$+ - * / \uparrow (\ \infty$	$\sum \int \Pi$

Table 2. Attributes for different symbol types

	super threshold	sub threshold	centroid
ascendent	$y_s + 0.8H_s$	$y_s + 0.2H_s$	$(x + 0.5W_s, y + 0.33H_s)$
descendent	$y_s + 0.9H_s$	$y_s + 0.6H_s$	$(x + 0.5W_s, y + 0.66H_s)$
central	$y_s + 0.8H_s$	$y_s + 0.2H_s$	$(x + 0.5W_s, y_s + 0.5H_s)$

liesInAboveRegion(s, a)
    1. Return getMinX$(s) \leq$ getCentroidX$(a) \leq$ getMaxX(s) &&
       getSuperThreshold$(s) \leq$ getCentroidY(a).

For other regions we proceed in a similar way.

2.2   Symbol Dominance

The *range* of an operator is the expected location of its operands, see Fig. 1. Chang [3] defines dominance as follows. A symbol s *dominates* a symbol a, if a is in the range of s, and s is not in the range of a. We say that symbols *dominate* their arguments. Arguments have lower *precedence* than the dominant symbol.

We define dominates(s, a) as a boolean relation which depends on the set of *operator classes*

$$T = \{-, \sqrt{}, \text{scripted}, \text{superscripted}, \text{non-scripted}, \text{sum-like operators}\},$$

the spatial regions and symbol attributes of s and a. The symbol '$-$' represents the horizontal bar and '$\sqrt{}$' the square root. If dominates(s, a) is true, it means that s dominates a.

To clarify the concept of dominance, we give some examples. Consider the sum symbol in Fig. 2(a). It dominates the symbol '∞', because the last is in the range (superscript region) of the first and we do not expect any symbol lying on some of the regions of '∞'. Analogously, the constant 'e' in Fig. 2(b) dominates the symbols '$-$' and '$\int$'. The horizontal bar lies in the superscript region of 'e', but the last does not lie above or below the symbol '$-$'. Observe that 'e' lies in the range of the integral, but the dominance in this case is resolved by comparing their size. Figure 2(c) also shows a case where symbol dominance is not clear. We cannot determine which one of the fraction lines dominates the other, because both of them lie in the range of the other and have the same size. We can avoid the confusion here by taking as the dominant fraction bar the one with the greater centroid's y-coordinate. Observe that we added some extra conditions to the definition of Chang, namely comparison between symbol's sizes and attributes, to determine dominance and to resolve ambiguity.

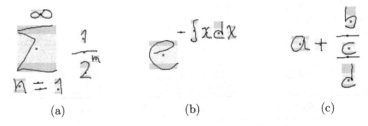

(a)   (b)   (c)

Fig. 2. Examples of expressions where (a) dominance is determined by the range, (b) dominance is determined by considering symbol sizes and (c) dominance between fraction lines is hard to determine

As we can see in this examples, dominance can be established by convention and can vary from an author to another. Different formulations of dominance define diverse *dialects* of mathematical notation.

2.3   Baseline Representation of Expressions

We describe mathematical notation as a hierarchical structure of nested baselines [9]. A *baseline* is a list which represents a horizontal arrangement of symbols in the expression. Each symbol has links to other baselines, which satisfy the spatial relations mentioned in Sect. 2.2, relative to it. For example, the expression $x_{ij} * y + \frac{a+b}{c}$ is determined by the baselines $(x, *, y, +, -)$, (i, j), $(a, +, b)$

and (c). The last two baselines satisfy the relations *above* and *below* relative to the horizontal bar, respectively.

This representation exploits the left-to-right reading of mathematical expressions. When reading an expression, one normally searches for the leftmost dominant symbol, then for the next leftmost dominant one and so on, until no more symbols are found. Given an ordered symbol list L, we can determine the leftmost dominant symbol in L through the function getDominantSymbol, which is defined as:

getDominantSymbol(L)
1. Let $n = $ length(L).
2. If $n == 1$ return s_1.
3. If s_n dominates s_{n-1}, remove s_{n-1} from L, in other case remove s_n.
4. Return getDominantSymbol(L).

Observe that this function uses the order of symbols in L.

In this way, given a list L, we construct its dominant baseline Db through function:

getDominantBaseline(Db, L)
1. If Db is empty, then set $Db = $ addSymbol($Db,$ getDominantSymbol(L)).
2. Set $s = $ getLastSymbol(Db).
3. Constructs a list $Hs = $ getRightNeighbors(s, L) of symbols in L which are right horizontal neighbors of s.
4. If Hs is empty, return.
5. Find the dominant symbol of the horizontal neighbors,
   $sd = $ getDominantSymbol(Hs).
6. Set $Db = $ addSymbol(Db, sd).
7. Use recursion: getDominantBaseline(Db, L).

We take special care in the definition of the function getRightNeighbors (step 3), to handle irregular horizontal layouts.

Now, we are ready to construct the baseline tree of the mathematical expression described by the ordered symbols list L by finding recursively dominant baselines. This is done by the function constructBaselineMST:

constructBaselineMST(L)
1. If L is empty, return.
2. Set $Db = \emptyset$.
3. getDominantBaseline(Db, L).
4. constructDominanceMST(Db, L)
5. For each symbol $s \in Db$, construct new symbols lists with its children obtained in the MST step, depending which spatial relations they satisfy and assign this lists to the corresponding links. The identity of this lists corresponds to the spatial relation they satisfy.
6. Set $L = Db$.
7. For each symbol $s \in Db$, use recursion applying constructBaselineMST to each of the child lists obtained in step 5.

Next section explains how this is done.

3   A Minimum Spanning Tree Construction and Symbol Dominance

The *minimum spanning tree (MST)* constraint method [6], considers the centers of the stroke bounding boxes as nodes of a completely connected weighted graph. Although this approach seems to be robust for stroke grouping (based on the minimization of a sum cost function), it lacks a robust method to carry out structural analysis. Compare Fig. 3(a) and Fig. 3(d).

Our experiments show that we can avoid many shortcomings in structural analysis if we use symbol dominance information to construct the MST. This method is described in the next three sections.

3.1   Weight Calculation Based on Attractor Points

We consider the previously recognized symbols as the nodes of a totally connected weighted graph. Then, we use Prim's algorithm to construct its MST: a new edge (s_t, s_n) is added to the MST if its corresponding weight $w(s_t, s_n)$ is the minimum of all edges, where s_t belongs to the MST and s_n does not belong to the MST. The function constructMST(Db, L) constructs the MST of the symbol list L. This is done by initializing the MST to $\{(s_1, s_2), \ldots, (s_{k-1}, s_k)\}$ where the symbols s_i belong to the dominant baseline $Db = (s_1, \ldots, s_k)$. In our method, the crucial step is the weight calculation of edges, where we use symbol dominance.

If dominates(s_t, s_n) is true, the weight $w(s_t, s_n)$ is the minimum distance between *attractor points* of symbols s_t and s_n. If dominates(s_t, s_n) is false, the weight corresponds to the distance between the centroids of s_t and s_n. Finally, if the relation right(s_t, s_n) or right(s_n, s_t) is true, the weight is the minimum distance among their corresponding black points as shown in the second a of Fig. 4. Figure 3(b) shows the first recursion step of constructMST without using dominance analysis.

The attractor points are located in the boundary of the symbol bounding box. The number of such points depends on the operator class. Figure 4 shows the attractor points corresponding to the different symbol classes when the first a and the integral (sum-like operators and square root) are dominated by x (scripted) and 2 (superscripted), the second a is dominated by + (non-scripted) and when the third a is dominated by sum-like operators and the horizontal bar.

3.2   Arguments to Special Operators

The range of symbols in the dominant baseline is not limited by the threshold attributes alone but also by "neighbor" operators [9]. Figure 5 shows how attractor points and symbol dominance help to define dominance regions. To draw the regions, we proceed as follows. Firstly, we take a pixel from the whole region and translate the symbol 'a', leftmost symbol in the region, such that its centroid and the pixel coincide. Secondly, we associate each symbol in the

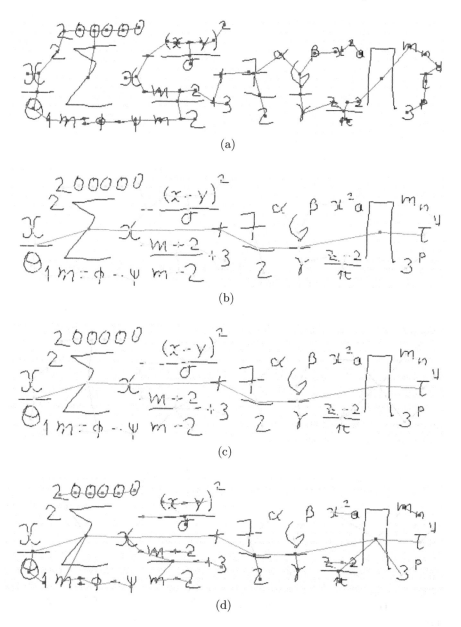

Fig. 3. (a) Minimum spanning tree of strokes. MST of the first recursion step of our method (b) without using dominance analysis and (c) using dominance analysis. (b) Final tree of spatial relations

baseline $(x, -, y, \sum, z, \prod)$ with different grey tones. Finally, the pixel is colored with the grey tone corresponding to the "nearest" symbol of the baseline, in terms of the edge weight used in the MST construction. Figure 5(a) shows the

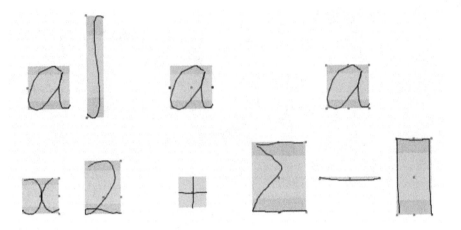

Fig. 4. Above: Attractor points of symbols not belonging to the MST. Below: Attractor points of symbols and operators belonging to the MST

regions for each symbol, using the distance between centroids as edge weights. We can appreciate in Fig. 5(b) that using symbol dominance to delimit regions, corresponds to the expected range of symbol operators.

Figure 5(d) shows how the range can be extended during MST construction. In this example, the regions of the symbols z and a are merged in such a way that the new symbol b lies in their range and ambiguities arising from argument association with $\prod$ are overcome. The regions were found as described before, but in this case we use the symbol b instead of a.

It can be seen why using the MST construction allows more flexibility to handle irregular layouts. For example, this is the case when we change an expression by adding some super indexes after entering it. The same applies when associating arguments to non-standard operators as ${}^*_*\prod{}^*_*$ as shown in Fig. 3.

Our method encounters problems when scripted symbols lie too close to the arguments of fraction or sum-like operators. The horizontal baselines of dominated symbols are merged incorrectly, when they are written too far away from operators and the last are written to close to each other. See Fig. 5(c) and Fig. 6(a) for an example of this. To avoid the problem, we multiply the corresponding weight by a factor $0 < \alpha < 1$ during MST construction, when the symbol in the dominant baseline is a sum-like operator or a fraction line. See Fig. 6(b).

3.3   Recognition of Matrices and Tabular Arrangements

The symbol '[' and ']' were taken as reserved symbols to construct matrices. The range of the symbol '[' is the bounding box which contains it and its corresponding closing square bracket.

After building the MST, we check for each $s \in Db$ whether it is an open square bracket or not. If it is, we proceed to identify row structures in the child

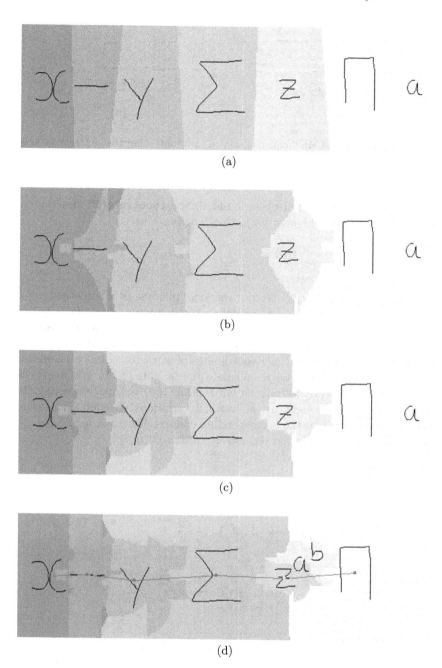

(a)

(b)

(c)

(d)

Fig. 5. Regions defined (a) using only the centroids, (b) using the attractor points and symbol dominance without distance factor and (d) with distance factor. (d) Growing regions in the MST construction

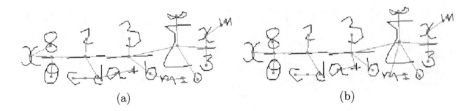

(a)   (b)

Fig. 6. The result of the MST construction (a) without using the α factor in weight calculation and (b) using the factor

list Ds of symbols dominated by s (found by the `countructMST` function). To this purpose, we define the *area projection function* f as

$$f(y) = \sum_{\substack{s \cdot Ds \\ y_s \cdot y \cdot y_s + H_s}} W_s H_s, \tag{1}$$

where $y_{Ds} \leq y \leq y_{Ds} + H_{Ds}$. We use the local maxima of a smoothed version of f, located at y_i, $i = 1, \ldots, n$, to define the attractor points (x_{Ds}, y_i) of s (see Fig. 7). The next step is to construct the MST of s and Ds using the "dynamically" constructed attractor points. Because we want to find rows in the symbol list, we multiply the x-coordinates of attractor points and centroids by a factor $0 < \beta < 1$ and we re-calculate the weights of the graph with this modification. This is a way to contract horizontally the distance between symbols in Ds and give more weight to the vertical variations of symbol's positions. Finally, we assign rows to the corresponding children lists of s, locate spaces in the rows and apply the method recursively to those lists.

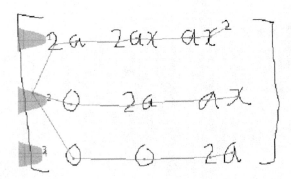

Fig. 7. The area projection function and the MST found in the matrix mode

4   Comments and Further Work

We presented a method for the structural analysis of on-line handwritten mathematical expressions based on a minimum spanning tree construction and symbol dominance. Our experiments showed that our method is robust to handle some layout irregularities. Our method handles non-standard layouts, like $\overset{*}{\underset{*}{\prod}}{}^{*}$. This can be easily extended to recognize expression which contains operators like $_nC_k$, or other operators which similar layouts. We also consider a method for the recognition of tabular arrangements, which can be easily extended to recognize stacked arguments of sum-like operators, like the one used in (1). This two characteristics are not found in other systems for on-line recognition. Fig. 8 shows some examples of expressions recognized by the current system.

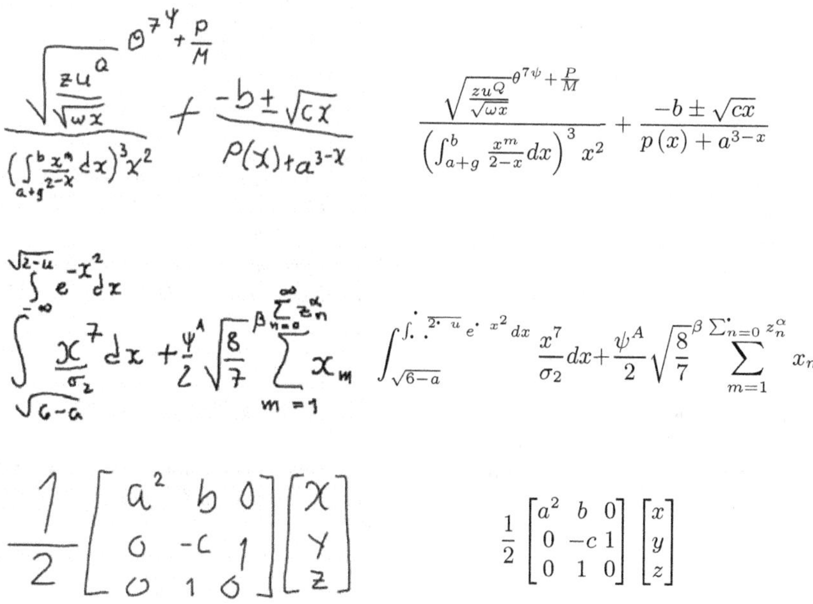

Fig. 8. Some expressions recognized by our current system

The recognition of on-line handwritten symbols is done using support vector machines and neural networks [8]. It is clear that some classification errors can occur. This could be problematic, for example, when recognizing the operator '$\int$' as '5', because our structure analysis assumes perfect symbol recognition. To avoid it, we can use an interface similar to the one we developed in [7], which allows immediate feedback and has undo-redo and visualization capabilities.

Determining heuristic values for α and β as described in the previous section, requires some experimentation. We have obtained satisfactory results by using the values $\alpha = 1/4$ and $\beta = 1/15$. We plan to construct a benchmark of on-line handwritten mathematical expression to determine the optimal values of the parameters α and β and the other ones required by our algorithm, as well as to obtain a numerical estimation of recognition rates.

The motivation of this research is to incorporate formula and gesture recognition capabilities in the electronic chalk board (E-Chalk), a multimedia system for distance-teaching [4, 8]. At present, E-chalk can convert the stored lectures into PDF format. One of our objectives is that lectures will be converted also into some electronic format like LaTeX.

Acknowledgments

The authors like to thank the anonymous reviewers for a variety of suggestions that helped to improve this paper. Ernesto Tapia thanks the Mexican National Council for Science and Technology (CONACyT) for its financial support during his Ph.D. studies via the credit-scholarship number 154901.

References

1. D. Blostein and A. Grbavec. Recognition of Mathematical Notation. In P. S. P. Wang and H. Bunke, editors, *Handbook on Optical Character Recognition and Document Analysis*. World Scientific Publishing Company, 1996.
2. Kam-Fai Chan and Dit-Yan Yeung. Mathematical Expression Recognition: a Survey. *International Journal on Document Analysis and Recognition (IJDAR)*, 3(1):3–15, 2000.
3. S. Chang. A Method for the Structural Analysis of Two-Dimensional Mathematical Expressions. *Information Sciences*, 2:253–272, 1970.
4. G. Friedland, L. Knipping, and R. Rojas. E-Chalk Technical Description. Technical Report B-02-11, Freie Universität Berlin, Institut für Informatik, 2002.
5. H. J. Lee and J. S. Wang. Design of a Mathematical Expression Undrestanding System. In *Proceedings of the Third International Conference on Document Analysis and Recognition (ICDAR)*, pages 1084–1087, 1995.
6. N. Matsakis. Recognition of Handwritten Mathematical Expressions. Master's thesis, Massachusetts Institute of Technology, Cambridge, MA, May 1999.
7. E. Tapia. JMathNotes: A Java-Based Editor for On-Line Handwritten Mathematical Expressions, January 2004. http://www.inf.fu-berlin.de/~tapia/JMathNotes.
8. E. Tapia and R. Rojas. Recognition of On-Line Handwritten Mathematical Formulas in the E-Chalk System. In *Proceedings of the Seventh International Conference on Document Analysis and Recognition (ICDAR)*, August 2003.
9. R. Zanibbi, D. Blostein, and J. Cordy. Recognizing Mathematical Expressions Using Tree Transformation. *IEEE Transactions on Pattern Analysis and Machine Intelligence*, 24(11), November 2002.

Making User's Sketch into a Motion Picture
for Visual Storytelling on the Web

Yang-Hee Nam

Division of Digital Media, Ewha Womans University,
11-1 Daehyun-dong, Seodaemun-gu, Seoul, South Korea
yanghee@ewha.ac.kr

Abstract. This paper introduces a cheap engineering solution of authoring and presenting user's own story in the form of animation on the world wide web. Most of existing story-making tools allow users to choose characters from a given database because model building task is time-consuming and requires some level of expertise. Comparatively, we suggest an easy 'three-dimensionalizing' method by incorporating user's own 2D sketches of characters, scenes and text to the story and by making them finally be presented in the form of 3D-like animation semi-automatically on the web.

1 Introduction

A Story is one of the important ways of communication and of cultivating creativity. For decades, most of elementary school teachers in Korea have given their students a so-called 'picture diary' homework so as to cultivate children's ability of thought, imagination and expression.

In this digital era, there have been digitally shared authoring tools such as wiki wiki web and storyspace [1]. These are text-based softwares regarding efficiency appropriate for serious writers. There have also been many commercial tools or games developed for visual story making such as SimCity, StoryMaker, ComicChat, and so on [2]. These can offer easy and fast ways of developing stories with corresponding visuals. The main purpose of these softwares, however, is usually not general story making but special purpose games or chatting. Also, the user's creativity tends to be limited to build expectable stories with some choice of characters and scene objects from the existing database.

Comparatively, we present a general story building environment where our research focuses on a way of incorporating user's own sketches of characters and scenes for the story. The story can finally be presented in the form of 3D-like animation on the web. Usually, there are two ways of creating user's own objects. One is to let users draw every necessary image frames for the animation. The other way lets users build their own 3-dimensional graphical models representing scenes and characters. The problem is that the both approaches are time consuming and quite difficult for general users to use. They thus make users difficult to focus on the story devel-

J. Lladós and Y.-B. Kwon (Eds.): GREC 2003, LNCS 3088, pp. 341–352, 2004.
© Springer-Verlag Berlin Heidelberg 2004

opment itself. Online authoring is, of course, not recommended in such time consuming approaches.

Our approach deals with the above problems by giving users 2D constrained sketching environment and by putting the cartoon-style sketches into a 3-dimensionalized scene. The sketches are drawn in 2-dimensional plane, but they stand and behave in a 3D world as paper-dolls that children often play with in a real-world. The 3-dimensionalizing process is based on automatic sketch analysis and generation of view sequences according to the story text.

The resulting web-based digital storytelling system will have further applications on various fields such as online education, interactive movies with multiple users' participation, and other interactive multimedia services [3].

The next section introduces an overall design of online storytelling framework, and the 3rd section describes sketch analysis methods for model building. Section 4 shows how the sketched objects are incorporated into the story animation with automatic camera control according to time. We finally give a conclusion and discuss our further research in Section 5.

2   Design of a Web-based Visual Storytelling System

This section discusses system requirements for shared digital storytelling. We first present our design of system components. By web-based visual storytelling system, we refer such a system in that the users can build their story text with the associated visuals while cooperating with other remote users. Also, a story will be developed with an appropriate timeline.

The main requirements for this kind of systems are identified as below:

- The ability of fast and easy modeling for the shape, attributes and behavior for main characters and scenes.
- The capability of scripting or inputing user's story text across time.
- Association with visuals and texts in an appropriate timeline.
- The capability of inter-communication between users commonly participating to an authoring process.
- Automatic and appropriate synchronization of authoring status between users sharing a story.
- The playback system for visualizing the spatio-temporal development of a story. This reveals the flow of text with the corresponding camera movement for the generating scenes.

Based on the above requirements, the client architecture of our web-based visual storytelling system is designed as Fig. 1. The main component named as Story Builder allows users the basic establishment for a target story such as date and weather condition. Also, it provides the most important part of the system - text input and visual sketchbook environment. These two different kinds of inputs can be associated each other using timeline manager. Users can also specify where to put their sketch objects into the scene using the visual sketchbook. And a remote user can help organizing scenes using helper tools.

Visualization Manager is responsible for generating the animation sequence of scenes built from the sketches. If it generates animation sequences directly with 2D images given by users, it should solve 2D interpolation problem which is known very difficult without manual indication of the frame correspondence. Requesting users to specify such a correspondence for image frames is non-sense in real-time authoring systems. It also requires users to draw many numbers of images in dense intervals of time.

On the other hand, our approach analyses the 2D sketch to build the basic 3D outline structure so that 3D-like animation effect can be generated by the continuous change of viewpoint and character poses. In this case, only one or two sketch is enough for describing a diary-length story.

Networking manager transfers the story updates of a client to the server so as to keep the consistency between the clients participating the story authoring. While updating the story, a user can also communicate with remote users about the storyline and get help from a remote user for the visual authoring task that could be relatively difficult for novice young users.

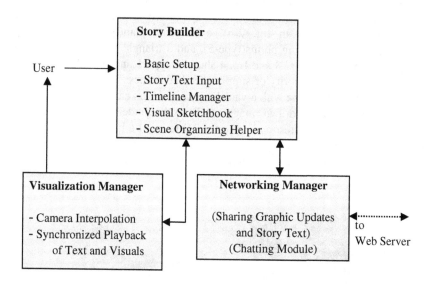

Fig. 1. Client System Architecture

3 Sketch Analysis for Making Story Objects Alive

This section presents the main idea for building a story animation from user's simple 2D drawing input. The basic concept is to make use of the information on the 3-dimensional structure implied in the sketch.

There has been an existing approach applied to generate a 3D-like navigation effect from an input image [4][5]. We can apply the approach for building an animation from a background sketch. We should also provide a method to put non-static objects into the scene and to move them. However, the existing approach to construct 3D model from 2D images are not efficient enough to apply for the real-time web based authoring [6][7][8]. Otherwise, we can model 3D objects with independent off-line tools and bring them later into web application environment, but it is also difficult and time-consuming for non-expert users. To avoid the needs of complex 3D modelling, we employ a 'paper-doll metaphor' for the main objects such as actors. In the following subsections, we introduce a paper-doll metaphor for modelling story objects and the sketch based background imaging method.

3.1 Projective Mesh Guidelines for Sketching a Story Background

Story background is a scene where the story happens. To construct a 3-dimensional background from a 2D image, we provide projective mesh guidelines to help users to set their background sketch plan. Projective mesh guidelines represent 3-D spatial plans when spaces are projected onto the 2D images. We employed 6 types of projective meshes that represent a space with a vanishing point(type-1) as shown in fig. 2(a), a horizontal plan(type-2) as in fig. 2(b), a diagonal plan(type-3), an arc-type plan(type-4), left-right vanishing points(type-5), and a triangle plan(type-6). Among many projective space plan, fig. 3 and fig. 4 shows a type-1 and type-2 mesh guidelines that are useful in the majority of simply sketched scenes. The type-1 mesh provides a sketch plan for the scene with a vanishing in it. Users can move the vanishing point interactively so that the drawn image can fit to the guideline. It is then easy to identify the sketch regions corresponding to the 3D faces of a hexahedron. The image in each region is mapped into the corresponding face as a texture. Now that the 3D scene is modelled, viewpoint animation can easily be generated.

(a) type-1 mesh overlapped   (b) type-2(horizontal)
onto the user sketch   mesh guideline

Fig. 2. Examples of projective mesh guidelines

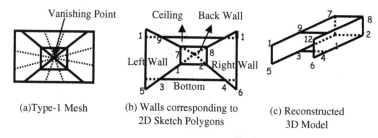

(a)Type-1 Mesh   (b) Walls corresponding to   (c) Reconstructed
                       2D Sketch Polygons   3D Model

Fig. 3. Image regions and their target 3D scene in the case of type-1 mesh [4]

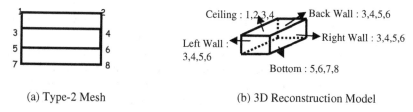

(a) Type-2 Mesh   (b) 3D Reconstruction Model

Fig. 4. Example of Reconstruction of type-2 (horizontal) mesh

3.2 Analysis of 2D Actor Sketch Using a Paper-Doll Metaphor

For putting the objects that play main roles as story actors into 3D animation, we suggest a so-called 'paper-doll metaphor' so that users can make and control their own actors easily enough. We are mentioning such a paper-doll having the following properties:

- People can easily draw and create paper-doll, while constructing a 3D doll model is a difficult task.
- In real-life, people cut a paper-doll running after one's contour. The doll has a flat shape without volume.
- Once it is cut, people can make it stand and move in a 3D space. All the motions of a paper-doll are basically controlled by bending some major joints in the body. Each joint motion has one-degree of freedom since a paper-doll can bend in the typical folding direction. Otherwise, the paper might be torn into pieces.

We thus define the paper-doll metaphor as controlling virtual actors according to the above properties. That is, the sketched image of an actor is digitally cut out according to its contour and is modelled as a flat polygonal shape without volume.

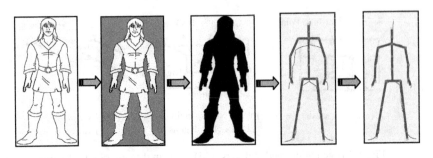

Fig. 5. Digital cutting and skeleton matching process for a digital paper-doll

Fig. 5 shows the process from automatic digital image cutting and skeleton matching against predefined body structure template. First, user draws an actor on a blank background. Otherwise, user can also load and use some popular character image. In both cases, the second step is extracing the contour of the sketched object by flood filling method [9]. As the silhouette extraction by flood filling fails if there is any hole in the shiluoette line, our interactive method warns users to draw connected curves at least for the outline. Yet the constraint does not request users additional effort or difficulty in drawing. In the third step, we cut out the character's outer region found in the previous step. During this process, the drawings of character's inner decoration are ignored. They will be considered later to map as a texture image to a 3D reconstructed model. The fourth step is carrying out a thinning on the identified object region [10]. Once the skeleton is extracted from a given sketch, we try to match between the skeleton and the corresponding template structure. During the final step, the positions of joints and the length of limbs of the skeleton template are adjusted according to the user character's relative part sizes. Using the upper and lower bounds of the spine, also the head and feet of the template, it is resized to fit the extracted bounds of the sketched object. This resulting skeleton structure will be used to control the motion of a paper-doll-like actor.

Though we can of course use more sophisticated image processing algorithm for this process of digital cutting and skeleton matching, we found it is very important that the effectiveness in time and ease of authoring on the web is kept for the usability.

Now, to use the skeleton structure for motion control, we have to know where the joints are and how their rotation axes is defined. We achieve this by predefining the template of 10 joints for human. The template has the information on the rotation axis for each joint so that the joint can bend around the axis just like folding a paper.

After matching each joint structure, the skin groups are built up by associating them with the limbs between relevant joints. Building up the groups of limbs and skin is done by dividing the polygon of the doll based on the bending axis line. As shown in fig. 6, each of the bending axes is defined as passing through the middle of the associated joint and perpendicular to the connecting limb. It thus crosses the contour line of the paper-doll. These bending axes correspond to the folding lines when children plays with a paper-doll. Since the angles of two adjacent limbs associated with a joint can have a significant difference such as in the case of shoulder joints, the axes are built up based on the average of perpendicular directions to each of two connecting limbs. The dotted rectangular region named Gn in fig. 6 indicates an polygon area belonging to the same skin group.

Based on these axes set up, users can specify the degree of rotation for each joint to generate a simple paper-doll motion. Each limb and the corresponding polygon groups act as if they stick together so that the motion of the limb is also applied to the associated polygons. After changing the character pose, the interior of the resulting silhouette is filled up with the skin group's texture warped by polygon based 3D transformation corresponding to the joint bending. Fig. 6 shows some of the examples of the resulting motion using paper-doll metaphor. The motion style is not accurate at all because our method emphasizes on the object creation using user's own sketch and easy real-time control of its 3D pose.

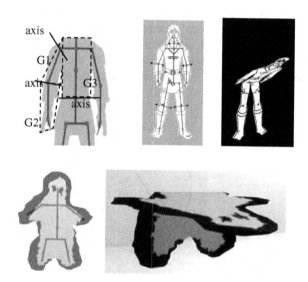

Fig. 6. Examples of bending motion using paper-doll metaphor

4   Automatic Camera Control for Visualizing the Storyline

Based on the simple sketch analysis introduced in the previous chapter, this section explains how the constructed 3D scene can automatically be presented as an animation. Since we have the background scenes and characters that are built as three-dimensional objects from 2D sketches, it is now possible to generate the animation by continuously establishing new position and direction of virtual 3D view. Now the problem is how to decide the sequence of camera positions and angles for the animation frames.

We employed an automatic camera control method to provide scene animation in addition to the actor motion. The automatic camera control makes users free from difficult set-up task of virtual camera [11][12][13][14]. Our method for camera parameter decision is visualizing the significant parts of characters or objects according to the storyline. The principles of this method is explained in detail in the author's previous work [15]. Briefly, according to the story text, the virtual camera detects the 'important target objects' of the scene first. Since these objects should be displayed in the current frame, the distance of virtual camera from them is determined so that camera's current field of view includes their bounding sphere region as fig. 7 shows. Also, the angle of the camera view is established as perpendicular to the important plane where significant interaction is occurring.

Now the problem is how to determine the important region that has to be visualized in the current frame. We employed two approaches. One is keyword spotting from the story text that user provided. We investigate the verbs in the story text sharing similar time bounds with associated visuals to decide where to show in current frame. Table 1 shows the target camera region and the corresponding examples of story keywords. Another approach is determining the scope of camera view by finding active actors(any actors with motion) and theirs interacting objects. The basic idea is same with the keyword spotting approach, but in this case we use the change of motion parameters as the clue for determining the target frame region.

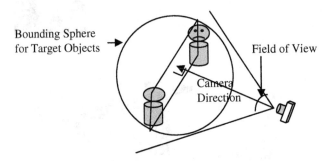

Fig. 7. Decision of virtual camera parameters to visualize the scene

Table 1. Target region to visualize with automatic camera control by story text spotting

Significant Region	Examples of Spotting Terms
Active actor's whole body + some portion of background	Walk, Enter, Approach
Active actor's whole body	Dance, Sit, Stand up
Active actor's face only	(Emotion Expression) Laugh, etc.
Active actor's upper body	(Upper body action) Shaking hands
Active actor's upper body + interacting objects	(Terms representing interaction with some objects) Touch, Interact, Pick up

Fig. 8. Insertion of actors into a scene and generated shots by virtual camera animation

Fig. 8 shows several example frames created by camera animation. The initial frame of fig. 8's first row shows the main actor standing in a position. In this scene, the virtual camera is zoomed out and visualizes the whole scene. Across time, the camera position is changed so that it can zoom the actor's upper body region. Other images show scenes created by virtual camera animation in real-time.

5   Implementation: A Shared Story Building & Animation Tool

Based on the proposed method that makes user sketch into 3D-like scenes and characters, we built up web-based shared storytelling system called DstoryOnline using Java applets and a server system. We also implemented using WildTangent library for the 3D graphics on the web.

Fig. 9 summarizes all the major process for making sketches into an animation real-time. The input story text is attached to the generated visual frames according to the timeline specification of the text. It then switches over to the next group of text according to the change of scenes. In this manner, the story text and the visuals are unfolded simultaneously. The synchronization of text flow and the sequence of the scene play is based on the timeline specified at the authoring time. Fig. 10 shows some example snapshots extracted from a continuous animation sequences generated as the result of authoring.

Those who connect to the site can join one of currently opened story rooms. They can participate to a common authoring space. To avoid the consistency problem, there are user-levels with different authoring capabilities in a story room.

The user who opened a story room first becomes the main author and the next users can only help and communicate with the main author. The users in a common story room cam share the visuals by selecting other user's 3D view and authoring sketchbook. A user can help another user's authoring process using helper's tools that provide the functions of object pointing and text-based chatting. Users can communicate

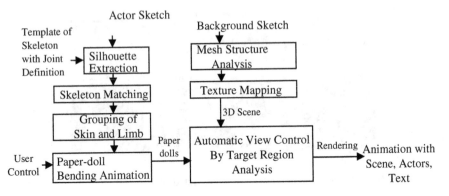

Fig. 9. From Sketch Analysis to Story Animation

each other through the chatting window. The problem of consistency can be more complex problem when a lot of users participate in the authoring in a same story room, but currently, a story is allowed to be shared by only two co-authors while the appreciation of the resulting story as an animation can be allowed to many users at the same time.

Fig. 10. Example snapshots of final presentation of stories

Whenever the set-up of writings and visuals is changed, the information is transferred to the server so that it can update and manage the status information of the story consistently. The information stored on the server includes the image of user sketched scenes and characters, the joint axes information of the character skeleton and the associated polygon skin group. The story text and changing values of actor motion parameters relating to the timeline is also stored on the server. Whenever the new information arrives, the sever broadcasts to other clients joining to the same story room.

6 Conclusions and Further Remarks

In summary, this paper describes an approach using sketch analysis and automatic view control to make it possible to simplify the process of visual story development and its presentation on the web. A web-based prototype system called DStoryOnline is constructed using Java to show the feasibility of the proposed methods. Since the scenes and objects are created based on user's quick sketches, the resulting scenes can look rough but quite interesting because the objects are user's personal creations. Finally, a story can be played as a motion-picture on the web, while attaching the corresponding story text across time. It is also verified experimentally that the real-time shared authoring is also possible at least by two people joining to the web.

This work is currently under extension to provide teacher's tool to help story creation of elementary school students. Based on our framework, the user interface for specifying motion parameters will be upgraded. Also, the keyword spotting mechanism will be more intensified by supplement the verb database.

References

1. Bolter, Joyce, Smith, *Story Space*, Computer Software, Cambridge MA: Eastgate Systems (1992).
2. Kurlander, D., Skelly T., Slesin D., Comic Chat, Proceedings of SIGGRAPH'96, New Orleans, LA (1996), 1: 225–236.
3. Kim, K. R., Lim, C. Y., A Study on the narrative structure and interaction of the interactive movie, Human-Computer Interaction Workshop (2002), Phoenix Park, Korea, CD-1.
4. Horry, Y., Anjyo K., Arai K., Tour Into the Picture : Using a Spidery Mesh Interface to Make Animation from a Single Image, Proceedings of SIGGRAPH (1997), 1:225–232.
5. Kang, H., Pyo, S., Anjyo, K., Shin, S., TIP Using a Vanishing Line & Its Extension to Panoramic Images", Eurographics (2001), Vol.20, No.3.
6. Beymer, D., Shashua, A., Poggio, T., Example based Image Analysis and Synthesis, AI Memo No. 1431, MIT (1993).
7. Kakadiaris, I., Metaxas, D., Bajcsy, R., Active Part- Decomposition, Shape and Motion Estimation of Articulated Objects: A Physics-based Approach, Proceedings Of the IEEE Computer Vision and Pattern Recognition, 1:980–994, Seattle, Washington, June (1994).
8. Agrawala, M., Beers, A., Chaddha, N., Model-based Motion Estimation for Synthetic Images, ACM Multimedia(1995).
9. Hearn, D., Baker, M. P. (ed.): Computer Graphics-C version, Prentice Hall (1997).
10. Zhang, T. Y., Suen, C.Y., A Fast Parallel Algorithm for Thinning Digital Patterns, Communications of the ACM (1984) vol. 27, no. 3, pp 236–239.
11. Drucker, S. M., et al., CINEMA: A system for procedural camera movements, In: David Zeltzer (eds.): Computer Graphics(Symposium on Interactive 3D Graphics) (1992) vol.25, pages 67–70.
12. Christianson, D.B., et al., Declarative Camera Control for Automatic Cinematography, In : Proceedings of the AAAI (1996).
13. Blinn, J., Where Am I? What Am I Looking At?, IEEE Computer Graphics and Applications (1988) pages 76–81.

14.   He, Li-wei et al., The Virtual Cinematographer: A Paradigm for Automatic Real-Time Camera Control and Directing, In Computer Graphics (SIGGRAPH'96 Proceedings) (1996) pages 217–224, August 1996.

15.   Nam, Y., Thalmann, D., CAIAS : Camera Agent based on Intelligent Action Spotting for Real-Time Participatory Animation in Virtual Stage, 5th International Conference on Virtual Systems and Multi-Media(VSMM), Scotland, UK (1999).

Invisible Sketch Interface in Architectural Engineering

Pierre Leclercq

LuciD Lab for User Cognition & Intelligent Design
University of Liège, Belgium
pierre.leclercq@ulg.ac.be
www.lema.ulg.ac.be/LuciD

Abstract. In this paper, we propose to discuss the concept of the "invisible interface", as an user interface compatible with the cognitive process involved in architectural sketching. We present the principles of such an interface, and illustrate them by our software prototype *EsQUIsE*.

1 The Sketch as a Design Tool

Sketches are widely used at the start of the design process by architects in building engineering. These drawings, initially abstract, gradually evolve into more geometrical representations of the desired object. Used at first to represent graphically the basic elements of the problem, they evolve towards more conventional representations of the project [16]. The sketch is used as a graphic simulation space: the basic elements of the project, set down in the earliest drawings, are progressively transformed until a complete solution to the problem is reached. Each sketch therefore represents an intermediate state between the first rough sketch and the definitive design solution (we have to underline that the sketches that we are dealing with here are "design drawings" rather than "presentation drawings" which are unconnected with the design process and only appear much later on, according to the Fraser and Henmi classification [6].

But the sketch is not simply an externalization of the designer's mental image [10,17, 18], it is also a heuristic field of exploration within which the designer discovers new interpretations in his or her own drawing, opening up an avenue to new perspectives for solutions. This fact explains the role played by the sketch in the search for solutions [1, 7, 8, 15].

The use of a sketch-based interface in a design assistance system should not be seen simply as an improvement to the interaction between user and machine, but as the means to integrate computer assistance into the very heart of the design process.

We have just seen that the sketch plays a major role in the designer's creativity. If we want to capture the project at the very moment of its conception without disturbing the course of the design process, the designer's freedom must not suffer the least hindrance. The problem of the interface is therefore a crucial one and concerns now a variety of approaches [2, 3, 4, 9].

In this article we will set out the necessary characteristics of such an user interface. Our research in this area over several years [11, 12, 14], as well as the develop-

J. Lladós and Y.-B. Kwon (Eds.): GREC 2003, LNCS 3088, pp. 353–363, 2004.

ment of our prototype EsQUIsE, has led us to specify various demands on the user interface of such systems.

We have called "invisible interface" an user interface demonstrating the four characteristics we consider essential for the early stages of a design: adaptability, naturalism, transparency and common-sense knowledge. This term expresses the fact that the system must fade completely into the background, and its presence must not be felt until the moment when the designer expressly requires its assistance. To understand fully the implications of the invisible interface we will look at the characteristics of EsQUIsE, a prototype application for the capture and interpretation of architectural sketches, in the second part of this article. In the third part we will define the invisible interface, then illustrate its characteristics in the functioning of our prototype.

2 The Sketching Prototype

EsQUIsE is a prototype application for interpretation of architectural sketches. Fully developed in Common Lisp, it captures the lines of an architectural sketch hand-drawn on a digital pad. It is then capable of deducing in real time the spaces enclosed within these lines and to associate them with characteristics appropriate to such places, by means of a character recognition module. The semantic model built up in this way is used to inform different evaluators about the performances of the building. EsQUIsE is made up of two modules that act consecutively (Fig. 1). The first, the entry module, captures then analyzes the graphic information in order to construct a geometrical model of the sketch. The second, the interpretation module, interprets the geometrical model according to the field of design in order to construct a functional model of the planned object, intended to provide appropriate information to various evaluators [13]. The figure 2 shows an example of a session screen copy.

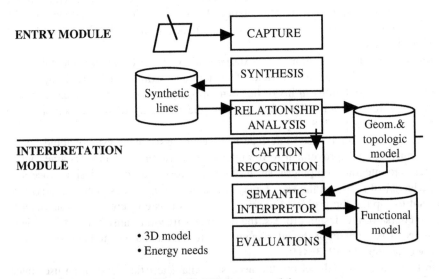

Fig. 1. EsQUIsE main modules

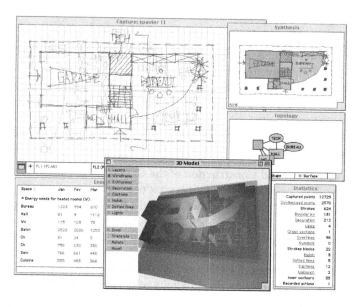

Fig. 2. Screen copy of the EsQUIsE prototype. Top-left image: capture of a hand-drawn sketch • Top-right: generation of the geometric and topologic models. Down-right: recognized items and 3D generated model • Down-left: evaluation of the model energy needs

2.1 The Entry Module

The role of the entry module consists in analyzing the drawing in order to construct the geometrical model of the sketch, in other words, the internal representation of the structure of the drawing: the significant graphic elements and the relationships they maintain.

The principal constraint on such a system is obviously the requirement that it should work in real time. Analysis therefore takes place in two phases. While the electronic stylus is being moved over the pad, the system captures the designer's movements. Then, as soon as a line is finished, the system takes advantage of the time lapse available before the start of the next line to run all the procedures to synthesize and analyze the layout.

Capture and Synthesis of Lines. The capture module receives the raw coordinates of the points relayed by the digital pad. It decomposes the sketch into lines, the first level of drawing recognition in our model. A line begins when the stylus is placed on the pad and ends when it is taken off. To limit the amount of information to be processed in later stages, an initial filtering of the data is carried out during the capture process.

The synthesis module consists of a series of successive filters intended to extract the essential characteristics of the lines, reducing by as much as possible the amount of information to be processed while conserving as faithfully as possible the appearance of the original line. To ensure that the sketch retains its "triggering potential", this step is carried out transparently for the user, who only ever works on his or her initial drawing, unaware of any interpretation being made by the system.

Recognition of Captions and Symbols. Taking advantage of the fact that the synthesis module has coded the drawing, a caption and symbol recognition procedure is run as soon as a line has been synthesized. The user can thus characterize quite naturally the elements in his or her composition. Analysis of the relationships between the captions and the rest of the drawing enables the system to identify the element defined in this way. EsQUIsE associates the captions with the outline they belong to, enabling it to deduce the characteristics of the rooms.

Analysis of Relationships and Construction of the Geometrical Model. The aim of the analysis of the drawing is to weave the network of relationships between the different graphic objects it contains. Relationships include, for example, inclusion, intersection, proximity and superposition of lines and contours.

Because the sketch is imprecise, we have developed a "fuzzy graphics" approach that takes into account a considerable margin of error in the identification of points, lines and intersections. Outlines, for example, do not need to be fully closed-off in order to be recognized. By analyzing the proximity of the ends of the lines, EsQUIsE is able to identify an imprecise outline.

2.2   The Interpretation Module

The job of the interpretation module is to translate the geometrical information, produced by capturing the sketch, into a functional model of the planned architectural object.

This interpretation is highly dependent on the specific semantics of the design field: figure 3, for example, shows some of the links established by EsQUIsE's interpretation module between geometrical concepts (on the left) and architectural concepts (on the right).

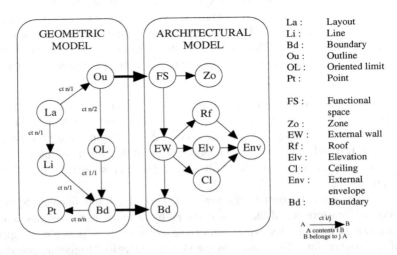

Fig. 3. Relationship between geometrical and functional models in EsQUIsE

We chose to represent the architectural model on a simplified structure diagram where the ordinate shows the level of abstraction at which the designer sees the problem (left part of Fig. 4). On the global level, the process evolves from highly abstract to more concrete, while, on the local level, the process evolves in a much less straightforward way: the designer sometimes decides to explore an idea in greater depth and at other times deciding to increase the level of abstraction so as to relax the constraints on the design.

In order to remain functional and relevant at every stage in the process, the model has to be able to adapt to these different levels of abstraction. It is therefore structured in several layers, each at a different level of abstraction.

The right part of figure 4 shows the three layers used in EsQUIsE's architectural model. In the center, the "frontiers level" is the model's first level of interpretation. It is deduced directly from the boundaries contained in the geometrical model. By analyzing the contact between the frontiers, the system constructs a more abstract representation of the building, made up of functional spaces and the adjacency relationships that they maintain. At the lowest - i.e. the most concrete - level there are the "detailed frontiers" that make up the model of the product, ready to be used in whatever ways are required during the production phase. This classification of information into different levels ensures that the model remains consistent throughout the process.

Because it is organized in layers with different levels of abstraction, the model built up in this way can support the different stages in the project being designed. This multilevel organization of the functional model also provides different access points for the project evaluators, according to their specific needs.

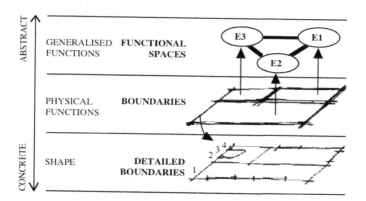

Fig. 4. The functional model of EsQUIsE, which supports the different levels of abstraction of the design process

For example, searching for similar compositions in a case base would be carried out on the basis of the topology; EsQUIsE can build the 3D architectural model with the boundaries level knowledge; whereas the "detailed frontiers level" would provide the measurements for standard CAD tools and for the energy needs evaluator.

3 The Concept of the Invisible Interface

The aim of the invisible interface is: understanding using the least possible means. It can be defined by its four characteristics: it is at the same time a adaptive, natural, transparent and intelligent interface. These terms are usually employed in the HCI domain; however, they recover different meanings according to author and context. So we suggest to define our own definitions of these terms, which we explain by the functioning of EsQUIsE.

3.1 An Adaptive System

Although every discipline uses more or less standardized graphic conventions, each architect has his or her own habits. The system must therefore be capable of supporting this unconventional dialogue mode by learning the designer's habits. For caption recognition, for example, EsQUIsE includes a learning module that builds up an alphabet for each user. In a more general way, we can say that the computer has to adapt to human behaviour, and more specifically to the fuzzy characteristics of sketches. As we saw in the previous summary of EsQUIsE, this step is managed by the synthesis module, which analyzes the hard line to build a computerized image of the project.

Figure 5 shows some examples of such mechanisms. The first window (top) shows the designer's original drawing and the second (bottom) shows the computerized version (you will recall that this second window is rendered invisible to the user who works only on his original line).

At first glance, we see that the synthesis module doesn't alter the general look of the drawing, which stays close to the original. However we see that some modifications have nevertheless been adopted. We also note that, apart from the synthesis of lines, designed to reduce the volume of computer data, the lines of the top-left corner of the rectangle has been extended, since the system considered the distance to the vertical line to be insignificant. Similarly, those parts of the lines jutting out above have not been considered to define the shape.

Unlike systems for the recognition of scanned images, the chronology of the drawing plays an essential role in our sketch recognition system. Each line is fitted into a pre-existing graphic context and is interpreted according to this order of appearance. When a designer draws two lines that are intended to meet, the contact point is never precisely positioned, the lines always being either a little too long or a little too short. It is therefore the chronology of the drawing that tells the system which line needs to be modified to preserve the consistency of the sketch. By combining chronological and geometrical information, the system can access a higher level of interpretation. For example, it can identify sequences such as captions, dotted lines, cross-hatching or blackening (figure 5), which are an aligned series of lines or graphic symbols that present the same characteristics.

For us, the adaptative interface is thus on the one hand able to adapt itself to the user himself or herself, by learning his or her working habits and, on the other hand, capable of dealing with the imprecision of human lines.

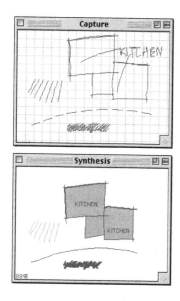

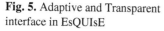

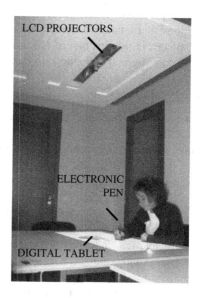

Fig. 5. Adaptive and Transparent interface in EsQUIsE

Fig. 6. The Natural interface. and the virtual desk

3.2 A Transparent Interface

A transparent interface means that the system does not require a pre-established dialogue procedure. One of the main arguments we have with a lot of sketch recognition systems is the fact that they impose a certain design method, which bears no relation to user's habits. In certain cases, the system imposes the symbols design order and, in others, the designer has to indicate when he or she is starting to draw a symbol and when it is finished.

In our system, the designer creates freely and the IT application monitors his or her actions. The context enables the system to identify the action carried out rather than the designer making use of a predefined function. A designer can thus take the tool in hand without any knowledge of its functioning. However, our system is not a recognition system suited for each user but is based on design habits peculiar to the architectural discipline. In EsQUIsE, the concept of transparent interface manifests itself in different ways. The first window (top) of figure 5, for example, shows a designer drawing sketched using EsQUIsE. The second window (bottom) shows the computerized image after synthesis. Although we note that the designer used only one colour and one thickness for his lines and doesn't give any instructions to the computer, EsQUIsE has been able to distinguish the various kinds of lines (the walls, the legends and their connecting lines) by examining chronological and geometrical relationships between user actions.

Using EsQUIsE does not require any use of the keyboard. The designer, who draws walls or writes captions, never specifies the significance of his or her actions. The system interprets the lines drawn on the pad in function of the context.

The transparent interface, perhaps more than the natural, is one of the necessary preconditions that enables a system to function at the conceptual design phase. Indeed, as we saw in the first part of this article, it is essential not to interrupt the design process by entering into dialogue with the computer.

3.3 A Natural Expression

All a designer needs to sketch a project is a piece of paper and a pencil. The aim of the natural interface is to conserve the simplicity of these tools, while at the same time achieving the same exceptional versatility.

Up to now, EsQUIsE has employed a screen pad (digital capture on an LCD screen) together with an electronic stylus as unique input device. This installation has already performed better than the traditional graphic tablet since in the latter case the parallax, which appears when a designer draws on the tablet and checks the on-screen results is eliminated. However, this system still had some drawbacks of which the most significant was undoubtedly the tablet's dimensions (18"), which limited the sketches' format and scale.

To remedy this situation, we are currently in the process of implementing a "virtual desktop" enabling the handling of much larger documents. In addition to this improvement, the virtual desktop extends the analogy to traditional working method by enabling multi-document handling on the desk (photographs, previous designs, etc.). We have carried out a prototype of the desk made up of a video projector with a mirror, enabling the screening of computer displays on a digital A0 tablet or on a 56" picture (Fig. 6).

Even though no scientific study of user behaviour in this new installation has been yet carried out, since this is still a prototype, we can however note two interesting results:

- the user's handle seems much more natural. Even though he or she mistrusts the apparently fragile screen pads, he or she soon feels comfortable on the virtual desktop;
- even though the desk's resolution is much lower than that of the screen pad, since it is limited by the projection, the system acquires details to which it didn't have access, as the scale chosen by the user is much greater.

Getting the most natural interface is obviously the primary aim of every pen computing system. However, current systems are far from being in competition with the traditional pen and paper. Carrying out a good natural interface involves giving consideration to both hardware and software parameters.

3.4 An Intelligent Interface Supplied with an Common-Sense Knowledge

A sketch is, by definition, incomplete. The designer only uses it to represent essential information, that which is specific to the current project. He or she focuses on certain problems in succession, postponing any decisions concerning other elements of the design. It is therefore quite common to come across one element that is fully defined in both shape and dimensions when the rest of the drawing is still very sketchily drawn. This way of working enables the designer to deal with the complexity of the project, going by his or her own experience to hierarchize the sub-problems that need to be resolved. The designer is only able to work in this way because he or she knows that the information that is not directly focused on is not going to cause difficulties later, or at least is only going to have a limited influence on the element being designed [11].

To fill in the information not specified by the designer, the system must be able to identify the context of the design being carried out. It is therefore capable of selecting the most relevant information in function of this context, rather than blindly settingstandard values for all its parameters. In order to feed appropriate information to the different evaluators while the project is still at the gestation stage, the system must be assisted by an implicit database specific to the particular field of design.

This omitted information must therefore be included in order to make up the functional model. By sharing this common-sense knowledge with the designer, the system can assign appropriate parameters to a design element well before these data are explicitly indicated – or even considered – by the designer. The use of this.implicit knowledge enables the system to construct a sufficiently complete model very early in the design process. The system adapts its data as and when the successive sketches are drawn, i.e. as the designer's model becomes increasingly precise.

In architecture, for example, the designer may draw a room and put a window in it. The software would search in its database and assign his/her usual sill height to the window. The designer might go on to call the newly created space "bath room". The software would consult its database and revise its decision, assigning the window a higher sill height, which would be more appropriate to the intimacy of its newly designated function. We organized this implicit database, till now by a direct coding in three hierarchically layers (Figure 7). The first layer consists of the designer's personal references: previous projects and design habits. The second layer is made up of the rules of good practice, European standards, norms, etc. Finally, the third layer contains universal references, which are independent of any context: characteristics of materials, density, conductivity, strength, etc.

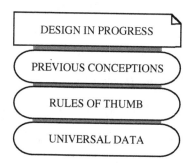

Fig. 7. Implicit knowledge of EsQUIsE

Because it is organized in layers with different levels of abstraction, the model built up in this way can support the different stages in the project being designed. Assisted by the implicit database, the system is capable of maintaining the consistency of the model, despite the incompleteness of the information it receives.

4 Conclusion – Summary

Our experience of designing sketch-based tools for architectural design support has led us to set out various demands on the user interface of such systems. It must be:

- adaptive (adapt its behaviour to the user)
- transparent (not impose a fixed dialogue protocol)
- natural(not change the habits of the designer)
- supplied with a common-sense knowledge (able to choose pertinent information according to context).

In our opinion, these four characteristics of the invisible interface are the necessary preconditions that enable a system to function at the conceptual design phase. The EsQUIsE prototype, which was developed according to these principles, has demonstrated the validity of such an approach in the field of architectural design. EsQUIsE works in two step phases. In the first step, it constructs the geometrical model of the sketch by detecting the relationships between the different elements that make up the drawing. Because this step is independent of any semantics specific to a particular field, it can be adapted to any discipline. Next, the interpretation module analyzes the geometrical model that has been built up, in order to give meaning to the sketch and constructs the semantic model of the architectural project. Thanks to an implicit knowledge base, belonging to each design discipline, this model could then provide very effective assistance to the design process because of the pertinent way it represents the object.

References

1. Ah-Soon C., & Tombre K. (1997). Variations on the Analysis of Architectural Drawings. *Proc. 4th International Conference on Document Analysis and Recognition*, pp. 347–351. Ulm, Germany.
2. Alvarado C., & Davis R. (2001a). Resolving ambiguities to create a natural sketch based interface. *Proc. IJCAI-2001*, pp. 1365–1371.
3. Alvarado C., & Davis R. (2001b). Preserving the freedom of paper in a computer-based sketch tool. *Proc. of HCI International 2001*, pp. 687–691.
4. Do, E. (1998). *The Right Tool at the Right Time - Investigation of Freehand Drawing as an Interface to Knowledge Based Design Tools*. Ph.D., Georgia Institute of Technology, USA.
5. Forbus, K., & Usher, J. (2002). Sketching for knowledge capture: a progress report. *IUI'02, California, USA*.
6. Fraser, I., & Henmi, R. (1994). *Envisioning Architecture: an analysis of drawing*. Van Nostrand Reinhold. NY.
7. Goel, V. (1995). *Sketches of thought*. MIT Press, Cambridge, MA.
8. Goldschmidt, G. (1991). The dialectics of sketching. *Design Studies vol. 4*, pp. 123–143.
9. Landay J. (1996a). SILK: Sketching Interfaces Like Krazy. *Proc. of Human Factors in Computing Systems (Conference Companion), ACM CHI '96*, pp. 398–399. Formal video program.

10. Lebahar, J.CH. (1983). *Le dessin d'architecte – Simulation graphique et réduction d'incertitude.* Éditions Parenthèses, Paris.
11. Leclercq, P. (1994). *Environnement de conception architecturale pré-intégré. Éléments d'une plate-forme d'assistance basée sur une représentation sémantique.* Doctoral thesis in applied sciences, Faculty of applied sciences, LEMA, University of Liège, Belgium.
12. Leclercq, P. (1999). Interpretative tool for architectural sketches. In *Visual and Spatial Reasoning in Design*, (Gero, J., & Tversky, B., Eds.), pp. 69–80. Key Centre of Design Computing and Cognition, Sydney, Australia.
13. Leclercq, P. (2001). Programming and Assisted Sketching. *Proc. Ninth Int Conf. CAAD Futures 2001*, (de Vries, B. et al., Eds.), pp 15–32. Kluwer Academic Publishers, Dordrecht, The Netherlands.
14. Leclercq, P., Juchmes, R., (2002). The invisible Interface in Design Engneering, in AIEDAM, Artificial Intelligence in Engineering Design & Manufacturing, Special Issue: Human-computer Interaction in Engineering Contexts, Vol.16, No. 5, Nov 2002, Cambridge University Press. (original and complete paper, synthesized here for GREC'03).
15. Mathus, P. (1994). *Analyse d'esquisses architecturales.* Thesis in architectengineering, LEMA, University of Liège, Belgium.
16. Mccall, R., Ekaterini, V., & Zabel, J. (2001). Conceptual Design as Hypersketching. *Proc. Ninth Int Conf. CAAD Futures 2001*, pp. 285–298. Kluwer Academic Publishers, Dordrecht, The Netherlands.
17. Rassmussen J. (1990). Mental models and the control of action in complexenvironments. In *Mental models and human-computer interaction 1* (Ackerman D., & Tauber M.J. Eds.), Elsevier Science Publisher B.V., Holland.
18. Suwa, M., & Tversky, B. (1996). What Architects See in Their Sketches: Implications for Design Tools. *Proc. CHI'96 Conference on Human Factors in Computing Systems*, pp. 191–192. Vancouver.

Report of the Arc Segmentation Contest

Wenyin Liu

Dept of Computer Science, City University of Hong Kong, Hong Kong SAR, PR China
`csliuwy@cityu.edu.hk`

Abstract. The Arc Segmentation Contest, as the fifth in the series of graphics recognition contests organized by IAPR TC10, was held in association with the GREC'2003 workshop. In this paper we present the report of the contest: the contest rules, performance metrics, test images and their ground truths, and the outcomes.

1   Introduction

This contest on arc segmentation held at the fifth International Workshop on Graphics Recognition (GREC'2003), Barcelona, Spain, July 30–31, 2003 is the fifth in the series of graphics recognition contests organized by the International Association for Pattern Recognition's Technical Committee on Graphics Recognition (IAPR TC10). A brief history of the contest series is presented in [1]. The purpose of this series of contests is to encourage third-party independent and objective evaluation of the industrial and academic solutions to the graphics recognition problem and therefore push the research in this area.

This contest is a re-run of the fourth contest on arc segmentation [1], but with new test images. In this paper we briefly present the final report of the contest, including the contest rules, test images and their ground truths, the winners and their performance, and discussions.

2   General Rules

The rules are exactly the same to those of the fourth contest [1], except for the new test images. The contest rules are summarized below.

- Recognition accuracy was measured on only solid arcs.
- The tested systems were run as black boxes on-site, with their configurations fixed during the contest. No human intervention was allowed.
- 12 real life or synthesized drawing images were tested. See Section 3 for detail descriptions of these test images.
- The input file format was binary TIFF and the output file format was VEC.
- Zero score would be given to participants for images that cause system crash or non-stop.

J. Lladós and Y.-B. Kwon (Eds.): GREC 2003, LNCS 3088, pp. 364–367, 2004.

- An overall average score based on each image's VRI [2] was used as the unique measure of performance of each participant's system. The performance evaluation software is also available at the contest website [4].

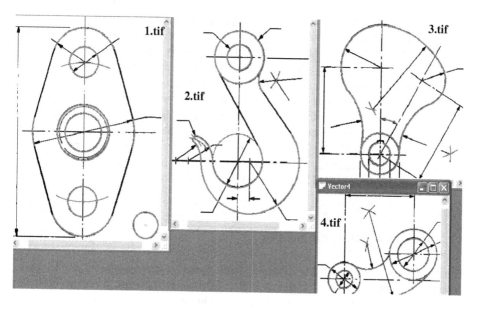

Fig. 1. The ground truth vector drawing for the four synthesized test images

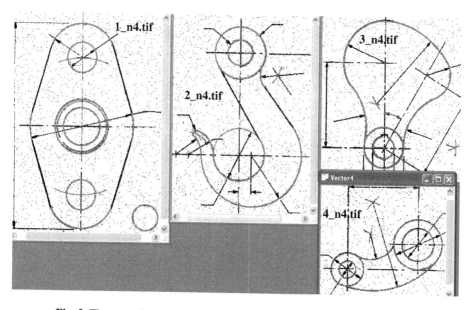

Fig. 2. The ground truth vector drawing for the four synthesized test images

3   Test Images and Their Ground Truths

In total we have used 12 test images. Four of them are generated by scanning four paper drawings in 256 grayscales and then binarizing with moderate thresholds. Their file names are 1.tif, 2.tif, 3.tif, and 4.tif, respectively, as shown in Fig. 1. The grayscale files of 1.tif and 4.tif are binarized again, but with bigger threshold, resulting thicker line widths in 1_230.tif and 4_230.tif, respectively. The grayscale files of 2.tif and 3.tif are binarized again, but with smaller threshold, resulting thinner line widths, in 2_100.tif and 3_100.tif, respectively. Some synthesized noises defined in [3] are added to 1.tif, 2.tif, 3.tif, and 4.tif, respectively and the results are 1_n4.tif, 2_n4.tif, 3_n4.tif, and 4_n4.tif, respectively, as shown in Fig. 2. The ground truth arcs of these images are obtained by manually measuring their geometry parameters. They are displayed in Fig. 1 and Fig. 2 in gray color over the test images. All ground truth vector files were stored in the VEC format. All these test images and their and ground truth files can be downloaded at the contest website [4].

4   Winners and Their Scores

This time, only two participants submitted their systems for the contest: Dave Elliman [5] and Song JiQiang [6]. The scores (*VRIs*) of their systems are listed in Table 1. Song's system obtained an overall score of 0.609 and while Elliman's obtained an overall score of 0.487. So the winner was Song JiQiang.

Table 1. The scores of the participants

Image (*.tif)	Song JiQiang's scores			Dave Elliman's scores		
	Dv	Fv	VRI	Dv	Fv	VRI
1	0.553	0.272	0.641	0.462	0.329	0.567
2	0.789	0.283	0.753	0.359	0.482	0.439
3	0.482	0.417	0.532	0.197	0.653	0.272
4	0.742	0.272	0.735	0.000	0.000	0.500
1_230	0.553	0.273	0.640	0.481	0.302	0.589
2_100	0.780	0.208	0.786	0.426	0.400	0.513
3_100	0.290	0.688	0.301	0.417	0.379	0.519
4_230	0.803	0.223	0.790	0.188	0.543	0.323
1_n4	0.446	0.428	0.509	0.488	0.159	0.664
2_n4	0.700	0.294	0.703	0.506	0.282	0.612
3_n4	0.199	0.750	0.224	0.327	0.425	0.451
4_n4	0.680	0.305	0.688	0.283	0.485	0.399
Average	0.585	0.368	0.609	0.345	0.37	0.487

5   Summary and Discussion

Compared with the previous contest, the test drawings this time are more difficult since there are many arcs tangent and connected to one another. The tangent points are hard to locate precisely, which also have strong impact on detection accuracy of the arc centers and radius. Hence, the overall scores of both participants are lower than the last time. The purpose of using all real life images with some extreme difficulties is to test the algorithms' robustness since almost all algorithms are quite good at segmenting simple isolated arcs/circles, as we saw in the last contest [1].

Again, we find from the contest results that although different approaches may work better on some images but worse on others, the overall performance on these difficult drawings is still not so satisfactory. This can be seen from their scores. After a rough analysis, we may draw a preliminary conclusion that a score of over 0.8 (VRI) may be relatively satisfactory/acceptable.

The impacts of binarization threshold and noise are no so clear since the impacts were not on the same directions. Sometimes, thick line width resulted in higher performance but sometimes, thinner width outperformed. The same cases happened for noises. Especially for Elliman's algorithm, which sometimes generated wrong arc directions, the impacts of noises and binarization threshold were even more difficult to obtain since the results were not trustable.

There is a special case for Elliman's algorithm on image 4.tif, which generated no arcs. Hence both detection rate and false alarm rate are zero. However, the VRI is 0.5, which is higher than many other images. Hence, we think we may have to re-define VRI the geometric average instead of arithmetic average of the two rates. We will try in the future contests.

Anyway, the contest had successfully attracted new participants and re-tested previously tested algorithms. We hope we can attract more participants in future contests and accumulate more and more data for a more comprehensive understanding of arc segmentation algorithms.

References

1. Liu W., Zhai J., and Dori D.: Extended Summary of the Arc Segmentation Contest. In: Graphics Recognition: Algorithms and Applications, Lecture Notes in Computer Science, volume 2390, Springer (2002), pp. 343–349.
2. Liu W. and Dori D.: A Protocol for Performance Evaluation of Line Detection Algorithms. Machine Vision and Applications 9 (1997) 240–250.
3. Zhai J., Liu W., Dori D., Li Q: A Line Drawings Degradation Model for Performance Characterization. In: Proc. ICDAR (2003), pp. 1020–1024.
4. http://www.cs.cityu.edu.hk/~liuwy/ArcContest/ArcSegContest.htm
5. Elliman D.: The Nottingham Symbol Recognition Algorithm. In: Post-Proc. of GREC2003, Lecture Notes in Computer Science (this volume), Springer (2004).
6. Song J. and Lyu M.R.: A Multi-Resolution Arc Segmentation Method. In: Post-Proc. of GREC2003, Lecture Notes in Computer Science (This volume), Springer (2004).

Symbol Recognition Contest: A Synthesis

Ernest Valveny[1] and Philippe Dosch[2]

[1] Centre de Visi per Computador, Edifici O, Campus UAB,
08193 Bellaterra (Cerdanyola), Barcelona, Spain
`ernest@cvc.uab.es`
[2] LORIA, 615, rue du jardin botanique,
B.P. 101, 54602 Villers-ls-Nancy Cedex, France
`Philippe.Dosch@loria.fr`

Abstract. In this paper, we present the synthesis of the first international symbol recognition contest, held during the fifth IAPR workshop on graphics recognition in Barcelona. We describe the framework of the contest (goals, kind of symbols, criteria of evaluation) and how the contest was organized. We expose in particular the way we have built the symbol database and which methods have been used to introduce noise in the model of the symbols, in order to evaluate the robustness of the recognition methods. The methods of the different participants are summarily described as well as the results obtained with these methods on the test images available during the contest. The evaluation protocol is presented, the results are analyzed and we conclude with some remarks for the next symbol recognition contest.

1 Introduction

Former contests held during past workshops on graphics recognition have dealt with the recognition of dashed lines (GREC'95)[1], the vectorization (GREC'97 and GREC'99)[2, 3] and the detections of arcs (GREC'01 and GREC'03)[4]. A symbol recognition contest, concerning one of the central problems in graphics recognition, has never been organized in past editions of the workshop, despite of its obvious interest. A first attempt to address the issue of symbol recognition evaluation was carried out in the more general framework of the 15th International Conference on Pattern Pattern Recognition (ICPR'00)[5]. The symbol library for that contest consisted of 25 electrical symbols, which were scaled and degraded with a small amount of binary noise.

If a lot of symbol recognition methods can be found in the literature, they appear to be sometimes very ad-hoc and domain dependent. According to the general conclusions of GREC'97 [6], there is a need for more generic symbol recognition algorithms. In this context, it appeared important to build a general framework to evaluate symbol recognition methods under several conditions and criteria. GREC'03 was a good occasion to start a work on that direction.

From an evaluation point of view, the question consists in determining the performance of symbol recognition methods when working on various kinds of

J. Lladós and Y.-B. Kwon (Eds.): GREC 2003, LNCS 3088, pp. 368–385, 2004.
© Springer-Verlag Berlin Heidelberg 2004

symbols, extracted from diverse application domains, under several constraints, with different levels of noise and degradation.

1.1   Goals of the Contest: Principles and Evaluation Methodology

As there are many factors which can influence the performance of a symbol recognition method, the main goal of the contest was not to give a single performance measure for each method, but to provide a tool to compare various symbol recognition methods under several different criteria.

The basic idea was to work with linear symbols, *i.e.* symbols made of lines, arcs and simple geometric primitives. If the description of this category of symbols looks very simple, it covers in fact a large variety of symbols, the most used in the domain of symbol recognition. Indeed, symbol recognition is a research domain covering a lot of application domains (architecture, electronics, mechanics, etc.) several data representation (mostly bitmap and vectorial), and several levels and kinds of noise and distortion. So, the determination of a set of constraints to define the kind of data for the contest is a tough task.

In order to be able to compare several recognition methods, some sound performance evaluation methods are required. Once again, there is a lot of possibilities to define them. Of course, the first result we expect from one method is an enumeration of the symbols found in the test images. But we can ask the methods to give us other values or features: the scale or orientation of the symbol with respect to the model, the confidence rate (if available), the location of the symbol inside a complex drawing, the computation time, etc. One possibility would be to give a global performance measure, combining all these aspects, possibly with a weight factor for each of them. But this possibility seems to be difficult to define and to exploit. We have preferred to favor another possibility: the evaluation of the recognition methods with respect to each of these aspects (considered alone), without establishing a general ranking of the recognition methods. It appears to be more interesting, from a scientific point of view, to analyze the impact of a kind of approach (structural, statistical, etc.) on the performance of the different evaluation items listed above.

1.2   Data: Type and Constraints

As symbol recognition concerns a large variety of data, drawing up an exhaustive list of interesting items that could be taken into account to define the data for the contest is complex. We have considered the following ones, mostly representative of the current research interests:

- The application domain, *i.e.* the technical domain where documents are used, which implicitly introduces some constraints on the kind of symbols [7].
- The data representation format, bitmap or vectorial. If vectorial, how the data is represented and how this vectorial representation is obtained.
- The segmentation, *i.e.* the fact that symbols are or not connected with other graphical parts of a document.

- The global transformations, such as rotation, translation and scaling, applied to the symbols with respect to their model.
- The degradation (bitmap-side noise) and the distortion (vectorial-side noise) of symbols.
- The scalability according to the number of symbol models, as some methods can work well on a limited number of symbols but significantly degrade their performance on a database with hundreds of symbols.
- The computation time, and how it evolves with the number of models, the degradation, the complexity (*i.e.*, number of lines) of the symbols, etc.

On the one hand, considering all these criteria for the purpose of evaluation of recognition methods constitutes a good framework. Each of these criteria can be evaluated alone, as well as combined with other criteria, giving us a very large number of test possibilities. On the other hand, graphics recognition methods are numerous [7, 8]. Some of them follow a statistical approach, other ones a structural approach and other ones a hybrid approach. An important point for the success of the contest was to propose a set test images which could be processed by most of these methods.

Thus, because of the large range of possible symbols and application domains, as well as the number of criteria and different recognition methods, a questionnaire was designed to get feedback from the possible participants. The analysis of the answers to this questionnaire helped us to take the final choices to define the symbol database and the final tests, as explained in sections 2 and 3.

2   The Symbol Database

2.1   General Aspects

According to the general considerations stated in the previous section and the answers of the possible participants to the questionnaire, we defined the set of data to be used in the contest.

First of all, we decided to use mainly two application domains, architecture and electronics, which were the most widely used according to the questionnaire and were representative of a wide range of shapes. We have used 50 different symbols (see figure 1), some of them with similar shapes, grouped in 3 sets containing 5, 20 and 50 symbols each, in order to address the issue of scalability too. In this first edition of the contest, we have only considered pre-segmented symbols, *i.e.*, images containing one instance of one symbol.

We also decided to support both bitmap and vectorial formats so that more methods could be evaluated in the contest. However, we do not apply any vectorization tool to binary images. Vectorial representation is always an ideal vectorial description of the image generated from the model of the symbol. Thus, it is not available when binary noise is introduced to images (see section 2.2).

Finally, we have applied several transformations, noise and degradation to the ideal model of the symbols in order to evaluate the robustness of the recognition methods. From the ideal model of each symbol, we have generated rotated and

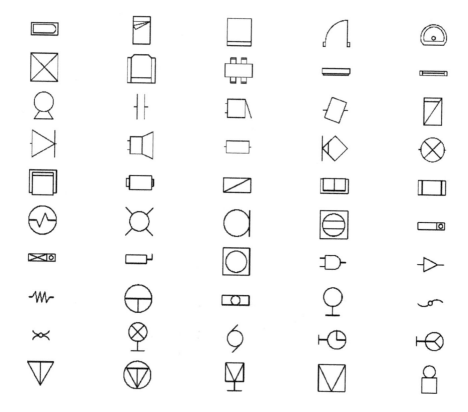

Fig. 1. 50 symbols used in the contest

scaled images to test invariance to global transformation. We have also applied
a method for binary degradation of symbols (see section 2.2) to simulate noise
produced when printing, photocopying and scanning. And finally, we have defined a model for vectorial distortion (see section 2.3) to generate images similar
to those produced when hand-drawing symbols.

2.2 Binary Degradation

Kanungo et al. have proposed a method to introduce some noise on bitmap images [9]. The purpose of this method is to modelize noises obtained by operations
like printing, photocopying, or scanning processes. The problem is approached
from a statistical point of view. The core principle of this method is to flip black
and white pixels by considering, for each candidate pixel, the distance between
it and the closest inverse region.

The degradation method is validated using a statistical methodology. Its
flexibility in the choice of the parameters lead us to adopt it. Indeed, a large
set of degradations can be obtained. The method itself accepts no less than 6
parameters, allowing to tune the strength of white and black noise, the size of

the influence area of these noises, a global noise (which do not depend of the presence of white/black pixels), and a post-processing closing based on well-known morphological operators. Of course, these 6 parameters may generate a large number of combinations, and thus, of models of degradation.

So, if the core method used for the degradation tests is formal and validated for its correctness, the determination of the set of parameters used for the contest is more empirical. We have tried to reproduce a set of degradation reproducing some realistic artifacts as those mentioned at the beginning of this section.

Nine models of degradation (see figure 2) have been determined. We have taken care to represent some "standard" noises: local, global, connectivity troubles... Despite of this effort, some of these models could seem to be far from the degradations usually noticed in real applications. Nevertheless, the purpose of the contest is also to measure the breaking point of the recognition method under these kind of constraints.

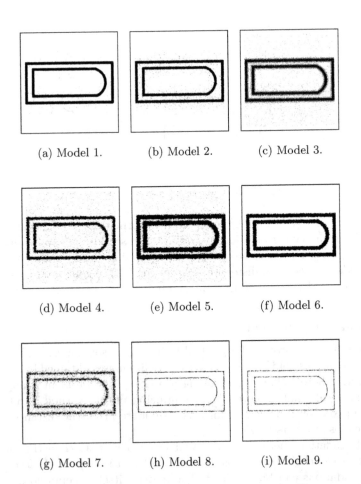

(a) Model 1.   (b) Model 2.   (c) Model 3.

(d) Model 4.   (e) Model 5.   (f) Model 6.

(g) Model 7.   (h) Model 8.   (i) Model 9.

Fig. 2. Samples of some degraded images generated using the Kanungo method for each model of degradation used

2.3   Vectorial Distortion

The goal of vectorial distortion is to deform the ideal shape of a symbol in order to simulate the shape variability produced by hand-drawing. The method for the generation of vectorial distortions of a symbol is based on the *Active Shape Models* [10]. This model aims to build a model of the shape, statistically capturing the variability of a set of annotated training samples.

In order to be able to apply this method, we need to generate a good set of training samples. This is not a straightforward task due to the statistical nature of the method. The number of samples must be high enough, and the samples must reflect the usual kind of variations produced by hand-drawing. However, it is difficult to have a great number of hand-drawn samples of each symbol. To be really significant, these samples should be drawn by many different people. Thus, we have decided to automatically generate the set of samples using a procedure based on the generation of deformed samples through the random modification of a different number of vertices of the symbol each time [11].

Each sample is represented using the model described in [12], which permits easy generation of deformed shapes. Each symbol is described as a set of straight lines, and each line is defined by four parameters: coordinates of mid-point, orientation and length. Thus, each deformed sample can be seen as a point x_i in a $4n$ dimensional space, where n is the number of lines of the symbol. Then, principal component analysis (PCA) can be used to capture the variability in the sample set. Given a set of samples of a symbol, we can compute the mean $\bar{x}$ and the covariance matrix S. The main modes of variation are described by the first eigenvectors p_k of the covariance matrix S. The variance explained by each eigenvector is equal to its corresponding eigenvalue. Thus, each shape in the training set can be approximated using the mean shape and a weighted sum of the eigenvectors:

$$x = \bar{x} + Pb \tag{1}$$

where $P = p_1, \ldots, p_m$ is the matrix of the first m eigenvectors and b is a vector of weights. This way, we can generate new images of a symbol by randomly selecting a vector of weights b. Increasing values of b_i will result in increasing levels of distortion (see figure 3). As the variance corresponding to each eigenvector p_i is equal to its corresponding eigenvalue λ_i, suitable limits for each weight b_i are $-3\sqrt{\lambda_i} \leq b_i \leq 3\sqrt{\lambda_i}$.

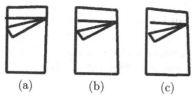

    (a)   (b)   (c)

Fig. 3. Examples of increasing levels of vectorial distortion

3 The Contest

From all the possibilities described in section 1.2, we have made some choices for the contest. The fact that this was the first edition of the contest did not make the choice easy, as we did not know how many participants will compete, and how hard the generated test images would be to recognize.

As explained in section 2, we decided to support only a subset of all possibilities: pre-segmented images, one degradation method, one deformation method, and some global transformations. Then, we defined independent tests for each category so that each participant, according to the specificities of its method, could choose the tests he wanted to run (or he could run).

As some methods require training data in order to work properly during the contest, the models of all the symbols and some sample tests were made available for all participants before the contest. The tests provided to the participants in the contest were similar, but different from the sample tests.

3.1 Description of the Final Tests Generated for the Contest

Following the previous considerations, we have generated a set of different tests, and we have grouped them into five different categories:

Ideal Images: there are three tests, each one involving an increasing number of symbols: 5, 20 and 50. Each test contains one single ideal image of every symbol involved in it. These tests aim to evaluate the ability of simple shape discrimination, as the number of symbols increases.

Global Transformations: rotation and scaling. There are three kinds of tests: tests with rotated images of the symbols, tests with scaled images and tests with rotated and scaled images. For each kind of test, three tests have been generated, each one involving an increasing number of symbols: 5, 20 and 50. This way we can also evaluate the scalability with affine transformations.

Binary Degradations: The nine models of degradation described in section 2.2 have been used to generate nine sets of tests, aiming to evaluate the robustness to different kinds of degradations. For each model of degradation, three tests, using 5, 20 and 50 symbols have been defined to analyze the scalability with degradation.

Vectorial Distortions: The model of vectorial distortion described in section 2.3 has been applied with three increasing levels of distortion to generate three kind of tests, each one with two tests, involving 5 and 15 symbols. The number of symbols is lower because the model for vectorial distortion only works with symbols with straight lines, and not arcs, and we only applied it to a subset of symbols.

Binary Degradations and Vectorial Distortions: The nine models of binary degradation have been combined with the three levels of vectorial distortions to generate a set of tests involving both kinds of deformations. All these tests only work with 15 different symbols.

3.2   Protocol of Evaluation

First of all, the main retained measure of symbol recognition evaluation is quite simple: it is a binary test, expressing the fact that the symbol represented in a test image is recognized or not by a recognition method. So, we planned not to consider other attributes, such as location, scale factor, etc. that participants might supply. However, participants were allowed (and encouraged) to provide more details about their recognition results. Some of these additional attributes have finally been analyzed, as exposed in section 5.

To manage the contest, several file formats were required. The basic idea during the contest was to give to each participant the possibility to choose which tests he wanted to compete in. So, each test has been considered as a stand-alone part. Therefore, it has to contain all the information that a participant need to know about a test: which are the models involved in the test and which are the test images. Our wish was to make the description as simple as possible. We finally decided to consider each test as a file archive, containing the symbol models, the test images and a description file. This description file is formatted as a .ini file, as the information it must convey does not require any complex structure.

Participants had then to supply their results in another format, based on XML. Indeed, the nature of the information describing a result may be more complex: name of the recognized symbol, location, scale factor, confidence rate, etc. These result files have then been matched against other XML files, corresponding to the description of the tests for the usage of the organizers, including the ground-truth. The description files for the usage of the participants have been generated from the description files for the usage of the organizers using a XSLT filter. All the formats described above (participant format, result format, organizer format) are freely downloadable from the Web site of the contest (http://www.cvc.uab.es/grec2003/SymRecContest/index.htm).

4   Participants

Finally, five methods developed by five different teams, took part in the contest. In this section we summarily describe the main features of each method, as provided by each team.

4.1   University of Rouen – La Rochelle

The system is based on the Object-Process Methodology (OPM) [13] and is divided into two parts: a library of recognition processes [14] and an application layer which controls the recognition process.

The whole recognition process is divided into three steps: a pre-processing step, a structural recognition step and a statistical recognition step. Statistical and structural bases are learned with different interfaces described in [15]. The pre-processing step is applied to degraded images and is based on blob coloring and morphological approaches [16], which are self-adapted, depending on a contextual measurement of the noise.

Structural recognition is based on inclusion graphs where the nodes correspond to the connected components and their loops, and the edges to the inclusion relations between them. Inclusion graphs are processed with a graph-matching algorithm [14].

Statistical recognition is applied to symbol loops, in order to recognize the set of symbols which can not be recognized only with the structural method.

4.2   National University of Ireland, Maynooth

This method is only suitable for vectorized segmented symbols. It fuses two kinds of methods: Descriptor Matching and Syntactic/Structural Matching.

Descriptor Matching aims to generate a number that will exclusively identify each symbol. Thirteen numerical descriptors are calculated based on properties of the symbol, such as the number of vertices, straight-line segments and arc segments, angle information, several length ratios, and so on. These values are combined using a weighted summation to give one descriptive value. The training set is used to generate the description value of all the library symbols. During recognition, considering the scale, rotation and noise distortion, a range of possible descriptive values is generated for a given image. Matching is performed by selecting the library values that lie within this range.

The method based on Syntactic/Structural matching builds a structural description of a symbol of the form: Base Entity (Type, Length), Entity1 (Type, Length Ratio, Angle, Distance), Entity2 (Type, Length Ratio, Angle, Distance) and so on. The Base Entity is the longest line segment in the symbol. Type is one of line, arc or circle. Length Ratio is the ratio of the lengths of the Entity to that of the Base Entity. Angle is the angle of a line connecting the midpoints of the entity and the base with the base entity. Distance Ratio is the ratio of the distance between these midpoints to the length of base entity. The training set is used to generate descriptions for the library images. For recognition, an entity matching strategy applied consisting of a search and scoring system based on matching corresponding elements.

Fusion of methods is needed because both of these methods have deficiencies. Description matching is affected by the scale, rotation, and distortion due to noise. On the other hand, syntactic/structural matching is computationally complex. Description matching is used as a first step. Normally each symbol will get only one matching model within its range. However, if this is not the case, syntactic/structural Matching is used to refine the classification.

4.3   City University of Hong-Kong

This method is based on vector-form graphics. Four types of geometric constraints are used to represent the graphical knowledge of symbols. Two algorithms have been developed for knowledge acquisition and symbol recognition, respectively. The system first uses the knowledge acquisition algorithm to learn the graphical knowledge of all models and store them for recognition. Then the system will recognize all symbols based on the learnt graphical knowledge. The input symbols to the system can be either vector-form graphics or raster images. If the input is a raster image, a vectorization processing is first applied. However, both raster images and vectorization results may have a lot of noise and distortions. Hence, a few pre-processing and post-processing methods are also used to reduce the noise and rectify the vectors to obtain a high quality vector-form graphics. Finally, the system uses the symbol recognition algorithm and all the learnt graphical knowledge of models to recognize all these symbols that have been described by vectors.

4.4 University of Nottingham

This method is based on a previous work in vectorization [17] and arc recognition algorithm [18], which provides the description of a symbol as a set of lines and arcs. Internally arcs are represented by the line corresponding to their chord, together with the convention that the arc is clockwise.

The algorithm used for recognition is the following. An image to be recognized, denoted by I is matched in turn against each of the templates T_k where $k = 1 \ldots n$ for n symbols to be recognized. A pair of lines (or arcs if there are no lines) are chosen, one from T_k and another from I. A geometric transformation is applied to the symbol I such that the chosen lines in each symbol are coincident. There are two possible transforms that may be applied, with the lines oriented in the same or the opposite sense. Both cases are investigated. Then, the same scale factor and rotation are applied to all the other lines and arcs in the image. The length of overlap of the corresponding lines in both symbols is taken as the matching criterion. A penalty is applied proportional to the area between the two lines.

The process is repeated using each possible pair of lines, which are longer than a threshold length in the template and the image until the best choice of reference lines are found. The transformation applied gives the orientation and scale which are returned. The same process is repeated for each template against the image and the best match taken. If this is above a threshold then the symbol is reported as recognized.

When the images are corrupted by noise, a clean up is attempted to reduced spurious lines and arcs, by snapping together the end points of lines that are close, and by combining the resulting chains of small lines into a single longer straight line.

The method has the advantage that it is able to segment images and to recognize them at the same time. However, this proved to be a disadvantage where one template contains an instance of another as a sub-clique as. A disadvantage of the method is that the time taken grows with the product of the number of lines in a symbol and template.

4.5 Fudan University, Shangai

The symbol recognition method is a three-step procedure including preprocessing, feature extraction, and classification. The classifier used here is Nearest

Neighbor, the simplest method, so that the robustness of the entire system relies on the preprocessing and the pattern descriptor.

The main aim of preprocessing is to improve robustness, for which filtering of noise is an usual approach. Here, the preprocessing follows the traditional processing. The specificity is that the filtering of noise is adaptive. This means that different degradation levels will result in different filtering effects.

Because the classifier used here is the Nearest Neighbor, the recognition accuracy is mainly dependent on the pattern descriptor. As vectorization in case of degradation usually yields vectors with considerable deformation and pixel-based approaches usually perform better in processing degraded images, here, pixels are used as the pattern primitive. A new pixel-based descriptor is proposed for symbol recognition. In general, different configuration of pixels corresponds with different shapes. The proposed descriptor is a statistical feature addressing the configuration of pixels.

5 Analysis of Results

In the analysis of the results of the contest, our main goal was not to give an absolute winner, but to show the robustness of the methods to the different evaluation criteria defined in the contest goals, and to state some general conclusions about common trends and problems. Thus, we will divide the analysis in six independent categories: performance on ideal images, robustness to scalability, affine transformations, binary degradations, vectorial distortions and the combination of binary degradations and vectorial distortions. We will also analyze some recognition errors common to several methods and the computation time of the method which has provided it.

Moreover, we have to take into account that not all participants took in part in all the tests, either because the method is not suitable for some type of images, either because they did not have enough time to run the method on all the tests.

5.1   Ideal Images

Figure 4 shows the results for the three tests with an ideal image of each symbol, each one with an increasing number of symbols (5, 20 and 50). The National University of Ireland did not participate in these tests because they only consist of bitmap images. Besides, the City University of Hong Kong and the Fudan University found an error in the description file of the test with 50 images which prevented them from running their method on that test. The results show an excellent recognition rate of 100% for all methods, except one, on the sets with 5 and 20 images. This is a good indicator of the ability of the methods to discriminate between different shapes. The results with the set of 50 symbols, although they only correspond to two methods, seem to demonstrate that recognition rate decreases due to confusions among similar symbols when the number of models increase.

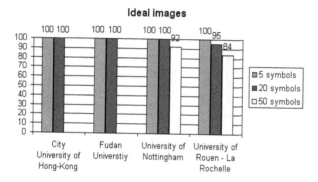

Fig. 4. Results of ideal tests

5.2   Scalability

One of the challenges for symbol recognition methods is their ability to scale well, *i.e.*, their ability to achieve similar recognition rates working with a high number of symbols than working only with a few symbols. In order to test this issue we have defined a measure of global performance for each method: for each participant we have computed the mean of the recognition rates for all the tests with 5 symbols, for all the tests with 20 symbols and for all the tests with 50 symbols. Results are shown in figure 5. As expected, performance the decreases with increasing number of symbols, although the variation is different depending on the method. However, it seems to be a common drop when passing from set with 20 symbols to set with 50 symbols. It is to be noted that in this set there are not only more symbols, but also very similar symbols. A more detailed analysis of scalability for each kind of test can be found in sections devoted to each kind of test.

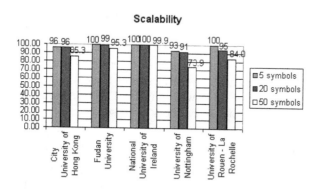

Fig. 5. Evolution of performance as the number of symbols increases

5.3   Rotation and Scaling

In figure 6 we summarize the results for images with rotation and scaling. In this case, the effects on performance depends very much on each method and type

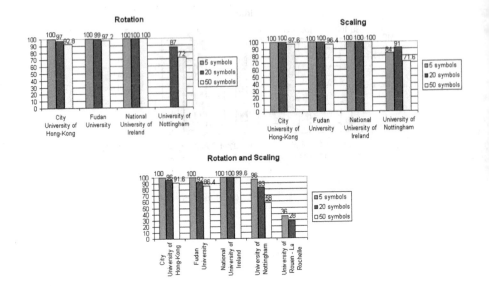

Fig. 6. Results of tests with rotation, scaling and combination of rotation and scaling

of transformation. The method developed by the National University of Ireland seems to be the most robust method with recognition rates over 99% in all tests, even in tests combining rotation and scaling with 50 symbols. The method by the Fudan University performs relatively well for rotation and scaling, although in both cases there is a slight performance drop when working with 50 symbols. However, for images combining both types of transformations, recognition rates are significantly lower. The method presented by the City University of Hong-Kong seems to be robust for scaling, but recognition rates decrease for rotation. When combining rotation and scaling, the results are similar, although slightly lower, to those achieved only with rotation. Thus, it appears that scaling has little influence in the performance of the method. Finally, the other two methods, which have only been run on some of these tests, those developed by the University of Nottingham and the University of Rouen-La Rochelle are not able to keep good performance rates with any kind of transformation, although it degrades more as the number of symbols increases.

5.4 Degradation

Only two methods have participated in all tests concerning images with binary degradations, as figure 7 shows. The other two methods, those developed by the University of Rouen-La Rochelle and the University of Nottingham have only been run on one or two tests with poor results, below 60%. The performance on these tests depends on the method, the model of binary degradation and the number of symbols.

The method which achieves the best overall performance in all tests is the method presented by the Fudan University. It shows very good results for tests

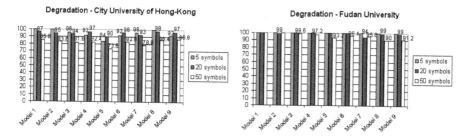

Fig. 7. Results of tests with degradation for methods by the City University of Hong-Kong and the Fudan University

with 5 and 20 symbols, with all recognition rates above 99% for all models of degradation. Only with 50 symbols the performance begins to degrade. However, even then it remains above 99% for models of degradation 1, 2 and 3. The models where the method fails correspond to those with heavy salt and pepper noise (model 4) with degraded border lines (model 5, 6 and 7) or with thinner lines (models 8 and 9). The worse results correspond to images with thinner lines than the original symbol.

The method presented by the City University of Hong-Kong shows a degraded performance in almost all tests, although it depends on the level of degradation, being lower as the number of symbols increases. As expected, the more noisy images are, the lower recognition rates are. The worse results correspond to model of degradation 5, which degrades heavily the shape of the lines. In this method, performance for models with thin lines seems to be better than for models with thick lines.

5.5 Deformation

The kind of vectorial deformation used in the contest does not seem to influence significantly the performance of methods. As the level of deformation increases, recognition rates keep almost constant. Only the combination of deformation and increasing the number of symbols has some remarkable effect on the method presented by the City University of Hong-Kong (see figure 8).

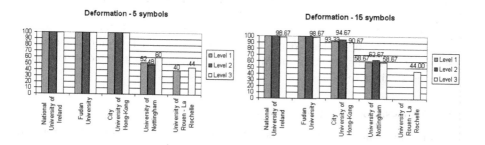

Fig. 8. Results of tests with deformation for both sets of symbols

5.6   Deformation and Degradation

As with tests containing degraded images, only two methods have participated in all tests concerning images with binary degradations and vectorial deformations (figure 9). The methods presented by the University of Rouen-La Rochelle and the University of Nottingham have only run one or two tests with poor results.

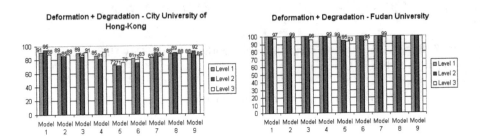

Fig. 9. Results of tests with deformation and degradation for methods by the City University of Hong-Kong and the Fudan University

For both methods, increasing the level or vectorial deformation does not affect significantly to their performance, similarly to tests with only degradation. For the Fudan University's method, recognition rates only drop a little with the highest level of deformation in some models of degradation, especially those which correspond to more noisy images, as model 5. The results achieved by the method presented by the City University of Hong-Kong seem to be a combination of the results achieved when applying each kind of transformation alone. Recognition rates follow a pattern similar to those corresponding to degraded images, but with a bit lower values, as an effect of the vectorial deformation.

5.7   Analysis of Errors

We have also tried to draw some conclusions from the most usual recognition errors. We have analyzed errors in all tests with 50 symbols (where all symbols have the same probability to occur), trying to identify the symbols with the highest error rates. We have found that there are several symbols with error rates significantly higher than the rest of symbols. In figure 10, we show the three symbols with more recognition errors. We also show, for each of these symbols, the three symbols which are the main source of confusion. We cannot draw strong conclusions, but we can see how it seems more likely to find errors in symbols with arcs or circles. We can also see that some of the symbols recognized instead of the original ones are similar to it, *i.e.*, they also contain a circular shape and some straight lines.

5.8   Analysis of Computation Time

Only one of the methods (that of the City University of Hong-Kong) has provided results about the computation time. We have analyzed these results and, in

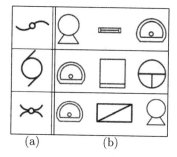

(a)   (b)

Fig. 10. (a) Symbols with more recognition errors. (b) Main confusions for each symbol

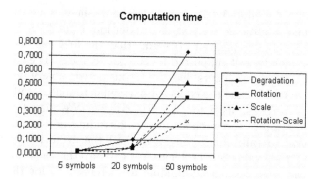

Fig. 11. Evolution of computation time as the number of symbols increases

figure 11 we show how the time increases as the number of symbols involved in recognition also increases. In this figure, the time is the average of computation time for all tests containing 5, 20 and 50 symbols. This was the expected behavior of any recognition method. We can also see how the time increases more when passing from 20 to 50 symbols, showing that the evolution is not lineal. This effect is more important with degraded images, maybe because the method works with vectorial data and vectorization may yield spurious lines when vectorizing degraded images.

Finally, figure 12 shows the different behavior of different symbols with respect to the computation time. We have observed that not all the symbols take

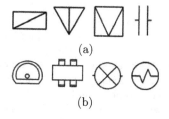

Fig. 12. (a) Symbols with the lowest computation times. (b) Symbols with the highest computation times

the same time to be recognized. Figure 12(a) corresponds to the four symbols with the lowest computation times while figure 12(b) to the four symbols with the highest computation times. As the method is vectorial, symbols with few lines have lower computation time than symbols with a lot of lines or circles, which might be approximated as a set of straight lines.

6   Conclusion

The first contest was a starting to point to inventory the diversity of data, methods, criteria that belong to the symbol recognition domain. Even if the first edition concerns only some restricted fields of application, it has been the occasion to determine the effort to be done to bring to the community a reference tool, able in some conditions to assist the evaluation of the large range of existing methods in symbol recognition. It seems that the first generated models of noise have been mostly well supported by the participants. The response of the community, with five participants, has to be considered as very positive.

Now, we have to continue the effort, in particular to make available all data, formats, models and test used for the first edition. We plan to increase the number of data, improve the methods used to introduce noise, and so on.

Here, we have to talk about the future and the evolution of the contest itself, as well as the evaluation problem. We can say that a web site is under construction, and that we aim at building a reference site for the problem of evaluating symbol recognition methods. Some things we have to work on: to get more images from other domains, to establish more degradation/deformation methods and models, to give the users the possibility to generate their own test data, to provide a tool for the automatic evaluation of the results so that anyone can check his results. Maybe, we have also to be more specific about the tests about one criterion, the tests with several criteria.

Acknowledgment

The authors would like acknowledge the participants for their participation to the contest and for their contribution to this article.

References

1. Kong, B., Phillips, I.T., Haralick, R.M., Prasad, A., Kasturi, R.: A benchmark: Performance evaluation of dashed-line detection algorithms. In Kasturi, R., Tombre, K., eds.: Graphics Recognition: Methods and Applications, Selected Papers from First International Workshop on Graphics Recognition, GREC'95. Springer, Berlin (1996) 270–285 Volume 1072 of Lecture Notes in Computer Science.
2. Chhabra, A., Phillips, I.: The second international graphics recognition contest - raster to vector conversion: A report. In Tombre, K., Chhabra, A., eds.: Graphics Recognition: Algorithms and Systems, Selected Papers from Second International Workshop on Graphics Recognition, GREC'97. Springer, Berlin (1998) 390–410 Volume 1389 of Lecture Notes in Computer Science.

3. Chhabra, A., Philips, I.: Performance evaluation of line drawing recognition systems. In: Proceedings of 15th. International Conference on Pattern Recognition. Volume 4. (2000) 864–869 Barcelona, Spain.

4. Wenyin, L., Zhai, J., Dori, D.: Extended summary of the arc segmentation contest. In Blostein, D., Kwon, Y., eds.: Graphics Recognition: Algorithms and Applications, Selected Papers from Fourth International Workshop on Graphics Recognition, GREC'01. Springer, Berlin (2002) 343–349 Volume 2390 of Lecture Notes in Computer Science.

5. Aksoy, S., Ye, M., Schauf, M., Song, M., Wang, Y., Haralick, R., Parker, J., Pivovarov, J., Royko, D., Sun, C., Farneboock, G.: Algorithm performance contest. In: Proceedings of 15th. International Conference on Pattern Recognition. Volume 4. (2000) 870–876 Barcelona, Spain.

6. Tombre, K., Chhabra, A.K.: General Conclusions. [19] 411–420

7. Chhabra, A.K.: Graphic Symbol Recognition: An Overview. [19] 68–79

8. Lladós, J., Valveny, E., Sánchez, G., Martí, E.: Symbol recognition: Current advances and perspectives. In Blostein, D., Kwon, Y., eds.: Graphics Recognition: Algorithms and Applications, Selected Papers from Fourth International Workshop on Graphics Recognition, GREC'01. Springer, Berlin (2002) 104–127 Volume 2390 of Lecture Notes in Computer Science.

9. Kanungo, T., Haralick, R.M., Baird, H.S., Stuetzle, W., Madigan, D.: Document Degradation Models: Parameter Estimation and Model Validation. In: Proceedings of IAPR Workshop on Machine Vision Applications, Kawasaki (Japan). (1994) 552–557

10. Cootes, T., Taylor, C., Cooper, D., Graham, J.: Active shape models: Their training and application. Computer Vision and Image Understanding **61** (1995) 38–59

11. Ghosh, D., Shivaprasad, A.: An analytic approach for generation of artificial handprinted character database from given generative models. Pattern Recognition **32** (1999) 907–920

12. Valveny, E., Martí, E.: A model for image generation and symbol recognition through the deformation of lineal shapes. Pattern Recognition Letters **24** (2003) 2857–2867

13. Dori, D.: Object-process methodology, a holistic systems paradigm. Springer-Verlag (2002)

14. Delalandre, M., HTroux, P., Adam, S., Trupin, E., Ogier., J.: A statistical and structural approach for symbol recognition using xml modelling. In: Structural and Syntactical Pattern Recognition. (2002) 281–290.

15. Saidali, Y., Adam, S., Ogier, J., Trupin, E., Labiche, J.: Knowledge representation and acquisition for engineering document analysis. In: Fith International Workshop on Graphics Recognition (GREC 2003). (2003) 33–43

16. Delalandre, M., Saidali, Y., Ogier, J., Trupin, E.: Adaptable vectorisation system based on strategic knowledge and xml representation use. In: Fith International Workshop on Graphics Recognition (GREC 2003). (2003) 250–261

17. Elliman, D.: A really useful vectorisation algorithm. In: Lecture Notes In Computer Science, 1941. Springer-Verlag (1999) 20–27

18. Elliman, D.: Tif2vec, an algorithm for arc segmentation in engineering drawings. In: Lecture Notes In Computer Science, 2390. Springer-Verlag (2001) 350–358

19. Tombre, K., Chhabra, A.K., eds.: Graphics Recognition—Algorithms and Systems. Volume 1389 of Lecture Notes in Computer Science. Springer-Verlag (1998)

Author Index

Lecture Notes in Computer Science

For information about Vols. 1–3094

please contact your bookseller or Springer